GOLF'S MAJORS

GOLF'S MAJORS

From Hagen and Hogan to a Bear
and a Tiger, Inside the Game's Most
Unforgettable Performances

GARY PLAYER
AND RANDY O. WILLIAMS

DEYST.

An Imprint of WILLIAM MORROW

DEYST.

GOLF'S MAJORS. Copyright © 2024 by Gary Player Enterprises LLC and Randy O. Williams. All rights reserved. Printed in the United States of America. No part of this book may be used or reproduced in any manner whatsoever without written permission except in the case of brief quotations embodied in critical articles and reviews. For information, address HarperCollins Publishers, 195 Broadway, New York, NY 10007.

HarperCollins books may be purchased for educational, business, or sales promotional use. For information, please email the Special Markets Department at SPsales@harpercollins.com.

FIRST EDITION

Designed by Jennifer Chung
Part opener background image © sanchesnet1/stock.adobe.com

Library of Congress Cataloging-in-Publication Data has been applied for.

ISBN 978-0-06-327784-7

24 25 26 27 28 LBC 5 4 3 2 1

CONTENTS

THE PGA CHAMPIONSHIP

THE US OPEN

THE OPEN CHAMPIONSHIP

PREFACE

My final appearance at a major championship was in April 2009 at the Masters. In total, I competed in over 160 majors on the regular tour, first at the Open Championship in 1956. I look back on that spring day in Augusta and my final competitive walk up eighteen with fond memories. With my beloved late wife Vivienne, our children and grandchildren watching, I stopped at end of the fairway and dropped to my knee to say a prayer of thanks and express my gratitude to this wonderful game.

Golf has played a significant role in my life for more than seven decades. This game took a poor boy from rural South Africa to traveling the world, competing against the best players, and dining with dignitaries from every country imaginable. A story like mine should be a script found only in fantasies.

My very first round of golf was at Virginia Park just outside of Johannesburg at the ripe age of thirteen. My father begged me to go play with him, and I reluctantly tagged along. As a boy, I was a fierce sportsman. Rugby and cricket were my games of choice. But I scored par on my first three holes that day. From then on, I was hooked. The prospect of becoming a world champion developed to be more than an obsession, rather my way of life. My plan was to practice harder than any golfer, ever, while also being a student of the game and learning from the great players before me.

Practicing is not always physical, as the mind proves to be the ultimate key to success when contending for major championships. We are just beginning to truly understand its effect on performance.

People often tell me about their son's or daughter's long hitting ability. That is maybe the least important attribute in my eyes. A player will get only so far off the tee. What wins tournaments happens inside one's head. Being able to harness bodily gifts and channel mental strength is the mark of a true champion. It was what allowed me to win the Open, the US Open, the PGA Championship, and the Masters— nine over nineteen years—as well as nine senior majors.

No doubt there were trials and tribulations I had to overcome throughout my career. It's difficult to explain how I won so many tournaments, and often I express my success as a divine intervention.

What does it take to win a major championship? This was one of the main reasons why I decided to write this book. As I have vigorously studied the successes of Bobby Jones, Ben Hogan, and many others, I wanted to key in on all who have won a major championship and how they overcame adversity on their way to victory. Some, as we know, were one-hit wonders. You look at players like the late Tom Weiskopf, who was one of the most talented golfers in history yet won only one major. Were they satisfied with that success and became too complacent with their place in history? Did their hunger to be at the top of the game disappear with the influx of prize money? Perhaps it was luck, but that is the residue of design.

In my era with Jack Nicklaus and Arnold Palmer, we played for legacy and growing the game around the world. Money came, but that was not the focus other than earning a living.

Superstar is a term that is used too loosely today. In my opinion, to reach true superstardom, you must win at least six majors or complete the career grand slam. Those who have achieved this feat have that "It" factor. But what is "It"? Discovering "It" became my mission.

When Randy Williams approached me to coauthor a book about the major championships, I knew it would be a monumental undertaking, as golf has such a storied history. But as a student of the game, dissecting the historic wins of my heroes like Bobby Locke, the battles waged between my contemporaries like Jack, Arnold, Tom Watson, and Lee Trevino, and the triumphs of today's stars like Rory McIlroy, would help complete my golf education. Though there are many secrets left to uncover.

This book certainly brings back fond memories, reconciles disasters, and uncovers how players handled themselves on golf's biggest stages, courses that have stood the test of time. There are triumphs, comebacks, heartbreaks, the value of longevity, and more. From my own personal experiences and observations of tournaments held before and after my playing career, this book will reveal the steps each player took to etch their name in golf's history.

So many of these tournaments came down to a final putt made under immense pressure. My hope is that this book inspires and informs readers about the battles we have witnessed over the years on the links. Golf is a generational game, and I am pleased to share this with you.

—Gary Player

You can win all the tournaments you want, but the majors are what you're remembered for. It's how you're measured as a champion in our sport. The majors are where it's at.

—TIGER WOODS

There is golf, tournament golf, and then there is championship golf.

—BOBBY JONES

I've said many times that a good player can win a golf tournament, but great players win major championships. When you think of the Majors, you think of the greatest tournaments in the world.

—ARNOLD PALMER

I think a major championship is the pinnacle of our sport.

—RORY McILROY

The major championships are the events in which you can compare golfers of yesterday with golfers of today, the only really true measurement.

—JACK NICKLAUS

It is precisely because they represent the summit of the game; the majors present the greatest challenge and the greatest glory the sport has to offer.

—GARY PLAYER

INTRODUCTION

There it is.

From some of history's greatest players you see how the four tournaments known as the majors (and collectively as the Grand Slam)—the Masters, the PGA Championship, the US Open, and the Open—are the absolute pinnacle of golf. Often determined by just one stroke after seventy-two holes of play, these are competitions played at a level of pressure guaranteed to test the nerve of even the game's very best. As you will see throughout this book, quite often it is simply just one swing, one good or bad break, that is often the difference between a lifetime of happy memories or reliving a haunting moment of what-if.

These are undoubtedly the world's toughest tournaments and the most sought-after prize, often taking years of failure to learn how to win, and most never do.

After writing a bestseller from an insider's perspective about the Super Bowl with Hall of Famer Jerry Rice (*50 Years, 50 Moments: The Most Unforgettable Plays in Super Bowl History*), I came away believing players in the National Football League were about the most competitive athletes on the planet. And they are, but the intensity of golf's greatest players in their drive to success in the summit events of their sport has been a real eye-opener.

When I approached the legendary Gary Player to cowrite this book with me, I got a quick education about the ferocity and drive the game's elite players possess.

As the winner of nine majors on the PGA Tour and nine more on the Senior Tour, Player told me all the money, all the other victories, the luxurious car, the fabulous house, when the golfer is competing at

St. Andrews, Oakmont, Kiawah and Augusta National—those things pale to the elite because they know they are playing for eternal glory, for history.

No one remembers who was the sand save leader, the straightest driver off the tee, the leading money winner of a given year, or how many Vardon Trophies they've won. No, what both the fan and the player remember is the performance that captured a major.

And when you are judged about how good you were in your career, they will look back and say, "Yes, well Gary Player won 165 tournaments, but he won eighteen majors," and the latter is what you are going to be judged on in the end. Everyone agrees.

It's been a lofty goal—to present an unprecedented insider's look at the most memorable performances on the sport's biggest stage, all in one handy volume, something fans can grab off their shelves and refer to and relive for years to come—but the enormous effort has been worth it.

Not only taking readers through the outstanding duels, epic collapses, the Davids defeating the Goliaths, and the all-time dominant performances in the greatest competitions golf has to offer, but to do so from the inside.

To achieve that, we wanted to provide readers about the hows and whys, so this book offers different and insightful behind-the-scenes perspectives of performing under pressure, strategies, and simply what was going on in the minds of those making history, as well as illustrating the various factors that came into play as they struggled to stay in contention.

Of course, being a one-volume work, it is not a comprehensive history. But being representative of the 466 grand slam tournaments spanning 163 years, clearly it is a daunting task that in the end can only be subjective.

Also, in covering such a massive project, not all of the content could fit in a single volume, thus you will find quite a lot of engaging bonus material on Gary Player's website as well as on the HarperCollins/Dey Street website.

Please note that while comparisons of champions of different generations is not an exact science—especially in golf, where equipment, travel, and courses have changed drastically over the decades—the best we can do is focus on a given time in a specific chapter and provide some perspective throughout the book as a whole.

It is a select compilation that aims to illuminate some of the game's most vivid and thrilling competitions. It is here you will find riveting stories of some of the most iconic players as well as more than a few unheralded golfers providing fantastic finishes and epic collapses (and everything in between) in their quest for glory.

It is representative of all different ways of winning . . . and losing. By peeling back the layers of the onion to reveal what fans don't know, we get inside the players' minds and simply learn why success in these four tournaments mean so much to them and how the very best succeeded, most only after years of struggle, and eventually learned how to come through in the clutch under staggering pressure.

From the amazing comeback victories to the heart-breaking failures, we will explore what happened behind those indelible moments. How even accomplished stars like Ben Hogan, Sam Snead, Johnny Miller, Tom Watson, Justin Thomas, and Rory McIlroy have also experienced the lingering pain of coming up short.

The scenarios are many and varied including:

· a career-defining shot like Augusta-native Larry Mize chipping in at the 1987 Masters
· Frenchman Jean van de Velde tossing away a three-shot lead on the final hole of the 1999 Open Championship
· Tiger Woods's fifteen-stroke victory at the 2000 US Open at Pebble Beach

This book will examine the story behind the story of all the different ways players have won (and lost) the game of their lives.

And although winning a major championship does not guarantee greatness, not winning one guarantees that you will never be considered great. Deep in his heart, every golfer knows this.

One of the joys of putting this together was seeing sort of a Walter Mitty effect coming into play here (James Thurber's story "The Secret Life of Walter Mitty," as you may recall, is about the human propensity toward escapism, an ordinary person who indulges in fantastic daydreams of personal triumphs) because this sport is personal, and in a very small way, weekend golfers like me can identify with the problems the greats are having. The golfer's expression of joy and disappointment are feelings we can relate to, again, on a relative scale; unlike a NASCAR driver, a power forward in the NBA, an Olympic gymnast, an NFL linebacker, or an NHL goalie, we know the golfer's problems in that we can sympathize with Phil Mickelson when his approach is buried under the lip of a sand trap or Brooks Koepka's tee shot lands out of bounds, because we have been there. And what brings us back is from time to time we hit a good one, too.

We will hear from champions and how they triumphed. We will hear from those who strived but fell short. Unique experiences and shared experiences. And when their voices are combined with Gary's perspectives, which he earned through six decades of competing in the game's biggest events, it speaks with an unequaled authenticity. The whole idea is to celebrate the game itself at the highest level and the players who put it all on the line at the pinnacle events of their careers. The heroes, losers, innovators, and unforgettable characters representative of over a century and a half of inspiring golf.

And it is my sincere hope that you will find in this book as much interest, enjoyment, and insight into the majors as we did putting it together.

—Randy O. Williams

GOLF'S MAJORS

THE MASTERS

THE MASTERS—THE VERY NAME CONJURES UP AN EVER-lasting image of a true outdoor cathedral set among tall Georgia pine trees, stunning azaleas, and dogwoods. Every April, by invitation only, many of the best players in the world brave the slippery slopes of the slanted and elevated fairways, punitive ponds and creeks, and maddeningly false fronts to even access the ulcer-inducing, undulating greens, all for the chance to achieve the dream of donning one of the most coveted trophies in all sports—the green jacket.

Augusta National Golf Club was founded by Bobby Jones, the legendary amateur champion, on a 365-acre property called Fruitland Nurseries in the early 1930s. He and his associate Clifford Roberts, an astute investment banker in New York, joined forces with famed Scottish architect Alister MacKenzie to bring it all to fruition.

Jones wanted a course that put an emphasis on strategy, and the result is the best example of what a major is all about. Every shot here offers an option. That is an important part of the equation.

You've always got a safe side of the fairway or the green to aim at, where, if properly executed, you know you'll likely have your ball sitting up on short grass. But take it from someone who has competed here fifty-two times: from those safe spots you are not, by any means, guaranteed par. With the wind a factor at various points, and the water in play at five of the back nine holes (eleven, twelve, and thirteen, aka "Amen's Corner," plus fifteen and sixteen) players also have risk-reward options on a number of holes, most notably the two par-5s located at thirteen and fifteen.

However, in order to even have a shot at glory here, the question is not whether to gamble but where to gamble. The answer is different for every golfer, but at Augusta you have to take chances in order to win. You can't just play safe all the time. It's a course designed to reward boldness and punish timidity. I love that.

Even since it launched in 1934, the Masters has been filled with great, great battles that often come down to the back nine on Sunday afternoon, working through the treacherous Amen Corner and the infamous Rae's Creek. For years, there was Ben Hogan, Byron Nelson, and Sam Snead putting on brilliant performances. Then Jack Nicklaus, Arnie Palmer, and myself had some of our best and worst major memories here. Arnold and I combined for seven Masters wins, but we each remained haunted long after by errant shots to the final green—his in 1961 and mine in 1962—that handed victory to the other.

Of course, who could forget Tiger Woods's tremendous display of power and finesse to win his first major in 1997. Then, after all his well-documented personal and professional ups and downs, he improbably grabs another green jacket twenty-two years later!

Such is the magnitude of the place, conducted at the same venue year after year like the Daytona 500, the Kentucky Derby, and the Indy 500, that it feels familiar even to the millions of fans who never have been there. Like those iconic events, the Masters is so ingrained into our memories that each shot measures up not only against the tournament at hand but also against history.

Why? Because every player knows that a Masters victory ensures them a hallowed place in the pantheon of the game.

"The Masters is a monument to everything that's great in golf," said Jack Nicklaus, a six-time winner.

1

THE SHOT HEARD
'ROUND THE WORLD

APRIL 4–8, 1935
AUGUSTA NATIONAL GOLF CLUB
AUGUSTA, GEORGIA

H e rose from the depths of poverty, a sixth-grade dropout who overcame a near fatal bout of pneumonia and emphysema in his late teens and went from caddying for 15 cents a round to become the first player to win all four majors. He invented the sand wedge and changed the game. He was "the Squire," famous for his wit and traditional plus fours (so called because they're four inches longer than traditional knickers). However, despite his many achievements, Gene Sarazen, one of only five to win the career grand slam, will always be known for one of the most famous strokes in the history of golf. And interestingly, it wasn't a winning strike (though it did lead to a playoff and eventual victory).

This is the story about the championship in which the "shot heard round the world" would lead Sarazen to his seventh and final major.

He had already achieved international recognition when he was only twenty, first winning both the US Open and the PGA Championship in 1922, then becoming a double winner ten years later—his second US Open and his only Open Championship in 1932. Sarazen (née Eugene Saraceni) will be forever known more for what he did with his four-wood on his second shot on the 485-yard, par-5 fifteenth hole on a beautiful course on a cold, wet afternoon in a fledgling tournament called the Augusta National Invitational Tournament. (It would become officially the Masters in 1939.)

While Sarazen's week ended with a lucky break, it nearly began with a bad one.

And even though Augusta rewards a player who is a good driver of the ball, Sarazen was about to find out other ways the driver could help him.

The country was still deep in the Depression. So, while staying at the stately Bon Air hotel downtown, Sarazen was careful with money. He had gone to sleep with $40 near his side on the dresser. Unbeknownst to him there had been recent reports of thefts at the elegant lodgings before his arrival.

There are various versions of what happened, but essentially the golfer was awoken in the wee hours of the morning of the first round by an intruder.

More concerned about the money than his personal safety, he barked at the intruder who was standing at the end of his bed, "Who are you? What do you want?" When the intruder didn't reply, Sarazen dove for his golf bag and pulled out the first club he laid hands on, which turned out to be his driver.

In his pajamas, he chased the intruder down the hallway, but when they fled downstairs, Sarazen returned to his room. They were never caught.

In relaying the story to famous sportswriter Grantland Rice for his weekly column, Sarazen called it "the queerest experience I ever had. But I was thinking of the forty dollars I had left on my dresser. These are tough days. I can use that forty dollars to feed my four cows."

Well, with his money and driver safe, the unnerving experience didn't seem to rattle Sarazen at all when the tournament began. He opened with a 68, just one stroke off the lead set by Henry Picard's 67.

Always impeccably dressed in a buttoned-up shirt and tie, Picard was very well liked and respected by his peers. The future two-time majors champion would go on to become a renowned teacher, and Ben Hogan among hundreds of others at different levels were benefactors of his teaching skills through the years.

As a matter of fact, according to the Golf Hall of Fame, Hogan, on the verge of quitting with just a lone victory in his first ten years as a professional, credits Picard for helping turn his career around.

Following a swing lesson on the practice tee at the Miami-Biltmore early in 1940, Hogan tamed his nasty hook. Picard suggested Hogan weaken his then-very-strong grip. He also advised Hogan to hit the ball with more power to close the club face. As a result, Bantam Ben, the person who rarely sought any outside counsel, would go on to win four times that year and get sixty-four victories overall, including nine majors.

"The greatest teacher I ever knew," Hogan once said of Picard.

High praise indeed.

Hogan admired and respected him so much that he dedicated his first instruction book, *Power Golf,* to Picard.

But back here at Augusta, Picard was focused on his own game, and it continued to be the best in the field. After rolling a 68 in the second round, he continued to be the leader at the halfway point. With a 71, Sarazen was four back.

Both Sarazen and Picard would have poor third rounds, 73 and 76 respectively.

As a result, there was a new leader.

Craig Wood, known as "the Blonde Bomber," shot 68 for a three-round total of 209, excelling despite stormy conditions (and a four-putt on the ninth). As a result, the native of Lake Placid, New York, the tall, strong, long-hitting, and unflappable Wood now owned a two-shot lead over Picard and three strokes over Sarazen heading into the final round.

Wood, obviously very talented, seemed to have a dark cloud over him at the end of a major event. He had lost the 1933 Open Championship in a thirty-six-hole playoff, lost the 1934 Masters by a single shot, and lost the 1934 PGA Championship in match play to Paul Runyan, his onetime assistant pro at Forest Hill and future Hall of Famer. After losing the 1939 US Open, Wood became the first player in golf history to lose all four men's majors in playoffs, or "extra holes." In other words, Wood became the first golfer to complete the "career Second Slam"—finishing second in all four majors.

Would the sun shine on Wood here at the second Masters?

It helped that Picard would end his chances by posting a 75.

Things were looking very good as Wood birdied four of the last eight holes in that final round. He was in the clubhouse being congratulated as the winner at 6 under par and a three-stroke lead. However, another dark cloud, this one in the form of Gene Sarazen, loomed at the fifteenth hole.

O. B. Keeler, writing in *The American Golfer*, reported the needling byplay between the two friends who were paired in that final round, as they stood in the fairway listening to the gallery's roar that greeted Wood's final birdie:

> Hagen: *"Well Gene, that looks like it's all over."*
> Sarazen: *"Oh, I don't know. They might go in from anywhere."*

After talking over club selection with his caddy, Thor "Stovepipe" Nordwall, Sarazen was taking his time sizing up his 4-wood when his pal Hagen barked out:

"Come on, hit it, will ya? I've got a date."

Turned out the fighting little Italian American had a date of his own, this one with destiny.

"I took my stance and rode into the shot with every ounce of strength and timing I could muster," Sarazen wrote in his book *30*

Years of Championship Golf. "The split second I hit the ball I knew it would carry the pond. It tore for the flag on a very low trajectory, no more than 30 feet in the air. Running forward to watch its flight, I saw the ball land on the green and then, while I was straining to see how close it had finished, the small gallery let out a terrific shout and began to jump wildly. I knew then the ball had gone into the hole."

Reportedly, inside the clubhouse, Wood's name had already been inscribed on the winner's check, but with one swing (235 yards, which was a long carry at the time, especially under the pressure of trying to win a tournament) Sarazen had made up three strokes on Wood. He parred the last three holes, which left him tied for the lead after four rounds.

A thirty-six-hole playoff resulted and, seemingly anticlimactically, Sarazen won by five strokes, 144 to 149.

All because it was that rare result, a double eagle, aka an albatross (when a player scores three strokes under par on a single hole, i.e., a 2 on a par-5), that put the 1935 Masters into golfing lore.

Grantland Rice, America's first star sportswriter (and also a founding member of Augusta National), called it "the most thrilling single golf shot ever played."

How rare is a double eagle?

A study done around 2012 estimated there are about forty thousand aces made in the United States every year, compared to about two hundred double eagles.[1]

Yes, but how many double eagles have contributed to victory in a major?

One thing was for sure. When the media dubbed Sarazen's albatross "the shot heard round the world," that was crucial in launching this small invitational event as a legitimate tournament.

First prize was $1,500. And the story goes that cofounder Cliff Roberts handed Sarazen a $50 bonus that certainly would help "feed the cows."

2

FORT WORTH'S FINEST:
BEN VS. BYRON

APRIL 9–13, 1942
AUGUSTA NATIONAL GOLF CLUB
AUGUSTA, GEORGIA

It was April 1942. World War II was raging in Europe. With gas rationing making it tough to travel to events, and core equipment components like rubber (for balls) and steel (for shafts) being siphoned off for the war effort, this would be the last Masters until after the global conflict ended. The Open Championship in Britain had already been suspended, as the courses there were converted to landing strips for the Royal Air Force.

But the 1942 Masters tournament would be one of the most memorable tilts that Augusta National would ever host as it featured two titans from Texas.

Ben Hogan and Byron Nelson—two men who grew up in the same caddy yard in Fort Worth, Texas, with a rivalry rooted in their days hustling for bags for loops with Glen Garden Country Club members, then competing against each other as teenagers in the caddy tournament.

After years of struggle to get to the top, these two players—polar opposites in personality and physicality, but also occasional room-mates on the road—would put on a show for the lucky gallery at Augusta that would make golfing lore.

Nelson, already a winner of three majors (1937 Masters, 1939 US Open, and 1940 PGA Championship), was a tall, angular fellow. Soft-spoken and gracious, he was one of the straighter arrows and straight-est hitters on tour. Hogan, though small in stature, was tough and wiry, and he could still hit the ball a long way for a person of his dimensions (about five eight and 140 pounds). The introverted young man, who had been struggling with his hook, was one of the hardest workers on tour, and now he had developed into one of the game's best ball strikers.

Hogan parlayed that into success and was the PGA Tour's leading money winner in 1940 and 1941.

However, in the opening round here, Hogan's game was not on the money. His first-round total of 73 was six back of the leaders and five back of Nelson. Meanwhile Byron bolted to the lead halfway through with a blistering 67 at 9 under par 135 total. Hogan, though he man-aged a 2-under 70, fell further off the pace and found himself now eight strokes back of the leader. In between them was a talented core led by Sammy Byrd (who gave up a baseball career with the Yankees to play golf), Jimmy Demaret (1940 Masters champion), Paul Runyan (a two-time PGA champion), and Horton Smith (a two-time Masters champion).

However, on a cool, dry Saturday the third round was dominated by Hogan. Using his experience battling the winds, his tremendous 5-under 67, which included four birdies on the back nine, was a full four shots better than anyone else in the top ten and five strokes better than Nelson's 72. Still at 207, Nelson was the fifty-four-hole leader with Hogan just three shots back in second.

The last round saw Byron start out poorly. After four bogeys on the first eight holes, Nelson found himself tied with Hogan at 6 un-der par. But after sinking his fourth birdie of the day, he left fifteen with a two-stroke advantage.

Hogan finished the round with a birdie that put him 8 under par. In his book, *How I Played the Game,* Nelson described the pressure he put himself under after a bogey at seventeen and needing a par just to get into a playoff:

"When I stepped up to my drive on 18, I noticed the tee box was kind of soft and slick. As I started my downswing, my foot slipped a little and I made a bad swing, pushing my tee shot deep into the woods on the right. By now I knew Ben had shot 70, and I had to have a par just to tie. When I got to my ball, I was relieved to find I had a clear swing. The ball was just sitting on the ground nicely, and there was an opening in front of me, about 20 feet wide, between two trees. I took my five-iron and hooked the ball up and onto the green 15 feet from the pin and almost birdied it—but I did make my part. I felt very fortunate to tie."[1]

Finishing three ahead of the field, Nelson and Hogan would play an eighteen-hole playoff for the green jacket.

In a rare nod to their stature, Nelson recalled, more than two dozen of the pros who had played in the tournament stayed to watch the two Texans battle it out in overtime.

Adding to the excitement, 1942 was also the first time that the Masters was broadcast live, by NBC radio.

Nelson had a wild front nine in the playoff. He started off with a double bogey after an errant tee shot opened things on hole one. He would birdie two and six but bogey four. Hogan's steadier performance put him at even through seven and a one-stroke lead.

However, at the par-5 eighth, Nelson nestled his second shot to within six feet of the cup, and rolled in the putt for eagle.

After both made pars at number nine, Nelson held a one-shot lead heading to the back nine. And what a back nine it would be. A couple of heavyweights landing some haymakers.

After three straight birdies beginning with the par-4 eleventh, Nelson's fine performance through Amen Corner had regained for him the three-stroke lead he had started the playoff with. However,

Battling Ben fired back with three straight birdies of his own, starting at thirteen, to cut the margin to one with just three holes to play.

But after Hogan bogeyed sixteen, he could not answer the bell. And despite bogeying eighteen, Nelson prevailed by one stroke, 69 to 70, winning his second and last Masters title.

The lucky gallery was treated to one of the best showdowns in tournament history.

It was a "masterful" performance between two great players, one that would help stretch pleasant memories until play resumed at Augusta National in 1946.

3

HOGAN'S FIRST GREEN JACKET LEADS
TO A NEW TRADITION AT AUGUSTA

APRIL 5–8, 1951
AUGUSTA NATIONAL GOLF CLUB
AUGUSTA, GEORGIA

For nine years Ben Hogan, now age thirty-eight, had sought one of golf's greatest prizes—winning the Masters.

Eight times he had a top ten finish at Augusta National. He had come in second place twice. Both were agonizingly close. In 1942 he lost an eighteen-hole playoff to childhood rival Byron Nelson. Then, after World War II canceled tournaments from 1943 to 1945, Hogan finished just one stroke back in 1946.

The tough little Texan had not only overcome a near-fatal car crash in 1949, but he had had won the US Open twice and the PGA Championship twice, so he was determined to get that green jacket.

Halfway through the 1951 Masters, Hogan's 142 (70-72) total gave him a share of second place, a position he resolved was not going to be where he'd end up on Sunday afternoon. However, he remained one off the lead and was again in the runner-up spot after a 70 on Saturday at 4 under par. What's more, he found himself in the middle of a deeply talented field that topped the leaderboard. The great Sam

Snead, the 1949 Masters champion, was tied for the lead at 5 under. Lloyd Mangrum, Cary Middlecoff, and his longtime adversary, Byron Nelson, were all still in the hunt.

When it came down to the crunch, coleaders Skee Riegel, a first-year pro, and Snead could not keep up with Hogan, who had a four-birdie, no-bogey final round of 68. No one else could produce a round under 70. Ben won by two strokes.

Finally breaking through at Augusta National meant a great deal to Hogan, and he came up with an idea to relive the joy of winning with fellow Masters champions.

And so Hogan sent the following letter to Augusta National co-founder and chairman Clifford Roberts:

Dear Cliff:

I wish to invite you to attend a stag dinner at the Augusta National on Friday evening, April 4th, at 7:15 p.m. It's my wish to invite all the Masters Champions who are going to be here, plus Bob Jones and Cliff Roberts. The latter has agreed to make available his room for the dinner party and I hope you can be on hand promptly at 7:15 p.m. My only stipulation is that you wear your green coat.

Cordially yours,
Ben Hogan

The letter was dated March 31, 1952. And the very first Champions Dinner did, indeed, take place on April 4, 1952.

The occasion was a hit and developed into a Tuesday night tradition when the defending champion selects (and pays for) the menu. The Champions Dinner—or, officially, the Masters Club Dinner—is a popular tradition that continues to this day.

Down through the years, a diversity of taste dominates the dinner.

And with so many winners hailing from all over the world, menus oftentimes convey a real sense of national pride. The majority of champions choose to serve traditional food from their home country, which has led to some interesting entrees.

Here's a "sampling":

Bernhard Langer: Wiener schnitzel (breaded veal) and Black Forest cake.

Mike Weir: The Canadian brought a lot of big game from the Great White North including wild boar and elk.

Sandy Lyle: Haggis (main ingredients: sheep's heart, liver, and lungs), boiled in a bag traditionally made from the animal's stomach. Add in onion, oatmeal, suet, and spices, and serve with mashed turnips.

Charl Schwartzel: A traditional South African "braai"—a barbecue that included lamb chops, steaks, and sausages.

Tiger Woods: Well, when you win five times you do your best not to repeat yourself. He's gone with cheeseburgers and milkshakes, chicken-and-beef fajitas, sushi and sashimi, and Porterhouse steak, among other offerings.

Others dipped into family recipes from the old country representing their heritage.

Fred Couples: Chicken cacciatore.

Vijay Singh: Seafood tom kah, chicken panang curry, baked sea scallops with garlic sauce, and rack of lamb.

As one might imagine, it was Lyle's offerings that presented the most critical feedback.

I remember a lot of people were pretending to eat it, but had napkins very handy. As a matter of fact, I don't think it was a coincidence that the number of napkins requested at Sandy's dinner far exceeded even those where you'd expect a lot of them like the fine Texas BBQs thrown by Jordan Spieth and Ben Crenshaw.

"Oh man, it was rough," said Crenshaw, wincing at the memory. "It was elaborate, though. Sandy had on his kilt. He had a big scabbard [a leather sheath for holding a knife] and cut the stomach out. It was a show."

Englishman Nick Faldo, a three-time winner, felt he finally got it right on the third go-round.

"First off, I went with steak and kidney pie. They didn't like the kidney [laughs]. For the second one I did shepherd's pie, but my third one was the most popular—it was fish and chips. I had it flown over from England. All the sauces, the vinegar that was brilliant. Everybody had the fish and chips. In all the years I've been going I would say that was probably top three of the most popular the among champions dining."

Faldo's fave? "Hideki's [Matsuyama] great Japanese menu that also included some fine steak was among the very best dinners."

So now you know, at Augusta, the only course that remains the same year after year is the field of play.

In an event that prides itself on long-standing traditions, one of the great Masters customs remains: the Masters Club Dinner started by the 1951 champion, Ben Hogan.

4

I

THE CLASH BETWEEN TWO SUPERSTARS
AND A SCENE-STEALING AMATEUR

APRIL 8–12, 1954
AUGUSTA NATIONAL GOLF CLUB
AUGUSTA, GEORGIA

During the period between 1949 and 1954—with the exception of 1950, when Jimmy Demaret won—the green jacket was worn by either Sam Snead or Ben Hogan, such was the dominance of the two greats at Augusta National at that time.

And perhaps their finest duel would be in 1954.

On second thought, *duel* is not the right word because there would be a little-known amateur who almost stole the show from the game's two giants.

Billy Joe Patton, a thirty-two-year-old accomplished amateur, grew up in North Carolina and began playing at age five. After graduating from Wake Forest and serving in the Navy, Patton—who would win the North and South Amateur three times and the Southern Amateur twice—earned an invitation to his first Masters after serving as an alternate to the US Walker Cup team.

He would make the most of the opportunity, which began the

day before the first round. The burly, bespectacled, crew-cut amateur came down from the mountains of the Carolinas, employed his quick-swinging style, and won the long drive contest held on Wednesday with a poke of 338 yards.

That success was certainly a confidence and momentum builder heading into the first round; the man from Morganton surprised everyone by starting things with a 70 and grabbing a share of the lead. Keeping his problematic wayward drives in check at Augusta, Patton followed that with a 74 and led the Masters halfway through the tournament at even par 144, one stroke ahead of Hogan and three strokes ahead of Snead.

Though he'd charm the patrons with comments like, "You didn't pay to see me play it safe," Patton's tendency to find himself off the beaten path caught up with him in the third round.

While Hogan rolled a 69 to take the lead as the only player under par (2-under 214) and Snead grabbed possession of second place with a 70, Patton's wild 75 placed him five strokes back of Hogan, who was not about to let an amateur ruin his goal of becoming the first player to win back-to-back Masters.

But a plucky Patton did his darndest to do just that.

While the two megastars couldn't generate anything in the early going of the fourth round, Patton jump-started his day by acing the par-3, 190-yard sixth with a five-iron that drove the ball into the cup on the fly. Adding back-to-back birdies at eight and nine to make the turn in 32 put him right in the mix. With Hogan scoring a double bogey at eleven and Snead bogeying twelve, Patton came to the par-5 thirteenth with the lead.

Buoyed by friends who had come from Morganton to support him and patrons hoping to witness an upset of monumental proportions, and influenced by their cheers of "Go for it Bill!" Patton did just that . . . but with disastrous results.

His ball went for a swim in Rae's Creek.

Undaunted, he took off his shoes and socks looking to splash out, but after rethinking it, he took a drop and finished the hole, still barefoot, posting a double-bogey seven.

You don't do that against two greats who eventually found their game. Snead birdied that same thirteen, and both he and Hogan birdied fifteen to force an eighteen-hole playoff, which Patton missed out on by one stroke.

Not a bad showing for a gentleman who made his living as a salesman for a lumber company. But now the big lumber came out.

These two titans were distinct from one another in that Snead was considered a natural who could "fall out of bed and score under par" while Hogan was the poster child of "digging it out of the dirt," grinding away through hours of practice.

"When I joined the tour, I watched others and I remember watching Sam Snead in an exhibition with Harvey Ward, Frank Stranahan, and Jackie Burke. Looking at Sam's swing I thought to myself, 'Now that is the way that it should be done,'" said 1973 Masters champion Tommy Aaron. "So I guess subconsciously I try to emulate Sam Snead's swing. Sam made the game look very effortless. With seemingly very little strain he could drive the ball a very long way."

Bobby Nichols, the 1964 PGA Champion, played many competitive rounds with Snead and Hogan and compared the two.

"Sam was such a natural athlete. He had a swing that was so easy, repetitive, and graceful. You just knew he was going to play well," said Nichols, a second-place finisher at the 1967 Masters. "I thought Mr. Hogan's swing was about the best of all, but Sam probably had the most natural ability of anyone that has ever played the game. Everything was so automatic."

What was automatic was knowing that Snead and Hogan would bring out the best in each other. Sure enough, the two played even for the front nine. Snead grabbed the advantage with a chip-in birdie at ten. However, he gave the lead right back with a bogey at twelve.

Now came the par-5 thirteenth, which both had birdied the day before to help get them into this position. Slammin' Sam decided to go for it in two, while Hogan chose to lay up. Snead took the lead with a birdie. Hogan had one last good shot at catching Snead when he hit his tee shot close at number sixteen. But he uncharacteristically three-putted and was now down by two. Snead played the eighteenth cautiously and made a bogey to win.

It would be Snead's third victory at Augusta National, and his seventh and final major.

I knew Sam Snead and Ben Hogan very well. And Snead was irritated when people said Hogan was the straightest hitter they ever saw. They'd say, "You know he [Hogan] put it in the same divot he did yesterday." And Snead would invariably say, "If he's that good, why didn't he hit it to the left or to the right of that divot?"

Snead and Hogan were both forty-one years old in 1954. And this victory made Snead the oldest Masters winner, a record he held until I won the 1978 Masters at age forty-two.

But even though he would not win another major, Snead, with that supple body, that beautiful rhythmic swing, that pure love of the game and desire to compete, would go on to play at a high level for decades. When he finally retired, his eighty-two victories were the most on the PGA Tour.

5

HONORED TO BE THE FIRST INTERNATIONAL
WINNER OF THE MASTERS

APRIL 6–10, 1961
AUGUSTA NATIONAL GOLF CLUB
AUGUSTA, GEORGIA

At the 1961 Masters tournament, I knew I'd be taking on both an army and an American tradition.

Not only was Arnold Palmer the defending champion, but he was so popular that his massive, dedicated gallery was dubbed "Arnie's Army" for their unswerving support. On top of that, I was coming to the par-72, 6,980-yard course, where no international player had ever won before.

I was aware that some great players from abroad, including Peter Thomson from Australia, Roberto De Vicenzo from Argentina, as well as my fellow countryman Bobby Locke, had fallen short of victory. I wanted to be the one to make players outside America realize that they could come to the best-run tournament in the world and win.

What was a key part in getting ready to go up against one of the most popular athletes in all sports?

Well, Arnold was my dear friend and I loved him immensely, but I had prepared my mind in advance. I was ready for Arnold and his army. I prepared my mind for the screaming and the shouting of his thousands upon thousands of followers. Of course, they always pulled for Arnold, but they were still kind to me.

On a gray, drizzly day where the normally slippery greens required careful approach, they were more amenable to scoring being soft and moist in the first round. I opened with a 3 under par 69 and that put me in second place, just one stroke back of Bob Rosburg and Arnie, who both had 68s.

The next day both Arnie and I created some separation atop the leaderboard.

With three birdies on the back nine including eighteen, I finished with a 68. Arnie's round included four birdies and a bogey for a 69. Halfway through we shared a four-stroke lead of 137 at 7 under.

It was no surprise to anyone following the game that we were clear coleaders favored to win. I believe that by the time we reached Augusta, we had won five of the thirteen tournaments between the two of us.

After my third straight round in the 60s (a 69—thanks to back-to-back birdies on the fifteenth and sixteenth holes), I had created some separation from my chief foe. Heading into the final round I was the only competitor in double digits. In first place, I was at 10 under, four shots ahead of Arnie, who finished with a 73 on Saturday.

Feeling good about my game and position, I was looking forward to the final round, but Mother Nature had other ideas.

I was even through eleven holes and Arnie was 2 under through nine when play was canceled due to heavy rains and flooding of several greens. The scores were erased, and the entire round would have to be replayed the following day.

Undaunted, I started out Monday with birdies on holes one and two to go 12 under, with Arnie at 7 under. I followed that with seven straight pars, but after a bogey at ten and with his three birdies on the front nine, my lead over Arnie had slipped to two.

Coming to the thirteenth, I was 11 under. This was a demanding

455-yard par-5 that doglegs left with a full right-angled turn. From the tee hard down the left side of the first leg, Rae's Creek runs along below thick woods.

I drove too far right deep into the trees lining the right side of the fairway. I should have taken a six-iron down the adjacent fourteenth fairway then put my third on the green, but I became impatient as the crowds were moving too slowly. I had instructed the marshals to move the deep gallery back along the right side of the thirteenth so I could have a clear shot into the fourteenth. I continued to ask for this courtesy, but the crowd was simply too large and unwieldy, so I gave up in despair and decided instead to jab the ball through the trees and back to the fairway. I used too much muscle and it ran into the creek.

I was too impatient! And it almost cost me. My mind was not right as my lead was slipping, and I was too excited and worried about the delay to think clearly. That thirteenth hole will always give me night-mares. And the resultant double-bogey dropped me into a tie with Arnie at 9 under.

After a bogey at fifteen, I was now out of the lead, one back of Palmer. And amateur Charles Coe, playing behind me in Palmer's group would produce three straight birdies starting at thirteen to get to 7 under.

At Augusta, you cannot boil it down to a few key shots; it's more about how good your mind is. So, after fighting to maintain my cool, I steadied my nerves and reminded myself I still felt I had a solid chance to win.

Yes, fans had watched Palmer come from behind to win the previous year's Masters, and they had seen him come charging up to win the previous summer's US Open with a final-round 65. But Augusta is a physically and mentally demanding course, and bogeys and double bogeys come into play even more when you are tired. Remember, Arnie had been chasing me for a couple days, and that takes a toll.

I have often said winning a major championship is a complete test of both skill and character, and an important component of success is to not only cope with adversity but in a strange way to actually embrace it. When under pressure, everything suggests an all-encompassing desire to escape and run for cover, but I came to develop a belief that one must go through with it, otherwise you could never live with the thought that you had given up.

And I was not about to give up.

Subsequently I closed with some great pars.

After a par at sixteen, I got it up and down at seventeen with a tough pin placement in the back right position. At eighteen, I landed in the bunker, then hit it out to within five feet of the pin and knocked it in.

Now with the lead at the seventy-second hole, Arnie hit his approach shot into the same the bunker as I had done earlier; however, his lie was a bit buried. Now if your ball is buried, you never have a wide-open face. You keep the clubface more square, and you hit down on it. And Arnold was never really an extraordinary bunker player. In this case he bladed it over the green and ended up with a double bogey.

I had finished with three pars, and I felt pretty good about that. There's no hole on that course you can't double bogey. Palmer still had to get those pars to beat me, and the only time you win is when the ball goes into the hole.

Everybody says how Arnold blew it. But *Sports Illustrated* magazine told the story as it actually happened. And it said, "Gary Player deserved to win it."

So, it was interesting to have somebody on my side because I wasn't going to have very many with Arnold, the great American icon, and nobody understood that more than me. I did not expect them to be on my side. Again, the importance of mental preparation.

I had defeated America's most popular golfer at its most popular event. And over time, my victory would spark a global movement in golf that's now commonplace.

It filled me with pride knowing that at just twenty-five I had earned an historic victory. The first international player to win the Masters.

6

THE NIGHTMARE LOSS
THAT STILL LINGERS

APRIL 5–9, 1962
AUGUSTA NATIONAL GOLF CLUB
AUGUSTA, GEORGIA

I have never experienced a bigger disappointment in golf than the 1962 Masters. Nothing even comes close to that.

Here was how it unfolded.

I knew that nobody had ever won the Masters twice in a row. That was my main thought, to see if I could do that.

I had not forgotten that I had ruined Arnie's chances to be the first to achieve that by defeating him here the previous year.

This year I captured the lowest round of the opening day with a 67, to lead by two over Julius Boros, a US Open winner ten years prior. (He would win it again the following year.)

Now Arnie secured the lowest score of the second round with a 66. His 8-under 136 total put him in the lead, but I was on his heels in second, just two back.

The third round saw a third party that would not only produce the day's lowest score but would figure in the three-way battle that would close this event. Thirty-two-year-old Dow Finsterwald, the winner of the 1958 PGA championship (the first PGA Championship held after the format was switched from match play to stroke play), put up a 65.

Thus, heading into the final round, the top of leaderboard looked like this:

ARNOLD PALMER	70-66-69=205	−11
DOW FINSTERWALD	74-68-65=207	−9
GARY PLAYER	67-71-71=209	−7

Dow, a former Vardon Trophy winner, birdied the par-5 second hole and drew to within one of Palmer. Meanwhile, after bogeys at one and three, I fell to six back of the leader. However, both Dow and Arnie made back-to-back bogeys at holes four and five. And after my fourth birdie, which came at nine, all three of us shared the lead at 8 under heading to the home half.

Dow had played Augusta well in the past. As a matter of fact, had he not called a two-stroke penalty on himself for taking a practice putt early in the tournament, he would have tied his good friend and eventual winner Arnold in 1960.

Here on the back nine, Dow would birdie thirteen and seventeen. After a birdie at eleven, I gave it right back with a bogey at twelve.

Well, if there is one moment in my life that haunts me, it is the sixteenth hole at Augusta. I had a two-shot lead over Arnold with three holes to play. And I was going to be the first player to win the Masters twice in a row. I hit first and put it twelve feet below the hole. Arnold missed the green to the right—pin high about seventy feet from the hole. So he chipped it, and the ball gathered speed. As we watched it, my caddy said, "We have won it because you can't stop the ball, as it has to go over the green from there because you simply cannot stop it."

And what did Arnie do? His ball came around the corner and down the hill a hundred miles an hour, and I thought for sure it was over the green. Instead it hit the flag and went in! And you can give somebody a hundred shots from there and it would never go in. Never. Anytime a player has missed that flag to the right, none of them have got it down in two, because it gathered speed.

I missed my putt, but I was still feeling good.

Arnold hit first on seventeen. I pulled out my driver. He hit a low hook that went into the Eisenhower tree and came down under it. I went fifty yards over the tree then had a nine-iron to the green. I'm guessing I landed about twenty feet from the hole.

Arnold took a five-iron and then ran it up to about twenty-five feet from the hole. And he knocked that in. Dow, Arnie, and myself finished four rounds knotted at 280.

We would comprise the first three-man playoff in Masters history. It would be an eighteen-hole playoff. No such thing as sudden death or a few aggregate holes.

In the playoff, Dow didn't really play well (including four bogeys on the front nine). I had a good outward half, which put me three strokes ahead of Arnold at the turn at 2 under. So once again, it came down to the same combatants as last year, Arnie and myself. But with such a hard-charging aggressive player as my remaining opponent, I could not afford the luxury of the slightest slip.

After nine holes I was out in 33. Palmer was out in 36. At the tenth hole I had a terrific shot to the green just behind the pin. Arnold hit a poor shot I would guess about thirty-five feet to the right of the flag. And a big break from right to left with that sloping green. I said to my caddy, "I think we have him here."

But sure enough, Arnie's shot came right around the bend and into the hole.

And I said to my caddy, "There is no question about it—God is an American."

Adding back-to-back birdies at thirteen and fourteen, Arnold was well on his way to a back nine of 31, for a 68 to beat me by three. I finished with a 71, and Dow at 77.

It happened more than sixty years ago, but I still feel the painful disappointment like it took place only yesterday. I have thought about that loss at least once a month ever since because losing that tournament was not possible. I loved Arnold. I loved him like a brother, but not that much to give him that tournament! Ha.

7

"WHAT A STUPID I AM"

Let me say this up front: despite the unfortunate incident at this tournament that would dominate many fans' memories of him, Roberto De Vicenzo was not only an outstanding golfer but a terrific sportsman. Like me, he won many tournaments all over the world. The popular and gracious Argentine was a great ambassador for the game. In 1970 he was voted the Bob Jones Award, the highest honor given by the United States Golf Association in recognition of distinguished sportsmanship in golf.

And know this—having played with him many times, including our pairing in the final round of the '67 Open Championship at Hoylake, where he won (and I finished third), Roberto was a tremendous striker, one of the three or four best I ever saw. There's no doubt in my mind that had he played a full schedule in America, he would have won a lot of major championships because he knew how to win.

Growing up in the suburbs of Buenos Aires, the son of a house painter and with six brothers and sisters, De Vicenzo would earn money fishing golf balls out of a pond at a nearby golf course, then graduated to being a caddy and learned the game.

He garnered success early. After turning pro he'd win tournaments not only in South America but in Europe and the United States as well. And he was used to being right in the mix on Sunday at the majors, particularly at the Open. Before winning it in 1967, he had come in third five times and was runner-up in 1950.

The big hitter was comfortable playing Augusta as well, having a top ten finish in 1967 at this event.

He opened the first round here with a 3-under 69, good enough for a share of second place. He was in a pack with Tommy Aaron, Bruce Devlin, Tony Jacklin, and Jack Nicklaus, just one back of the leader, Billy Casper (who would win this tournament two years later).

With a very good second round, I moved up to grab a share of the lead with Don January at 5-under 138. On the strength of a fine birdie at eighteen, I took sole possession of the lead and headed into the final round at 6 under. However, breathing down my neck was a bevy of deep talent that also had dreams of a green jacket. Raymond Floyd and Bob Goalby were among those just one back. Roberto and Lee Trevino were just two back.

Goalby—like me, the son of a miner—was a tremendous competitor. A terrific athlete who excelled in baseball, he attended the University of Illinois on a football scholarship and served in the United States military during the Korean War.

The 1958 PGA Tour Rookie of the Year started out the last day with three birdies on the front nine. At the turn he was just one back of the leader, De Vicenzo, who was at 9 under. (I finished out of the running with a final-round 72.)

With a seven-birdie day including three straight beginning at fifteen, Bert Yancey made a good run with a 65, but that would not be enough.

De Vicenzo, celebrating his birthday, put a charge in the gallery by opening with an eagle. The crowd went wild and began singing "Happy Birthday" to him.

He followed that with back-to-back birdies.

A big man, the Argentine was a great driver of the ball; however, he admittedly was not a great putter. He could putt well enough and could win tournaments because the rest of his game was so strong. He drove the ball long, and he regularly hit the ball so close that he did not have to be a great putter. Still, the flat stick was working well so far on this day. His front nine 31 tied the course record.

Then with a birdie at ten, De Vicenzo took a two-stroke lead over Goalby. But in a tremendous display of his own scoring power, Goalby not only produced back-to-back birdies at thirteen and fourteen, but on fifteen he matched Roberto's eagle with one himself. A tremendous three-iron shot to get to within eight feet of the cup gave him the lead at 12 under.

Thinking to himself what a birthday present a Masters championship would be, De Vicenzo birdied seventeen, but at eighteen his approach carried over the green and into the gallery. Despite the bogey, he went to the scorer's table tied for the lead.

Angry at his bogey at the penultimate hole, Goalby settled down and, after a stern self-talking-to, parred eighteen. Seeing Roberto at the scorer's table, he said to his friend, "Well, I will see you at the playoff tomorrow."

However, in walking past him and seeing his puzzled, nonresponsive look, Goalby wondered if there was something wrong, especially since the Argentine had finished a half hour before him.

Indeed there was.

Still upset by bogeying the last hole, De Vicenzo quickly glanced at his scorecard and hurriedly signed it. The problem was that his playing partner, Tommy Aaron, had incorrectly marked Roberto down for a 4, when in fact he birdied the hole and it should've been recorded as a 3. And De Vicenzo missed it. The rules prohibited a correction once a card was signed; thus he finished at 10-under 278 (officially credited with a closing 66, instead of the 65 he actually shot), while Goalby was 11-under 277. So instead of a tie and subsequent eighteen-hole playoff the following day, the green jacket went to the man from Illinois, not from Argentina.

Aaron explained what happened:

Just as Roberto holed for yet another birdie to the roar of the crowd at seventeen, almost simultaneously an even bigger roar rose from the fifteenth green, where Goalby had made eagle to tie for the lead at 12 under. It was such an electric moment that I inadvertently forgot to record Roberto's score before leaving the green. Standing at the final tee, all I could think was, "You know, if he can par this, he'll have a great chance of winning." But after making a bogey five, he was understandably upset.

Aaron continued:

We are sitting there and Roberto was so disappointed he had his head in his hands. I remember the gallery leaning over the rope asking me what I shot while I am trying to check my scorecard. That is how close spectators were to you. There is just a small round table with a member sitting with us who was on the scoring committee. Roberto was approached by an official informing him that was wanted in the press room. And with that he grabs the card, scribbled his signature without checking it at all, and walked off to meet the press.

My first thought was, "God I hope that card is correct. He didn't even look at it." So I am sitting there and the card is right in front of me. Well I looked at it the scoreboard at eighteen and I thought there is something wrong here. That does not look right. I look at his card and went right to seventeen. And I thought, "Oh my God, I didn't even look at the seventeenth, I was so focused on eighteen." So I told the official there that I need to see Roberto right now. As he asked, "What is the matter?" And I told the official that he had signed an incorrect scorecard. Roberto comes back and I say, "Roberto, there is nothing I can say except that I am sorry."

I have not told many people this because it sounds so bad, however I truly feel it was just an emotional reaction of his, and all these years later I'm still convinced those words were totally innocent, a reflection of the shock he was in when he said, "Well, let's just change it."

"Roberto," I said, "we can't do that, it would be breaking the rules."

He quickly gathered himself and said, "Yes, of course. That's right."

So, I sat there with him as two or three other groups finished their round. He didn't say anything and I just reminded him there wasn't anything we could do and that I was sorry.

He was okay with that and he never blamed me. A terrible thing that happened, but the circumstances. I mean, I will check my card three, four, maybe five times. I will replay the round in my mind. Now there's somebody you could bounce the scores off of.

It was a horrible thing and I felt terrible about it, but so many players don't understand how important that is. They take a very cavalier, casual attitude toward the scorecard. I'm talking about not only many of the weekend players, but even some of the tour players used to do that.

Sitting down with Goalby just before the award presentation during a televised interview, trying to muster the strength to cover his heartbreaking mistake, De Vicenzo said: "I have been a professional for many years and I never think, 'What a stupid I am.' Because when you play in a tournament you have to check the scorecard very carefully and I make the wrong thing today . . . I feel sorry for myself and I don't think I'll get another chance to get this close and win the tournament like this week." Then turning to look at the winner, De Vicenzo added, "But I want to congratulate Bob Goalby for playing so good."

Goalby, looking over at Roberto, responded, "I don't really know what to say because Roberto is one of my good friends. We've been playing twelve, thirteen years together, and I really regret what happened because it seems like it's not really the way to win the golf tournament. I really don't know what to say."

Aaron, who won the Masters in 1973 (where, ironically, he corrected a scorecard error in the final round when his playing partner, Johnny Miller, recorded a 5 and not a birdie 4 on thirteen), added: "In truth, there were no winners that day. Roberto was the most tragic, but poor Bob got tons of hate mail, and I took some hits as well, despite a defense from Jack Nicklaus: 'There's no way it was Tommy's fault,' he told the media. 'It was Roberto's responsibility to check his card.'"

Many sports fans somehow viewed Goalby's Masters title as something improperly attained when in fact he played superbly, closing with a 66 with five birdies and an eagle, so Roberto would not have won even if his scorecard mistake never happened. People forget he would've just qualified for a playoff.

Though he kept his true feelings to himself for many, many years, weathering the controversy with grace, Goalby finally felt he had to get it off his chest. In a 1989 interview with the *Los Angeles Times* he said this:

"I've always felt like a victim, as much or more than Roberto. None of the problems with scorecards were my fault. But I have forever been singled out as the guy who won the Masters because of some damn clerical mistake. I don't think I ever got credit for what I did that week."[1]

Of the many hundreds of negative letters he received, one suggested, "They ought to put you and Sonny Liston in cement and drop you in the ocean."

Goalby won eleven times on tour and was a runner-up in both the PGA and US Open tournaments. He was a golf broadcaster for many years on NBC. He boldly led the Tournament Players Division to break away from the PGA of America and help form what now is the PGA Tour (with significant support from Palmer and Nicklaus). Then he joined with veteran pros Gardner Dickinson and Dan Sikes in 1980 to organize a tour for players fifty and older (now called the Champions Tour).

Roberto's infamous comment lives on as part of the golf lexicon today.

"What a stupid I am" was a quote heard 'round the world and was featured on the cover of *Sports Illustrated*. But the affable Argentine was smart enough take advantage of the mental error.

He cashed in nicely as a spokesman in a series of ads for Avis, the car rental company that branded itself as being "No. 2, but trying harder."[2]

Roberto De Vicenzo won many awards during his playing days and scored more than two hundred international victories. In 1989 he was inducted into the World Golf Hall of Fame.

8

NICKLAUS-WEISKOPF-MILLER = MAGNIFICENCE

APRIL 10–13, 1975
AUGUSTA NATIONAL GOLF CLUB
AUGUSTA, GEORGIA

Competition. That's what drives the greats. And the majors are the absolute pinnacle of golf, competitions played at a level of pressure guaranteed to test the nerve of even the greatest golfers. They are simply the world's toughest tournaments and the most sought-after prize, often requiring years of failure before a player learns how to win. The 1975 Masters will go down as one of the greatest examples of the very best competing against one another down to the wire.

I arrived at Augusta that year as the defending champion, having won the second of my three green jackets. However, I finished here back in the pack, which goes to show you: one had to be at the top of their game that week in order to have a chance, because out here there's too much talent and too much desire to win.

And one of the reasons why my good friend Jack Nicklaus has won more majors than anyone was that, like myself, he simply enjoyed the challenge of proving himself in competition against the very best.

"That's the fun of it," he'd say.

Three leading players came into the Masters this week at the top of their game. And their back-and-forth battle would hold the sporting world spellbound as it dramatically climaxed into one of the greatest finishes in golf history.

Twenty-seven-year-old Johnny Miller was in the prime of his career, coming between his wins in the 1973 US Open and the 1976 Open Championship. A dominant force, he was the hottest player on tour coming to Georgia. He won eight times the previous year and became Pro Golfer of the Year in 1974. This year his winning ways continued; he had taken three of the first five events of 1975.

Tom Weiskopf, thirty-two, was a tall, athletic man who owned one of the best swings in the game. With that wide arc, the Ohio native had a motion that was both graceful and powerful. Already a three-time runner-up at Augusta, Weiskopf had been in good form recently; he'd followed his second place at the Heritage Classic with first in the Greater Greensboro Open (now known as the Wyndham Championship) immediately preceding the Masters.

Now the winner of that Heritage Classic just happened to be the other player in this drama, Jack Nicklaus.

Nicklaus was three years older than Weiskopf, but they both grew up in Columbus, Ohio, and played for the Ohio State golf team. In recent weeks, the twelve-time major winner had won the last two tournaments he entered—the Doral-Eastern Open and the aforementioned Heritage event.

And the thirty-five-year-old Nicklaus wasted no time climbing to the top at this event. Showing the formidable skills of long, accurate driving, clutch putting, and mental tenacity that had earned the fourteen-year veteran four green jackets already, his 68-67=135—9 under total—gave him a five-stroke lead heading to the weekend.

Weiskopf had a share of fifth place, six back at 3 under. But with 75-71, Miller barely made the cut.

One person that unfortunately did not make the cut was the first Black player since the tournament's inception in 1934.

Lee Elder, a forty-year-old journeyman on the pro circuit since 1967 who had qualified after winning the Monsanto Open the previous April in Florida, had come up the hard way. Born in Dallas, Texas, in 1934 and one of ten children, he lost his father, who was killed in World War II, and his mother soon thereafter. As a way to support his brothers and sisters he became a caddy but developed skills of his own.

Dropping out of high school and constantly in search of money, the young man began playing big-money matches under the tutelage and support of the legendary hustler Titanic Thompson. Later he refined his game under former tour player Ray Mangrum and a legendary Black golfer, Ted Rhodes.[1]

After serving in the military himself, Elder came out feeling he had the game to compete at the highest level. However, the PGA Tour was off-limits to him due to a Caucasian-only rule that would be enforced until 1961. So in the meantime, he would dominate the minority-led United Golfers Association, winning four national titles on some pretty shoddy municipal courses.

But at Augusta, with its comparatively pristine conditions, Elder had the help of a very seasoned caddy for the Masters. Harry Brown carried the bag for eight years there for Roberto De Vicenzo (see chapter 7).

Despite a few calls by some rednecks on the back nine for him to miss a putt, overall Elder was warmly received by spectators and applauded for good shots just like the other competitors.

He finished the first round with a 74. And despite gamely competing under enormous pressure, with a second-round 78, Elder missed the cut.

Miller, who narrowly escaped a weekend exit, instead stormed back into contention with a fantastic third round. After opening with a par, on the long second hole, Miller used a terrific bunker shot to set up a shirt birdie, which put him now ten strokes back of the leader. He would get to even par after holing a birdie from fourteen feet on the next hole. A well-struck two-iron set up a birdie at the longest par 3 on the course, hole four. And with a birdie at the tough fifth, Miller's mindset was to continue to be aggressive with his hot hand.

The streak continued when he teed off the sixth with a five-iron, which led to a one-foot birdie. Now despite missing the green with his second shot, Miller faced a thirty-five-footer to a pin sitting atop a crown. When that went in, his sixth straight birdie broke the record set by Hale Irwin and myself in 1974.

Miller set a course record of 30 for the front nine. He added another birdie on the back nine and finished with the lowest round of the day at 65.

His stunning performance somewhat diluted another great round. This happened to be turned in by Weiskopf, who rolled a 66. They were in a league of their own. The next player had a 69. Nicklaus, paired with Palmer, had an off day with a 73. Something happened that more often than not when he was paired with the King.

Through the years Nicklaus always said that the two titans would get caught up in their respective galleries urging them each to beat the other, only to lose track of the entire field.

With three-fourths of the tournament completed, Weiskopf, at 9 under, held a one-shot lead over Nicklaus. It was his first lead in the Masters after any round. And Miller, who was lingering back in twenty-seventh, had moved all the way to third place, just four back.

Sunday would turn out to be a phenomenal performance between these three.

However, way before those three would get started, there'd be another phenomenal performance by a superb player. Defending US Open champion Hale Irwin would produce a bogey-free, eight-birdie round of 64, only to tie for fourth place at a distant 5 under.

But this day was a battle between Weiskopf, Nicklaus, and Miller. Nicklaus was paired with Tom Watson in the next-to-last group, while Miller and Weiskopf were in the final group.

The two Ohioans swapped birdies through the first nine, and they were tied at 11 under after ten holes. Miller, with five birdies and two bogeys coming to Amen Corner, was just three back. After Nicklaus bogeyed fourteen, with Weiskopf's birdie on the same hole, there was a two-shot swing, and he now had the lead back by one.

Weiskopf was at 11 under, Nicklaus was at 10 under, and Miller was at 9 under.

On the 520-yard par-5 fifteenth, after a good belt off the tee, Nicklaus was under pressure. He was trailing Weiskopf by one stroke, and he knew he had to have a birdie at the very least. He selected a one-iron for his second shot from 240 yards away.

"I was on one of those little bumps in the fairway, uphill lie, and a 1-iron is a hard club to stop on that green," recalled Nicklaus. "I took it and hit it straight up in the air. It comes off the golf club and you watch the flight and you say, 'Ooh, was that fun.' A shot I will always remember."[2]

And the Golden Bear owned some of the most memorable shots in the majors when it came to the difficult-to-control one-iron.

At the 1967 US Open, Nicklaus hit a 238-yard one-iron shot onto the green at the seventy-second hole. He made the putt, establishing a new US Open scoring record. Then seven years later at the first US Open that Pebble Beach hosted in 1972, Nicklaus sealed the title by striking the flagstick with a wind-piercing one-iron for a tap-in birdie.

On the 190-yard par-3 sixteenth, Nicklaus struck a so-so five-iron that landed about forty feet short and left of the flag. His playing partner, Tom Watson, planted his ball into the water. After finding his first effort unplayable in the edge of the pond, there would be a slight delay as Watson went back to re-tee.

This allowed Nicklaus to look back and observe both drop putts at fifteen, and the roars of the crowds told him they were both for birdie.

Now Nicklaus was one behind Weiskopf and one ahead of Miller.

Watson's ball had landed on the green to an area that would provide Nicklaus a good read for his.

With the delay, Weiskopf and Miller watched the group ahead of them while milling around back at the sixteenth-tee box.

"I remembered that final break from a twelve-footer I had made for birdie in winning my first Masters back in 1963. As I looked over my putt, the thought of my mind at first was 'Make par.' Then, as I stood up after a last look at the line, I realized it was crystal clear in my mind's eye. I told myself, 'Make it,'" recalled Nicklaus in his book *My Story*.

"I stroked the ball solidly, starting it exactly where I intended to. As the ball got within about twelve feet of the hole, I was so certain it was going in I thrust my putter high in the air. As the ball actually fell in the cup, both Willie and I went into what can only be described as war dances. It was an unforgettable moment for both of us. Holing a putt of that length over that difficult a line at that moment was just a humongous break. The excitement was almost unbearable."[3]

Weiskopf took all this in as he stood back at the tee, watching the great player raise his putter and uncharacteristically jog around the green in celebration. Then Nicklaus ran off to the seventeenth green without looking back, knowing how key that shot was. Quite aware his opponent had just made a very tough putt under enormous pressure to tie him for the lead, Weiskopf was understandably disheartened, but he had to regroup quickly and get his nerves under control.

Alas, with a tee shot that was short, Weiskopf three-putted the hole to fall one behind Nicklaus, who parred number seventeen.

Nicklaus 12-under, Weiskopf 11-under, and Miller 10-under.

At the 400-yard par-4 seventeenth, Weiskopf parred the hole to stay one back. But Miller was about to make another move.

Nicklaus was assessing his putt on the seventy-second hole when a huge roar suddenly erupted from the seventeenth green. He knew someone had birdied. Buying a little time by circling his ball again, a tricky twelve-footer with a hard break left, he had to decide to be more aggressive if it was Weiskopf who made the putt, or lag it up if it was Miller. He decided on the conservative approach. He missed on the low side of the cup, which allowed for a straight uphill follow-up, which he made for his par.

Miller made a clutch birdie putt that was so perfect that the millisecond it left his blade, he showed some exuberance of his own, raising his hand in an energetic wave well before the ball reached the hole. He had it made and he knew it, joining Weiskopf to be just one back with one hole to play.

Nicklaus 12-under, Weiskopf 11-under, and Miller 11-under.

Despite the enormity of the situation (a birdie would earn a play-off spot), both Weiskopf and Miller hit solid drives and fine approach shots at the 420-yard final hole. So, once again (as I have stated many times throughout this book), it came down to the putter. Nicklaus peered out at the green from the scorer's tent, looking on like the thousands of other highly engaged spectators.

With a fifteen-footer to tie for the lead, Miller ever so slightly misjudged the break and veered just slightly left past the hole.

Seeing what happened, Weiskopf measured his eight-footer quite carefully—after all, he had to keep his hopes of a green jacket alive.

It wasn't meant to be. The ball stayed right never touching the hole.

"I saw Johnny's ball break and I played for the same break," a disappointed Weiskopf said. "I hit it good. I hit it the way I wanted to. The ball didn't break. It's the break of the game. But there will be other days."

Unfortunately, there'd be no other days in terms of major victories for Weiskopf. After his obvious disappointment of a fourth time being runner-up at Augusta, he had bravely vowed, "I know one thing. I will win this tournament one day, and my green coat will be tailor-made." Despite that, the closest he'd get would be a share of ninth place the following year.

He would have a few more top five finishes, including a runner-up performance at the following year's US Open, but he would never win a second major.

Weiskopf was almost as good a golfer as I ever saw, but he won only one major. And one major on the senior tour, the US Open. It just goes to show that having a beautiful swing does not automatically translate into winning majors. I wish Tom could've won more, because he deserved to.

Miller, too, would never win a green jacket, finishing runner-up in 1981. I remember playing with him at Augusta, and he just fired at the pins hole after hole. I will never get over it. His iron shots to the flags were like darts on a dartboard. I mean, it was hard to believe.

For Nicklaus, it was a record-breaking fifth Masters title. (He'd go on to win a sixth in 1986—see chapter 11.) It was clearly done in a way that the Golden Bear prefers, dueling hole after hole against the very best to the end.

The common perception was that it simply had to be an agonizing ordeal wreaking havoc on one's heart and nerves for more than four hours. However, Nicklaus, grinning from ear to ear, had a completely different take on it.

"Fun" was how the thirteen-time major winner described the play at the press conference afterward. "To be out there in the middle of something like that is fun," he would insist. "You're inspired, you're eager, you're excited. You almost want to break into a dead run when you hit a good shot. It's what you've prepared yourself for, what you wait a year for. To know you can look back some day and know you were a part of something like it, that's just great."

Two-time Master champion Ben Crenshaw made this observation about the Golden Bear:

"You look at Jack Nicklaus and Tiger Woods and a few others, they excelled in the big arena. And one reason why? They loved that competition. They got themselves into position so many times. I must say Nicklaus's record is incredible. Not only for the wins, but how many times he was right there in the mix with all those seconds and thirds. Out of this world."

Competition at the highest levels. That was what Jack's world was all about. With the hard-charging Miller and the determined Weiskopf, the 1975 Masters raised not only Augusta but the majors in general to an even greater status.

9

FLOYD'S MASTERY OF THE FORGOTTEN FIVE-WOOD

APRIL 8-11, 1976
AUGUSTA NATIONAL GOLF CLUB
AUGUSTA, GEORGIA

Raymond Floyd was born the son of a golf pro in Fort Bragg, North Carolina, and would go on to win four majors, twenty-two PGA Tour events, and the Vardon Trophy. He would also become a member of the World Golf Hall of Fame. Yet his prowess in another sport nearly prevented all that from happening.

You see, just after graduating from Fayetteville High School in 1960, the teenager was offered a sizable bonus to become a pitcher in the Cleveland Indians organization. Instead, he chose to attend the University of North Carolina in Chapel Hill. However, after just a semester hitting the books, Floyd decided to hit approach shots, leaving the campus to become a professional golfer in 1961. (Later on he'd pitch batting practice to his beloved Cubs on occasion while living in Chicago, serving up meatballs to the likes of the great Ernie Banks, Ron Santo, and Billy Williams. With his well-known competitiveness, though, he surely would have liked to see what those hitters could have done against his best stuff.)

It took a while for all that promise on the links to fully come to the fore because even in 1969, the year he won his first major (the PGA Championship where he defeated me by one stroke!), Floyd's reputation was that of a partier known more for late-night drinking and carousing.

The young man made no apologies for being single and coming from a small town, wanting to live it up. And he did, sharing good times at nightclubs, racetracks, and various sporting events. Floyd was buddies with the Rat Pack, Broadway Joe Namath, and Clint Eastwood, among others. Floyd even owned a piece of a bar in San Francisco called Coke's, where sometimes he played guitar onstage and was an investor in the Ladybirds, a topless band.

Still, when he was focused, he had the game many envied.

"I was just amazed at how good Ray Floyd was. How he could strike the ball," recalled former US Open champion Jerry Pate. "I tell him to this day, watching him hit those Wilson staff one-irons with his upright backswing and hit down on it, I teased him because he's about ten years older than I. My father used to say, 'Watch him, son, that Ray is standing on those one-irons.' Ray could hit that one-iron like a bullet."

And even though his career didn't speed to the top like a bullet, after getting married (to Maria Primoli, an airline stewardess from Philadelphia) and then becoming the father of two sons, Floyd began showing a marked commitment to the game.

Floyd was ready to play a leading contender role in the majors, and he had a game made for Augusta National. One of the players taking note of this was the 1973 Masters winner, Tommy Aaron.

"Raymond had many of the same qualities as Nicklaus. He was very focused. And a lot of confidence in himself. He had a tremendous short game. A great putter. Really just a good all-around player. A great competitor who was tremendous under pressure," Aaron said. "[For example,] he'd be off the green where many other players might putt, but he would pitch it and tried it hole it like Phil Mickelson would later on. Out of the bunkers as well."

There's no question that Floyd had a high-level short game, but a longer club would be pivotal in his historic run at the 1976 Masters.

In his days before all the distance-explosion equipment, the burly North Carolinian, tired of double bogeys, decided that the way he was going to handle those sand-based Bermuda greens, which were harder than cement and hard to hold, was go with a club that lofted the ball on a higher trajectory. While five-woods were rarely seen except in ladies' sets, he felt that was the right club to better land his approach shots on those crucial par-5s.

So he went to Bert Dargie, a third-generation golf clubmaker whose grandfather brought the craft to Memphis from St. Andrews, Scotland. Upon asking Dargie if he had any five-wood clubheads, Floyd was told, "Nobody makes five-woods for men. I have some we make for women."

Undaunted, he left the shop with a handful of them. While a couple cracked at the hosel after constant practice, Floyd did see that the results were just what he needed for Augusta.

The new club in his bag clearly paid off at the 1976 Masters right from the first tee. In the first three rounds, Floyd had eleven birdies and an eagle on the par-5s.

His confidence translated into an opening-round 65, two shots better than defending champion Jack Nicklaus. That lead over Nicklaus and the rest of the field grew to five after a solid 66 the following day. It was a record-setting performance, bettering the previous thirty-six-hole tournament record by four strokes.

And he was just getting started. As a result of his 70 on Saturday, Floyd's fifty-four-hole total of 201 (15 under) was a new Masters record. He now led second-place Nicklaus by eight after three rounds.

When asked about what he admired about Raymond Floyd, Bill Rogers, 1981 Open Championship winner, didn't hesitate to say, "His competitiveness, he was just tough as a boot. Raymond was one to model yourself after. He always looked like he had control of the moment."

And at Augusta in 1976, Floyd had control of the Masters like few had before or since.

Here's a good example of how that handy new club worked wonders for him. In the third round at the difficult par-5 thirteenth, Floyd faced a second shot that required a carry of about 220 yards. A tributary to Rae's Creek winds in front of the raised green, and four bunkers threaten behind. With the five-wood, Floyd proceeded to fly over the main trouble and land gently into a greenside bunker. From there he hit a fine sand shot to within two feet of the cup, for another one of his many birdies on the par-5s.

This 1976 version of the Masters would be the exact opposite of the all-time great three-man battle from the year before when Nicklaus, Tom Weiskopf, and Johnny Miller battled down to the last roll of the last putt at the seventy-second hole.

Never during the last round did Floyd ever lead by fewer than seven strokes. At one point he had put ten shots between himself and the men who were competing in the other Masters.

Floyd played the final fourteen holes without a bogey. With a final birdie on that par-5 fifteenth, he'd go on to tie Jack Nicklaus's then-tournament-scoring records of 17 under par 271.

So dominant was his play, Floyd won by eight shots over runner-up Ben Crenshaw. (Despite three eagles, Nicklaus finished a distant third, eleven strokes behind the winner!)

"He [Floyd] was such a great front runner," said Crenshaw, "His performance at the 1976 Masters may have been one of the most convincing victories the golf world had seen."

When you are hitting the balls into the green at Augusta, sometimes the green can get very firm so you can hit a nice high shot, which you can do with those little fairway woods. Believe me, they make a massive difference. They hit the ball a lot softer than an iron shot. So that five-wood was a very confidence-providing tool for Raymond.

And you must remember, Raymond Floyd was as fine a competitor as there has ever been. I played against him in many tournaments, and this man was a fierce, fierce competitor.

10

A PLAYER FROM WAY BACK

APRIL 6–9, 1978
AUGUSTA NATIONAL GOLF CLUB
AUGUSTA, GEORGIA

Some golfers are fortunate to snatch victory from the jaws of defeat. Many more have suffered defeat when victory seemed assured. While earning any grand slam title is a thrill, there are few things sweeter than winning a major in come-from-behind fashion, and that happened to me in winning my third green jacket at Augusta.

My final victory at the Masters in 1978 was considered by many the least likely yet most spectacular of my major wins.

Why? Well, some "experts" in the media thought I was fading because I had not won in America since the 1974 Memphis Classic, even though I was doing quite well in other parts of the world.

"I just won the South African Open for the eleventh time. I have won over [one hundred] tournaments all over the world, so I find that kind of talk damn frustrating," I remember telling a reporter.

There's nothing worse than when people give opinions on things when they're really not privy to what's going on.

I hadn't won a major, but you know you can be very close, and the difference between winning and losing is a fraction. And after one person in Greensboro said, "Gary Player doesn't stand much of a chance. He's a falling star," my reply to myself was, "Well, ha, ha we will see how right he is."

I knew what I was capable of doing.

I wasn't necessarily stronger than anybody else, but I was fitter than anybody else in the field even at the age of forty-two.

And I knew early about fitness. It's only when you go back to Augusta now and walk the golf course, you find it is so difficult to do. The average person would be exhausted, and the next day your body would have aches and pains. I played thirty-six holes in practice rounds. After lifting weights and doing calisthenics, I was so fit, and I was hitting the ball well. Also, you have to be confident. The big thing is that you've got to believe in yourself. Too many people rely on what other people are telling them.

Then there was the competition. In the field there were more than a dozen past Masters winners including Tom Watson, the defending champion, as well as five-time winner Jack Nicklaus. The two men were in their primes; coming into this event, the former beat the latter at the famed Duel in the Sun at Turnberry in the previous Open Championship.

There were also US Open champions like Johnny Miller, Hale Irwin, and Hubert Green. PGA champions like Lee Trevino and Lanny Wadkins, as well as Open Championship winner Tom Weiskopf, all proven performers under pressure.

While there were many dangerous shot makers on hand, the combination of swirling winds and rather tough hole locations, unusual for early rounds, made putting an even greater challenge than normal at Augusta.

I had my misadventures, including a shot that ended up in Rae's Creek, and I lost a few positions, but I rolled another 72 and was still within five strokes of the coleaders, Lee Trevino and Rod Funseth, heading into the weekend.

Defending US Open champion Hubert Green was making his presence felt with a fine 69 and a tie for fifth. Jack's continued putting woes dropped him back with a 73, but even though the Golden Bear roared back with a 69 on Saturday, he would actually lose ground, as Hubert followed up his own 69 on Friday with a brilliant 65 to take a three-stroke lead after the third round.

I scored a 69 to move in tie for tenth at 3 under.

So, heading into the final round, Hubert was leading with a very hot putter.

And in mastering Augusta's greens, one-putting nine times, Green did it in a unique style.

Using a distinct crouch, he would place his right forefinger down the shaft of a putter that was older than him. But it worked because he only needed twenty-seven strokes on the greens, which had bamboozled most of the competition.

Answering a question from the media in the interview room where he was looking at the leaderboard, Green said: "Well, I'd rather be three ahead than three behind. I know I can still lose, and it still isn't over, but I like the way I am playing. Being in this spot puts more pressure on me."

And that's the name of the game. From the mouth of a majors champion, that's what it's all about, delivering under pressure in the crucial moments on the road to glory.

Standing on the tee on the first hole of the final eighteen, I started out seven strokes behind leader Hubert. Despite starting the pressure-packed back nine, I was still five strokes back. However, I knew I could do it.

The week before, I had changed the putting stroke I'd used for the previous twenty-four years. I used to jab at the ball, but I changed to stroking it. I knew everyone says the firm-wrist stroke is better.

All these young guys had been putting so well with it that I finally decided I had to try it, as my wife had suggested.

I hit a five-iron onto the tenth green. Drawing on my years of experience playing the particular undulations here, I then dropped a twenty-five-foot putt for a birdie. I hit a seven-iron to the dangerous twelfth and made a fifteen-footer for a birdie. My confidence was growing. And despite falling down lunging at a four-iron on the par-5 thirteenth, I kept my poise, and the shot settled on the green only fifteen feet from the pin. I two-putted for a birdie.

I couldn't help but feel strong and in control, and much of it was due to the flatstick. On the par-5 fifteenth, I two-putted from eighty feet for a birdie. I then dropped a treacherous fifteen-foot downhill runner for a birdie at sixteen. Finally, I came to the seventy-second hole, and after sticking a six-iron shot to the green, I faced a slippery downhill twenty-two-foot birdie putt.

Nobody had ever holed a putt from above the hole to win the Masters before I did that. I was now in sole possession of the lead at 11 under par.

As the putt fell and the crowd roared, Seve Ballesteros walked across the green with great enthusiasm, hugged me, and said, "Garrreeee, you teach me to win Masters today."

I embraced my caddy, Eddie McCoy, and said, "Well, you got your roof."

This was in reference to earlier in the week. When we arrived at Augusta, Eddie told me, "I need to get a roof on my house." I said. "Well, we got to win it and you'll be going to get a roof."

Now if my chip shot on the eleventh hole didn't spin out, and I could've dropped my makeable putt for an eagle on thirteen, I'd have had an even better score.

My putter was hotter than the ninety-degree heat we were playing in.

Now I had a chance to cool off, but not the way I would have preferred. Now the leader in the clubhouse, I had to sweat it out while waiting nearly an hour for the final groups to finish. I nervously looked on, as one by one, the challengers came through having their opportunities.

Playing the waiting game. It was agony, sheer agony.

Rod Funseth, the second-round coleader, birdied the par-5 fifteenth hole but parred the last three, including a putt left on the lip at the sixteenth. Still, he had a putt on eighteen that would have forced a playoff. Funseth had the same putt for a tie on the eighteenth green that I had sunk. He gave it just as good a roll but narrowly missed.

Recalling my own record in such events, I did not want a playoff. I still remembered that playoff loss to Arnold Palmer at Augusta in 1962.

Despite a horrendous lie, defending champion Tom Watson smoked a two-iron for an eagle at thirteen, and remained in the mix with a pair of birdies until his undoing at eighteen. After his drive with a four-wood sent him behind some trees to the left, his forced slice flew over the gallery then missed a tournament-tying eight-footer. He finished with a bogey and one back of me.

And while his trusty old putter worked like a charm the previous round to help provide him a three-shot lead heading into Sunday, Hubert Green's flatstick eventually let him down when it mattered most.

On eighteen, Green made a brilliant approach shot that landed him to within a yard of the hole. As he stood over his putt that would've forced a playoff, his concentration was suddenly disrupted by the voice of a broadcast commentator. It was actually a friend of his, Bill Kelly of CBS Radio. Starting up his routine all over, Green then missed to the right on a putt that was straight in and flat. Asked afterward about the incident, Green only blamed himself. It also provided proof to golfers everywhere that there is really no such thing as a gimme.

I called my wife, Vivienne, who was home in Johannesburg, waking her up at 3:30 in the morning to credit her for convincing me to change my putting stroke.

Her advice had worked. My performance would go down in golf lore as one of the most amazing last-round rallies of all time, as I had just twenty-seven putts, including eight one-putts.

In perhaps my finest hour at Augusta, I had become the oldest Masters champion at the time (Jack Nicklaus would break my record at the age of forty-six in 1986), but to win again seventeen years after my first Masters victory was a great feeling. The win also had added meaning in that my ninth major tied me with my idol, Ben Hogan.

11

THE GOLDEN BEAR'S MASTER CHARGE

APRIL 10–13, 1986
AUGUSTA NATIONAL GOLF CLUB
AUGUSTA, GEORGIA

Babe Ruth, Muhammad Ali, Bill Russell, Jim Brown, Wayne Gretzky, and Jack Nicklaus—there have been few athletes that have started off spectacularly, then continued steadily upward, almost without interruption, for so many years. And regarding the great measuring stick of our sport, winning majors, Jack had won more than Ben Hogan and Arnold Palmer combined. But not lately.

It had been six years since the forty-six-year-old Nicklaus had won a major. His last victory at a tour event came at his own tournament in May 1984—the Memorial on his Muirfield Village course in Ohio.

There were rumblings that he was past his prime, some even derisively calling him "the Olden Bear."

Heading into this event, Nicklaus missed the cut in three of the seven tournaments he entered and withdrew from a fourth. Of the ones he finished, his most impressive showing was a tie for thirty-ninth at the Hawaiian Open.

Seeking guidance from Jack Grout, his only teacher since age ten, Nicklaus found a problem. He was using too much hand action and less body work. It was a reminder that his powerful hips and thighs and strong shoulder turn were the foundation of his power. The refresher lesson came right on time because that aspect of his game contributed a lot to his brilliant success at Augusta National, where he had earned five green jackets.

However, for a course he knew so well, a 74 in the first round got him off to a lackluster start. That was on par with the pundits who never considered him among the favorites at this fiftieth Masters.

In fact, one of those favorites led the field halfway through the tournament. That flamboyant Spaniard, Seve Ballesteros, already a two-time winner here, was all alone in first place at 5-under 139. Nicklaus was six back.

However, after play in the third round was completed, some familiar names had moved up the leaderboard. Among them were Bernhard Langer and Tom Watson. Future three-time major winner Nick Price catapulted himself to a share of second place with a record-breaking 63. With Ballesteros, Langer, and Donnie Hammond, he was just one back of Greg Norman.

Still looking for his first major, the brash Australian was playing with supreme confidence. Norman's irons were finding the greens like radar. However, with a 69, Nicklaus would be just four back to start the final round. With progressively lower scores heading into the final day, the putter now joined his power game, and the Bear was quietly making noise deep in the forest of competitors back in ninth place.

What would unfold on Sunday would be one of the most exciting final rounds in Masters history, with five different players who would at least have a share of the lead.

Ballesteros gained a piece of the lead on the front nine, helped by a hole-out eagle at eight. Texan workhorse Tom Kite, who had given away a green jacket just two years earlier, also eagled eight and was just three back.

Norman, now tied for the lead making the turn, did not start out well on the back nine. He double-bogeyed the par-4 tenth, and it was Ballesteros and Kite fighting for the lead. Despite birdies at eleven and thirteen, the tenacious Texan fell two back of Ballesteros as the Spaniard produced an eagle to go 9 under.

Meanwhile, Nicklaus had three straight birdies beginning at hole nine. Despite a bogey at twelve, he was now just three behind the leaders. But after following that with a birdie at thirteen, the Golden Bear was starting to get a sniff of something good downwind.

Addressing his ball, a shade over two hundred yards from the pin at the par-5 fifteenth, Nicklaus bombed a four-iron right at the flag. After it landed in front of the hole and bounced left, he would sink the twelve-footer for an eagle. The result moved him to within a shot of the lead that had been held by Ballesteros and Kite through fifteen.

Now in the thick of the hunt, his muscle memory kicking in, Nicklaus nearly aced the hole with his five-iron. It went past, then spun back until it rested three feet from the cup. Back at fifteen, hearing the roar from the birdie, Ballesteros proceeded to hit his four-iron into the pond fronting the fifteenth green. Bogey.

Meanwhile with a birdie at fifteen, Kite now had a share of the lead with Nicklaus and Ballesteros.

At seventeen, as his eighteen-foot birdie attempt headed toward the hole, Nicklaus walked after it with the club raised in his left hand. Millions watching on television heard CBS Sports' Verne Lundquist exclaim, "Maybe . . . Yes sir!"

Nicklaus now had the lead. And after parring the seventy-second hole with a forty-foot uphill putt pulled to within inches of the cup, he finished with a closing back-nine 30 for a fourth-round score of 65. The roar for the Bear as he hugged his caddy and son Jackie was as memorable as lead announcer Jim Nantz's comment from the TV booth: "The Bear has come out of hibernation."

Still, the unprecedented sixth green jacket was not his yet. Norman, "the Great White Shark," was enjoying a surge of his own. He had four straight birdies starting at fourteen. (On the seventeenth, he made an outstanding approach under and between two trees that ran up the fairway and onto the green, then settled twelve feet away from the cup for the fourth birdie.) Norman was now standing at the eighteenth tee tied for the lead. The fifty-four-hole leader could now become the seventy-two-hole winner with one more birdie. (Kite would miss his birdie try at eighteen to finish one back.)

After a solid three-wood shot off the tee, Norman chose a four-iron to reach the flag located some 185 yards on the back of the green. It would be a club selection he'd lament for years afterward. Practically the instant he made contact, the Shark knew it was too much club; he realized a split second too late that he should have accounted for the adrenaline rush he was experiencing and clubbed down.

His ball sailed high and right, pushing it into the gallery. The result was a highly unlikely up-and-down result. With Norman's subsequent bogey, the forty-six-year-old Nicklaus had made history by winning the Masters for the sixth time.

"I'm certainly not as good as I was ten or fifteen years ago. I don't play as much competitive golf, but there are still some weeks when I'm pretty good," Nicklaus said with an ear-to-ear grin afterward.

I watched it very carefully in the clubhouse. He won the Masters at forty-six, and I had said to my wife when I won at forty-two that I didn't think anyone would beat that. I was the oldest to win it when I did. Then Jack came along and did it at forty-six. Remarkable!

So, it shows you what I have often talked about in this book, and that is longevity. To appreciate what Nicklaus has accomplished, consider that he won his six Masters titles over a span of twenty-three years, nearly a quarter century of success at the highest level.

And that is why you've got to recognize Jack Nicklaus as the greatest golfer who ever lived. Because not only does he have the most major championships, but the longevity, that's a very big thing.

And how much more of a thrill can a man have to be the oldest man to win the Masters and to have his son on the bag? That's peaches and cream, man.

12

LOCAL BOY MAKES GOOD

Born in Augusta, Georgia, and with a middle name of Hogan, Larry Mize was bound to make a name for himself at the Masters. And it all started as a teen when he operated the scoreboard at the third hole and dreamed of someday wearing the green jacket.

Then it was off to attend college at nearby Georgia Tech (where the Masters creator Bobby Jones studied as well). Turning pro in 1980, the slender, six-foot Mize, despite a flair for iron play and a fine touch around the green, would come up short in the victory department. Entering the 1987 Masters, the twenty-eight-year-old had just one previous win to his name: the Danny Thomas Memphis Classic in 1983.

And even though he had three runner-up finishes in 1986, including the Kemper Open (where Greg Norman beat him on the sixth playoff hole), none of the pundits viewed the local entry to be among those battling for the title come Sunday afternoon. Maybe one of the sixteen former champions, including the previous year's winner,

Jack Nicklaus, or perhaps one of the eight other major winners in the field, but not Mize.

Well, the local got their attention when he rolled a 2-under 70, then followed that with a 72 to grab a share of second place halfway through the competition. One of the keys to his fine results so far was that the greens were super hard and fast, which played to the Augustan's strengths.

In the third round, 1984 Masters winner Ben Crenshaw was holing everything in sight on his way to a 67 and a share of the lead at 4 under.

Roger Maltbie, a twelve-year tour veteran looking for his first major, was also at 4 under. He was the thirty-six-hole leader at Turnberry when Jack Nicklaus and Tom Watson had their Duel in the Sun at the 1977 Open Championship (he'd finish twenty-sixth there).

There is also the story where the colorful Californian, who would have a long career as a TV golf analyst, once went looking for a lost paycheck. After winning the 1975 Pleasant Valley Classic in Massachusetts, the Tour rookie showed off his $40,000 winner's check to fellow patrons in a bar, then somehow left it behind. Fortunately, they placed a stop on it and he was issued another.[1]

But there seemed to be no stopping Maltbie here as he went from an opening 76 to a 66 (low round of the second day), then a 70 to climb to the top.

Meanwhile, Mize's journey really began with a "good" bogey after his tee shot at twelve found Rae's Creek. Pleased to avoid a bigger number, he would go on to score three birdies on the back nine. With a confidence-building 72, he was just two back with eighteen holes to play.

It was a bunched leaderboard after fifty-four holes. Seve Ballesteros and Curtis Strange were also at 2 under, while Norman and Bernhard Langer were just one off the lead.

Because third-round coleaders Crenshaw and Maltbie would end up with too many bogeys, resulting in each shooting 74 in the final round, that opened the door for the pursuers.

Mize, despite back-to-back bogeys at three and four, grabbed a share of the lead after his third birdie of the day at hole seven. And after back-to-back birdies at twelve and thirteen, he had a one-stroke lead. However, he would fall one back of the new leader, Norman, after a pair of consecutive bogeys starting at fourteen.

Nevertheless, by ending with a clutch birdie on the seventy-second hole, Mize found himself the clubhouse leader at 3 under. All he could do now was sit and wait in Jones Cabin near the tenth tee, as the other contenders finished their rounds.

As Langer and Strange would fade, Ballesteros, looking for his fifth major victory, was on the march. With birdies at fifteen and seventeen, the dangerous Spaniard was now tied for the lead. However, he landed his approach shot in a bunker at the treacherous par-4 eighteenth. If he could not get it up and down, a bogey would end his tournament. After a solid par, he joined Mize in the cabin to see how Norman would finish.

Following a birdie at the par-5 fifteenth, Norman grabbed a share of the lead, but he quickly gave it back with a bogey at the next. Then he managed to birdie seventeen to tie Mize and Ballesteros yet again. Now at eighteen, landing his approach twenty feet away, Norman had a chance for the outright victory. Could the coveted green jacket be the Shark's? No. His putt missed by less than an inch on the underside of the hole.

In a way, it was déjà vu all over again. Just a year before at that same seventy-second hole, he was set to win with a birdie, and even a par would tie Nicklaus. Instead, his shot to the green veered off right and settled among the patrons, and the resultant bogey left him sharing second place with Tom Kite.

So here it was, Augusta's David taking on two global goliaths of the game in a playoff for a major title.

Starting on the par-4 tenth hole, the comparatively shorter hit-ter Mize hit a tee shot that got a roll on a downslope and actually ended up twenty yards closer to the flag than his opponents. He had a seven-iron into the green, while the others each required a five-iron.

Ballesteros landed just off to the right fringe, and Norman finished just off the back edge. The former's putt rolled four-plus feet past; the latter's went closer to the cup but also missed. That left Mize with a ten-footer for the win.

However, not wanting to be too aggressive and have a three-foot comebacker downhill, Mize did not hit it firm enough. His putt ran out of steam and died in front of the hole on the low side. Surpris-ingly, Ballesteros missed his comebacker and was eliminated. Thus he embarked on the lonely walk back up the hill to the clubhouse.

At the eleventh it became a two-man battle. And this time it was a return to normalcy, as Norman outdrove Mize by at least twenty yards.

With the pin located at left middle, bringing the pond more into play, Mize wanted to draw his approach in. However, his five-iron flared way right of the green and settled around 140 feet from the flag. After Norman landed just off the putting surface on the fringe, he was thinking birdie. But Mize, in surveying his shot, tried to re-main positive, thinking that if he could get it close, he could put pres-sure back on Norman, who was still about fifty feet away.

With the greens extraordinarily hard and fast, knowing the ball would not likely check up, and with the pond lurking in back, the Augustan felt he had only one option: a bump-and-run through the fringe.

Well aware this was no time to be tentative (that was what cost him his golden opportunity on the first playoff hole), Mize pulled out his '56 Jack Nicklaus Muirfield sand wedge (which was actually his backup) and proceeded to knock that long chip low and firm. As the ball was turning left and rolling slowly, he held his wedge at waist level and gazed at the ball, which eventually went right into the hole for an amazing birdie. An ecstatic Mize leaped exultantly as it dropped, and he tossed his club into the air.

Now the pressure *really* was on Norman. He had to sink the long putt just to stay in the game.

He started walking over to shake the winner's hand before the ball even reached the hole.

Even though he fell to Jack Nicklaus at Augusta in 1986, and collapsed at the '96 Masters (see chapter 15), Norman has always maintained that his untimely de-Mize in '87 was more devastating. The Shark said it was the one that "gutted him the most." This major had him weeping on the beach outside his Florida home at 3 a.m., and he has said it took him four full years to get over it.[2]

It was a playoff where Larry Mize took on two superstars. In an A-Mize-Ing moment in Masters history, with his stunning chip-in, Larry became the first champion to come from Augusta itself. In an event full of tremendous lore, this career-defining shot would be seen over and over. If there had been a marquee it would have read: *A Chip Down Magnolia's Memory Lane.*

It was not a bad time to get a measure of revenge for losing to Norman in a playoff earlier at the Kemper Open.

"I picked a doozy to win," Mize said. "I'd probably rather win this than any other. I beat the two greatest players in the world."

13

♟

HEARTBREAK FOR HOCH,
A FIRST FOR FALDO

APRIL 6–9, 1989
AUGUSTA NATIONAL GOLF CLUB
AUGUSTA, GEORGIA

The 1989 version of the Masters would feature a surprise veteran superstar leader seeking his first green jacket halfway through. In the end, after switching putters and mastering the tricky greens of Augusta, a future superstar would come from behind to snare his first of three coveted sport coats. And in between, a thirty-three-year-old journeyman would infamously lose his shot at glory.

After a bogey-free 67 in the first round, on day two, when low scores were scarce, forty-nine-year-old Lee Trevino added a 74. His 3-under 141 total gave him a share of the lead with Nick Faldo, the 1987 Open champion. Two strokes back, in a group that included past champions Seve Ballesteros and Ben Crenshaw, was Scott Hoch.

Though Hoch did win the Vardon Trophy for lowest scoring average—70.08—in '86, the Orlando, Florida, resident had won only three PGA tournaments lifetime. But after a long rain delay, the third round was completed on Sunday. Former leaders Trevino and Faldo would balloon to 81 and 77 respectively. Hoch moved into a share of second place, just one back of leader Crenshaw, who was at 3 under through fifty-four. He was playing like this was his time.

Years later, Faldo would talk about the challenges of the greens, but what he said certainly could have applied to his poor third round here.

"Well, the hardest thing is the grain of the grass grows off the greens toward you. So, you are chipping into the grain and it is pretty severe. And if you hit it fat, you'll make an absolute mess of it. If you overcompensate and don't land it on the correct spot, a lot of greens are raised slightly so you are chipping uphill and then landing it on a downslope. And if you get either one of those wrong, you're in a heck of a mess. If you're short, it comes back to your feet, if you're long, it's gone. So the short game at Augusta is quite scary," noted the lanky Englishman.

Even though Trevino's attempt at a career grand slam was gone, Sunday afternoon provided an exciting matinee as six different players held at least a share of the lead on the back nine.

First and foremost, Faldo, who started the fourth round five shots back, switched out putters and birdied four of his first seven holes. Seve Ballesteros appeared in good position to earn another Masters title as he birdied four of the first five holes. And after a fifth birdie on the front nine, he shared the lead at 5 under with Mike Reid and Hoch.

Reid, a slender, bespectacled journeyman who was an All-American at Brigham Young University, chipped in for a birdie on the twelfth hole to take sole possession of the lead for the first time in the tournament at 6 under. However, after missing a short par effort at fourteen and following that up with a double bogey after hitting his approach into the water at fifteen, chances for his first major evaporated. Ballesteros, the winner here in 1980 and '83 and the reigning Open Championship champion, hit a six-iron that missed the green at sixteen and rolled into the water. That double-bogey ended his bid.

Another former Open champion, Greg Norman, was once again

in a familiar spot, contending at Augusta on Sunday. After six birdies on the back nine, Norman walked to the seventy-second hole with a share of the lead at 5 under.

Fifty-four-hole leader Crenshaw had an up-and-down day, but after a birdie at seventeen, he too was at 5 under. However, like Norman, he would miss out on the playoffs by one stroke after they both bogeyed the last hole.

Hoch, playing with Crenshaw, actually had a chance to win the tournament at the seventy-second hole, but he missed his birdie try from twenty-five feet.

In producing the low round of 65, Faldo's flatstick was phenomenal on the back nine at Augusta. He dropped the ball into the cup from all over, including a twelve-foot birdie on the thirteenth as well as a big-breaking fifteen-footer on the sixteenth and a thirty-foot birdie on the second-to-last hole of regulation. He attributed it partially to proper pitching based on years of playing the course under its competitive pressures.

"The scare factor on the second shots or generally the second shots is if you miss the greens in the wrong places, it's very easy to do. Regarding chipping it's an absolute truth, no exaggeration that you have to get it within a two-foot circle," explained Faldo.

"You better make sure you have the right speed and the right blade because if you get it wrong, obviously everything gets magnified there. If it is a little too strong, it can be off the green. If it is a little weak, the break gets it and manipulates it. And if you catch the wrong slope you can find yourself now forty feet away."

Tied at 5-under 283, Faldo and Hoch would be the participants in a sudden-death playoff. Starting out at ten, both hit the fairway, but Faldo pushed his approach in the short right-side bunker. Hoch then played safely, hitting the front middle of the green and leaving an uphill birdie putt. After Faldo managed to chip out to fifteen feet, the savvy veteran Hoch lagged his twenty-five-foot stroke to within two feet, forcing Faldo to make that par try. He missed and settled for bogey.

In the cold mist with darkness upon them, Faldo hoped his brilliant short game that afternoon would not be wasted. He could only stand there and watch as Hoch faced a putt of less than two feet to win his first major.

What happened next is part of golf lore. In a Masters moment for the ages, not only did Hoch miss, but his ball didn't even hit the hole. It was a dead pull the instant it left his putter.

"I just thought, 'Well, he's opened the door for me.' Then it felt like destiny," said Faldo, recalling that moment.

Faldo took his hot putter and sank a twenty-five-footer on the second playoff hole to win.

He didn't deny that his play on the tricky greens were beyond super that day, but the new champion also credited another kind of shot that was key to the victory. "I holed probably five putts that I would never make again, but I had a three-iron into eleven in the playoffs, which was one of the best shots I ever hit."

Hoch would have success later on both the regular tour and the Champions Tour. He would win eight of his titles after that Masters and climb to as high as eleventh in the world in 1997. Unfortunately, he will likely be most remembered for the short missed putt on the first playoff hole that denied him a victory at Augusta National. For a time, the phrase "Hoch as in choke" was used derisively to describe him. But playing on two US Ryder Cup teams and earning nearly $20 million over his career would ease his pain.

Faldo was the first golfer from England to win a Masters. And his great approach shots and play around the greens would be no fluke, as he would earn two more Masters victories. As a matter of fact, he would repeat as champ in 1990, becoming the first back-to-back winner since Jack Nicklaus in 1965–66. And Faldo would win again in the 1996 Masters.

14

WIN ONE FOR THE MENTOR

APRIL 6–9, 1995
AUGUSTA NATIONAL GOLF CLUB
AUGUSTA, GEORGIA

It was the start of an emotional week for an emotional player. Ben Crenshaw had spent the early part of it saying goodbye to his lifelong instructor, friend and mentor Harvey Penick. On the day before the start of the 1995 Masters, he had flown from Augusta back to Austin, Texas, to serve as a pallbearer for the Hall of Fame teacher and author of the classic instructional book *Harvey Penick's Little Red Book: Lessons and Teachings from a Lifetime in Golf*.

Very few players shared the kind of relationship Ben had with Harvey.

Crenshaw was introduced to the game by his father, Charlie, a schoolteacher, who placed him under the guidance of Harvey Penick when he was just eight.

Penick, who was so respected as a teacher that *Sports Illustrated* called him the "Socrates of the Golf World," cut down a seven-iron for him, showed him a proper grip, and watched as Crenshaw effortlessly whacked balls onto the green seventy-five yards away.

"Now let's go to the green and putt the ball into the hole," Penick told his new student. "If you wanted it in the hole, why didn't you tell me the first time?" responded the first-time golfer, as Penick recalled in his classic book.

Young Ben seemed like he was born to "putt the ball into the hole."

After his father had purchased a $20 club for his teenage son at Harvey's golf shop, that putter became known as "Little Ben." The rest is history.

He won seventeen amateur events, including the individual NCAA title three straight times from 1971 to 1973 while an All-American at the University of Texas. Crenshaw had the strongest amateur résumé since Jack Nicklaus.

He then started out by winning his first PGA Tour start (the 1973 San Antonio–Texas Open), and the following week he finished second. He was the can't-miss kid.

He missed only when it came to the majors. For years he'd have some fine performances at each of the four majors, but he could never break through to the winner's circle.

Twice he had a share of the lead at the seventy-first hole, and twice he double-bogeyed away golden opportunities (1975 US Open, 1979 Open Championship). He'd lose another on the third hole of a playoff in the 1979 PGA Championship. It seemed as if he'd be just another player with enormous promise that went unfulfilled.

That gratifying first majors victory came at Augusta in 1984. Crenshaw was the leader after the first round, and he was the leader after the final round, closing with a super 68 to defeat Tom Watson by two strokes.

This was despite a near career-ending case of Graves' disease the following year that mostly affected his short game. When putting or chipping, his nervousness and jitters made it difficult for him to find his touch. He would get treatment, and after recovering he'd have other opportunities. But still no victories. At Augusta in 1987, Crenshaw led on the back nine, but he bogeyed the seventy-first hole to miss a playoff by a stroke. In '89 he bogeyed the seventy-second to miss yet another.

Through the years, Crenshaw persevered and learned a lot from all the near misses.

"You have to get your nose in there in the beginning. To know what it feels like [that] incredible pressure you are under. And it is a battle within yourself to know they've turned the pressure up quite a bit. You feel it intensely because any golf course a major is on it is a scrutiny of your game. It is tough for everyone," explained Crenshaw.

He continued: "I saw this line in a book a long time ago. Bobby Jones said, 'Look, there's tournaments, then there's majors. The majors are like going to the circus looking at the high-wire act, but in the majors they take the net away.' I thought it was one of the best lines conveying the pressure a golfer is under."

Well, entering the 1995 Masters and one of the sport's great venues in Augusta National, where the best compete for the season's first major crown, Ben arrived with a heavy heart. His game was nowhere near the level it was when he'd won the green jacket eleven years prior.

The devastating personal loss, combined with his own lackluster play in the PGA Tour season leading up to the Masters, led many to count Crenshaw out before this tournament even started. But it wasn't hard to see why.

He had three missed cuts in his last four starts. Hadn't broken 70 in two months. And for the stat clincher—he was ranked sixty-ninth on the PGA Tour in putting. That's correct. Ben Crenshaw—sixty-ninth.

But this would be a different week for Crenshaw, and it started with a tip.

"Tuesday before the tournament, my longtime Augusta caddy, Carl Jackson, made a suggestion to place the ball a little bit back in my stance, and to turn my shoulders more. It worked right away, especially for my confidence," recalled Crenshaw.

That confidence was reflected in the results of his overall play. He was right in among the leaders with scores of 70 and 67 halfway through. He was just two back of leader Jay Haas and tied with David Frost and Phil Mickelson at 7 under.

Along with this reawakened confidence, another thing working in Crenshaw's favor was some deep, deep knowledge garnered after years of hard lessons. Said Crenshaw, "It's the nature of the golf course that it's very difficult to learn. The greens are difficult. You zero in on your distances to the greens, it fluctuates so much because it is an up-and-down golf course with a lot of change of elevation. It is so thrilling to play."

After a terrific 69, Crenshaw now shared the lead with Brian Henninger heading into the final round. (The 187th-ranked player in the world would fade the following day with a 76.)

Putting well over the first three rounds again played a key role to garnering a share of the lead for Ben. But as anyone will tell you, the greens have to be played smartly over four rounds because it is common knowledge they are the course's primary defenses, with double and even triple bogeys prevalent, especially on Sunday.

Again, this is where experience is key. While it starts with knowing where to place your approach shots, there's an army of concerns like the varying pin positions, the speeds, and the false fronts.

"I don't think there are enough practice putts that you can hit at Augusta. Because the greens are so undulating, it seems like you never got the same putt. You hit an approach shot and you're left with a putt and you go, 'I've never had this putt before,'" explained Crenshaw.

Ironically, putting was the topic of the last conversation between the Austin teacher and player.

Just two weeks before the Masters and Harvey's death, Ben was in the bedroom of the elderly man who was bedridden and could hardly speak.

"Harvey said, 'Look, first of all, trust and believe in yourself. Number one. Number two—make sure that you get your hands just ahead of the ball. In other words, sort of a forward press. And take two practice strokes.' Those were some of the last words he said to me."

Ben recalled that conversation and carried it around in his mind for that final round. (He would later say, "I had a fifteenth club in the bag this week. That was Harvey.") But there were other contenders vying for the jacket.

One was the Great White Shark.

Greg Norman started the day three strokes behind Crenshaw and Henninger, but he leaped early into contention with birdies at the second and sixth holes. And with a birdie at thirteen he had a share of the lead. But a bogey at seventeen would end his chances, and he finished three strokes back.

Another was Davis Love III.

He had to win the Freeport-McMoRan Classic in New Orleans the week prior just to qualify for this event—he had blown a two-stroke lead by bogeying the last two holes, but won in a playoff. With a birdie on the seventy-first hole here, Love had tied Crenshaw for the lead, and his par at eighteen gave him a terrific 66, but now he had to wait for Ben to finish.

Ben got a fortunate bounce off a tree after a pulled drive at fourteen (in the gallery his wife, Julie, said to herself, "Another Harvey Bounce"), then a key moment arrived at the devilish par-3 sixteenth. Using a six-iron for the 170-yard hole, the forty-three-year-old's draw landed to the right of the flag. He would finish it with a birdie. After grabbing the same result at the par-4 seventeenth, he had a two-stroke lead with one hole to play.

After tapping in for bogey, giving him a one-stroke win over Love, Crenshaw let his bottled-up emotions flow out.

Gentle Ben bent over, put his face in his hands, and wept, comforted by his caddy, as his putter and hat fell to the ground. It was a scene that brought tears to the eyes of many on hand at Augusta National and on television that day, and became one of the more indelible moments in majors history.

In a game that can be so heartless, Crenshaw was able to provide the most wonderful gift possible to the memory of Harvey Penick, as he shed tears of joy, tears of relief, and tears for his mentor, by heeding the words of his teacher to trust himself.

And as the sun set, Crenshaw stood at the winner's ceremony and said, "Fate had dictated another championship, as it has done so many times."

He still feels the same way nearly thirty years later.

"I honestly believe to this day that God was honoring Harvey through me. When you're forty-three, you don't know how many chances you're going to get. It was like somebody put their hand on my shoulder that week and guided me through it. He was there with me. I felt it. I was playing free. There's no question that was my most important and lasting victory and to do it for Harvey Penick, it will always make me smile. Especially there [Augusta]. I love that place so much."

It just shows you what a gentleman Ben was and what loyalty means.

If you expect loyalty from people, you are going to have your heart broken.

Loyalty is a gift. So is what Ben Crenshaw did. To get on an airplane to fly down to Harvey Penick's memorial services, my goodness, I have such admiration for what he did.

God rewarded him with a Masters win. In all my years competing at Augusta National, Ben breaking down after finishing at eighteen was the most heartwarming victory I ever saw in the Masters. Filled with love and loyalty.

Love is the almighty force of the world. And he exemplified that.

15

THE DAY THE SHARK DROWNED

Greg Norman was already a two-time majors champion.

His first came at the Open in Turnberry in 1986 with a five-stroke victory.

Then in 1993 at Royal St. George's, he began the final round one stroke behind Nick Faldo, the defending champion. Norman's 64 in blustery conditions is considered one of the best in majors history. It garnered him his second Claret Jug.

Fast forward to 1996, the Australian had already won the prestigious Doral-Ryder Open on the PGA Tour and was in the middle of a ninety-six-week run as the world's number-one-ranked player.

Life was good. Ferraris, boats, mansions, helicopters, money, Norman seemingly had it all, but he wanted the green jacket. It was something he had coveted since finishing fourth at Augusta National in 1981, where he began building his adopted moniker, "the Great White Shark," into a branding symbol that launched a global commercial empire.

Yes, that cotton-poly blend basic sport coat can be found in most department stores for under $200. But it takes on a whole different aura with a simple logo and a few buttons initialed ANGC, believe me.

Norman had come close to adorning it a few times, most notably in 1986 with second-place finishes after Nicklaus made his famous attack (see chapter 11). The following year Larry Mize did him in with an amazing chip shot in the playoffs (see chapter 12).

However, things started out a bit iffy before Norman even reached the first tee. In a practice round the day before the start of the tournament, the superfit Aussie felt something he rarely if ever did: a surge of pain in his back. That forced him to end his day early. Fortunately, he was able to secure the services of Fred Couples's therapist.

Waking up Thursday, Norman must have been feeling awesome because he tore through Augusta's par-72, 6,925-yard layout with a record-tying opening round of 63. With birdies on nine of the last twelve holes for a two-shot lead over Phil Mickelson, it was the best opening round at Augusta National since Nick Price rolled 63 there in 1986.

With a fine 69 in the second round, Norman held the halfway lead at 132, 12 under par. Four shots back in second place was Nick Faldo. The thirty-eight-year-old Englishman hadn't contended in a major in two years. Besides the ongoing retooling of his game with coach David Leadbetter, Faldo had to endure the notorious ceaseless onslaught of the British press in going through a nasty divorce from his second wife, Gill, and suddenly a very public romance with twenty-one-year-old former Arizona State golfer Brenna Cepelak.

Norman increased his lead over Faldo to six strokes heading into the final round.

The man was showing how complete his game was, and it certainly looked as though this time the green jacket would be his.

"At that time, Greg drove the ball better than anybody. Very long and controlled. He hit his iron shots extremely high that held the greens," said fellow countryman and television broadcaster Ian

Baker-Finch, reflecting on it years later. "He had that Arnold Palmer, swashbuckling, go-for-broke approach. And he was an excellent chipper. As well as an excellent putter. I think he was the best putter in the world for a couple years there."

With everything working to a T, how could Norman fail over the final eighteen?

Well, after sinking a clutch par on the fifty-fourth hole, Faldo would be paired with Norman. These two top talents weren't strangers to each other (nor were they chums).

They had dueled before, perhaps most notably at the 1990 Open championships at St. Andrews. Tied for the lead halfway through, Faldo went low (67), while Norman skied (76). The Englishman then cruised to his second Open title with a five-shot win.

But this one was shaping up to be Norman's turn for a major title. After all, no player in Masters history had lost a six-stroke lead.

After fifty-four holes, standing at 13 under par 203, it appeared the Shark was ready to take a bite out of several Masters records. This included what looked like an easily reachable scoring mark of 17 under par 271 held jointly by Raymond Floyd and Jack Nicklaus. And with his dominance reminiscent of Floyd's performance twenty years prior, Norman could become the fifth player to go wire to wire (sole possession of first place after each round) at Augusta.

Everything about Norman from tee to green had the appearance of a steady yet firm control of his game, to the point where many were thinking he already had one arm into the green jacket sleeve.

And then, as one of the last to leave the locker room after the third round, Norman went to the bar to grab a water when well-regarded British golf journalist, Peter Dobereiner said to him, "I don't think even you can f&*% it up from here, Greg."

On top of that, noted golf swing analyst Peter Kostis, working for CBS television, had noticed an ominous sign. After a couple times at the driving range over a few days, he had noticed Norman was experimenting with a stronger grip then went back to a weaker one another day. And from the comparative erratic ball striking from the third round, Kostis thought that would be trouble in the final eighteen. He mentioned it to a journalist, thinking it was off the record. But it got out and Norman was furious. He complained to Kostis's boss, producer Frank Chirkinian, a good friend.[1]

Sure enough, stepping to the first tee of the final round, Norman missed the fairway en route to an opening bogey. There was no turning back.

Meanwhile, the very methodical Faldo arrived uncharacteristically late.

"I was busy watching NASCAR," Faldo recalled with a chuckle years later. "Then I wandered down and my caddy, Fanny, told me, 'Okay, you've got fifty-seven minutes'—normally I practice for one hour and twenty minutes. So basically I just told myself to get on with it without thinking too much. But as the round progressed each shot became more and more important. I was just able to continue hitting just really good golf shots."

While Norman had roped that snap hook into the trees for an opening bogey, Faldo was workmanlike, making par, birdie, par, par over the opening four holes.

Faldo remembers the lesson he was reminded of as he observed his playing partner early in that round.

"I could feel the nervousness emanating from Greg. I remember him gripping and regripping the club, a bit of uncertainness that wasn't there previously," said Faldo. "And I think if an opponent knows you can hit a really good shot, it puts a little more pressure on them."

What Norman could not do was find the A+ game he had produced over the three previous rounds. After a bogey at nine, Norman's lead over Faldo (who had birdied holes two and six) was down to two at 11 under. As they headed to the back nine, things unraveled quickly, and more water than he could handle was filling the Shark's gills. After back-to-back bogeys on ten and eleven, Norman's double bogey at twelve had now given his opponent a two-shot advantage.

On the par-5 thirteenth Faldo wanted to get in position for a birdie, but he was in a bit of a quandary about club selection. He had an old MacGregor persimmon five-wood for shots about 215 yards with carry, but the slope on this fairway led him to go with a more predictable two-iron.

He explained his reasoning in eventually settling on the long iron. "You have to appreciate that because the slope is so steep, that old persimmon had a very flat soleplate and it just wouldn't sit," recalled Faldo. "I put it down, and the face would go left and right. That scared me. I didn't like that. You can't go left and you can't go right on that hole, because of the water, which easily brings bogey into play, so, considering the lie, I eventually went with the two-iron. It turned out to be a heck of a shot."

After they both parred 14 and traded birdies on 15, Faldo, at 11 under, still had a two-stroke lead with three to play. Norman still had the firepower and skill to make up the deficit.

But something two-time majors winner and longtime broadcaster Johnny Miller would later say about the Englishman would summarize what happened next:

"Like a big python, Nick slowly squeezed you to death. He was the most ruthless player of his era. When Norman was in the midst of blowing that lead at the '96 Masters, Greg found out as many others would, there was little point in trying to struggle. If you lost your composure just a bit and tried to fight him off, he just killed you faster."

Sure enough, at the par-3 sixteenth, Norman hooked his shot into the water short and left. The resultant double bogey doubled Faldo's lead to four.

After they both parred seventeen, Faldo finished off the Shark by birdieing eighteen for a 67 and a five-shot win. Norman, despite a 78, finished second.

In earning his third green jacket, it was typical Faldo when he was at his best. It was Faldo's third green jacket.

Norman owned two majors of his own, but with his numerous

shortcomings in these grand slam events, his critics will forever question his ability to handle pressure.

"I hope I'm remembered for shooting 67 and not for what happened to Greg," Faldo said afterward. "But, obviously, this will be remembered for what happened to Greg."

And even though the vast majority of professional golfers don't come close to winning major tournaments, let alone score ninety victories around the world, Norman was still the man behind one of the most notorious collapses in Masters history. To his credit, however, Norman faced the media immediately after his biggest downfall.

"Much credit to him for doing that. I couldn't have done that," said Faldo. "But all credit to Greg. To stand there and take it on the chin at such a vulnerable time. As a matter of fact, that's what I said to him on the last green, 'Don't let the bastards beat you down,' because I knew what he was in for. I genuinely felt for the guy on that day because I know for sure I would have been scarred if that was me."

16

THE DAWN OF A NEW ERA: TIGER TIME

APRIL 10–13, 1997
AUGUSTA NATIONAL GOLF CLUB
AUGUSTA, GEORGIA

We've all seen, read or heard about the young prodigies who took their sport to another level. And in this game, you had sharp-shooting teen sensations Bobby Jones and Jack Nicklaus. However, starting on the back nine of the first round of the 1997 Masters was a now fully formed phenomenon named Eldrick "Tiger" Woods.

He had shown early signs of being a potential game-changer with three consecutive US Junior titles, followed by three consecutive US Amateur titles; he also became NCAA champion at Stanford. At age nineteen, Woods participated in his first PGA Tour major, the 1995 Masters, and tied for forty-first as the only amateur to make the cut. The experience would serve him well, as did picking the brains of greats like Nicklaus, Palmer, Floyd, Couples, and Norman during practice rounds at Augusta. When he turned pro at age twenty in August 1996, Woods already had three tour wins when he headed back to Augusta the following April.

His plans were no secret. At a pretournament press conference Woods stated: "I just came here to win."

That may have appeared premature when the now twenty-one-year-old produced four bogeys and tallied a 40 for the front nine on the first day (after missing the cut the year before). But that was precisely why this would turn out to be a special week.

Adjusting a swing change on the fly (bringing the club almost parallel to the ground because his backswing was too long), and with the encouragement from his seasoned caddy, Fluff Cowan, Tiger roared back, beginning with a birdie at ten. Then back-to-back birdies starting at thirteen, an eagle at fifteen, and a fourth birdie at seventeen produced a sizzling 30 for a 2-under 70, just three back of the lead. It was the first time in seven rounds Woods had broken par at Augusta.

Defending champion Nick Faldo, who was paired with Woods that first round, later said, "What he did on the back nine, one could say that was the real beginning of Tigermania. So it was nice to have been a part of that. It was quite something. He just left us in his dust."

The six-time majors winner had not seen anything yet. The dust cloud would grow and choke all competitors following in his wake.

Taking on the par-72, 6,925-yard track the next day, Woods started round two three back, but he would end the day three ahead. Led by a fabulous eagle at thirteen, Tiger's 66 provided him with his first lead in a professional majors championship. Scotland's Colin Montgomerie was in second place at 5 under.

Bogeys would not be a problem for Woods (and he'd never three-putt the entire tournament). Having scored the best round of the day Friday, and also scoring the best round of Saturday (65), Woods *tripled* his lead to nine shots.

At 15 under 201, the closest competitor to Woods was Italy's Costantino Rocca, who was at 6 under. Eight-time major winner Tom Watson, who followed a 68 with a 69, was eleven strokes back in fourth, while Montgomerie's 74 dropped him into a tie for sixth.

Despite being someone on the verge of winning their first major,

Woods resorted to being a typical twenty-one-year-old at night. Playing ping-pong, shooting hoops, and becoming absorbed in video games with college pals while dining at Arby's, he stayed at a rented house with his parents, Earl and Kultida.

Watson, a two-time Masters winner, was totally impressed and was basically saying it was all over.

"Looks like the kid is going to win his first Masters," said Watson. "It's going to be great for the Masters. This golf course is suited for his game. I don't know how many courses are not suited for his game, as good as this kid is."

Even seasoned golf writers concurred.

Golf Digest's Dan Jenkins compared the situation to one of the most dominant sports performances in history when he wrote, "Tiger Woods on Sunday at the '97 Masters was the biggest lock in sports since Secretariat at the Belmont."

And the kid did not disappoint. He won going away just like the majestic thoroughbred. After a 4 over par 40 on the opening nine, he played the final sixty-three holes in 22 under, and with five birdies for a final-round 69 at 18-under 270, Tiger won by twelve strokes.

In securing his first major title, Woods's performance created the largest victory margin in Masters history, passing Nicklaus's nine-shot winning effort in 1965. He would later surpass this with a fifteen-stroke margin of victory at the 2000 US Open in Pebble Beach (see chapter 56).

Six-time Masters winner Jack Nicklaus, who finished twenty shots back here, could only shake his head in admiration, saying: "It's a shame Bob Jones isn't here. He could have saved the words he used for me in 1963 for this young man, because he is certainly playing a game we're not familiar with."

It would be a sport-changing performance, and one that all started with a bogey on first hole and ended with the heartfelt embrace between father and son. As millions watched on television, CBS broadcaster Jim Nantz perhaps summed it up best when he told the audience, "There it is, a win for the ages."

And one of the biggest winners going forward would be that electronic box in the living room, as Woods's victory set television ratings records for golf. The final-round broadcast on Sunday was seen by nearly 45 million viewers in the United States. They had found a ratings goldmine in the charismatic twenty-one-year-old. He'd go on to draw in casual fans to their home screens by the millions.

The 1997 Masters was the coronation of golf's new king.

Tiger became the first Black golfer to win a major and the youngest player, at twenty-one, to win at Augusta National. No one saw it coming. In a sense it was reminiscent of twenty-two-year-old Cassius Clay in 1964, when he stunned the oddsmakers by dethroning world heavyweight boxing champ Sonny Liston in a seventh-round technical knockout. Like Clay, who shook up the world with his coronation in the boxing ring, Tiger did something similar in the golf world.

On April 13, 1997, nearly fifty years to the day after Jackie Robinson broke the color barrier in Major League Baseball, Woods would change the environment and style of the sport at a place where no Black man was allowed to join the club until 1990 and all the caddies were Black until 1982.

Woods's victory became a cultural milestone in general, prompting millions who had never been interested in golf to pay attention. As a result, advertisers paid attention to new markets, and player purses increased and TV ratings zoomed.

What also zoomed as a result of Tiger's stunning display of power (he averaged 323 yards off the tee on the measured holes—nearly twenty-five yards longer than the next player), were course designers scrambling to lengthen their layouts, including Augusta.

The victory was transformative for the sport in general, which caused an explosion in the equipment and apparel businesses but also sparked a generation of hopefuls who wanted to be like Tiger. Some of the current stars like Rory McIlroy and Justin Thomas, as well as more than a few leading professionals on the LPGA Tour, readily admit Woods fueled their dreams as they watched him at the 1997 Masters.

17

FOR RORY, THE WRONG KIND OF FADE

APRIL 7-10, 2011
AUGUSTA NATIONAL GOLF CLUB
AUGUSTA, GEORGIA

Rory McIlroy led after the first round. He led after the second round. He led after the third round. He looked like a lock to making the green jacket symbolic of his first major victory. But a combination of his bad fade on Sunday and Charl Swartzel's tremendous closing 66 made the superbly talented Irishman's experience something all the greats from Ben Hogan and Sam Snead to Arnie and Jack have . . . losing a tough one in a major.

I should know. I've been in Rory's shoes, too. Losing the 1962 Masters to Arnold Palmer still irks me to this day.

After shooting a fabulous 65 to colead after the first round, McIlroy, who had missed the cut at the previous Masters, was cautiously optimistic about his fine start.

"After the second round here last year it was probably the low point of the season for me. I think that Augusta National, it takes years and years of figuring out and they make tiny little adjustments here and there, but I feel a lot more comfortable on the golf course this year than I did the previous couple of years, which is great. And it showed in the way I played today. I played some really good golf out there."

Indeed, he did, and McIlroy continued his "really good golf" by finishing the second round with a 69 and sole possession of the lead.

The third round was more of the same. After playing the first twelve holes in 1 over par, McIlroy birdied thirteen, fifteen, and seventeen to gain a four-shot lead heading into the final round.

2009 Masters champion Ángel Cabrera from Argentina stormed into second place with a 67, and South Africa's Charl Swartzel finished with a 68 to tie with Cabrera, KJ Choi, and Jason Day at 8-under 208, the closest group to McIlroy.

The leader talked about being composed and feeling "stress-free."

"Patience and patience. Yeah, I stayed—stuck to my game plan really well, stayed really patient. You know, things weren't going that well for me, 1 over through twelve holes, and then played the last six holes in 3 under. It was great. Yeah, that was the key thing for me, just really staying patient."

McIlroy then described his four birdies, which gave him the cushion heading into the final day.

"First birdie of the day came at the fourth hole, poured a three-iron, probably the best swing I put on it all day and got it on the back tier five or six feet and was able to make that. Hit a three-wood and a six-iron to the thirteenth, exactly where I wanted to, just on the bottom of the slope there and two-putted around thirty feet. Fifteen, I hit driver, six-iron pin high right just where I wanted to and two-putted again from twenty, twenty-five feet. Then got away with my tee shot a little bit on seventeen. I had a bit of—I didn't have a gap, but I was far enough back from the trees that I could hit it high and sort of hook it a little bit and hit a wedge from 155 and got it to the back of the green somehow, and it was a bonus for that putt to go in. I've been waiting for one to go in all day," he said with a chuckle.

Would he be in a merry mood Sunday evening? Well, he certainly conveyed a sense of calm before the storm, saying, "I haven't had any trouble sleeping the last three nights, so hopefully it'll be the same."

McIlroy woke up to take in a big rugby match with Ulster, his favorite team playing Northampton. He was trying to keep away memories of what had happened at the previous year's Open Championship at the Old Course at St. Andrews that prevented him from scoring his first major win: he tied the tournament's eighteen-hole scoring record with a 63 in the first round, but in very high winds on day two he soared to an 80. He came back to finish tied for third.

On this day, McIlroy was fairly steady through the front nine, but with an opening birdie and an eagle on three, Schwartzel was gaining fast. At the turn McIlroy had a thin one-stroke lead arriving at the tenth.

The Irishman's train to Butler's Cabin derailed there. After a disastrous triple bogey at the par-4, 495-yard "Camellia" tenth, McIlroy could never get back on track.

While he dropped seven strokes on the back nine, Schwartzel birdied the final four holes to win by two shots. His 66 was the low round of the day and earned him his first major victory.

Schwartzel became the third South African to win the Masters, along with myself and Trevor Immelman (2008). It came at a very good time, as 2011 marked the fiftieth anniversary of my 1961 Masters victory, which made me the first international player to win the Masters. An achievement I am very proud of.

With his poor closing effort finishing with an 80, McIlroy took a blow to his pride. Unsurprisingly, he pointed to the tenth hole as the turning point.

"I'm very disappointed. You know, I was leading this golf tournament with nine holes to go, and I just unraveled. Hit a bad tee shot on ten and then never, never really recovered. You know, it's going to be hard to take . . . I knew it was going to be very tough for me out there today, and it was. I felt good that I hung in well for the first nine holes, and then as I said, just sort of lost my speed on the greens, lost my line, lost everything for just two, three holes—ten, eleven, twelve—and couldn't really recover after that."

Geoff Ogilvy, who tied for fourth with Tiger Woods and Luke Donald, talked specifically about his good friend, Rory:

"Rory makes one swing at ten and gets really unlucky, this is to fight the battle all the way and because every shot is very difficult. It was a shame, but there is precedent because it's happened to several others at the Masters. It was very uncharacteristic of Rory," continued the Australian. "He has not done very many things like that in his career. But that is one of the beauties of that place that makes it so special, because it is so difficult to win. Just one bad swing and the whole thing can become unraveled. And you simply don't get that many opportunities at Augusta. We all felt for Rory that day."

And nobody felt worse than Rory, but he knew that everybody loses, even the very best, and he also knew the greats bounce back. For McIlroy that return to excellence came just two months later, when he roared back in record fashion.

His wire-to-wire win in the US Open at the Congressional Country Club's Blue Course in Bethesda, Maryland, was a dominant performance. And it was never close.

He led by three after the first round, by six after the second round, and by eight after the third round. He won by eight strokes.

McIlroy broke all kinds of records at this major: fewest strokes ever in a US Open, and most strokes under par, in addition to various round records. He shot all four rounds under par, all in the 60s.

That's bouncing back.

Rory has the best golf swing in the world today, and I still believe he will end up winning the Masters someday.

18

BUBBA'S HOOK INTO HISTORY

APRIL 5-8, 2012
AUGUSTA NATIONAL GOLF CLUB
AUGUSTA, GEORGIA

As a thirty-three-year-old big-hitting lefty from Bagdad, Florida, who brandished a driver with a macho pink head and shaft for cancer awareness, there was no reason Bubba Watson should have been a consideration to be one of the favorites after three starts at Augusta resulted in finishes of twentieth (tied), forty-second, and thirty-eighth (tied).

However, while the leading picks were Tiger Woods, Phil Mickelson, Rory McIlroy, and world number one Luke Donald, none of them were self-taught like Watson, who learned the game by hitting Wiffle balls around his house. Bubba arguably possessed just as great an imagination and as vast an arsenal of shots as anyone in the field. That would be on display in historic fashion here at the 2012 Masters, which was the seventy-sixth one played.

With his pink driver performing well on the demanding Augusta tee shots, Bubba produced a fine 69 to start things off. His 3-under score gave him a share of fourth place.

Also searching for his first major title, Lee Westwood was in the lead at 5 under with a 67. In thirteen prior Masters appearances, the Englishman's best finish was second place in 2010.

In recounting his round, Westwood, a player with thirty-three international victories including four in 2011, explained how the course suited his game.

"I missed a short one on four for par, and then I hit an eight-iron to four feet on five, eight-iron to ten feet on six, nine-iron to six feet on seven, and then chipped it stone dead on eight and missed from about ten feet on nine. So I had a run of holes there where I hit it close," said Westwood. "But if you look at my stats this year, they have this proximity-to-the-hole stat and I'm fairly high up on that, and this is a second-shot golf course. I figured if I drive the ball well, which I generally do, then I'm going to have a chance to get it close to flags and from there, it's just an issue of how many putts I hole."

Bubba kept holing putts good enough to grab a share of third place at 4 under 140 after two rounds. He was just one back of Jason Dufner and the 1992 Masters winner, Fred Couples.

Even with a green jacket and ten career top ten finishes at this tournament, Couples was both stunned and thrilled with his play.

"Very shocking and it was a great day. You know, I've said it for twenty-eight years, this is my favorite golf tournament in the world."

For Watson, despite being among the leaders in the middle of the competition, his thoughts weren't far from being a new father. (Watson and his wife, Angie, became the new parents to a one-month-old adopted baby boy, Caleb, just two weeks before the Masters 2012 tournament.)

"That's what I'm thinking about," he said after the round. "Here, this is just a golf tournament. Win, lose, or draw, it doesn't matter the whole scheme of things. It would be nice to be a green jacket, but if I don't win it, no big deal. My son is at home, our new son is at home. Obviously, that is more important to me than trying to make a putt to win a golf tournament."

Another lefty trying to win a golf tournament was Phil Mickelson. And after going low on Saturday with a 66 (a long way from his opening 74), the three-time Masters champion, just one shot off the lead, was poised for snaring another jacket.

However, both Mickelson and the fifty-four-hole leader, Peter Hanson, could not maintain their momentum.

A veteran of the European Tour, he took on some quick bogeys and by the time Hanson shanked his tee shot on the par-3 twelfth short of the water, for another bogey, the native of Sweden fell from contention.

Phil fell a bit after pushing his tee shot left at the par-3 fourth and it caromed off a greenside grandstand. It resulted in his second triple bogey of the week, and he'd finish two shots short of the playoff.

Meanwhile, Louis Oosthuizen was making a play. The South African winner of the 2010 Open Championship at St. Andrews had started the day two back of the leaders, but with one memorable swing he vaulted into the lead.

At the par-5 second hole, Little Louie, with one of the smoothest strokes in the game, found himself 253 yards from the hole. He used a four-iron, and his shot landed on the front of the green, hiked the slope, and rolled some ninety feet into the cup for that rarest of scores—a double eagle.

Oosthuizen had never made a double eagle in his life. It was the first double eagle on Pink Dogwood and just the fourth in Masters history.

It was witnessed by Bubba, his playing partner, who now fell four back of the lead. However, despite a bogey at twelve, Bubba, who at six foot three towered over his playing partner (yet is still an inch shorter than his wife, a former professional basketball player in the WNBA), was progressively rising to the occasion.

Bubba then birdied holes thirteen through sixteen to tie for the lead. Coleaders at ten under, the partners in the penultimate pairing both parred seventeen.

On the seventy-second hole each were on the green in regulation.

Oosthuizen missed a thirty-five-foot birdie try, as did Bubba from approximately twenty-five feet. With pars they proceeded to a sudden death playoff.

After each of the competitors parred the playoff eighteenth, they proceeded to the next, the tenth.

The tenth, a 495-yard par-4, has historically been one of the more difficult in Masters history, with its 4.31-stroke average the highest in relation to par. It has a steep downhill dogleg left; if one can access the slope in the fairway with their tee shot, easy yardage is added with a generous roll. However, if that doesn't happen, it's a long way down there for shot number two.

In any event the hard-sloping right-to-left green is protected by a bunker right and a huge slope to the left. Most players are pleased to make par and move to the eleventh tee with a sigh of relief.

But there'd be no relief for Bubba, at least not after his pink driver betrayed him by landing his ball deep into the woods, right of the fairway. Realizing the predicament his playing partner was in, Oosthuizen decided to play it safe with a three-wood off the tee, but his shot found a bit of trouble as well. Landing also to the right in the first cut of rough, the ball sat more than 220 yards from the green.

Oosthuizen followed that up with an approach shot that failed to reach the green, and the ball came to rest on a deceptive upslope.

Asked if Bubba had any chance of reaching the green from his position, three-time Masters champion Nick Faldo, broadcasting for CBS, responds, "I doubt it, to be honest."

Bubba and his caddy, Ted Scott, long had a theory they operated under. As he walked toward his predicament, it came into play.

"We were walking down the fairway going, we've been here before [he'd already made a par from the right trees on number ten in regulation]," said Bubba. "And Teddy reminded me of our mantra when he said, 'If you've got a swing, you've got a shot.'"

Despite nothing less than the Masters riding on the outcome, still, a punch-out was not even in the equation for this creative artist.

With his ball resting on pine straw and no clear path to the green, attempting a shot most PGA Tour players wouldn't even consider, Bubba crowded the ball with his pitching wedge, closed the clubface severely at address, closed his stance, and blasted from the inside out as hard as he could. He hit a 155-yard snap hook around the magnolia with so much movement on the ball, with an action kind of like a billiard player, it landed on the green spinning sideways and came to rest within twelve feet of the cup.

"It was just a classic excuse for him to conjure up another piece of magic," said Faldo.

Faldo's broadcast partner, Jim Nantz, added, "He plays the game really unlike anyone else, and that's part of the reason he's so popular."

"I hit fifty-two-degree, my gap wedge, hooked it about forty yards, hit about fifteen feet off the ground until it got under the tree and then started rising," said Bubba with a victorious laugh. "Pretty easy."

Not bad for one of the few players who doesn't have a swing coach, and never has.

"I had no idea where he was," Oosthuizen said. "Where I stood from, when the ball came out, it looked like a curve ball. Unbelievable shot. That shot he hit definitely won him the tournament."

Indeed, after Oosthuizen just missed with his par putt, Bubba sank his for the victory.

As part of a tearful victory celebration shared with his mother and friends, a deeply faithful family man, Bubba's mind became filled with thoughts not only of his wife and child but also of his father, a former Green Beret who battled posttraumatic stress disorder and who passed from throat cancer in 2010.

Free-flowing and fun-loving with a seemingly unlimited arsenal of shots, the self-taught Bubba walks to the beat of a different golfer.

So, it is kind of a contrast—his victory here at Augusta.

Whereas the Masters is ordered and traditional, Bubba is hang-loose and seemingly a spur-of-the-moment type of individual often associated with creative artists.

"I got in these trees and hit a crazy shot and I saw it in my head and somehow I'm here talking to you with a green jacket on," he said afterward.

A wedge from the woods. It is a shot that will live on in the tournament's rich lore.

19

AN IMPROBABLE COMEBACK
AS TIGER ROARS AGAIN

APRIL 11–14, 2019
AUGUSTA NATIONAL GOLF CLUB
AUGUSTA, GEORGIA

After a long period of well-chronicled marital, substance abuse, surgery, and coaching issues that took him to the depths of professional and personal despair, the now forty-three-year-old Tiger Woods, fourteen years removed from his last Masters title, was about to make a bid for a return to glory. Time, spinal-fusion surgery, and perseverance (including predawn trips to the gym, ice baths, measured range sessions, and heaping doses of gratitude) had helped Woods rejuvenate a broken body and spirit.

Let me tell you something about Tiger.

When Tiger and I played golf, contrary to what psychiatrists and people tell you to play, was to go out there and relax and have fun. Hogwash!

I got so irritable I would bite one of my children's heads off if they came near me, and Tiger Woods was the same.

I will never forget when he walked through the locker room at

Augusta in 2019 with his bodyguards. His focus was so intense that it couldn't be explained it to the average person. But I could see it. I have been in that same zone.

Tiger's mind was now clear. His storied fall from the top of the game was in the past. And he was ready to win.

Indeed, he did. Tiger won the Masters for the fifth time (thus breaking my record of thirteen years between titles at Augusta).

For Woods, the key to getting to this position was winning the Tour Championship the previous September at the East Lake Golf Club in Atlanta.

"I feel like I can win. I've proven that I can do it [at East Lake]," said Woods at a pre-Masters press conference. "I just feel like I've improved a lot over the past twelve, fourteen months, but I've more than anything just proven to myself that I can play at this level again. I've worked my way back into one of the players that can win events."

Well, the four-time Masters winner would have some formidable opponents who were also plenty capable of winning. Bryson De-Chambeau, aka "the Scientist," found his formula and birdied six of his final seven holes to grab a share of the opening round lead with a 66. He shared the top spot with burly Florida native Brooks Koepka, who was the winner of two of the three previous majors but missed the previous year's Masters while he recovered from wrist surgery. Koepka was the only competitor to go bogey free here.

Three-time Masters champion Phil Mickelson was one back. World number two player Dustin Johnson and Ian Poulter were two back at 4 under. Adam Scott and Jon Rahm were part of a group at 3 under. So Woods was facing some deep talent from the start. Part of a batch of ten players tied for eleventh place at 70 (2 under); it matched his opening result in three of his four previous Masters wins (in 2005 he opened with 74).

It should be noted that the previous Masters winner who came from outside the top ten after the first round had been Woods, who was tied at thirty-third and seven strokes behind Chris DiMarco after the opening eighteen in 2005.

The talent at the top just got deeper as five players, all major champions, shared the lead at the end of the second day. The most in the tournament's history.

T1	JASON DAY (AUSTRALIA)	70-67=137	−7
	BROOKS KOEPKA (UNITED STATES)	66-71=137	
	FRANCESCO MOLINARI (ITALY)	70-67=137	
	LOUIS OOSTHUIZEN (SOUTH AFRICA)	71-66=137	
	ADAM SCOTT (AUSTRALIA)	69-68=137	

Coleader Koepka prided himself on the strength of his game between the ears: "I just think I know I can beat a lot of people mentally. I know some people don't think I'm mentally tough, or tough in general, but I think I am," he said. "I think I've proven that with three trophies. I feel like no matter how things are going, whether they are going really well or really poorly out there, I can grind it out, and especially during a major. I know just to hang in there because there's always something around the corner."

Lurking around the corner was Woods. With a 68, he was just one back halfway through the tournament.

The third round had favorable weather conditions that were conducive to low scoring. Tiger shot a 5 under par 67 on Saturday, his best round of the tournament, to move into a tie for second with

Tony Finau (64). But it would be the amiable Italian, Francesco Molinari, who was the star of stars this day.

The young man from Turin, whose brother Edoardo also played on the tour, entered the final round of the Open Championship the previous summer at Carnoustie, trailing by three strokes. He would shoot a bogey-free 69 (and no bogeys over his final thirty-seven holes) to become not only the first Italian winner of this major but the first Italian winner of any of the major championships.

One of the players he passed at Carnoustie on the way to a Claret Jug was Woods, who finished sixth.

Now, here at Augusta, with four straight birdies on the treacherous back nine, Molinari's bogey-free 66 gave him the fifty-four-hole lead with a 203 total and 13 under.

But weather would mess with normal Sunday pairings in a couple of ways. With massive storms already blanketing the western part of the state and in anticipation of them arriving later in the day for Augusta, organizers took the unprecedented step of deciding to send final-round threesomes off the first and tenth tees. And starting tee times some five hours earlier than normal was a significant change. Thus the final group of Woods, Francesco Molinari, and Tony Finau would tee off at 9:20 a.m.

Also, winds could (and would) wreak havoc.

"It will be interesting to see if that wind comes up like it's forecast, fifteen, twenty miles an hour around this golf course is going to be a test. And I've got to be committed, hit the proper shots and then hopefully time it," said Woods.

Tiger certainly was helped by the anticipated poor weather. Otherwise there'd have been no threesomes, and he would not have been in the final pairing. But he was, and that, plus having essentially the entire gallery pulling for him, aided his cause. Still, Woods was under pressure to win a first major title after having not held the lead after fifty-four holes.

But for the fourteen-time majors winner, that was par for the course. "The day I don't feel pressure is the day I quit," said Woods. "At least if you care about something, obviously you're going to feel pressure. And I've always felt it, from the first time I remember ever playing a golf tournament to now. That hasn't changed."

What also had not changed, at least in the early stages of the fourth round, was the steady play of Molinari, who seemed to be handling the pressure well.

Opening with six straight pars, the Italian walked off the eleventh green still maintaining a two-shot lead. At 13 under he had a couple strokes on Koepka and Woods.

Others would make runs. Dustin Johnson, Patrick Cantlay, Jason Day, and Xander Schauffele, among others. Still, at this point, they were all chasing the defending Open champion from Turin.

The par-3 155-yard twelfth, known as Golden Bell, would be ringing the bells of several players in contention. And largely because of what Woods predicted the day before about being able to time the swirling winds at Amen Corner, which had blown away the title chances of many a challenger.

Koepka's tee shot hit the bank and rolled into Rae's Creek. Ian Poulter had the same result. In the next and final group, Molinari's reaction said it all. Not wanting to get it too high for the gusting wind to take it, he pushed it, and instead of making the bunker, it became a wet ball. Missed by a foot, and that was more than enough for trouble to appear. Tiger, showing his experience, played it safe, and his ball landed on the green while Finau's ball also went swimming.

They all double-bogeyed while Woods dropped it in for par. It was an example of a philosophy based on years of playing Augusta.

"Conservative when needed, and aggressive when allowed," said Woods.

That experience was quite evident, when I saw on television what Molinari, Koepka, and the other guys did. Each of them made a double bogey on the hole with a nine-iron in his hand. They all went for the pin, and the rule is you never shoot at the pin unless you are behind and you have to.

And here are these guys in front, who should've aimed for the middle of the green. So what did Tiger Woods do? He came along and uses his experience just playing for the middle of the green because you can hit the most perfect shot there. I have played more tournaments at Augusta than anybody—fifty-two—so I know what I am talking about.

There's just one thing for you to do with that hole. You shoot for the middle of the green, get your par, and you get out of town.

"Yeah, the mistake Francesco made there let a lot of guys back into the tournament, myself included," said Woods.

To his credit, Molinari would steady the ship and birdie the next hole to get one back, while Koepka would eagle that hole to get both back. But Woods would birdie thirteen as well to take the lead at 12 under.

Veteran tour player Billy Mayfair tells the story of how the mind of a champion works:

"I clearly remember playing with him at Bay Hill one year. We are on the thirteenth hole. A windy cold day in Orlando. And he had flighted a ball to the back edge of the green. It was kind of an odd shot. I'm always looking to pick someone's brain and walking down the fairway I asked Tiger, 'Why did you hit that shot? It seemed kind of odd,' and he looked right at me and said, 'That's what you have to do is hit that high straight eight-iron on thirteen at Augusta.' The Masters was still a month away and he's already preparing for it."

After the birdie at thirteen, Woods would also birdie the par-5 fifteenth. Now at 13 under, he had the lead for the first time all day as Molinari found water (just like Ballesteros did in the final round in 1986 to end his chances) and a double bogey again at fifteen to fall three back.

Koepka, who also birdied fifteen, trailed Woods by one. And though Cantlay's eagle at fifteen also put him at 12 under, he'd take himself out of contention with back-to-back bogeys. Johnson (with an impressive three straight birdies starting at fifteen) and Schauffele would finish at 12 under, but that would not be enough.

Koepka dropped an absolutely riveting draw eight-iron to about four feet and converted for a second straight birdie, this one on the par-3, 170-yard sixteenth. The roar was so loud he had to back off his tee shot up ahead.

Woods now had a two-stroke lead at 14 under.

So to stay in it, Koepka had to birdie the last two holes. He had a twelve-foot birdie look on seventeen that stayed high, and after a massive drive down eighteen he hit his approach to within six feet. Another good chance at birdie, but another par result as he pulled the putt left.

Woods had a fine drive at the seventeenth that resulted in an easy par. With a two-shot lead teeing off at the seventy-second hole, Woods whacked a three-wood down the right side, then proceeded to miss the green. But a pitch shot set up a two-putt bogey and a one-shot victory for his fifth green jacket.

Tiger, who knew the perilous woods of Augusta so well, had patiently hunted down each of his prey one by one. Over the last six holes, on the strength of three birdies he had dropped major champions Molinari, Koepka, and Johnson, as well Xander Schauffele, the tenth-ranked player in the world.

After dropping in his final putt at eighteen, Woods broke into a huge grin and raised his arms high, then he fell into a long embrace with his caddy, Joe LaCava. Then he hugged his son, Charlie. He had won this tournament first as a son hugging his father, Earl, in 1997, and now he was a father himself. After hugging his daughter and mother, he'd later say in the posttournament interview on CBS, "To have my kids there, it's come full circle."

It was, Woods would say, one of the greatest accomplishments of his stellar career.

"It's overwhelming just because of what has transpired," Woods said. "I could barely walk. Couldn't sleep. Couldn't walk. Couldn't do anything."

Perhaps it took a multimajors winner who had overcome his own injuries to really sum up what happened at the 2019 Masters.

"Absolutely incredible. You just look at the last five years and what he's had to go through; I mean, to come back, get back playing and back to where he was, get his body back in shape. You know, it's one thing to do it on the range; one thing to do it when you're practicing, and then to be able to come back out here and have the Tiger of old back—as a fan, I love it. I think it's awesome. I'm glad he's back" said Koepka.

20

A MAJOR BREAKTHROUGH FOR
GOLF-MAD JAPAN

APRIL 8–11, 2021
AUGUSTA NATIONAL GOLF CLUB
AUGUSTA, GEORGIA

Each April throughout his youth, while Japan's iconic cherry blossoms (sakura) blanketed the country in soft pink splendor and grabbed the attention of both locals and visitors, Hideki Matsuyama's focus was on the splendor that was on display among the azaleas and dogwoods half a world away.

For every morning of the tournament, year after year, the young man would wake up at 5 a.m. and watch the Masters, dreaming of the day he might compete for a green jacket. The first time for his own annual ritual of taking in the action at Augusta National on TV came in 1997, when Tiger won (and became his hero).

Having learned golf from his father, a former club champion, Hideki, nearly a quarter century later, would become the first Japanese player to win a men's major championship when he won the 2021 Masters Tournament (Japanese women have won two majors).

Before this breakthrough, there've been some very, very good Japanese players who've played quite well in the majors.

Masashi "Jumbo" Ozaki, a big hitter who is the all-time victory leader of the Japan Golf Tour, had three major top tens with his best finish a tie for sixth place at the 1989 US Open.

Tommy Nakajima garnered six career top tens in majors, his finest performance being a third-place finish at the 1988 PGA Championships.

Shingo Katayama, known as "Cowboy Shingo" for the distinctive hats he wore, had a pair of fourth-place finishes: the 2001 PGA Championship and the 2009 Masters (which he closed with a fine 68—to that point the best Augusta finish by a Japanese player).

Masahiro Kuramoto tied for fourth place at the 1982 Open Championship. Shigeki Maruyama has three career top tens at the majors, his best finish a fourth-place tie at the 2004 US Open.

Perhaps the most notable player from Japan was Isao Aoki from Chiba. The Hall of Famer, who learned the game as a caddy during his youth, had four top ten finishes in the majors. The most memorable was the 1980 US Open at Baltusrol Golf Club.

There, he shared the lead with Jack Nicklaus heading into the final round. Nicklaus was coming off the first poor year of his pro career. In 1979, he went winless on the PGA Tour for the first time since his professional career started in 1962.

Aoki, with a pair of back-to-back top ten finishes in the 1978 and 1979 Open Championships, was appearing in only his second US Open.

After blistering Baltusrol with three straight 68s, Aoki skillfully took on the Golden Bear until finally succumbing, finishing with a 70 to Jack's 68 for the two-stroke loss. But that runner-up result was the best majors finish by a Japanese player until Hideki.

For Hideki, manifesting his youthful dreams of a Masters victory really took hold in 2011. He arrived with a heavy heart—just a month earlier Japan and his home of Sendai had been ravaged by a terrible earthquake and a series of tsunamis that resulted in more than fifteen thousand deaths. Nevertheless, his first experience at Augusta was quite successful. His 287 resulted in his being awarded the Silver Cup as the leading amateur.

Fast-forward ten years.

Now age twenty-nine, with a lot more experience competing under the pressures of a major and ranked twenty-fifth in the world, Hideki was about to make history. Still, there would be hurdles from both a very unforgiving course and relentless competitors.

One of those was Justin Rose. Winner of the 2013 US Open at Merion, the Englishman also had some solid play at Augusta under his belt, which included five top ten finishes here. And the way things started out, it looked like he'd be in the mix again with an outstanding 65 to take the first-round lead. His score was all the more impressive because only eleven golfers finished under par, and the only other two to shoot below 70 were Brian Harman and Hideki, both with 69s.

"The greens were firm and fast. It was very important to hit your second shot on the proper side of the pin, and I was able to do that," said Matsuyama in accounting for his good opening-day result.

The second round involved a rare occurrence. After opening with a 76, Matthew Wolff was disqualified from the Masters for signing an incorrect scorecard following his second round.

Justin Rose's scorecard correctly said 72, and so he continued to be the leader halfway through at 137.

And while Rose would draw up another 72 in the third round, Matsuyama would follow up his 71 with an astounding 65 (the lowest score by three shots) to take a four-stroke lead into the final round.

A rain delay during the third round seemed to help him because while others were refueling in the locker room or just relaxing in the clubhouse, Matsuyama sat in his car. And as the rain fell all around the vehicle, he serenely played games on his cell phone.

The players returning about eighty minutes later to a golf course that was now noticeably more forgiving, especially the dampened, significantly slower greens. With the wind having all but vanished, Matsuyama's game really took flight.

Playing his final eight holes in 6 under par (including an eagle at fifteen), putting him at eleven under par for the tournament, Hideki was one round away from winning.

"Thankfully for the rain, I was able to put some spin on the ball and checked up and got close to the pin. I did play well today. And my game plan was carried out, and hopefully tomorrow I can continue good form," Hideki said after the round.

Normally shadowed by a plethora of Japanese media following his every move, conditions were quite different at these Masters.

Due to COVID-19 and related travel restrictions, the number of media and spectators allowed was greatly reduced. Also due to the pandemic, the 2020 Masters was postponed from its traditional April date and played in November instead. Holding or sharing the lead after each round, Dustin Johnson won it with a tournament-record score of 20-under 268.

But if Matsuyama was to be the recipient of the green jacket from Dustin, he'd have to get by some formidable contenders over the final eighteen.

New players had moved into contention. Justin Rose and Australian Marc Leishman were joined in second place by Xander Schauffele and a Masters rookie, Will Zalatoris.

Schauffele, playing with Matsuyama, had grandparents who lived in Japan, and said he knew enough of the language to make some jokes with Hideki earlier on. But now, as he was trying to break through to the majors winner circle as well, it was game on. The San Diego native had runner-up finishes at both the 2019 Masters and 2018 Open Championships.

Zalatoris, twenty-four, from Dallas, Texas, was a wiry, data-driven player not unlike Bryson DeChambeau. Will, a former Texas State Amateur champion used DECADE, a course-management system developed by Scott Fawcett, a forty-seven-year-old data guru. Its math-based approach to strategy combined PGA Tour scoring statistics with shot-dispersion patterns to inform players on club selection and lines to aim for. Avoiding mistakes took precedence over flag hunting.[1]

As Matsuyama eluded mistakes of his own, things looked promising for him. About halfway through his final round he had pushed his lead to six strokes. However, the proverbial wisdom that "the Masters begins on the back nine on Sunday" came into play here as well.

He lost some strokes, as Xander made a run.

Matsuyama felt compelled to go for it in two on the par-five fifteenth, which he had eagled earlier in the tournament. But his approach with a blistering four-iron came in low and hot, sailed right over the green, and rolled into the water out back.

"It was a four-stroke lead, and I felt I needed to birdie fifteen because I knew Xander would definitely be birdieing or maybe even eagling," Matsuyama would say later of his strategy.

On the strength of four consecutive birdies on holes twelve to fifteen, Schauffele was just two back as they arrived at the par-three sixteenth tee.

However, Schauffele's quest for his first major ended here. His tee shot bounced back into the water. After taking a drop, he hit his next shot over the green and into the gallery. When he eventually found the hole, it was for a triple bogey, his first in a major.

Matsuyama took a two-stroke lead to the eighteenth tee, made bogey at the last, and won by a stroke over Zalatoris.

The twenty-four-year-old Masters rookie had holed an eighteen-foot par putt on the last hole for a 70 and sole possession of second place. It was the best performance by a first-timer to the Masters since another Dallas youngster, Jordan Spieth, was runner-up in 2014 to Bubba Watson.

His own fine result certainly was pretty special for Hideki Matsuyama.

And it was a double victory for golf-mad Japan: Matsuyama's win on Sunday was the second victory for a Japanese golfer at Augusta

National in the previous eight days. On April 3, the seventeen-year-old Tsubasa Kajitani, from Okayama, won the Augusta National Women's Amateur tournament.

For Matsuyama, it was his first tour victory since winning three times in 2017, and he became the seventh player to win both low amateur in the Masters and a green jacket.

A photo of that moment when his caddie, Shota Hayafuji, bowed to the course after his win, spread quickly on social media. People appreciated the show of respect.

As defending champion Dustin Johnson placed the green jacket on him, Matsuyama said, "I'm really happy"—and no doubt so was an entire nation of golf-mad supporters.

He would return home to a hero's welcome.

"Hopefully I'll be a pioneer in this and many other Japanese will follow," said Matsuyama, speaking through interpreter Bob Hunter. "I'm glad to be able to open the floodgates hopefully, and many more will follow me."

THE PGA CHAMPIONSHIP

LAUNCHED IN 1916 WHEN A DEPARTMENT STORE MAG-nate, Rodman Wanamaker, a dedicated sports enthusiast, formed the PGA Professional Golfers' Association of America, the fledgling PGA Championship got a great boost after the father of modern professional golf, the enormously popular Walter Hagen, not only won it in 1921 but then took the title four consecutive years from 1924 to 1927.

A visionary entrepreneur, operating stores in Philadelphia, New York City, and Paris, Wanamaker was a marketing whiz who bestowed upon the annual winner a mammoth trophy that bears his name. (It stands at 28 inches high, 10½ inches in diameter, and 27 inches from handle to handle, and weighs 27 pounds.) Over a century later, the Wanamaker Trophy is still one of the most recognized in all sports.

The tournament is also well recognized in the golf world. Through the decades, the PGA Championship has overcome perhaps more hurdles than the three other major events to stay one of the four Grand Slam events.

For many years the tournament drew criticism for having a lack of talented competitors from abroad, for being moved about restlessly on the golfing calendar, and also for its selection of comparatively lackluster venues, which were determined more by political considerations than golfing refinement. The role of television also greatly impacted this major. In the late '50s and early '60s, this medium was playing a growing role in popularizing golf, and networks felt the PGA Championship's match play format (where you sought to beat an opponent, not par), while potentially exciting, was simply too risky. Broadcast executives were concerned that too many of the big names could be knocked out too soon. So, the PGA of America agreed in 1958 to switch it to stroke play.

Still, with the combination of the organizers upgrading their venues to present some of the great tests of the game—courses like Pebble Beach, Baltusrol, Oakmont, Southern Hills, Riviera, and Winged Foot—along with some thrilling performances by John Daly, Tiger Woods, Rory McIlroy, and Phil Mickelson, among others, the PGA Championship has proven it belongs in the Grand Slam rotation.

Besides, it always features more players in the top one hundred of the Official World Golf Ranking than any of the other majors, making it the deepest field.

21

GOLF'S NEWEST MAJOR DEBUTS
WITH A DRAMATIC FINISH

OCTOBER 10–14, 1916
SIWANOY COUNTRY CLUB
BRONXVILLE, NEW YORK

As a result of a series of meetings that began in mid-January 1916 chaired by Rodman Wanamaker, the son of the pioneering founder of Wanamaker's department stores (now Macy's) with a group of golf professionals (including the esteemed Walter Hagen) and several leading amateur golfers, the resulting new organization, the Professional Golfers' Association (PGA) held its first championships later that fall. The winner would be the first holder of the Wanamaker Trophy, five hundred dollars, and a diamond-studded gold medal.

The field of thirty-two enjoyed some terrific fall weather competing at the Siwanoy Country Club in Bronxville, New York, a Donald Ross course that was just a couple years old and located about twenty miles from midtown Manhattan.

The match play format Wanamaker and the cofounders preferred (they would change to stroke play in 1958), was based on the News of the World Match Play tournament, which had been organized by the British PGA since 1903, although it had not been played since 1913 because of World War I.

There were some tweaks, but the PGA's version was played over five days with all matches contested over thirty-six holes; matches in the News of the World Match Play were over eighteen holes except for the final, with the event being completed in three days.

The field of thirty-two golfers qualified through sectional tournaments. The biggest draw, Hagen, aka "the Haig," who would win his matches in the Round of 16 and the Quarterfinals, would lose here in the semifinals to Jock Hutchison (2 up). But in 1921 he'd win his first of a record-setting five PGA titles. Only Jack Nicklaus would win that many.

Also advancing out of the round of sixteen was Cyril Walker. An undertold, yet tragic story.

Born in Manchester, England, then emigrating to the United States, Walker would be credited with six wins on the PGA Tour. But his biggest victory by far would be against a field that included the likes of Hagen, Sarazen, and Bobby Jones in the 1924 US Open.

A diminutive man—one newspaper called him the pocket-sized Ben Hogan of his day (that is saying something)—in his prime, Walker weighed just 120 pounds, fifteen less than Ben.[1]

Despite the smallness in stature, Walker could belt the ball and was among the longer hitters of that era. At a time when the ball didn't have nearly the flight capabilities of today and they were using sticks that were comparatively low-tech, that skill was a key part of his victory at the wind-swept 6,880-yard Oakland Hills course outside of Detroit.

It was such a demanding course that after winning the 1951 US Open there, Ben Hogan would famously say, "I tamed the monster."

And let me tell you something, having won the 1972 PGA Championships on that same very challenging course, I feel that was indeed a very impressive win by Cyril Walker as he outplayed the great Bobby Jones, who was trying for his second consecutive US Open title.

But he had a nasty disposition and his play was slow. Reportedly his routine would include examining around his ball for even the smallest pebble or leaf; and checking the wind not once but several times, then taking up to a dozen practice swings before every shot. One newspaper reported his glacial pace led to the players who were following him in a big tournament to be supplied a deck of cards to pass the time. The combination of his temper and his slow play eventually led to his being outcast on the fledgling pro circuit.[2]

Perhaps the ultimate example came out on a trip to the West Coast. He adamantly refused tournament officials' repeated warnings to speed up his play during the second round of the 1930 Los Angeles Open. After Walker reportedly took over an hour to play just three holes police were called in, and he had to be physically removed from the course.

Though he'd work as a club pro for a few more years, a growing dependence on alcohol would lead to tragedy.

After a gig as a caddy in Miami, then trying to hang on as a dishwasher, his body and mind were now ravaged by alcohol. Down and out with nothing left and nowhere else to go, the haggard Walker shuffled into a local jail cell on the rainy night of August 5, 1948, and asked the police sergeant for a place to sleep.

The next morning during his rounds, a guard found Walker dead, slumped over in a chair. His passing at age fifty-five was attributed to pleural pneumonia.[3]

Jock Hutchison, who would defeat Walker, 4 and 3, to advance to the semifinals where he'd knock Hagen out of the tournament, was also a British expat who moved to the United States. Born in St. Andrews, Jock would win the Open Championship held there at the Old Course in 1921.

Bobby Jones made his Open Championship debut at that event. In the first round he had been paired with Hutchinson, and while he witnessed Jock's hole in one on the par-3 eighth hole, Jones's grace under pressure and gentlemanly sportsmanship skills were still in the future. After hitting into a bunker on the eleventh hole in the third round, then unsuccessfully taking four swings at the ball, Jones picked up the ball and stormed off the course.

Staying on course at Siwanoy, Jim Barnes and Willie MacFarlane also advanced to face each other in the semifinals where Barnes's 6-and-5 triumph carried him to the finals against Hutchison.

These combatants were no strangers to one another. Meeting in a regional qualifier to get into this event, Barnes and Hutchison tied at 147. So after a nine-hole playoff the following day to decide the winner, Hutchison took the medal by a stroke with a score of 38.[4]

Hutchison got off to a fine start, going 4 up after eight holes. But Barnes, another expat from Britain and a rather tall fellow for the times (six foot four), used his length as well as reconnecting with his keen short game to draw to within one at the end of the morning eighteen.

After lunch, Barnes continued to build momentum in the final round. He grabbed the lead for the first time with a birdie on the seventh hole and kept it through the turn. However, on the back nine he had a drop-off, and Hutchison snatched back the lead with just three to play.

The inaugural PGA championship was a tight battle coming down to the wire. After Hutchison missed a five-footer on seventeen, the now-tied contestants both faced four-footers at the final hole after four strokes on the par 5. A measurement was needed to determine who putted first, and Barnes was an inch closer.[5]

After Hutchison missed his, Barnes sank the winning putt.

The exciting debut of what would later become known as one of the majors could not have gone better for the organizers.

Barnes eventually won four majors total, and Hutchison won two.

One of those titles for Barnes would be back-to-back PGA crowns. However, the successful defense of his PGA victory would come in 1919, because the tournament skipped 1917 and 1918 due to World War I.

22

HAGEN VS. SARAZEN: THE GREATEST 38-HOLE MATCH PLAY CHAMPIONSHIP OF ALL-TIME

SEPTEMBER 24–29, 1923
PELHAM COUNTRY CLUB
PELHAM MANOR, NEW YORK

In many ways the 1923 PGA Championships was the first heavyweight title fight in golf.

Here was a rare marquee matchup in a major, not like those empty exhibition matches of today. This was for something that counted . . . for a lot.

Walter Hagen was the winner of this event in 1921. Gene Sarazen won it in 1922.

Hagen had won all three majors in existence at the time, the PGA and the Open Championship (though they weren't referred to as majors at the time), and the US Open twice.

Sarazen, just twenty, in addition to being the defending champion of this event, had won the US Open earlier in the year, defeating Hagen by three strokes.

Without a doubt they were the two best golfers in the world at the time.

While their talents were obvious, another selling point that kept the street-corner newspaper boys busy was the combatants' contrasting personalities.

Growing up poor and starting out as a caddy to help support his family, Sarazen was comparatively quiet. Hagen was a global personality, a larger-than-life international bon vivant who helped raise the profile of the sport with his dashing presence and winning ways.

Two greats stepping into the ring, which would be the Pelham Country Club, just about fifteen miles outside of Manhattan. It was Jack Dempsey vs. Gene Tunney. It was War Admiral vs. Seabiscuit.

Under the match play format (at the PGA Annual Meeting in 1957, the PGA Championships would change to stroke play), the field of sixty-four qualified by sectional tournaments, then competed in six rounds of match play, all at thirty-six holes in a single-elimination tournament.

Though both favorites were supremely talented, their opponents had some skills of their own. In the quarterfinals, Jim Barnes gave Sarazen all he could handle. There was the physical contrast (Sarazen was five five and Barnes six three), but both had impressive credentials.

The Englishman (who moved to the United States in 1906 and turned pro but retained his British citizenship) won four majors: the very first PGA Championship at Siwanoy in 1916, the 1919 PGA, the US Open in 1921, and the Open Championship in 1925. Barnes's two PGA titles were the first in the event. Leading wire to wire, he defeated Hagen and Fred McLeod in the 1921 US Open by nine strokes, a record which was not broken until the year 2000 by a guy named Tiger.[1]

After the first round, Sarazen had built a 3-up lead. However, showing why he had earned those big wins, Barnes fought back, and after an eagle at the thirty-fifth hole he squared the match. In a bit of foreshadowing, it took a birdie at the final hole for Sarazen to claim victory.

Fred McLeod was Hagen's opponent in the quarterfinals.

Like Barnes, the native of Scotland had his own impressive credentials. Winner of the 1908 US Open, he also was runner-up in two others—the 1919 PGA Championship and the 1921 US Open. However, his title chances ended here as Hagen dispatched him, 5 and 4.

Another Scotsman, Bobby Cruickshank, like Sarazen, was short (at five four he went by assorted nicknames like "Wee Scot" or "Wee Bobby"). They would meet for the second time in consecutive years in the semifinals of this event.

Different score (3 and 2) but the same result, as Sarazen, a native of Harrison, advanced to the championship match, 6 and 5, largely due to terrific putting.

Rochester-native Hagen gained an unrelenting 12-and-11 victory over George McLean to create an all–Empire State finale. It was a much-anticipated finale that would meet and exceed the hype.

There were a couple theories why Hagen hadn't defended his crown the previous year. One was that with this tournament was in its infancy, and the modern concept of "major championships" had not yet emerged. So without that prestigious career heft that comes with a victory in a grand slam event, some say Hagen did not return to defend his title because he had better offers—like playing exhibition matches that paid a lot more money.[2] In another version, Sarazen felt Hagen disrespected him. Some accused Hagen of skipping the '22 event to avoid the then-twenty-year-old US Open champ. Whatever the reason, this would be a great test of the two very best going at each other in a scheduled thirty-six-hole match.

Two unyielding, ultracompetitive golfers had at it. Sarazen birdied the first and last holes but sandwiched in five bogeys, one more of each than Hagen, so they were all even after the morning round.

For the afternoon's eighteen, the little Italian American jumped out early. After birdies at three and five, and after Hagen bogeyed the seventh, Sarazen had a three-stroke advantage.

With three holes remaining, the defending champion was still in command two holes up with three to play. Against the ropes, Hagen summoned his vast reservoir of determination and grit, and while Sarazen bogeyed two of the final three holes, Hagen finished up with pars.

Even after thirty-six, they went to sudden death.

After thirty=seven they were still deadlocked after each score birdied.

However, on the thirty-eighth, a drivable par 4, dogleg left, Hagen's tee shot found a bunker about twenty feet away, and he couldn't get out with his first effort. Sarazen, barely saved from hooking out of bounds by some trees, was twice as far back and in the heavy rough. With a poor lie, odds weren't good he'd get onto the putting surface.

However, like a golfer's version of a brash, young Muhammad Ali, the supremely confident Sarazen surveyed his situation, then suddenly turned to the crowd and announced, "I'm gonna get this so close, it's gonna break Walter's heart." (Maybe this was where golf enthusiast Babe Ruth got the idea for his called shot in Game 3 of the 1932 World Series against the Chicago Cubs at Wrigley Field?)

Sarazen's shot landed to within two feet of the cup, and his birdie putt was the winner.

But the Haig would not go quietly away into the night. As a matter of fact, he stormed back in an unprecedented flurry and proved why today he's still considered one of the all-time greats.

Hagen would go on to win the next four PGA Championships! That is four straight. Back-to-back-to-back-to-back. And on top of that, he'd own three more Open Championships (see chapter 62).

Sarazen became the first golfer to win the US Open and PGA Championship titles in the same year. And, of course, he secured a permanent place in the sport's lore with his double eagle at the 1935 Masters (see chapter 1).

23

THE HAIG'S UNMATCHED FOURTH STRAIGHT PGA TRIUMPH

OCTOBER 31–NOVEMBER 5, 1927
CEDAR CREST COUNTRY CLUB
DALLAS, TEXAS

Nattily dressed, supremely confident, gregarious, a bon vivant with a larger-than-life aura about himself, and simply a world-class talent, golfer Walter Hagen was the Babe Ruth of his sport. In the same year that the Yankee slugger finished an amazing season with a .356 batting average, 165 RBI, and 158 runs scored, his sixty homers more than the totals of any other team in the American League that year, Hagen would set an amazing record that will probably never be broken.

You see, the Haig's victory in Dallas made him the only golfer in history to win the PGA Championship four consecutive times. Gene "the Squire" Sarazen never did it, and neither did Ben Hogan, Jack Nicklaus, or Tiger Woods. The only other comparable performance would be the four straight Open Championships won by Tom Morris Jr. between 1868 and 1872 (the Open was not played in 1871). It was also Hagen's fifth and final PGA Championship trophy and the ninth of his eleven career wins in majors.

Here was how the tournament played out.

The venue, Cedar Crest, was designed by noted architect A. W. Tillinghast, one of the most prolific architects in the history of golf (Winged Foot, Bethpage Black, and Baltusrol, among many others).

This par-71 parkland course winds through trees and has relatively small greens, some of which have steep runoffs, thus accuracy is at a premium.

Opened in 1919, it hosted the Dallas Open in 1926. Macdonald Smith, a native of Carnoustie in Angus, Scotland, who'd have twenty-five victories on the PGA Tour, was the winner here. This course was also the site from where Harry "Lighthorse" Cooper honed his talents. His mother, Alice (I don't think this is where the legendary rock star—who is an avid golfer himself—got his moniker from) was a pro (rare back then) and his father was the head professional at Cedar Crest. Harry's nickname "Lighthorse," by the way, came from his speed of play. He would enjoy a long career as a teacher and pro, racking up thirty PGA Tour victories, and was inducted into the World Golf Hall of Fame in 1992.

However, the 1927 PGA Championships would be the only major Cedar Crest held.

The match play format for this PGA Championship called for twelve rounds (216 holes) in six days:

Monday—thirty-six-hole stroke play qualifier; top thirty-two professionals advanced to match play

Tuesday—first round, thirty-six holes

Wednesday—second round, thirty-six holes

Thursday—quarterfinals, thirty-six holes

Friday—semifinals, thirty-six holes

Saturday—final, thirty-six holes

And in the Monday qualifier, Walter Hagen started out very well. He was the medalist at 141.

Things didn't start out so well, however, in the three-time defending champ's first round. After ballooning to an 80 in the morning round, Hagen found himself four down at one point, and had to rally to defeat Jack Farrell, 3 and 2.

Another player given a scare was former PGA champion Gene Sarazen. J. G. Curley actually had a chance to win but missed a two-foot putt. The Squire was able to advance after extra holes.

The second round featured hometown hero Harry Cooper against Al Espinosa. One of the earliest Hispanic golfers to play on the pro tour in the United States, the California native would be credited with nine PGA Tour victories. And even though Al didn't win a major, he did record eleven top ten finishes.

Espinosa would come close twice. At the 1928 PGA Championship he'd lose to Leo Diegel in the championship match. At the 1929 US Open he'd be defeated by Bobby Jones in a playoff. There'd be no playoff here, as the four-time winner of the Mexican Open took care of the local favorite, Cooper, and advanced, 5 and 4.

With Tommy Armour's win over Tom Harmon and Hagen defeating Tony Manero, a quarterfinal match would pit the defending US Open champ (Armour won at Oakmont in June in an eighteen-hole playoff over Harry Cooper) with the defending PGA champ.

In that match, Hagen relied on some fine putting to advance to the semifinals.

Even though he blew an early lead, Espinosa was able to slip by Mortie Dutra, 1 up. Sarazen lost to fellow Italian American Joe Turnesa, 3 and 2. Johnny Golden defeated Francis Gallet with the same score.

Turnesa, a native New Yorker, was one of seven brothers, all golfers (their father worked at Fairview Country Club in Westchester County, New York, as the greenskeeper). He'd score fourteen PGA Tour wins. None of those would be majors, but like Espinosa,

Turnesa came very close twice (the 1926 US Open to Bobby Jones and here to Hagen).

Legend has it that Hagen woke up late on the penultimate day of the tournament after a night of drinking and was down five on hole thirteen, and the sun was shining in his eyes. The flashy Hagen rarely wore a hat because he was known for his attractive black hair. He was getting ready to tee off, when a kid in the gallery shouted, "Mr. Hagen, would you like my cap?" He showily took the cap, birdied the hole, and won the match. He won again the following day, capturing the fourth of his career eleven majors. And who was the kid who loaned Hagen his cap? A fifteen-year-old Byron Nelson.[1]

Hagen not only performed at the highest level but was quite adept at gamesmanship. And the latter was on display the semifinals. Throughout the match, Hagen had conceded any putt by his opponent mostly within three feet, but sometimes reportedly as much as five or six feet. Messing with Espinosa's mind would pay off.

Espinosa was 1 up heading into the thirty-sixth and final hole. As Espinosa lined up to attempt a three-foot putt, he looked to Hagen presuming he'd get the free pass, but the champ just smiled and then turned his back to chat with the gallery.

Sure enough, Espinosa then missed the match-winning putt. The match ended one hole later, when a shaken Espinosa three-putted.

Match play was difficult to begin with, testing one's mental and physical endurance with thirty-six-hole days back-to-back . . . and Hagen was at his best when the contest was hanging in the balance.

In the other semifinal, taking advantage of his opponent's woeful putting, Turnesa actually had a 9-up lead after the morning round and closed out the match, 7 and 6.

Apparently Turnesa didn't consult with Espinosa, because he would fall victim to the Haig's same clever strategy he used in the semifinals. Hagen conceded all putts within three feet all the way through to about the thirtieth hole. And sure enough again it was an effective ploy, as Turnesa couldn't hole anything on the way in.

Even when it mattered most, at the final hole, Turnesa had a putt, which would have sent the match into overtime. Instead the ball rolled up and hung on the lip of the cup, and there it stayed. It would be the difference as Hagen had won his fourth straight PGA Championship.

Incredibly, that victory bumped Hagen's match play record at the PGA Championship during the 1920s to an amazing 30-1. His lone loss in that span came in the 1923 finals—which went thirty-eight holes—to Gene Sarazen. Hagen's four consecutive PGA Championship victories has to be one of the all-time great achievements in major golf.

In another example of his intimidation skills, Walter's pretournament habit of asking "Okay boys, who's coming in second?" might have been tongue-in-cheek, but nevertheless, he made his point.

He was often called the Father of Professional Golf. While it would have been interesting to see how he would've fared against Bobby Jones if the PGA had allowed amateurs, still, has there ever been a greater match play golfer than Walter Hagen?

24

A PGA TITLE: THE CENTERPIECE OF BYRON'S HISTORIC STREAK

JULY 9–15, 1945
MORAINE COUNTRY CLUB
KETTERING, OHIO

It all began uneventfully enough back in March, with Byron Nelson and his good friend Jug McSpaden, aka the Gold Dust Twins, for all their 1-2 finishes, winning the Miami International Four Ball by beating Denny Shute and Sam Byrd, 8 and 6.

The pair had formed a bond after each signed up for military service but were both rejected due to health—McSpaden with severe sinusitis and Nelson with a disorder that caused his blood to clot four times slower than normal. But starting in 1942 and on into 1944, the pair played exhibition matches to raise a lot of money for the war effort and made 110 Red Cross and USO appearances, traveling via troop trains and military aircraft and often joining celebrities Bob Hope and Bing Crosby at those outings.

How sharp was Nelson's game when he arrived at the only major of the year?

In his book, *The Game I Love,* Sam Snead wrote, "During his streak year of 1945, Byron was magical. He had grooved his swing and was pretty happy with it, so during the streak he stopped practicing. He would arrive at the course, warm up a bit, hit out a dozen balls, hit a few putts to get comfortable with the speed of the greens, and then go shoot 65!"

But if he planned on securing both his ninth-straight win and the Wanamaker Trophy, Nelson would have to get past some formidable competitors and a different format as well as an ailing back.

The latter he took care of via nightly heat, massage, and osteopathic treatments. As for the format, Nelson had defeated Snead in the 1940 PGA Championship and was confident in his match play skills.

Regarding the competition, he was hoping to avenge his loss in the final match to Bob Hamilton in the previous year's PGA championship.

Finally, he had another reason to achieve a good result here. Nelson wanted to retire to his native Texas to become a gentleman rancher with his own spread for himself and his wife, Louise.

In his memoir, *How I Played the Game,* Nelson said: "Each drive, each iron, each chip, each putt was aimed at the goal of getting that ranch. And each win meant another cow, another acre, another 10 acres, another part of the down payment."

His first match was a tall order facing the diminutive great Gene Sarazen. A native New Yorker, the Squire was a seven-time major winner and had won the career grand slam. Sure enough Sarazen quickly grabbed a 2-up lead after just two holes. However, Nelson, playing gingerly with the ailing back, managed to rally and roll to a 4-and-3 win. His hopes of getting a chance at revenge by playing defending champion Hamilton was not to be as Bob lost to Jack Grout (future instructor of Jack Nicklaus) 4 and 3.

These thirty-six-hole consecutive rounds would test Nelson's back, and perhaps the biggest came here in his second match against Mike Turnesa. One of seven golfing brothers from Elmsford, New York, Turnesa was a six-time winner on the PGA Tour.

The end of the match saw Nelson 2 down with just four holes left.

He nailed consecutive birdies at the thirty-third and thirty-fourth holes to square the match. Nelson then proceeded to make eagle at the next hole and halved the final hole. It was a heartbreaking loss for Turnesa, who was 7 under par, but Nelson was 10 under par with rounds of 68 and 66.

After the match, Turnesa told reporters, "I was seven under and still lost. How the hell are you supposed to beat this man?"

Nelson's next opponent, former back-to-back PGA champion Denny Shute, would be wondering the same thing after their quarterfinal match when Byron advanced 3 and 2.

In the semifinal, Nelson faced Claude Harmon. In becoming the 1948 Masters champion competing as a club pro against full-time tour players, Harmon's 279 total tied the then–tournament scoring record as he defeated a deep field that included Ben Hogan, Cary Middlecoff, Sam Snead, Jimmy Demaret, and Nelson.

In a match delayed by rainy weather, Nelson overcame a shaky start to take a three-hole lead by the halfway mark, and went on to win with relative ease, 5 and 4.

For the final, Nelson would face Sam Byrd. Byrd had defeated a pair of former PGA Champions, Vic Ghezzi and Johnny Revolta, to reach the title match.

The stocky, athletic Georgian had given up professional baseball to become a professional golfer. A Yankee outfielder beginning in 1929, Byrd was called Babe Ruth's Legs, a reference to the fact that he often would appear as a pinch runner and defensive replacement for the Bambino toward the latter part of the slugger's career. A great driver of the ball, Byrd had four wins on the PGA Tour and would win twice more in 1945.

On the strength of four straight birdies on the closing holes, Byrd took the morning match. In the afternoon tilt, Byrd was up 3 after an early birdie. However, with the winds now gusting to over thirty miles per hour, the advantage now played into Nelson's hands; he had grown up in Texas under such conditions. Overcoming the heat, the crowds, the winds, and an ailing back to take control of the contest, Nelson birdied the twenty-ninth hole then won the next three to defeat Byrd 4 and 3.

This would be Nelson's fifth and final major.

Nelson finished 37 under par for the 204 holes he played. And in a record-setting year where he won eighteen times and finished second seven times, this was his most important win, the only major played that year. With his game at such a magnificent level, imagine what he could've done if those three other majors were held.

Nelson was so dominant in 1945 that he captured his eleven straight victories by an average of 6.67 strokes. And his 68.33-stroke average was a whole stroke better than anyone the previous season. Naysayers continue to downplay Nelson's achievements because he faced depleted fields due to World War II, but it must be remembered that in 1945, Ben Hogan played in eighteen tournaments while Sam Snead competed in twenty-six.

By the way, after winning five events in 1946, Nelson was able to buy that spread in Texas. So, at just thirty-four years old, he retired to his 740-acre new home in Roanoke outside of Dallas, which he called Fairway Ranch.

25

BARBER RAZOR SHARP ON THE GREENS

JULY 27–31, 1961
OLYMPIA FIELDS COUNTRY CLUB
OLYMPIA FIELDS, ILLINOIS

Golf is a very tough game. Most tournaments come down to the wire. Some don't, but if you look at history they usually go down to the wire. That is when you've got to have a special mind. And a special putting stroke.

Well, you know everyone talks about long-hitting. I'd like to remind people that long-hitting is an asset, but not a necessity. What is a necessity is knowing that a one-inch putt counts the same as a 350-yard drive. This was never more evident than in the 1961 PGA Championship held at Olympia Fields south of Chicago. Why?

Well, I was witness to one of the greatest clutch putting performances in majors history, and it was put on by Jerry Barber. At five foot five and less than 140 pounds, he had won five times on the PGA Tour before this event, not because he was a long driver of the ball, but rather because of his accuracy and his putter.

The forty-five-year-old, bespectacled Barber, who grew up one of nine children on a farm in Illinois, also possessed a steely competitive spirit. So that combination of mental tenacity and big-time skills with the flat blade kept him in the hunt in many tournaments.

This tournament would be held on Olympia Fields' North Course, a par-70, 6,722-yard layout that featured some significant elevation changes, a meandering creek, and scores of native oak trees.

Designed by two-time Open Championship champion Willie Park Jr., the North Course hosted the 1925 PGA Championship, which was won by Walter Hagen.

At one time it was one of four courses there, but after the club fell into financial difficulties during World War II, it was forced to sell off half of its land. Course No. 4 became the North Course, and the remaining holes from the other three courses were reconfigured to make the South Course.[1]

Barber, the plucky father of five, opened with a solid 69, just two back of the leader, Art Wall Jr., the 1959 Masters champion.

However, crazy weather would rule these proceedings.

Friday's second-round results were washed away when a light drizzle suddenly gave way to an intense storm that dumped more than an inch of rain on the course. So, with all scores tossed (fifty-four of the 166 rounds had been completed), the entire round was replayed on Saturday, thus making Sunday a thirty-six-hole affair.

After Saturday's results were tallied, Barber had added a 67 to his 69 and moved into sole leadership of the tournament halfway through at 4-under 136. That was a two-stroke margin over Don January and Doug Sanders, who were both seeking their first major. Despite another storm on Sunday, January, a thin Texan with a graceful swing and who enjoyed his cigarettes, would become the fifty-four-hole leader after finishing with a 67. Barber's solid 71 put him two back in second place.

In the afternoon's final round, after opening with a birdie, the quiet Texan strung together eight straight well-executed pars. Meanwhile,

Barber was all over the place, chipping in for par on one hole and bogeying another. Still, he managed to stay just two back of January heading to the back nine.

That wouldn't last, however, as Barber double-bogeyed the tenth while January continued to rack up pars to the point where upon reaching the sixteenth tee he had a four-stroke lead.

Perhaps memory was playing on Barber's mind. Just two years prior, he nearly won the PGA Championship in Minneapolis, tying for the first-round lead, and after rolling a 65 in the second round he had the outright lead at the halfway point. He still led the tournament after fifty-four holes but lost by a shot to eventual winner Bob Rosburg.

They both parred sixteen, with Barber nailing a tough twenty-footer. On seventeen, despite a poor tee shot, the best Barber could do was land a fairway wood about forty feet past the flag. January could have sealed the win with an eight-foot birdie, but he missed. Barber drained the long putt and still had a fighting chance despite being down two with one hole to play.

Perhaps with nerves showing, both competitors drove their tee shots on the seventy-second hole into separate bunkers. Barber's bunker play placed him sixty feet above the hole on the green. January blasted to within fifteen feet of the green, then chipped to within the same fifteen feet from the cup. While Barber was peering through his thick glasses to size up this perilous putt, January recalled what he was thinking at that moment.

"I figured I'm going to make a five, he's going to make four or five, and I'm going to shake his hand and leave as champion," said January, who had finished fifth in this major the year before. "So I'm standing there rehearsing my speech, and he holes it. I couldn't believe it. After that I couldn't make my putt if it had been a No. 3 washtub."[2]

Even though the thirty-one-year-old wasn't washed out of the competition, after watching his competitor sink three straight magical putts, it likely could not have helped his confidence heading into an eighteen-hole playoff the following day.

Exemplifying his skills on the green, Barber said this about his sinking 120 feet worth of putts over those three remaining holes: "After I holed out that shot on the 3rd hole, I made up my mind I would never give up. Golf is a funny game. Even when I was so far behind at the end, I kept reminding myself that something would happen—maybe the sky would fall in."[3]

Though the sky would not fall in, at least certainly not from rain, this time the nearly five thousand spectators would endure the sweltering heat of Chicago in midsummer for the Monday playoff.

In the first playoff of the PGA Championship's stroke play era, January twice held two-stroke leads. But once again Barber, a club pro at the Wilshire Country Club in Los Angeles who neither smoked nor drank but would gobble down vitamins by the handful, rallied to finish with a 67—a one-stroke edge over January, who bogeyed the last hole.

Gracious in victory and showing some wry humor, Barber said he told January coming off the final hole, "The best player didn't win today—but I'm glad I did."[4]

January later took part in the second playoff of the PGA's stroke play era, beating Don Massengale to win the 1967 PGA Championship and his lone major title.

How good was Barber on the green? In ninety holes of play, he never three-putted. At forty-five years, three months, and six days old, he had become the smallest and oldest winner of the PGA Championship (the age record would hold until Julius Boros won the 1968 PGA Championship at age forty-eight).

The win defined Barber's career; he later drove a Cadillac with a license plate "1961 PGA." Barber was later named Player of the Year in 1961, the same year he was captain of a winning Ryder Cup team.[5]

This was my first PGA Championship. While I finished with a share of twenty-ninth place, I learned a lot that would propel me to victory the following year (see chapter 26).

Jerry's rally in regulation and subsequent victory is still considered one of the greatest putting displays of all time.

26

MY THIRD MAJOR:
FINALLY, A RETURN TO FORM

JULY 19–22, 1962
ARONIMINK GOLF CLUB
NEWTOWN SQUARE, PENNSYLVANIA

I worked very hard to win nine majors on the PGA Tour and each one is important to me, but the 1962 PGA Championship at Aronimink will always have a special place in my heart. Why? Because it came at a period where my career was at a serious crossroads.

After my "winter of discontent," where I felt I had underperformed in those tournaments early in 1962, I flew home to South Africa deeply concerned about the state of my game, as I had finished out of the money for the first time in more than twelve months and fifty straight tournaments.

However, when I rejoined the tour by competing in the Masters, as the defending champion I was determined to become the first player to win back-to-back green jackets.

With the lead in the final round, I was playing with Arnold Palmer and there were three holes to go. And I got him by two shots. I had him.

However, he made a comeback over Augusta National's back nine in the final round, shooting 31 to make up three strokes and tie for the seventy-two-hole lead with myself and Dow Finsterwald. Then, in the first three-person playoff in tournament history, Palmer carded a 68 to beat me by three strokes (Dow was a distant third).

I finished second in the Masters. This may sound like nothing to get too worked up about, but I definitely felt I deserved to win that one more than I did the previous year.

You know, it is funny: If someone were to ask me what the worst moment of my life was, golf-wise, the most unforgettable, I would say the '62 Masters (see chapter 6). But it was at the Open Championships in Troon that July where things really bottomed out, for several reasons.

On the last hole I needed a par to make the cut. I hit a shot that went straight at the flag. A perfect shot. But it ran over the green. My ball finished an inch out of bounds, and I missed the cut by one stroke.

I had left the Open Championship with my tail between my legs. That was how I described it to a few journalists at the time. And that was how I was quoted in the newspapers. Now the whole golf world knew it. I was really depressed, and I even called my agent to question this global pursuit. I don't think I had ever been so dejected about golf before in my life.

In every situation in life you have two choices: You can be positive or you can be negative. And on that plane, I was already a long way down the road toward the one choice that doesn't win you even a club championship let alone a major. But you see sometimes misfortune is a gift, so I made the switch (in attitude). I got back the passion and the hunger that has always driven me.

I got on the earliest transatlantic flight possible to Philadelphia, then I went to the golf course early and practiced hard working out my strategy for the week and building up my confidence. I had arrived so early the holes weren't yet punched in the practice green, so I used

empty milk bottles as targets. Then I played at least eighteen holes a
day leading up to the tournament, then headed to the range, where I
would work until dark.

Even though I had never seen Aronimink before, I wanted to make
sure I outpracticed everyone. I never wanted anybody to hit more balls
than me. I learned this from Ben Hogan and have watched dedicated
players like Vijay Singh and Tom Kite adopt a similar approach. At
the same time, I continued my complete workout. Stretching. Weight-
lifting. Plus running on the treadmill to keep the speed. And endurance for four rounds.

In that era of persimmon woods and big-dimpled golf balls, it was
a relatively long test at more than seven thousand yards. This included
the monster 610-yard ninth hole, which no one would reach in two
that week. But to me the key playing this course, designed by the
renowned Donald Ross, was keeping the ball in play, which was the
most important factor throughout the tournament because the rough
was high.

Big hitters like Arnold Palmer and Jack Nicklaus (making his first
appearance in the PGA Championship) were paired together for the
first two rounds. Arnie, the winner at Troon, rolled 71-72 while Jack
scored 71-74. Doug Ford (the 1955 PGA champion), with a pair of
69s, had the lead heading into the third round. I was just one off the
top with midway numbers of 72-67.

While Arnold and, to a lesser extent, Jack often strayed into the
trees with their drivers, I fared better by using a new four-wood off
most tees. Another contributing factor was that the knowledge of
the greens I'd picked up that week was really helpful. With a third-
round tally of 69, I began the final round with a two-stroke lead over
second-place George Bayer and Bob McCallister.

My playing partner, Bob Goalby, four behind at the start of the
day, birdied the fourteenth and sixteenth holes of the final round to
get within one. It seemed the tournament had reverted to the old

match play format, which it had dropped five years earlier, as for all intents and purposes it had come down to just Bob and myself.

Bob was a very fierce competitor and an all-round sportsman in college. Just a tough opponent. But I kept telling myself that I was putting so well, which you have to do to win any tournament.

You know everyone talks about long-hitting. I'd like to remind people that long-hitting is an asset, but not a necessity. I have mentioned it before, but it bears repeating, what is a necessity is knowing that a one-inch putt counts the same as a 350-yard drive. And I was putting so effortlessly I felt like I could make everything.

It seemed like each time he would hole a twenty-footer for a birdie, I would come back and sink a thirty-footer, and so we went on. I had a comfortable lead on him, but birdies from Bob on the fourteenth and sixteenth saw him cut my lead to one stroke.

Obviously, you're trying to handle the extra tension that naturally comes when you know you could win a major championship, and with Bob being such a wonderful competitor, I knew I had to play very, very well. The shot I hit at the last hole I remember like it was yesterday. Taking a three-wood, I aimed it one hundred yards left of the flag and hit the biggest slice around the corner and onto the green.

I was safely on the green, but at fifty feet from the pin, Bob was half that distance from the hole. My firm rap put the ball two feet past the hole. Now Bob had a chance to tie the match and force an eighteen-hole playoff. However, he missed and finished at 67. I sank my putt for the victory.

I played well and won the championship mainly by keeping the ball in play and driving with a four-wood, hooking it off the tee. That took me away from the right-handed bunkers and those on the left side out of range.

When I reached down to retrieve the ball, I paused to give thanks to God for making it possible. The success I enjoyed at Aronimink reminded me of an important lesson, one that carried me through the rest of my career: Sometimes adversity is a gift. You think things are bad at the moment, but because I left England early for the PGA and practiced hard, then went on to win the PGA, tough times aren't always purely bad times, and attitude counts for a lot.

Golf is a great character builder, they say. I suppose that's true, but I was reminded during this stretch of my career that it makes stern demands on the character as it goes along. Winning this championship had restored my faith in the game and the life I was leading, and I reestablished confidence in myself.

At twenty-six, I had won my third major and the third leg of the Grand Slam. It felt great to be back in form, reinvigorated and back in the winner's circle.

27

DEGREES OF DIFFICULTY

JULY 18–21, 1963
DALLAS ATHLETIC CLUB (BLUE COURSE)
DALLAS, TEXAS

One of the distinct challenges of this sport is that in addition to going up against not only your opponent and yourself and the varied topographical layouts, you face Mother Nature. When competing in the elements, we must universally contend with unpredictable weather, playing in winds, rains, mist, frost, and fog of varying degrees. And, of course, heat and cold.

Regarding the latter, in all my years in professional golf, I don't believe I ever experienced a greater range of temperature change in playing two consecutive majors than in 1963. I don't think any of us who competed in the Open that year at Royal Lytham and the PGA Championship in Dallas, Texas, could imagine the contrast in playing conditions being any broader.

To best illustrate this, my good friend Jack Nicklaus went from wearing three sweaters in England to soaking up sweat with three towels in Texas (and that was just during the front nine of the first round)! The temperature never fell below 100 degrees the entire week.

By the early afternoons it would rise to 110 and over. It might have been the Blue Course, but it was red hot.

And Jack arrived a little steamed at himself, for he felt made a rare error at the final hole, a bogey that left him one stroke outside the playoff, thus costing him a chance at his first Claret Jug.

We started at 51 degrees with a small ball on bumpy, dried-out links land. A few days and many thousand miles later, we were teeing it up in more than double that temperature—110 degrees—with a large ball on steamy, soggy parkland. This was one of the many tests we faced.

Jack vented some of his frustration and got back into competitive mode by winning the long-drive contest with a shot over 341 yards (and for his prodigious poke, he earned a gold medal clip that he'd use for the next fifty years).

"Nicklaus had all the tools," said 1973 Masters champion Tommy Aaron. "He had tremendous length when he wanted to. And he did not always try to hit the ball as far as he could, like players today. In winning that driving contest in Dallas at the 1963 PGA Championships, I believe it was over 340 yards. That was with old, dead Titleist balls. And a wooden club with a tiny face! That tells you the power he had."

But even Nicklaus was powerless to get Mother Nature to turn down the heat, and in his book, *My Story* he recalls how he dealt with it:

> From the moment we arrived until the moment we left, I doubt the temperature ever fell below one hundred degrees. By the early afternoons it would have risen to one hundred ten or more. The second you walked out of the motel room your shirt was soaked, and by the time you came off the golf course you could literally wring out every article of clothing . . . At least three players were forced out of the championship by heat exhaustion, and fans keeled over like ninepins every day. Gary Player even laid aside his 'strength-giving' all-black out-

fit for an all-white ensemble. Apart from playing and eating, I spent almost the entire time in our motel room, praying the air-conditioning wouldn't go kaput. Everyone was dripping all week.

The boiling conditions increased the need to keep the greens damp to prevent them from dying of heat. That made for comparatively easy scoring conditions in the opening round on the relatively new course, built in 1955, and its 7,046 yards.

Dick Hart, a twenty-seven-year-old assistant club pro from the Hinsdale (Illinois) Golf Club, rolled a 66 helped by a hole in one on the 216-yard sixteenth hole. He maintained a three-stroke lead halfway through, however, looming near the top of the leaderboard were such players as the new US Open champion, Julius Boros; former PGA champion, Doug Ford; and next year's Open champion, Tony Lema.

With everyone fighting fatigue brought on by the heat, there was a change in the leaderboard after fifty-four holes. And even though I was determined to make a good showing as the defending champion and shot a 67 in the third round (see chapter 26), it would not be enough to overcome my early rounds of 74-75. I would finish with a share of eighth place.

Australian Bruce Crampton needed just twenty-eight putts. With an eagle and five birdies, he took a two-stroke lead and finished with a superb 65 at 5-under 208. Another former PGA champion, Dow Finsterwald, moved into sole possession of second place with a brilliant 66. With a 69 (and a bag full of soaked towels), Nicklaus worked his way up to third place.

But it would be an unheralded golf pro, Dave Ragan, a former All-American at the University of Florida, who would make a run early in the final round to get in the mix that would include him, Crampton, and Nicklaus.

Ragan had four birdies in the first seven holes to get among the leaders. But a wild drive at seventeen ended his chances after a bogey.

Crampton melted on the back nine after finding too much rough on fourteen, while Nicklaus, after sinking a thirty-foot birdie putt on 15, seized command for his first lead of the week.

However, on the par-4, 420-yard seventy-second hole, the hot, tired, and baked twenty-three-year-old hit his tee shot into the rough. Facing a shot that went down a hill, across water and onto an elevated green, Nicklaus did not forget his tough lesson from the prior week's Open championship. Instead, he took his medicine and just pitched the ball out into the fairway.

He won his first PGA championship here with a 5-under 279. Nicklaus would often say through the ensuing years that this was an example of learning from failure. It was also at the core of what many believe was his greatest strength, and that was mental tenacity and self-assurance.

It would be the first of five PGA Championships for Nicklaus, although this one nearly scorched him. At the award presentation, he felt the heat coming off the metal handles, and realized it had been sitting in the blazing sun for a while. Nicklaus quickly pulled his hands back and had to grab yet another towel, this one to hold up the prize.

The three playoff contestants at the 1913 US Open, held at the Country Club in Brookline, Massachusetts.
Left to right: Harry Vardon, Francis Ouimet, and Ted Ray.

The *Pelham Sun* previews the 1923 PGA Championship being held at Pelham Country Club.

Gene Sarazen tees off at the ninth hole of the 1923 PGA Championship.

The seventeenth fairway during the final match of the 1923 PGA Championship between Gene Sarazen and Walter Hagen.

Hagen's lengthy putt on the seventeenth green as
Sarazen looks on.

Scenes from the 1950 US Open at Merion Golf Club,
won by Ben Hogan.

Sam Snead won seven major championships between
1942 and 1954.

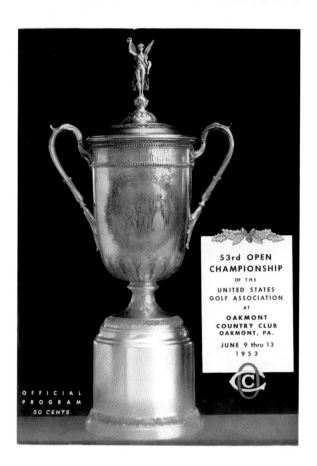

53rd **OPEN**
CHAMPIONSHIP
OF THE
UNITED STATES
GOLF ASSOCIATION
AT
OAKMONT
COUNTRY CLUB
OAKMONT, PA.

JUNE 9 thru 13
1953

OFFICIAL
PROGRAM
50 CENTS

55TH U. S. G. A. OPEN CHAMPIONSHIP
STAFF
THE OLYMPIC CLUB
SEASON
TICKET HOLDER
GROUNDS ONLY
257
Not Transferable
JUNE 13-19, 1955

55TH U. S. G. A. OPEN CHAMPIONSHIP
CADDIE
THE OLYMPIC CLUB
SEASON
TICKET HOLDER
GROUNDS ONLY
297
Not Transferable
JUNE 13-19, 1955

OFFICIAL PROGRAM
U.S.G.A. 55TH
OPEN
CHAMPIONSHIP
Olympic Country
Club
SAN FRANCISCO

2477

THURSDAY, JUNE 16

USGA 66 OPEN CHAMPIONSHIP

THE OLYMPIC CLUB
AT LAKESIDE
SAN FRANCISCO, CALIF.

GROUNDS & CLUB HOUSE
SEASON TICKET
(TRANSFERABLE)

Hancock Bros. San Francisco

PRICE
$1.00

FORTY FOURTH NATIONAL CHAMPIONSHIP
JULY 19-22, 1962

PGA

ARONIMINK GOLF CLUB
NEWTOWN SQUARE, PENNSYLVANIA

WHAT IS...

the Open?

66th USGA OPEN CHAMPIONSHIP
THE OLYMPIC CLUB, SAN FRANCISCO · JUNE 16-19, 1966
OFFICIAL SOUVENIR PROGRAM · ONE DOLLAR

2477

WEDNESDAY, JUNE 15

USGA 66 OPEN CHAMPIONSHIP

THE OLYMPIC CLUB
AT LAKESIDE
SAN FRANCISCO, CALIF.

GROUNDS & CLUB HOUSE
SEASON TICKET
(TRANSFERABLE)

Hancock Bros. San Francisco

A happy Hogan meeting with the press after winning the tournament.

Hogan eyes a shot at the 1953 US Open at Oakmont Country Club.

It was Hogan's record-tying fourth US Open victory.

Between us, Arnold Palmer and I won sixteen majors on the PGA Tour.

Here with defending champion Arnold Palmer in 1961, I'm proud to be the first international player to win the Masters.

The Aronimink Golf Club, which hosted the 1962 PGA Championship, site of my third major victory, was a par-70, 7,045-yard layout.

A crowded bridge crossing at the 1962 US Open.

Jack Nicklaus follows the flight of a shot from the fairway at the 1962 US Open.

I'm so proud to bring home another Claret Jug.

Doug Sanders and Jack Nicklaus at the 1970 Open Championship in St. Andrews, Scotland.

Johnny Miller tries to hack out of the rough at the 1973 US Open at Oakmont.

Miller celebrates dropping another putt at the 1973 US Open at Oakmont.

Coauthor Randy O. Williams with two-time majors winner Ben Crenshaw.

1973 US Open winner Miller gets the trophy . . . and the girl (his wife, Linda).

Overhead view of the seventeenth hole at Crooked Stick Golf Club, host of the 1991 PGA Championship.

Twenty-five-year-old John Daly was originally the ninth alternate at the 1991 PGA Championship.

Seve Ballesteros (left) and Nick Faldo (right) at the 1991 PGA Championship.

Nicklaus, a five-time winner of this major, at the 1991 PGA Championship at Crooked Stick.

PGA CHAMPIONSHIP

	HOLE	1	2	3	4	5	6	7	8	9	10	11	12	13	14	15	16	17	18	MESSAGES
LEADERS	PAR	4	4	3	4	5	3	4	4	5	4	5	4	3	4	5	4	3	4	
DALY J		10	11	11	11	12	12	12	12	12	12	12	12	13	13	14	14	12	12	LOW ROUND
KNOX K		8	8	8	8	8	6	6	5	6	7	7	7	7	8	8	7	7	6	TODAY
STADLER C		6	6	5	6	5	5	5	5	6	6	6	5	5	5	5	5	4	4	GALLAGHER
LIETZKE B		8	8	8	8	8	7	7	7	8	8	8	8	8	8	9	9	9	9	67
GILDER B		6	6	5	5	4	5	5	5	5	5	5	5	5	5	5	6	6	5	SEE YOU
MAGEE A		7	7	7	7	7	7	7	7	7	7	6	6	4	4	4	5		3	AT
PATE S		2	2	2	2	2	2	2	2	3	3	3	3	3	4	4	4	4	4	BELLERIVE
GALLAGHER J		2	3	3	2	2	2	2	3	3	4	5	5	4	5	6	6	6	7	IN
HUSTON J		4	4	4		4	5	5	5	3	4		3	4	5	5	5	9	5 4	1992
RICHARDSON		3	2	2		1	1	1	1	2			3 3	4	4	5	6 6	5		

The leaderboard at the 1991 PGA Championship reveals that Daly is the only one in double figures.

Daly, winner of the 1991 PGA Championship, at the trophy presentation.

Lee Janzen would win the 1998 US Open at the Olympic Club in San Francisco by one stroke.

1998 US Open runner-up Payne Stewart, who was known for his colorful attire, would win it the following year, then tragically would perish in a plane crash five months later.

France's Jean van de Velde weighs his options at the seventy-second hole of the 1999 Open Championship at Carnoustie Golf Links.

A couple of golf's heavyweights—Tiger Woods and Tom Watson.

The Wanamaker Trophy in all its glory.

A deep gallery follows Phil Mickelson down the fairway at the 2021 PGA Championship, held at Kiawah Island Golf Resort. Mickelson, age fifty, would become the oldest winner of a major that day.

Jon Rahm wins his first major, the 2021 US Open at Torrey Pines Golf Course.

American Collin Morikawa celebrates his victory at the 2021 Open Championship at Royal St. George's Golf Club.

28

THE OLD ACCOUNTANT DENIES THE KING'S QUEST FOR A CAREER GRAND SLAM

JULY 18–21, 1968
PECAN VALLEY GOLF CLUB
SAN ANTONIO, TEXAS

To be honest, being able to complete the career grand slam before Nicklaus and Palmer was a great challenge. We loved each other like brothers, but at the same time we were very competitive. And while Arnold won seven majors, the PGA Championship was the only one that eluded him. This would be his eleventh try, and it was a heck of an effort.

Palmer didn't arrive in the Lone Star State at the top of his game. Even though he began the year well with a runner-up finish at the Los Angeles Open and was victorious out in the desert at the Bob Hope Classic, the majors didn't see the King at his best. He missed the cut at the Masters, played poorly in the US Open (finishing fifty-ninth), and failed to make a charge in the Open at Carnoustie (where I managed to secure my second Claret Jug).

Nevertheless, as the only three-time winner of the Texas Open proving he could play well in the heat, Palmer was pumped to go out and get that elusive Wanamaker Trophy right here at Pecan Valley.

The hilly, 7,010-yard course is one of a small number of twentieth-century major championship venues that no longer exist. One of its distinguishing features was the plentiful large pecan trees that loomed in the field of play, demanding an ability to shape the ball right or left and low or high. Add in a meandering creek, and you had a fair number of holes that required layups.

That would play havoc with the big hitters (bombers Jack Nicklaus and Tom Weiskopf would be among those who would miss the cut). And if you landed on the green at some point, that was no gimme, either. Grainy and undulating greens made for some particularly difficult reads.

The first three rounds saw a couple of less-heralded but quite capable players exchanging leads back and forth.

Texan Marty Fleckman, a three-time All-American out of the University of Houston who helped his team win an NCAA championship, was making the best of his Nicklaus-designed equipment and swing tips from Byron Nelson. He opened with a 4-under 66 and a two-stroke lead over Frank Beard.

Beard, a bespectacled former All-American at the University of Florida, had turned pro in 1962. He was comfortable playing in the heat as he won the 1965 Texas Open. And in 1967 Palmer came in second to him twice, as Beard took the crown at both the Houston Champions International and the Tournament of Champions.

Halfway through here, Fleckman and Beard shared the lead at 2-under 138. However, the leaderboard was quickly filling with more prominent players vying for the lead: Doug Sanders, Miller Barber, Julius Boros, Palmer, and Lee Trevino all were within four strokes.

To their credit, hitting more fairways than anyone else and putting well on Bermuda greens, both Beard and Fleckman maintained a share of the lead after rolling 72s, and they were two strokes ahead of everyone at even par after fifty-four holes.

Palmer headed the prominent group just behind the leaders at 2 over. Bob Charles, a former Open champion, was not only a rare lefty, but he also came from a place that produced far more world-class rugby players than golfers—New Zealand.

One of the pretournament favorites also in that pack, and just a pair of shots behind the leaders, was Texas's own Lee Trevino, the new US Open champion. The city fathers had greeted the Merry Mex at the airport with a mariachi band, and many of his friends from Dallas came to support him. This was his chance to shine in his home state and its large Mexican American population.

But as Lee tells the story, maybe a little too much support. Maybe a little too much Merry.

"I got to make a confession to you. I have never revealed what happened to me. I had a condo right next to the clubhouse at Pecan Valley. Well, what happened was these people in Florida had just invented Gatorade. They came by my place and said, 'It's going to be hot tomorrow, so we want to leave this case of Gatorade for him.' So we have about fifteen to twenty people in the condo. Most were drinking tequila mixed with Gatorade. I'm not drinking it. I have my beers. So I go to bed about eleven. I wake up thirsty, so I go to get some water in the fridge. So I see this pitcher with Gatorade in it. Thinking it was pure Gatorade I drink about half of it. When I got up the next morning, hell, I was so drunk I could not find the sofa! I had won the US Open earlier and had a chance to double. I think honestly that I wanted to win it too much for the people of San Antonio. I had such a huge following there."

While Lee would fade with a final-round 76 that would send him back to twenty-third place, another stocky player from that pack was going in the other direction.

An American of Hungarian descent, Julius Boros was an accountant from Connecticut who came to the game late. As a kid he would hop the fence into the Fairfield Country Club with his brothers and sneak in a few holes here and there. But it wasn't until he was nearly thirty that he'd put away the ledger books for clubs and try his hand on the PGA Tour.

He had a nonchalant approach. Very rarely rushing about, and often smoking a cigarette, Boros had what five-time majors winner Peter Thomson called, "The most rhythmic, beautiful player who never really hit the ball in anger."

Boros rarely took a practice swing or spent much time lining up his putts. He was a swing in constant motion from address. And with his laid-back and effortless-looking swing, his catchphrase was "Swing easy, hit hard."

"His hands were real loose on the club. Julius Boros could have used a long tube of toothpaste without the cap on it. And hit golf balls and never squeeze any of the toothpaste out," explained Trevino. "When he took the club back you could see his wrists at the top, you can see his hands bent and fingers opening up. Then he comes down and the fingers tighten up a bit and the club releases all by itself. Julius Boros never released a golf club in his life. He had the clubs in his hands so light, in other words, the club kind of released by itself. Sam Snead was like that. Snead said, 'You got to hold the club like a little bird.'"

And Julius had experience defeating Arnold in a major. In 1963, Boros won his second US Open title by defeating Palmer (and Jacky Cupit) in an eighteen-hole playoff at the Country Club in Brookline, Massachusetts. In the final round here at Pecan Valley, while Fleckman and Beard eventually faded, Boros, Palmer, and Charles surged.

Arriving at the seventy-second hole, Palmer made a charge to the point where a birdie at the finish would give him the lead. However, he hooked his drive into the left rough among the looming pecan trees and into a television stand, where he got a free drop. But his army went into a frenzy of hope after he blasted out a tremendous shot from 230 yards to within eight feet of the cup.

Hunched over in that familiar position of his, narrow stance with his toes pointed inward and his knees nearly touching, Palmer, amid the dead silence of the thousands who made up his gallery, stroked a ball that initially looked like a winner. But he had played too much right-hand break and it stayed out.

Still, though, Arnie got into the clubhouse at 281, tied with Bob Charles, for the clubhouse lead.

It came down to the accountant.

It was a numbers game. Boros sliced into the woods on the seventeenth and bogeyed. But as he stepped to the final hole, he still had the lead by one. However, the drama grew greater as a poor second shot with his three-wood left him about thirty yards short of the green. Nevertheless, the cool, calm Boros rallied, placing his wedge shot to within three feet of the cup. But with these tricky greens, this was no gimme. Just the day before, Boros had missed shorter putts on the fourteenth and fifteenth holes for a double bogey and a bogey, going from a 68 (and a share of the lead) to a 70.

Covering the action, Dan Jenkins, the great *Sports Illustrated* writer, described the final shot.

As Boros took his stance over the putt that would win him the PGA, a less than golf-wise Texan in the gallery giggled and said loudly, "You worried about making that un, June-is?"

At once, hordes of volunteers in their red hats hollered, "Quiet!"

Of course, "June-is" was very upset and worried. He must've taken at least two seconds before he stroked it in.[1]

Perhaps Jenkins summed it up best about Boros: "A middle-aged man struck a marvelous blow for tired, portly, beer-drinking, slow-moving fathers of seven."[2] Boros was forty-eight years and four months old, making him at the time the oldest winner not just of the PGA Championship but of any of the four professional majors.

Boros would hold that record for more than fifty years, until Phil Mickelson, at age fifty, won the PGA Championship at Kiawah (see chapter 35).

29

MY MIRACLE AT "THE MONSTER"

AUGUST 3–6, 1972
OAKLAND HILLS COUNTRY CLUB (SOUTH COURSE)
BLOOMFIELD HILLS, MICHIGAN

In 1972, I was high on the World Money List and World Scoring Average and had won more than a dozen tournaments between 1969 and 1971, despite a runner-up finish at the 1969 PGA Championships, and placing third in the 1970 Masters and fourth in the 1971 PGA Championships. Winning a sixth major remained elusive, but I arrived in Michigan in peak condition and was ready to take on not only defending champion Jack Nicklaus but what I had previously stated was the toughest course in America.

A par 70 at over 7,000 yards and over 118 bunkers, Oakland Hills, located just outside of Detroit, would be no pushover. It was termed "the Monster" in 1951 by Ben Hogan, a two-time PGA Championship winner, when he won the US Open there. He famously quipped—"I'm glad I brought this course—this monster—to its knees."

Nicklaus, winner of the year's Masters and US Open and runner-up in the Open Championship, stated that Oakland Hills had "less breathing room" than any championship course he had ever competed on.

Well, after a pair of 71s, I was just three back of the lead heading into the third round. One ahead of Nicklaus and two ahead of Lee Trevino and Billy Casper.

Despite taking the tournament lead after three rounds on the strength of five birdies for a 67 and a fifty-four-hole total of 209, I don't know what it was. Perhaps it was from waking up to a steady rain. But on Sunday morning I decided to get a boost by phoning my family back home. And after speaking with my wife, Vivienne, and our kids, I will never forget my father came on the phone and said, "Win it for me, Gary."

Well, my father was a miner, working for years and years eight thousand feet underground. Never made more than one hundred pounds a month in his life. You know I loved my dad. He was a big man of six foot two (being half a foot shorter, I don't know where the hell I came from), and he would cry like a little whipped pup.

He was a man who works in a gold mine with a son who was a world champion. You could imagine that he was very sentimental. And he would cry quite a lot. He was back home and was starting to get old. When he said that, with all the support and sacrifice he made for me, I made my mind up to play as well as possible to do just as he asked.

However, things didn't start out so terrific for me in the final round. I bogeyed three of the first four holes. And I gained a two-stroke lead late on the back nine, but after back-to-back bogeys on fourteen and fifteen I came to the par-4 sixteenth with just a one-stroke lead. I had worked incredibly hard for this major, but after driving my tee shot into the rough, I felt it slipping away from me. And now a majestic Weeping Willow tree bordering the lake was looming, and it could seemingly ended my chances for a second PGA title. I was a bit edgy.

Now it is ironic. When I played a practice round before the tournament, I hit a ball off the sixteenth fairway through the green. There must've been a little bit of wood underneath the ground because when I hit it, the divot did like a zigzag.

I thought, 'What a strange divot,' but I did not pay much attention to it. Now in the final round I drove into the rough. It was soggy. I had to shoot over the willow trees. But there was a seat stick right in line with the flag. I lay on the ground like a three-fourths pushup. I saw that seat stick inline with the flag, so I stood up and walked across the fairway, and there was that zigzag divot. In the practice round, I had hit an eight-iron from there. Now, I was facing a dual challenge of getting the ball airborne quick enough to clear the tree, but with enough power to carry the water to a flagstick I could not see. I went with a nine-iron here because the grass was wet and it was going to jump, to fly.

It was an all-or-nothing gamble. The slightest mishit, or if the nine-iron proved to be not enough club to carry the pond, I'd be staring a bogey at minimum and possibly even a big number.

The flag was in the most difficult position I had ever seen in my life, just eight feet from the water. I hit it over the trees and three feet from the hole, and made the putt.

One of those players chasing me was Tommy Aaron. Standing at eighteen, Aaron felt if he could sink his ten-footer for par, he'd have a good shot at winning with lowest score in the clubhouse. He had completed his round and now had to wait for others to finish to see if his score held up. But my birdie at sixteen ruined those thoughts.

It was one of the greatest, if not *the* greatest, shots of my career.

But great shots, much like great championship victories, are often the result of careful planning and hours of toil on the practice range. And putting in the time and effort builds your confidence until you know you have the ability to execute the shot under pressure.

That shot enabled me to cover the Monster's last three treacherous holes in 1 under par on a day when just about everybody else played them over par, and it helped me to a two-shot victory and my sixth major.

Most of all, it was a win for my dad.

30

TWAY HAS A BLAST AT LAST

AUGUST 7–11, 1986
INVERNESS CLUB
TOLEDO, OHIO

I t is one thing to win a major, it is another to win it wire to wire. In the history of the PGA Championships, it has been done only five times. (Though it must be pointed out that from 1916 to 1957, the tournament used a match play format. There is no such thing as a wire-to-wire winner in a match-play tournament.)

Here at Inverness, fresh from winning the Claret Jug as the Open champion at Turnberry, the supremely confident Greg Norman was on the verge of joining that exclusive PGA wire-to-wire club. He opened with a 65 for a one-shot lead. After a second-round 68, the Great White Shark now led by four.

On Saturday, managing the tiny, undulating greens bordered by looming trees all down the fairways, Norman hit long, straight drives and sank putts from everywhere to roll his third straight round in the 60s on the 6,982-yard, par-71 track. His 69 put him at 11 under, and that was good enough to maintain that four-stroke lead heading into the final round. It looked like a clean sweep was within his reach—

yes, even for Norman, who was infamous for his last round mishaps and misfortunes (see chapter 15).

Enter the next player to tear out some of Norman's soul. Bob Tway.

A tall, lanky former three-time all-American out of Oklahoma State University, Tway was only in his sophomore season on the PGA Tour yet was second only to the thirty-one-year-old Norman in the prize money race. Heading into this major he had already won three events. His third-round 64, one that included eight birdies—which tied the tournament record at the time for lowest third-round score—moved him into second place, four behind Norman.

Heavy rains on Sunday stopped final round play for the day in midafternoon. In the final group, Norman and Tway managed to complete just one hole, so play was resumed on Monday afternoon.

After Tway bogeyed hole nine while Norman birdied it, the Shark still had a four-stroke lead heading to the back nine. However, with Norman's double-bogey on the par-4eleventh, where he tried to blade his shot out of a fairway divot and landed in a bunker for his troubles, Tway found himself just two back. Then Tway birdied thirteen and Norman bogeyed fourteen after bending a drive under a tree and was forced to pitch out back onto the fairway. The two were now tied with just four holes left.

With both parring the next three holes (the twenty-seven-year-old Oklahoman aided himself greatly by making a pair of sensational chip shots to save his score on two of those holes), they were still tied at 7 under coming to the seventy-second hole.

The eighteenth was a 354-yard par-4 recognized as one of the tougher finishing holes in the game. Tway teed off first. His one-iron effort went right, forcing him to deal with an unfavorable address because his feet would be a foot below the ball on a hill. Norman's drive was just fine, and even though his second shot landed on the green, the amount of backspin from his wedge led the ball back into fairly deep grass just off the putting surface.

Meanwhile, Tway's nine-iron found one of the five bunkers surrounding the hole.

Setting up for what would be not only the greatest moment of his career but one of the most memorable shots in major's history, Tway positioned his shoes into the sand and peered over the bunker mound to glance at the pin placement. He adjusted his swing to account for the speed and slope of the green. Then he swung, and the ball lightly landed about a foot onto the putting surface and began rolling . . . and rolling.

Then in the silence one could hear the "kerplunk" of the putt dropping into the cup (as well as the "kerplunk" of the Shark's heart sinking). With Norman looking on in disbelief, the normally stoic Tway began jumping up and down in celebration.

Tway would later say, "I was not trying to make the sand shot. I was just trying to get safely on the green for one putt and a par. To make a shot like that at eighteen is something. The odds against it I don't even know. I may never make one of them again in my career."

Crestfallen, Norman, who just the day before had pitched in from sixty feet to save par at the thirteenth, would need another brilliant play here to tie and force a playoff. It didn't happen. His chip zoomed ten feet past the hole, and he missed the par comebacker to lose by two strokes.

Having led all majors that year after fifty-four holes, the new owner of a "Saturday Slam," always gracious in defeat, magnanimously stated that the better man had won and that Tway had deserved it.

Well-known for his candor with the press, even though he escalated to a 40 on the back nine, the Great White Shark was a little taken aback by their harping on his inability to effectively deal with the late-round pressures of a major.

In the posttournament press conference, a reporter asked Norman if "the monkey" was again sitting on his back after yet another blown opportunity. Norman snapped, "I don't understand you guys. Don't go saying the monkey's back on my back."[1]

Peter Jacobsen, who shot a 71 and finished third at 279 when he birdied the last hole with a ten-foot putt, was in that final pairing. The veteran player from Portland, Oregon, who earned seven victories on the PGA Tour, had this to say about Norman:

"This going to sound funny, but I think Greg Norman is one of the most underrated players of our time because people [primarily] remember those final rounds when players would chip in or hole out shots from the bunker, crazy things, but Greg was certainly one of the most underappreciated and underrated players. Greg did everything well."

Well Greg Norman is a very charismatic man. And for several years was the best driver of the golf ball in the world, but he didn't have the big-match temperament to take him on to win more majors. When he lost this tournament, they all said how unlucky Greg Norman was after Bob Tway holed the bunker shot on the last hole to win. He came back in 40! He completed the back nine in Four Zero. You don't win a club championship, you don't win a ladies' club championship with a 40 on the back nine.

Though he'd win Player of the Year in 1986, Tway would never make a major splash again, but the one he did will endure the sands of time.

31

A LONG SHOT LEGEND THAT BEGAN
AT CROOKED STICK

AUGUST 8–11, 1991
CROOKED STICK GOLF CLUB
CARMEL, INDIANA

John Daly taught himself to play as a kid by fishing golf balls out of a pond on a nine-hole municipal course in Dardanelle, Arkansas (pop. 3,621). He developed an exceptionally long backswing, one that went well past being parallel to the ground, while raising his hands as far as they could go, turning that junk-fueled but amazingly flexible chunky torso like no one before him. Eventually he would win both the Missouri and Arkansas State Amateur Championships during high school. He attended the University of Arkansas on a golf scholarship, but he decided to leave early to try his hand at the pro game.

The twenty-five-year-old chain-smoking unknown, a bomber with touch around the greens, had failed Q-school several times. He competed in a couple of stints on the Sunshine Tour in South Africa as well as the Ben Hogan Tour (now the Korn Ferry Tour) before a T-12 finish at the 1990 PGA Tour Qualifying Tournament finally earned him 1991 PGA Tour privileges. He was about to go from un-heralded golfer to an unbelievable folk hero in just one tournament.

Though the long-hitting, self-described redneck found his massive drives often enough to place fourth in the Honda Classic and third in the Chattanooga Classic, he also missed eleven cuts throughout 1991 and had not made enough money to qualify for the PGA Champion-ship at Crooked Stick in Carmel, Indiana, which is just outside of Indianapolis.

And after learning he was ninth alternate for the year's final major, figuring the odds were too long of getting in that field from that far back, Daly decided to just chill at home in Memphis, hang-ing out with his pals and dining twice a day at his favorite chain restaurant—McDonald's. However, in between cheeseburgers and cigarettes, Daly would get a call from Ken Anderson of the PGA of America. Anderson informed him that a couple players had dropped out for various reasons and that he had moved up a few notches.

By the time Anderson had called back again on late Wednesday afternoon to say he was now third alternate, Daly decided to hop in his car. He and his fiancée, Bettye Fulford, drove all the way to Car-mel. At the very least Daly felt he could hang out with Fuzzy Zoeller, his best pal, on tour and have a few drinks. When they got to their hotel after two o'clock in the morning, Daly found a flashing light on his room's phone. Having smartly informed the PGA office which hotel his agents had booked for him, sure enough the first miracle had happened. It was Anderson again. This time Daly was told he was to tee off later that afternoon.

Turned out the last person to drop out was Nick Price, who had to give up his spot late in the game because his wife, Sue, was ready to deliver their first child at any moment.

Still bleary-eyed from the ten-hour drive, Daly woke up to a Mc-Donald's breakfast burrito. With no time for a practice round, and unable to even see the course, he gladly accepted Price's offer of using his seasoned full-time caddy, Jeff "Squeaky" Medlin.

Miracle number two.

Price, who would win this PGA Championship the very next year, had a very different game than Daly (who didn't?). But the veteran Medlin quickly adjusted in helping decide on the right club, and it often began with something like this . . .

As they approached the tee box throughout the week, as Daly surveyed the grounds, Medlen handed him the driver and one important piece of strategy: "Kill it, John."

It was an era long, long before today's commonplace bombing of the fairways, so it was a veritable freak show to a stunned gallery when their instant blue-collar hero was tearing apart a 555-yard par-5 with a driver and six-iron, and 465-yard par-4s with a driver and a sand wedge.

Feasting off cigarettes, sodas, and the rapidly growing support from the fans, Daly was tearing up the lengthy 7,289-yard course.

However, during a midafternoon rain delay, as thousands of an estimated twenty-five thousand spectators scrambled for shelter, thirty-nine-year-old Thomas Weaver was struck by lightning. Despite the best efforts of a nurse and several doctors from the crowd rushing to his aid, he died.

Later on, after hearing what happened, learning that Weaver had left behind a wife (Dee) and two daughters (Emily, who was twelve, and Karen, who was eight), Daly donated $30,000 to Weaver's family for a college fund. Both daughters would go on to study medicine, with Karen becoming a doctor in Indianapolis.

When play did resume, Daly finished with a 69, just two back of the leaders. Following that up with a 5-under 67 (thanks to such prodigious efforts like reaching the par-5, 600-yard fifth hole in two), Daly now had the lead going into the third round. He gave a lot of credit to the chemistry he had with his bag man.

"He was a damn good caddy—so experienced, so focused. It was amazing how fast he got to know my game. He could club me right away, like we'd been working together for years. That's not easy," explained Daly in his book, *My Life in and out of the Rough*. "At the pro level, there are a lot of gradations. One guy's 8-iron is another guy's 7. One guy fades everything, another guy draws it. Low trajectory, high trajectory. And so on . . . Right from the first tee, Squeaky saw how good I was hitting driver, and he didn't want any negative stuff—no backing down and playing safe and hitting the 3-wood—so he'd hand me the driver, and in that voice of his that got him his nickname, he'd say the same thing: 'Kill it, John. Just kill it.'"

Here he was an unknown leading the world's toughest field. It was not lost on the fans. As Daly played in the first round with Bob Lohr and Billy Andrade, a handful of onlookers rapidly grew to hundreds lining the greens and fairways. Daly soon found himself buoyed by spectators reaching out to this rookie from Arkansas and slapping high fives.

However, there was a potential incident where Daly could've been slapped with a severe penalty.

He had rolled another 69 to go 11-under 205 and opened up a three-shot lead over veteran Kenny Knox and 1982 Masters winner Craig Stadler. Apparently though, several rules fanatics watching the tournament on television said Daly had violated rule 8, section 2, part B on the eleventh green. They frantically reached for their phones, and one connected with a tournament official to explain what he saw.

The rule essentially states, "When the players ball is on the putting green, the player, as partner or either of his caddies may before, but not during, the stroke point out a line for putting, but in doing so the putting green shall not be touched. No mark shall be placed anywhere to indicate a line for putting."

As Daly was lining up a thirty-five-foot eagle putt on the 533-yard, par-5 eleventh hole, his caddy touched an area about a foot away from the cup with the bottom of the flagstick he was holding. According to the Rules of Golf, the line of a putt cannot be indicated by touching the green with any object.

Daly settled for a birdie. After completing his round, officials escorted him and Medlin to a television truck, where he was asked what line he was using on the putt. Daly told officials he was aiming to the left of the cup—where, in fact, he started his putt. Medlin had touched the green about a foot to the right of the cup. Daly was spared two penalty strokes after officials ruled that there was no infraction.

"It was a shock, but everything is OK now," said Daly.

What was somewhat shocking was how fast Daly was becoming a folk hero. He reached an even broader audience when the owner of the National Football League's Indianapolis Colts, Jim Irsay, sent a limo for Daly and Bettye to their Saturday evening game as guests of honor. Led onto the field, Daly was greeted by thunderous applause from forty-eight thousand fans as the Hoosier Dome's giant video screen rolled action footage of his booming swing at Crooked Stick.

The Golf Gods had blessed Daly with colossal clubhead speed that enabled him to fly tee shots over fairway bunkers and take massive shortcuts on dogleg holes. Where fellow competitors needed to use three-irons to hit into greens, he was hitting with seven- and eight-irons.

Those fine pros, Bruce Lietzke, Jim Gallagher Jr., and Knox never really came close to challenging Daly on the final day. Inspired after arriving on Sunday morning to find a note in his locker neatly folded from his idol Jack Nicklaus—which read, "Go get 'em John"—he did.

And on the strength of four birdies, Daly would win his first major by the same amount he led the day going in, by three strokes. He was the only player to finish in double figures under par, at 12-under 276. As he walked up the eighteenth fairway after hitting an eight-iron to the middle of the green, Daly pumped his right arm to charge up the already deafening ovation from the stands. It was a special time, one which Daly has often looked back on. He has said how important those spectators were to his victory.

Quite arguably the most unforeseen major champion since Jack Fleck (see chapter 44), Daly would later reflect on his legendary win at Crooked Stick on his website: "I made a promise to win it for the fans. After the victory is when I realized that the fans had won it for me. All the excitement and encouragement I received kept me pumped up, and helped me close out the final round."

The most talented player during the Tiger Woods era besides Tiger was John Daly. John Daly had as much talent as Tiger Woods, except the one man was 100 percent dedicated, and made the right decisions (on the golf course); and the other man (Daly) was the opposite, because he did not apply himself correctly.

Still, you just don't win one of golf's four major championships having never seen the course, let alone getting into the field as an obscure alternate. I truly feel that John Daly's magical performance at Crooked Stick remains one of the biggest underdog stories in all of sports history.

32

THE TIGER-TAMER FROM KOREA

AUGUST 13–16, 2009
HAZELTINE NATIONAL GOLF CLUB
CHASKA, MINNESOTA

Since the early twenty-first century, when Tiger Woods established himself as the dominant golfer in the game, it seems that the players who have given him the most trouble in the clutch periods of a major have been less heralded competitors. It has been challengers with names like Bob May, Chris DiMarco, and Rocco Mediate rather than the marquee stars of the era known by one handle such as Els, Duval, McIlroy, Scott, and Mickelson. So, while the former challenged the number one player in the world, taking him to the end in three memorable majors with very admirable efforts, each still came up short. Now it would seem that whether his foe went by one name or two, Tiger had everyone by the tail.

But what about someone who wasn't popular enough to go by their last name alone? What about someone who went by two initials and a surname?

Enter Yong-Eun Yang, or Y. E. Yang.

The son of vegetable farmers in South Korea, he came to the sport comparatively late. Stout of build (he once aspired to be a body-builder, but a knee injury in his late teens ended that dream) he never even heard of the game until he was nineteen. After he completed mandatory military service in his homeland, he traveled to New Zealand, where he practiced and played intensely there to pursue a golf career. Maybe some of these TV commentators will now concede to how beneficial weights are.

Before winning his first event on the PGA Tour (the Honda Classic in the spring of 2009, when he was ranked 460th in the world), Yang had started out on the Asian Tour. He took the Korean Open and earned entry into the well-regarded HSBC Champions Tournament at the Sheshan Golf Club in Shanghai, China, in November 2006.

Why is that important to this story?

Well, it is not very well-known, but the young Korean, essentially just starting out in his career, took on Tiger, who was on track to win the esteemed event. Instead, Yang came away as the upset victor. He knocked off runner-up Woods with a superb 3 under, final-round 69. That is a confidence builder.

Knowing he tamed the Tiger once, Yang was not afraid to do it again—this time at a major, the 2009 PGA Championships. He would face the hungry fourteen-time major winner who hadn't forgotten that loss in China, but there also would be many other players in the field at this menacing, oversized, par-72, 7,674-yard course who knew how to win a major. In total ninety-seven of the top one hundred ranked players in the world were participating here.

And two of the very best took the measure of the monstrous par-5s (number three, 633 yards; number seven, 572; number eleven, 606; and number fifteen, 642) to grab the top two spots on the leaderboard after the first round.

Woods, who was going for a record-tying fifth PGA title, opened with a 67. Thanks to five birdies and no bogeys, he had a one-stroke lead over defending champion Padraig Harrington.

"It's always nice to get off quick. But the first round, you can play yourself out of a golf tournament. Certainly, [you] cannot win the golf tournament on the first day," said Woods.

Despite conditions on the second day being tougher, with strong winds toying with putts, Woods's good start continued. He built some separation and broke away from the pack with a run of three straight birdies on the back nine.

Players like Harrington had to cope with the particularly fierce afternoon winds. (Blustery gusts had players backing off more than a few times to rethink their shots). His 73 still had him in second place, tied with four others. Y. E. Yang on the strength of an eagle, followed a 73 with a 70, and was six back at the halfway juncture.

But all indications pointed to a tough road to overcome the pace set by Tiger. In addition to the continuing blustery weather, all eight times Woods had led at the halfway point of a major, he had gone on to win. He was well aware of that and liked where his game was at to make it nine for nine.

However, something unusual happened on Saturday. A typical third-round "moving day" usually saw Tiger moving up the leaderboard or, in this case, creating further separation and expanding on his first-place position.

What Tiger did instead was play more conservatively, primarily due to weather.

The problem for him was that those hungry competitors nipping at his heels did not. With a 69 and 67, respectively, both Harrington and Yang cut Tiger's lead in half. These two now shared second place just two back at 6 under.

US Open champion Lucas Glover and Sweden's Henrik Stenson, winner of that year's Players Championship, each scored a round of 68 and were tied for fourth place. Three-time major winner Ernie Els, looking for his first PGA Championship, had it going for a while; he got as close as one shot from the lead but finished with three straight bogeys, which left him five back.

Despite halving his deficit heading into the final round, the defending champ was aware of the credentials of the player leading the event.

"Obviously to get a win, you've got to beat him by three tomorrow; that's a tall order," said Harrington, "but . . . everybody in the situation who is behind is going to think, well, you know, we have nothing to lose. You've got to have that attitude."

Particularly pleased that he managed to gain five strokes when he thought maybe he'd just get one or two due to the wind, Yang, thanks to a go-for-broke style of attacking Hazeltine on his way to the low round of the day, a 67, was feeling good about his position. Combined with the boost of having caught up and defeating Woods before, this made the Korean quietly confident.

"You never know in the world of sports and the game of golf. So just try to make every shot, just focus on every shot that I have. And then tomorrow I may end up inside the top ten, top three, and even win the PGA Championship. You never know. And that experience would certainly help."

Paired with Woods in the final round, what helped Yang was knocking down the flagstick on the par-5 third hole for a key birdie early on to cut the deficit to one.

Meanwhile, after a disastrous snowman (meaning a score of 8 on any individual hole) at the par-3 eighth, the shortest hole on the course, Harrington was done. Finding water twice, the quintuple-bogey 8 led to a final-round score of 78. Uncharacteristically it was not unlike what befell Harrington in his final round just the week before, yet in this case he was leading Woods at the WGC event late before finding water and running up a triple bogey. He would finish in a tie for tenth here.

In a sign of things to come about an untimely inconsistency with his putting, when Woods three-putted number four, he dropped into a tie with Yang. Twice Tiger would retake the lead only to give it back with bogeys. It had long been a two-man race, and when they arrived at the par-3 thirteenth it was all square at 6 under.

Another opportunity presented itself for Woods here. After his challenger found the bunker, Tiger landed a fine shot to within eight feet. It certainly looked like a two-shot swing was unfolding here, especially after Yang failed to get his bunker shot inside Woods's ball.

Instead, after Yang calmly dropped his putt for par, Woods missed his very makeable birdie try. They were still knotted at 6 under when standing at the tee of the par-4 fourteenth.

While Yang's tee shot finished short of the green, Woods appeared to have the advantage yet again, as his ball had a good lie in the greenside bunker. After Woods made a fine play out of the trap, thinking his opponent would birdie the hole, Yang felt he had to get it close to match birdies.

Instead, what happened became a key moment of the tournament. Yang chipped his ball from eighty feet and rolled it across the slick green, and it dropped in for an eagle.

The crowd roared. Even though Woods made a birdie, his perfect record of winning every major when he had a fifty-four-hole lead was in jeopardy. Symbolic of how the day was going for him, Woods had a chance to tie things up on the very next hole, but his twelve-foot birdie effort lipped out.

After both parred sixteen and then bogeyed seventeen, Yang was holding a slim one-stroke lead at the seventy-second hole.

The par-4, 475-yard eighteenth presented a situation where many might have expected that the nerves would now kick in for Yang, who had never been in a position to win a major before. But Woods, with fourteen of those titles under his belt, would conjure up one of those magic moments he'd produced time and again.

Tiger needed to make birdie (or have Yang bogey) to force a playoff. No one would blame Yang if he became yet another competitor who folded under the pressure of a Sunday with Tiger. However, fate had other things in mind on this afternoon.

Yang cooly stroked a stunning 210-yard hybrid to clear a tree and then over a bunker to twelve feet. Then he sank the putt to seal a three-shot victory after Woods finished with a bogey.

After raising his arms in triumph, Yang acknowledged the cheering gallery in an extended moment of elation. The enthusiastic weight-lifter, who now could afford the gym he always wanted, was showing good form when he became the first winner anywhere to clean and snatch his bag over his head.

Yang, in explaining how he maintained his calmness under such pressure to became the first Asian-born male player to win a major, attributed much to his simple joy of the game.

"As I started to pick up golf, I fell in love with it. And ever since I've been probably—I have the best job in the world doing what I love the best, I love the most," said Yang.

The thirty-seven-year-old Korean, the fourth of eight children, the 110th-ranked player in the world, had his eye on the Tiger and never blinked. Down the stretch, when it mattered the most, Yang played the last five holes in 2 under, while Woods, the world's number one golfer, played them in 1 over.

This was arguably the most unexpected victory since a twenty-year-old former caddy named Francis Ouimet beat Harry Vardon and Ted Ray at the 1913 US Open (see chapter 38) or at least on par with Jack Fleck, the unheralded golf pro from Iowa who defeated Ben Hogan at the 1955 US Open (see chapter 44).

"I knew the odds were against me. I tried to be the least nervous I have ever been and went for broke," said Yang. "I've sort of visualized this quite a few times—playing against the best player in the history of golf, playing with him in the final round in a major. I have always dreamed about this."

Like Ouimet and Fleck before him, Yang overcame long odds, and his dream came true.

33

RORY FINDS GLORY ON THE EDGE OF DARKNESS

AUGUST 7-10, 2014
VALHALLA GOLF CLUB
LEXINGTON, KENTUCKY

Fresh from a wire-to-wire victory at the Open Championship at Royal Liverpool, Rory McIlroy was intent on becoming the first player since Padraig Harrington in 2008 to win consecutive majors when he arrived for the PGA Championship just a couple weeks later at Valhalla.

Valhalla, opened in 1986, ranked number one in Kentucky and among "America's 100 Greatest Courses" by *Golf Digest*, went through extensive changes from its original architect, Jack Nicklaus, and his design firm, after it hosted the 2011 Senior PGA Championship (won by Tom Watson). Nicklaus and colleagues did much re-bunkering. Also, the reconstructing/recontouring of the greens provided for a lot more pin placement possibilities with the aim of providing a greater test of golf for the game's best players.

And the test of the best started right out of the box.

With twenty-three current and former majors champions in the field, it would see Rory still displaying the hot hand with an opening 66.

And even though rough weather came in on Friday, McIlroy persevered through drizzly and soggy conditions to post a 4-under-par 67 to go with his first-round 66 to snare first place. No stranger to inclement weather, the young man from Ireland overcame two bogeys with four birdies and an eagle.

"Another very solid day's work," said the leader by two at 9 under at the halfway mark.

McIlroy's hot hand continued to be on display, and once again he closed the third round really well, with birdies on three of his last four holes for a 67.

But to maintain his lead, he needed every stroke. The scoring average for the round was 69.6 (the lowest in PGA Championship history to that point), and at one point it created a compact leaderboard that saw five players tied for the lead at 10 under on the back nine.

Phil Mickelson, one of those climbing the board with a 67 of his own, was now tied for fourth. He credited fans for one reason why he did so well:

"It really is amazing when you look at the [inclement] weather conditions and the challenges logistically to get here from a spectator's point of view, how many people have shown up to support this tournament. It is just great energy. It's great energy to have so many people and be so supportive not just of myself, but all the players. They have been great."

Knowing full well that one measure of greatness is having success in the Grand Slam events, Rickie Fowler, looking for his first major victory, also rolled a 67 and was in in a good position in third place, just two behind McIlroy at 11 under.

The final round would see Fowler and Mickelson paired together. Phil was confident about his short game and what he felt he had to do the last eighteen:

"I need to play aggressive and make some confident swings early on and make some birdies. I'm going to be trying to make up ground on some guys that are playing really good golf and will be making birdies tomorrow, so I'll have to make a lot of them."

However, for the leader who one-putted nine of his last twelve holes, confidence reigned supreme.

"To shoot another 67 without really having some of my best stuff for the round was really pleasing," said McIlroy. "I feel like I'm really confident right now [and] no matter who is on that leaderboard; I feel like I have a pretty good chance in beating them."

Well, whoever ultimately hoisted the twenty-seven-pound Wanamaker Trophy would have to wait longer than normal. Another rain delay pushed back tee times so late that a degree of darkness and the possibility of a carryover to the following day would come into play.

Things didn't start out well for McIlroy early in the final round. He lost the lead with a pair of bogeys after six holes. Meanwhile, in the group just ahead of him, Fowler and Mickelson were tearing it up, registering four birdies and five birdies, respectively, on the front nine. There was also a new contender in play, as Sweden's Henrik Stenson who, like Fowler, was also looking for his first major title, played up a storm with five birdies of his own.

All three passed the leader. Was darkness setting in early on McIlroy's back-to-back majors effort?

There'd be no raining on his parade here however. At one point down by as many as three shots, McIlroy pulled it together, starting with an eagle at the tenth to get within one shot.

It would turn out to be a key hole for his title run, but even McIlroy wasn't sure what was happening when he smoked a three-wood from 281 yards on the par-5 tenth. He later admitted that eagle required some good fortune.

"I hit three-wood from I think it was 284 total. The ball flight was probably around thirty feet lower than I intended. And the line of the shot was probably around fifteen yards left of where I intended. It was lucky, it really was," explained McIlroy. "You need a little bit of luck in major championships to win, and that was my lucky break. I didn't hit a very good shot there, but it worked out well and I made eagle from it."

Then while each of the aforementioned contenders had a bogey, McIlroy proceeded to score a pair of birdies (on holes thirteen and seventeen) to snag the lead back.

However, standing on the eighteenth tee with a two-stroke lead, he was not only playing against some great competition on a very challenging course. He was quickly reminded there was another foe in play: Mother Nature.

Darkness was rapidly setting in, and on top of that a thunderstorm was looming on the not-to-distant horizon.

In a terrific show of sportsmanship, Mickelson and Fowler—who were playing just ahead of McIlroy and his playing partner, Bernd Wiesberger—had just hit their tee shots off the par-5 eighteenth. They agreed to allow that final pairing to hit up just after them so that even if tournament officials decided to halt play due to darkness, McIlroy and Wiesberger would have the option of finishing out the hole. McIlroy would later say that if not for his opponents' gesture, he definitely would not have been able to finish the round.

As it turned out, Fowler lipped out but Mickelson made it close. Needing an eagle to tie McIlroy, Mickelson's chip from off the green just narrowly missed, but his birdie brought him to within one, forcing McIlroy to make his par.

Which he did in a rather strange scenario. As flashes from thousands of cameras lit up the near-dark green, McIlroy sunk his clinching putt.

The new champion was quick to thank his main competitors for what they did in unusual circumstances.

"You know, to get this thing finished and get this thing over and done with, the guys let us play up with our drives, and they didn't need to do that, they could have just left us on the tee box there and just play normally, but they showed a lot of class and a lot of sportsmanship by doing that," said McIlroy. "I thanked Rickie and Phil in the scorer's area."

With this victory at Valhalla, McIlroy became the first player since Tiger Woods in 2008 to win three straight starts on the PGA Tour (he'd previously won the Open Championship and the WGC-Bridgestone Invitational), and the first since fellow Irishman Padraig Harrington to win consecutive majors. Harrington won the same two in 2008—the Open Championship and PGA Championship.

For Mickelson, it was his second runner-up finish in a PGA Championship and his eighth overall second-place finish in a major.

The four major championships that McIlroy has won were done in grand style. And there is no question that even today he has the best golf swing in the world by a mile.

After watching him all these years, I feel confident, in spite of the fact that he has not won a major since 2014 and in spite of the fact that he should have won the Open Championship in the final round in 2022 but didn't due to bad course management. I still believe Rory is going to go on and win a lot of majors.

34

THE EAGLE THAT LANDED A MAJOR

AUGUST 6–9, 2020
TPC HARDING PARK
SAN FRANCISCO, CALIFORNIA

This would be a very unique and distinct major for several reasons. Because of the global pandemic, the PGA Championship would be the first held in 2020 because the others had been postponed or cancelled. This event's organizers had been working for six years on all the logistics, food and concessions, security, and sponsor components for an expected forty thousand spectators each day, and those plans had to be scrapped. So the organizers had just a sixty-day window to write an entirely new plan that included COVID-19 protocols. The highly regulated plan, about as thick as a phone book, had to be approved by the city.

It would also be held on a course that at one point was so neglected it had become a "weed patch," according to Tom Smith, the general manager of TPC Harding Park. "They parked cars here in the fairway while the US Open was played in 1998 over at the Olympic Club."

Opened in 1925 and named after President Warren G. Harding, Harding Park Golf Course was designed by Willie Watson and Sam Whiting, who also designed the nearby Olympic Club Lake Course.

Harding Park began hosting major amateur tournaments soon after opening—most notably, the USGA National Public Links Championship and the San Francisco City Championship, one of the oldest consecutively played competitions in the world. And in 1944, the course began hosting PGA Tour tournaments.[1]

But the municipal course gradually fell into disrepair. And after it became a parking lot for the US Open at nearby Olympic Club, a powerful foursome gathered to do something about it.

"Sandy Tatum, former USGA President, champion golfer for Stanford University [he helped them win back-to-back NCAA Men's Golf Championships in 1941 and 1942] and an accomplished attorney in the Bay Area, along with financier Charles Schwab, the PGA Tour's Tim Finchem and the mayor San Francisco Willie Brown, each brought their expertise and a shared vision to bring Harding back to its glory," said Smith.

Extensive renovations were completed in 2003 that featured a complete redesign to the course and expanded it from 6,743 yards to nearly 7,200 yards in length, but still maintained the character and integrity of the original layout. Harding Park began to host PGA Tournaments again.

This time, the TPC, part of the property division of PGA Tour, was brought in to help the city of San Francisco manage the property.

One of the players who would be glad that Harding Park had returned all the way from its "weed patch" days was PGA Tour rookie Collin Morikawa.

He had gotten quite familiar with the course after playing many rounds during his four years attending the University of California, Berkeley, where he was a four-time All-American and Pac-12 player of the year. Morikawa would parlay that local knowledge to major success.

TPC Harding Park's GM noted the course has a what-you-see-is-what-you-get layout. He described the challenges of the cypress-lined course, where the rough is thick outside the narrow fairways (average twenty-five yards), and the ball doesn't fly as far in the damp air, and the lies are unpredictable and one has to shape the ball well in both directions. The course tests all aspects of the game.

"It is fairly straightforward. It's a matter of placing your shot right where you can see it. Perhaps undertold is the fact that it is Mother Nature that makes the course quite challenging," explained Smith. "We are right against the ocean. We are right at sea level. The temperature is fairly cool. The air is somewhat heavy with high humidity. So all those factors makes the course play longer. At the same time there's no trickery. It's a pretty straightforward golf course. There are no blind tee shots, you just need to make the shot your shot."

Looking to make their shots were ninety-one of the world's top one hundred ranked players. One of those was Brooks Koepka.

On a day when the scoring average was 71.12, the lowest for an opening round in PGA Championship history, Koepka was looking to become the first player in ninety-three years to win the PGA Championship for the third straight year. He was right in the mix, just one back of the leaders with a 4-under 66.

Sharing the lead with American Brendon Todd was another former PGA Champion, Australian Jason Day. Each finished with a 65. Morikawa was four back with a 69.

Both Koepka and Day would finish day two strong, and their 134 totals placed them in second with a group tied at 6 under. But the story of the day was Haotong Li, the 114th-ranked player in the world, who shot a bogey-free round of 65 to take a two-stroke lead after thirty-six holes.

The little-known twenty-five-year old from China had three international victories but had yet to win on the PGA Tour. But now in just his twelfth start in a major, with back-to-back birdies early on, he added three more to grab the clubhouse lead.

In the third round, yet another former major champion made his presence felt.

The 2016 US Open winner, Dustin Johnson, had a pair of back-to-back birdies on the back nine and a personal majors record eight overall for the round. This put him in a good position to get his second major, being the sole leader at 9-under 201.

Well, the third round certainly did not appear difficult for the rookie Morikawa, who had started the weekend six back. A pair of birdies on the front nine and one on the par-5 tenth led him to post a 7-under 65 to head into the final round tied with Koepka and Paul Casey, who was just two back in fourth place with a fifty-four-hole total of 203. While he was pleased with his third-round result, Morikawa's mind was already looking ahead to the final round.

"I've got to be ready for hole one, and then be physically and mentally prepared through eighteen. I can just control what I can do, so hopefully get off to a good start tomorrow."

He certainly did. After producing back-to-back birdies on three and four, Morikawa went to 9 under and just one back of the leader, Dustin Johnson.

DJ, however, did not have history on his side entering the final round of the PGA Championship. He had not converted any of his fifty-four-hole leads in a major. He also had the lead at the 2010 PGA Championship at Whistling Straits, but a ruling went against him that would cost him a playoff spot.

After an opening birdie here, Johnson bogeyed hole three. There were now eighteen players within four shots.

One of those was the Englishman Paul Casey. The avid cyclist might as well have been cruising down the road on his bike because he was in a similar zone. After two birdies on the front nine, his birdie on ten to start the closing half put him into a tie for the lead at 10 under. But there were others climbing up the leaderboard. After most had come through the fourteenth hole, there were seven players within one shot of the lead!

Someone was going to have to do something spectacular to earn a measure of separation. It would end up being the young man with the most knowledge of the course.

When he stepped up to the tee at the somewhat shortish 294-yard, par-4 sixteenth, the five-foot-nine, 160-pound Morikawa decided to drive to the pin. Now here was a player who came into the PGA ranked 110th in driving distance, and had given up some twenty-five yards off the tee to leading contenders in this event like Tony Finau, Bryson DeChambeau, and Cameron Champ.

Morikawa explained his crucial decision: "There's a hazard on the left on sixteen, but that's pretty far away. I just had to be fully committed, and J.J. [Jakovac, his caddy] asked me, you know, 'Are you sure? Is this what you want to do?'

"I'm like, 'Yes, this is driver. This is perfect.' You know, stepped up, hit a really good drive, and obviously it ended up where it did."

Showing steady nerves of a much more seasoned player, the twenty-three-year-old made a brilliant tee shot that settled on the green, leaving him just a seven-footer for an eagle.

However, knowing the magnitude of every single shot late on a Sunday major, the Kid from Cal was well aware he had to complete what he started and get the ball down in one.

"I had to make that putt. Two strokes is a lot different than one stroke coming down eighteen."

Morikawa calmly dropped it in the cup for a two-shot lead. That would be the margin of victory, as he would finish with a 64 at 13-under 267. Third-round leader Johnson shot 68 and tied for second with Casey, while Koepka fell well back and closed with a 74.

Being the first major conducted without spectators, Morikawa was not able to feed off the energy, from the joy shared by massive galleries, but he was philosophical about the situation.

"I think without a crowd it plays very different. If there were thousands and thousands of people, I think everyone would have heard the shout on sixteen for sure. But whether crowds were here or not, I still had to get it done, so I'm really happy about what just happened."

Morikawa secured his third career victory and first major title with a blistering back-nine 31 that included one of the most memorable clutch eagles in golf history.

35

PHIL ACES FATHER TIME

MAY 20–23, 2021
THE OCEAN COURSE
KIAWAH ISLAND, SOUTH CAROLINA

Upon arriving here for the 103rd PGA Championships at this island paradise outside Charleston, there were not any significant signs from Phil Mickelson of what was about to happen.

Lefty hadn't hoisted a major championship trophy since 2013 at Muirfield. Soon to be fifty-one, he hadn't finished in the top ten in a major championship since the 2016 Open Championship at Royal Troon. With zero top twenty finishes in the ten months leading up to this event, he had fallen outside the top one hundred in the Official World Golf Ranking. Las Vegas was not impressed with his résumé of five major titles and nine top ten finishes in this event, and many sports books put him at 300–1 odds to win.

But odder things have happened to Phil. He had a slimmed-down look from a healthier diet and lifestyle that included meditation, and he was now looking at the game through a rosier prism, albeit via dark sunglasses. And with his brother Tim on the bag, and feeling good after polishing his long, smooth swing with coach Andrew Getson, Phil was ready to take on the Pete Dye–designed course in search of his sixth major and his second Wanamaker Trophy.

Of course, this event, always with one of the most talented fields, included some formidable competition who had their own eyes on the same prize. There was Brooks Koepka, who despite not being a hundred percent after knee surgery, was looking to win this major for the second time in three years, having won four majors since the last time Mickelson contended. Collin Morikawa was set to defend his crown after winning at Harding Park the previous year. Louis Oosthuizen was coming off a third-place finish in the previous US Open and had a runner-up finish at the 2017 PGA Championship at Quail Hollow. Three-time major winner Padraig Harrington, at forty-nine and participating in his twenty-first PGA Championship, was determined to show he was still a contender. Young guns like Jon Rahm, Scottie Scheffler, and Will Zalatoris were all quite confident they had the game to be in the mix come Sunday.

They would all be facing nasty ocean crosswinds, devilish bunkers, and the knowledge that this par-72, 7,876-yard coastal track was also the longest course in majors history.

At a pretournament press conference, Phil said, "The guys out here are so good. They are so talented. The course setups are very penalizing that you've got to be focused every shot, and if I lose my focus on any holes out of seventy-two, the field here is going to eat me up and so that's the big challenge for me to get in contention."

Well, if the first round was any indication, Phil was focused. His 2-under 70 put him one off the lead.

The spectators, limited to roughly ten thousand because of pandemic protocols, were clearly expressing their support for Mickelson. Feeding off that, he rolled a 69 to share the lead with Oosthuizen halfway through the tournament.

Mickelson was 6 under through the first eleven holes; however, he bogeyed three of his final six. It was practically the opposite of his first round, when he shot 2 over on the front nine but was 4 under in a bogey-free back nine.

Koepka, just one back after a 69-71, explained how the weather and course challenges on Friday at Kiawah appealed to his nature.

"I love it when it's difficult. I think that's why I do so well in the majors. I just know mentally I can grind it out. Like when it's windy like this, it's not so much putting, it's more about ball striking, and I felt like I struck it really well today. I feel like that's why I've done really well. You've got to understand that sometimes par is a good score, and you've just got to accept it and move on."

In the third round, Morikawa, the defending champion, followed up a 75 with a 74, and Padraig and Louis scored 73 and 72, respectively. Phil and Brooks both rolled 70s, thus providing Mickelson a one-stroke lead heading into the final round.

Koepka, who was down five early in the back nine but finished 6 under par for the championship, was excited when informed that he'd be in the final pairing with Mickelson for the last round. He said, "It'll be nice. At least I can see what Phil is doing and then I don't have to turn back and look and see what he's up to. Looking forward to it. Got a chance, and everybody will be in front of me, so I know what I've got to do. This golf course you can make one little mistake and it can be costly. That's why it's a major championship."

A major championship indeed, for many of the pretournament favorites brought their Sunday best. Zalatoris and Scheffler closed with 70s for a share of fourth along with Morikawa, who battled back with a 68. Irish greats Shane Lowry and Harrington earned a piece of third place with 69s. But it would be a three-player race for the trophy.

Koepka dueled Mickelson from the start of the final round. On the opening hole Brooks birdied while Phil bogeyed. But Lefty got the advantage back after the two-time PGA champ double-bogeyed the next hole.

For the only man to sleep on the lead in major championships in the 1990s, 2000s, 2010s, and 2020s is fifty and playing in his twenty-eighth PGA Championship, a highlight came from the sand at five. When he was just trying to get up and down to prevent any more momentum from slipping away, Mickelson saw his bunker shot take four small bounces and then run into the right center of the cup for an unlikely birdie.

Heading to the back nine, on the tenth hole from short range, Phil stroked a birdie and suddenly held a four-shot lead.

His fans had been there before. In the past, they had to deal with the angst that came with witnessing Phil the Thrill making questionable decisions in clutch moments down the stretch, and they were mortified when ensuing wildly errant shots proved costly.

Mickelson led by five shots with six holes to play. But his legion of followers clutched their hearts, recalling past digressions when his advantage was cut to two after he bogeyed at the thirteenth and fourteenth. Could this be yet another near miss? Phil already had eleven runner-up results at majors.

But this was the new Phil. Right?

Oosthuizen stayed in the mix, producing a birdie at the sixteenth. Despite this, Phil-nation saw their leader press on with a calm demeanor and determined resolve behind those aviator specs. Taking advantage of some adrenaline, he launched the longest drive of the day, a 363-yard drive right down the middle of the fairway. And so, after a birdie of his own at sixteen, Mickelson regained a three-stroke lead.

Though he made a bogey on the par-3 seventeenth after having to chop out of thick rough, Phil looked at ease.

However, after hitting a nine-iron to within eighteen feet of the pin and essentially securing the victory, chaos ensued as Phil, Brooks, and their caddies became suddenly engulfed by a sea of fans as they tried to reach the green. Despite some nervous moments at this unexpected stampede, they got there safely after security came to their rescue. Koepka, who was inexplicably 3 over par on the two par-5s on the front nine, still had a chance to force a playoff on the final hole. He would need to make his twenty-two-footer for birdie and have Mickelson three-putt from fifteen feet. However, Koepka missed and made par while Mickelson two-putted for his sixth major title.

With the victory, being just three weeks shy of fifty-one, Phil set a new record as the oldest player to win a major on the PGA Tour. Julius Boros was forty-eight years and four months old when he won the 1968 PGA Championships at Pecan Valley Golf Club in San Antonio, Texas.

Mickelson became only the fourth player to win PGA Tour events in four different decades, joining Sam Snead, Raymond Floyd, and Davis Love III.

I am very proud of having set a record at the time for becoming the oldest player to win the Masters (age forty-two in 1978). I have often stated that longevity is too often overlooked in evaluating the success of one's career, and that taking into consideration the time span between a first and last majors championship victory really should be a key factor.

I have been saying for more than forty years that one day someone at fifty will win a major. And I was poo-pooed all that time. Now I'm telling you that one day a person of sixty or more will win a major. It wasn't far off with Tom Watson. At fifty-nine he nearly won the Open at Turnberry in 2009. People are getting younger by exercising and better diets, and there are secrets to longevity, so you will find somebody at sixty winning a major.

"This is just an incredible feeling," Mickelson said on the eighteenth green at the Wanamaker Trophy presentation ceremony. "I just believed that it was possible but yet everything was saying it wasn't. And I hope that others find that inspiration. It might take a little bit of extra work, a little bit of harder effort to maintain physically or maintain the skills, but gosh, is it worth it in the end . . . there's no reason why I or anybody else can't do it at a later age."

36

MITO'S MISTAKE AND JUSTIN'S JOY

MAY 19–22, 2022
SOUTHERN HILLS COUNTRY CLUB
TULSA, OKLAHOMA

Despite terrific play from many contenders (Rory McIlroy, Will Zalatoris, Cameron Young, and Matthew Fitzpatrick, among others) this major will be known for a costly mistake by a player performing in his first PGA championship and a past champion's return to glory with an amazing rally.

Here's the story of Mito Pereira and Justin Thomas in their quest for glory. A quest that would ultimately hinge on experience.

As far as the venue, Southern Hills has enjoyed a lot of experience regarding the majors. It has hosted three US Opens and five PGA Championships.

Cameron Young, who was the 2021–2022 PGA Rookie of the Year and would tie for third place in this major, described the course's nuances:

"For one, it is very, very long. And I think there are several holes with the slope of the fairway don't suit the hole necessarily. Like number five is a very long dogleg left, but the whole fairway kind of slopes away from you left to right. And if I remember correctly the prevailing wind is off the left there. So it makes it very tough shot to hit, and there are other holes like that out there at Southern Hills. Like number nine, and number seven and ten, where the fairways just kind of roll in the direction opposite of the dogleg," explained the New York native. "The greens are very tricky. There's a lot of slope, especially for a golf course that we played that was closed probably 7,500 yards if not more."

Nick Price, the 1994 PGA champion here, called Southern Hills "a ball striker's paradise."

One of the game's better ball strikers, Rory McIlroy, a two-time winner of this event, opened with a scintillating 65. Starting the tournament on the back nine, the Irishman birdied four holes in a row on his first half and avoided a bogey until the sixth hole, his fifteenth. He finished the round by making an eighteen-foot putt for birdie on the ninth.

"I feel like this course, it lets you be pretty aggressive off the tee if you want to be, so I hit quite a lot of drivers out there and took advantage of my length and finished that off with some nice iron play and some nice putting."

Nice.

2017 champion Justin Thomas, fighting through allergies and a sinus infection despite a pair of bogeys on the front nine, made three birdies on the back nine to shoot 67 (3 under), the lowest score in the afternoon.

Mito Pereira was one shot back with a 68.

But the twenty-seven-year-old Chilean torched the Hills with the lowest score in the second round, a 64. Two under heading to the back nine, Pereira had four birdies to finish at 8 under, just one off the lead of Zalatoris, who scored a 65.

He attributed playing there while at Texas Tech University as helping.

"I played in college here in 2015, I think. They change it a little bit, but for sure it's a tough course, tough greens to read. They're really slopy," said Pereira.

Zalatoris was positioned atop the leaderboard at the halfway point after producing a marvelous 66-65 combo. The wiry Texan, who just a month earlier finished second in the Masters Tournament with a score of 9-under-par, one stroke behind champion Hideki Matsuyama, credited the luck of the draw in being able to play the back nine with minimal wind and being bogey free. He was pleased with his result.

But gale blasts and colder temperatures would play havoc for players competing in the third round. Crosswinds and unpredictable gusts forced balls off line all over the place, including at least a cup and a half on many greens.

Because of this, Zalatoris dropped three back with a 73. It began with a poor start, where he lost four shots on his front nine. Despite the big score, the twenty-five-year-old said he'd lean on some expert opinions on how to prepare for the final round.

"I've been fortunate enough to grow up around Lanny Wadkins and Lee Trevino, and obviously those guys are major champions. Just stick to my game. Got nothing to lose tomorrow."

A pair of other young players, Cameron Young and Matthew Fitzpatrick, rolled 67s.

The highlight for Young, a former roommate of Zalatoris at Wake Forest, was driving the green on the seventeenth and sinking a twenty-four-foot putt for an eagle to finish at 5 under and alone in fourth place.

The Englishman closed strong. With birdies on four of his last ten holes, including both seventeen and eighteen, Fitzpatrick, now at 6 under, had a share of second place with Zalatoris.

After a pair of 67s, Thomas ballooned to a 74 and was now seven strokes in back of the leader heading into the final round.

And with his third straight round in the 60s (68-64-69), Pereira took a three-stroke lead at 9-under 209.

Despite being in an unfamiliar spot, Pereira, 100th in the Official World Golf Ranking, mentioned what his approach would be for the biggest eighteen holes of his life.

"It's by far the biggest tournament I played, the biggest round of golf, and tomorrow is going to be even bigger. I just—I don't know how to say, just try to keep it simple, try to do the same things that I've been doing, try to not even look at the people that's around me."

Well, Pereira had a difficult time doing the same things he was doing because in that final round, after back-to-back bogeys at the seventh and eighth holes, his three-stroke lead shrank to just one. That was only because he was able to save par from a bunker on the ninth to make the turn at 7 under, one shot ahead of Zalatoris and Young.

The leading contenders had their troubles—Zalatoris had bogeys at twelve and fifteen, and Young fell two behind after hitting his tee shot on the par-3 fourteenth into a bunker, then three-putted for a double-bogey on the sixteenth. But Justin Thomas began to make up his seven-shot deficit with four birdies (and two bogeys) through twelve, including a sixty-four-foot putt at eleven.

But the next-to-last hole proved to be the difference maker. Hitting what he would later deem the then-best shot of his career, Thomas teed up on the par-3 seventeenth with a seven-iron.

Drawing his ball into the middle of the green, the pride of the Alabama Crimson Tide's winning golf squad knocked in his sixth birdie of the day to move to 9 under par. He was the clubhouse leader with his third 67 of the tournament.

Pereira reached the green on the par-5 thirteenth hole in two shots and two-putted for a birdie, but his tee shot on the next hole flew over the green. He made another bogey, dropping his lead again to just one shot.

Zalatoris had three-putted for bogey on the sixteenth before holing a seven-foot birdie putt at the seventeenth to reach 5 under. He then closed out with a par on the eighteenth to tie Thomas for the clubhouse lead at 5 under.

Pereira barely missed a birdie putt at seventeen that would've provided him a two-shot cushion, and arrived on the seventy-second hole needing a par to win a major. He would later say he wasn't nervous, but in what could have been a career-defining victory, he took the absolute most unfavorable time to make the worst shot of his tournament. By blocking his tee shot with what looked like an atypical follow-through for him, Pereira drove his ball into a small meandering creek on the right side.

From there, with the penalty drop, he had 190 yards left and still had a chance to make a bogey that would get him in the playoff. However, the ball traveled over the green, leaving a tough pitch that he could get to only twenty-two feet. He needed two putts and—just like that—seventy-one holes of championship-caliber effort was over. The double-bogey 6 meant not even a playoff for the Chilean.

That left Thomas and Zalatoris to square off from 5 under in a three-hole playoff.

The two remaining contenders both started off with birdies. Thomas went 1 up after birdieing the next hole. After Zalatoris missed a lengthy birdie putt on the third playoff hole, Thomas needed only to two-putt for par to win his second major title.

A twenty-nine-year-old native of Louisville, Kentucky, Thomas—who comes from a family of PGA professionals, with his father, Mike, being a longtime PGA club professional in Kentucky and his son's swing coach, and his grandfather Paul, playing in the 1962 US Open and the 1993 US Senior Open before eventually passing away from COVID-19—had scored his second Wanamaker Trophy in five years.

His seven-shot comeback after fifty-four holes tied John Mahaffey in 1978 for the largest in PGA Championship history. Mahaffey entered the final round seven shots behind Tom Watson. Mahaffey shot a sensational final-round 66 to get into a sudden-death playoff with

Watson and Jerry Pate. All three men parred the first playoff hole, and Mahaffey sank a twelve-footer for birdie on the second hole to win the title.

For Thomas, it was the third-largest rally in any major championship. Only Paul Lawrie, who came back from ten shots in the final round of the Open in 1999 (best remembered for Jean Van de Velde's meltdown—see chapter 74), and Jack Burke Jr., who climbed from eight shots back at the 1956 Masters, had bigger comebacks.

One of the reasons for the successful comeback was tied to a "tough love" session at the driving range the night before the final round between Thomas and his caddy, Jim "Bones" MacKay.

"Yeah, I'm fully confident in saying that I wouldn't be standing here if he didn't give me that—wasn't necessarily a speech, but a talk, if you will," said the new champion. "I just needed to let some steam out. I didn't need to bring my frustration and anger home with me. I didn't need to leave the golf course in a negative frame of mind. I just went down—I played pretty well yesterday for shooting 4 over, and I felt like I'd played terrible. And he was just like, dude, you've got to be stop being so hard on yourself. You're in contention every single week we're playing."

MacKay, fifty-seven, had been the long-time caddy for Phil Mickelson (winning five majors during a twenty-five-year partnership)—the defending champion who became the oldest winner of a major at fifty but who had opted not to defend his title.

If Mito Pereira had won, he would have been the first Chilean to claim a majors championship and just the third from South America to do so (Argentinians Roberto De Vicenzo and Ángel Cabrera being the others). He was disappointed yet philosophical about the finish: "On eighteen, I wasn't even thinking about the water. I just wanted to put it in play, and I guess I aimed too far right. I just hit in the water.

In all my years of competing, it's one of the hardest things to do, there are not many players that can lead a major championship and win. Very few.

Inexperience had cost him the tournament. He put up a game façade when facing the media afterward, but he said with a sense of forlorn regarding his tee shot on the seventy-second hole, "I wish I could do it again."

He'll be wishing that for a very, very long time.

37

KOEPKA'S COMEBACK

MAY 18–21, 2023
OAK HILL COUNTRY CLUB (EAST COURSE)
PITTSFORD, NEW YORK

In the mentally demanding game of golf, self-assurance is a precious and elusive commodity.

And thirty-three-year-old Brooks Koepka had enjoyed great success. In his previous twenty-one majors championship starts, the Floridian had four victories, four runners-up, and fourteen top 10 finishes. But when he shattered his knee, he shattered his confidence.

The horrific injury to his knee cap and patella tendon happened in March 2021. As Koepka recalled: "I just slipped. I was at home. I dislocated my knee and then I tried to put it back in, and that's when I shattered my kneecap and during the process tore my MPFL [medial patellofemoral ligament]. My leg was sideways and out. My foot was turned out, and when I snapped it back in, because the kneecap had already shattered, it went in pretty good. It went in a lot easier!"[1]

And it nearly tore up his career. It certainly played with his head. On the Netflix documentary series *Full Swing*, Koepka appeared clearly at a crossroads, uncharacteristically wondering aloud if he could compete with the likes of Scheffler and other young stars any longer. "I'll be honest with you: I can't compete with these guys, week in, week out. A guy like Scottie, he can shoot 63 every day. I don't know."

After initially balking, Koepka joined the LIV Golf League, the Saudi Arabian–financed circuit that reportedly paid him $100 million in guaranteed earnings to lure him away from the PGA Tour.

I suspect he joined the LIV tour because he had to be concerned to some degree about whether his body would last. And that is similar to Bryson DeChambeau's reason for joining, but only those two players themselves can answer. Everybody's got an opinion, but they are the only ones who really know the truth about it.

Though not nearly 100 percent back physically over two years after the freak injury, Koepka nevertheless had a real good chance to win his first green jacket with a two-stroke lead after fifty-four holes at the 2023 Masters. However, his subconscious mind played with his normally massive self-belief. Still not fully confident in his physical capabilities, Koepka played conservatively in the final eighteen and lost to Jon Rahm by four strokes.

After a second round of 66 here at Oak Hill, Koepka was in the mix again at a major. The two-time champion made five birdies on his closing nine holes, including both the seventeenth and eighteenth.

With his confidence building after finally being able to fully use his repaired knee in his swing, Koepka made three birdies on the back nine, including a forty-six-foot putt on the seventeenth to reach six under for the tournament. His second straight 66 put him atop the leaderboard once again after fifty-four holes.

Given where he was a year before, or even six months before, the muscular Koepka felt all the rehab was finally paying off.

"Yeah, I thought all I had to do was be healthy. That was just the only question mark. But you know, having an off-season to kind of just bust my butt and be in the gym every day, to working on things, doing different—doing different recovery, it's been—it's been really good," said Koepka.

So with the mind, knee, and swing all clicking in sync for the first time in a long time, Koepka showed that old familiar mental tenacity when he began his fourth round and his quest for a fifth major, something only nineteen other players in the history of the game have achieved.

Canadian Corey Conners and rising star Viktor Hovland, a twenty-five-year-old from Norway, were looking to claim their first major, and both were just one back at 5 under. But Koepka had started out on fire.

He made three straight birdies to increase the gap to three shots after four holes and get to 9 under. However, Hovland was ready for a fight. The poised young Norwegian made back-to-back birdies on the front nine and trailed Koepka by just one at the turn.

Meanwhile a southern California club pro, Michael Block, was capturing the hearts and minds of fans and media. After his third straight 70, he was tied for eighth place, becoming the first PGA professional to be inside the top ten after the third round since Jay Overton in 1988.

Playing with Rory McIlroy in the final round, Block's amazing performance included a hole-in-one at fifteen. His fifteenth-place finish (the best by a club pro since Lonnie Nielsen tied for eleventh in 1986 at Inverness), guaranteed he'd have to find someone to cover for him giving lessons in Orange County, as he was assured a spot at the PGA Championship the following year at Valhalla.

"The most surreal moment I've ever had in my life," the forty-six-year-old Block said. "I'm living a dream."

Koepka, knowing the anguish and hell he had gone through to get his game back to the level he was at before the freakish incident, remained poised despite the challengers for the Wanamaker Trophy lurking around him. They included Scottie Scheffler, whose four birdies on the back nine propelled him to within two shots of Koepka as he shot a five-under 65, tying the lowest round of any player in the tournament. But down the stretch it would be that pesky Norwegian who provided the greatest opposition.

As he stood at the tee of the par-4, 458-yard sixteenth hole, Hovland was just one back at 8 under. It would be a pivotal hole.

Hovland first drove into a fairway bunker. He then mishit his recovery shot and his ball became embedded in the bunker facing. After a drop, he could only pitch out. With a double bogey result to Koepka's birdie on the same hole, it was all over.

Koepka had his third PGA Championship, but Hovland took away some hard-earned lessons.

With a share of fourth place at the 2022 Open Championship, a share of seventh at the Masters, and a share of second here, Hovland saw the positives of three straight top tens in the majors.

"It sucks right now, but it is really cool to see that things are going the right direction," Hovland said. "If I just keep taking care of my business and just keep working on what I've been doing, I think we're going to get one of these soon. Brooks is a great player."

Koepka shot 72-66-66-67 for a 9-under-par 271. Hovland (68) and Scottie Scheffler (65) tied for second place, two shots behind. Koepka joined Jack Nicklaus and Tiger Woods as the only players to win three PGA titles in the stroke play era.

With the victory, Koepka became the first golfer to win a major golf championship as a member of LIV Golf (though some sort of alliance between the two tours has since been announced, exact details are not yet available as of the publication of this book).

Having finally overcome the lingering injury and self-doubt, Koepka tried to explain what this major means to him.

"It's incredible. I look back to a couple of years ago and where I'm at now. To be able to be here is special. It means a hell of a lot more to me."

THE US OPEN

ESTABLISHED IN 1895 (THIRTY-FIVE YEARS AFTER THE Open Championship), the US Open, unlike the limited invitational field of the Masters, is truly open and provides an equal opportunity for any qualified golfer to showcase his skills.

In other words, the competitors are primarily determined by ability alone in a series of qualifying events, as opposed to an invitation or a specific record. The result is the chance for the hungry amateur and club pros to play against Tour professionals.

In the US Open, golfers compete on the best courses in the country, under rigorous conditions such as traditional narrow fairways, heavy rough, firm ground conditions, and often the speediest greens. These are set by the USGA, which is driven to find the best player. The US Open is often viewed as the most difficult of the four majors to win. Thus, the greater corresponding joy of being victorious.

Though in its first decade it was conducted for amateurs and Great Britain's large wave of immigrant golf professionals (including

Scotland's Willie Anderson, who became a four-time US Open Champion in 1901, 1903, 1904, and 1905), in 1913, the US Open really took off when Francis Ouimet, a twenty-year-old American amateur, stunned the golf world by defeating the famous English professionals Harry Vardon and Ted Ray in a playoff.

The national championship went to a higher level amid the brilliant performances of Bob Jones Jr., who won the US Open four times (1923, 1926, 1929, 1930). Not only did he spark the event's first spectator sellout crowd, but in addition to becoming regular front-page news, the popular Georgian's success created a boom in entries that caused the United States Golf Association to introduce sectional qualifying in 1924.

Over the decades, this event has been shaped by the arrival of national television coverage, as well as better technology, improved course maintenance, and more emphasis on fitness and training. But the one common drive of all the great champions, from Ben Hogan to Hale Irwin and Brooks Koepka, is to secure one's place in history by winning the toughest tournament there is.

38

GOLF'S GREATEST UPSET

British greats Harry Vardon and Ted Ray were on an exhibition tour of the United States and were such big stars the USGA delayed the 1913 US Open until September just so they could make it to the tournament. (Do you think the USGA today would reschedule the national championship so that Tiger and Phil could finish their exhibition in Las Vegas, or Dustin and Bryson could make their LIV tour event in Broken Arrow, Oklahoma?)

Ray, the longest hitter in the game (sort of a twentieth-century version of John Daly and his grip-it-and-rip-it style, but in tweed jackets and an ever-present pipe in his mouth), had won the most recent Open Championship in Muirfield in wire-to-wire fashion. Vardon was already a five-time winner of the Open Championship and had a previous US Open victory. These two were among the world's most accomplished players.

So, when they arrived in Brookline (just outside of Boston), many figured it'd be just a two-man battle between these English gentlemen, in an era when the game was dominated by the Brits and Scots.

Little did they know, these history-making stars, that when they left the Country Club, they'd indeed be part of a record performance, but on the losing end to a local store clerk who had to beg his manager to get the time off from work.

That clerk was Francis Ouimet, a gangly, unknown twenty-year-old self-taught amateur golfer and son of hard-working blue-collar immigrants. He lived in a small house on Clyde Street, where, from the second-floor bedroom he shared with his brother, he could see the seventeenth hole of the Country Club.

During his youth, Ouimet would often cut through the course on his way to school and pick up lost balls, which ignited his interest in the game. He would do some caddy work there. He'd also sneak onto the course and play a few holes, learning the game that way, or simply wander for hours observing the swings of the well-to-do members.

Upon arriving for the qualifying round, Ouimet was disheartened to learn that his caddy Jack Lowery would not be available. Why? He was caught skipping school by a truant officer. Unafraid of a similar fate, Jack's ten-year-old younger sibling, Eddie, made himself Johnny-on-the-spot and quite eagerly took his brother's job.[1]

The youngster, spunky yet barely taller than the bag he'd be toting, insisted he could do the job.

"Eddie takes three street cars, skips school, shows up at Brookline and runs up to Francis," said Mark Frost, author of *The Greatest Game Ever Played*. "It's about 10 minutes to [Ouimet's] tee time. [Eddie] explains that Jack isn't coming cause he had to go back to school. And Francis says, 'Well, thanks for coming to town,' and starts walking away. And Eddie says, 'I could caddie for ya.' And Francis says, 'Eddie, you're shorter than my bag, you can't do this.' And Eddie ends up convincing Francis that he's the guy who should carry his bag in the Open."

While he was comparatively unknown, Ouimet was indeed the state amateur champ so he certainly was adept with his niblick, mashie, spoon, and brassie, but even with his extensive local knowledge, there was no way he'd make the cut let alone take on the biggest names in the sport.

Or could he?

In a tournament scheduled for two days, thirty-six holes both days, the young man didn't start out on fire. He double-bogeyed the first hole. He doubled the second hole.

Ouimet opened with a 77. At the end of day one, Vardon was tied for the lead at 147. Ray was two strokes behind, tied for third. Ouimet had a better second round; his 74 put him in a tie for seventh with Walter Hagen and two others four back.

Now with the help of his kid psychologist and rookie caddy Eddie Lowery constantly in his ear with words of encouragement, Ouimet vaulted to a share of the lead with another 74, the lowest score of the round.

Heading into the final round that Friday afternoon, the local clerk was now level with Ray and Vardon at the top of the leaderboard. Word spread among the community, and suddenly streetcars were filled with Bostonians rushing to witness how a local boy would fare in the finale against the world's best down the stretch.

They wouldn't be disappointed but—spoiler alert!—they would have to come back the following day to see it through to the end.

Ouimet started slowly in Friday's final eighteen, shooting a 43 on the front, but with Vardon and Ray already in the clubhouse with 79s, the kid played the last six holes in 2 under to tie. All three at the end of regulation were at 304 (12 over).

The key shot came at the seventeenth (where else than his "home" hole, right?). With support from a hometown crowd surrounding the green, and little Eddie telling his player that he could handle the harrowing, multibreaking, downhill, knee-knocker twenty-foot putt, Ouimet rammed his stroke so hard it smashed into the cup, popped up then down in for the bird. How could this not be a sign of destiny?

Ouimet slept like a baby in the comforts of home. The following morning, on his way across the street, he saw that more than ten thousand folks had come to witness David take on not one but two Goliaths in the playoff. And many of them had never seen a golf tournament before.

This would not just be any Saturday in the park. This day would be a game changer for the sport.

They played in misty conditions. It was a close battle—all were tied at even-par 38 at the turn. It wasn't until the tenth hole that someone made a move, and it wasn't either of the pros. After snaring a one-shot lead there, the kid from across the street added another stroke to his advantage after twelve.

However, the clincher could only happen at one hole. You guessed it, Ouimet's "home" hole at seventeen.

The amateur golfer calmly sunk a fifteen-footer for a birdie there. His victory would be clear and decisive, as he finished with a 72 while Vardon could manage only a 77, and Ray, 78.

The fans hoisted both Lowery and Ouimet, the first amateur and only the second American to win the national championship, onto their shoulders in celebration.

More than two centuries after the battles at Lexington and Concord, this battle at Brookline saw a young Bostonian start another American revolution, this one in the sports world.

Ouimet's stunning achievement actually made the front pages of the world's newspapers, something extremely rare for the athletic field in general.

While the underdog story produced a book and a subsequent Hollywood movie based on Mark Frost's tome *The Greatest Game Ever Played*, arguably the biggest impact would be what it did to open up the sport in general. The victory by a working-class amateur ignited national interest in the sport and expanded its reach beyond just the well-to-do across the United States.

According to the Ouimet Scholarship Fund, which was founded in 1949 to assist students involved in the golfing community pay for college, the number of Americans playing golf soared from 350,000 in 1913 to more than two million a decade later. The number of courses tripled during that time period, and many of those were public.[2]

And what of little Lowery? The pipsqueak that not only lugged the bag as big as he was for all those pressure-packed rounds but constantly served up reminders to his player to be laser-focused on the current shot?

"My little caddie, Eddie Lowery . . . not much bigger than a peanut, was a veritable inspiration all around; and a brighter or headier chap it would be hard to find," Ouimet wrote for the *American Golfer*.

"Peanut" would go on to do all right for himself.

A skilled golfer himself, Lowery went on to become a multimillionaire when he moved to California and built the largest Lincoln-Mercury dealership in America. In the San Francisco Bay Area, he'd sponsor many amateur golfers, including Ken Venturi (1964 US Open champion) and Harvie Ward (1955 and 1956 US Amateur champion), who worked for Lowery at his dealerships.

Speaking of Venturi and Ward, it was Lowery who had both of those amateurs tee it up in 1956 at the tough Cypress Point course in Monterey against two American Goliaths—Ben Hogan and Byron Nelson—in a friendly match. It is considered the greatest fourball match ever.

Brilliantly recounted in Mark Frost's 2007 book *The Match: The Day the Game of Golf Changed Forever,* the two teams traded birdies and eagles the entire round, but Hogan and Nelson won, 1 up, when Hogan sank a ten-foot birdie putt at the eighteenth.

As for Ouimet, he'd never turn pro. He tied for fifth in the 1914 US Open, and tied for third in the 1925 US Open, then won the US Amateur in 1931.

So, what was in that bag little Lowery toted into history? Here's a list of Ouimet's clubs and their rough modern equivalents:

Driver

Brassie (two-wood)

Spoon (three-wood)

Wooden cleek (five-wood)

Sammy (utility club with a rounded back)

Jigger (low-lofted iron for bump-and-run shots)

Midiron (two-iron)

Mashie (five-iron)

Mashie niblick (seven-iron)

Niblick (nine-iron)

Putter

39

MARATHON MEN

JULY 2–6, 1931
INVERNESS CLUB
TOLEDO, OHIO

Imagine playing an entire extra tournament, yes, a whole other seventy-two holes to determine a winner for our national championship (as if the USGA's treacherous accoutrements were not enough to deal with in regulation).

Mix in some historic equipment in play with such sweltering heat that this US Open was dubbed "the Inferno at Inverness," and you have one of the most distinctive majors in the sport's history.

The longest playoff in major championship history happened here at this historic golf venue in Toledo, Ohio, which to date has hosted four US Opens (1920, 1931, 1957, and 1979) and two PGA Championships (1986 and 1993).

Inverness is generally described as a positional golf course that requires more finesse, where having a shorter club doesn't make the shot easier, as many of these greens are comparatively smaller. So, the core of the matter is not only being able to keep on line (did I mention the narrow fairways?) but to play every shot in the bag.

Today's golf fans know Inverness Club for the thrilling finishes in the 1986 and 1993 PGA Championships. The first major at Inverness Club was no different. It took place in 1920, when the Donald Ross course was in its infancy.

The favorite was Harry Vardon, a seven-time major champion and the most dominant player of the time. Carrying a five-stroke lead with just five holes to play, it appeared the future Hall of Famer was a sure winner. However, after three-putting on three holes on the back nine, all he could manage was a share of second place as Britain's Ted Ray edged him by a single stroke.

Though neither one would be playing at Inverness for the 1931 US Open, the field was still very impressive. Looking to take on the par-71, 6,529-yard layout were such marquee figures as Walter Hagen, Tommy Armour, and Gene Sarazen. However, the undersized gallery was attributed more to the missing star than the melting heat (hotter than a firecracker over this Fourth of July weekend).

After winning the US Amateur, British Amateur, US Open, and Open Championship in 1930—an unprecedented accomplishment that came to be known as a Grand Slam—Bobby Jones retired from competition, and though he would be present at Inverness, he'd only roam the course as a spectator.

Now that Jones would not be defending his title, those aiming to take his crown still faced a pair of new challenges in the form of equipment. Explaining that they wanted to make the sport more "challenging," the United States Golf Association USGA mandated the use of a larger and lighter ball (1.68 inches in diameter, 1.55 ounces) that season. (The rule would be dropped after just one year, and the USGA returned to a ball of at least 1.62 ounces. The 1.68-inch diameter specification would remain in place.)

It quickly garnered the moniker "balloon ball," as it didn't carry as far, was hard to control in the wind, and difficult to putt with. The other change was the introduction of some players using steel shafted-clubs. Jones would be the last US Open winner to use hickory shafts.

With so much to talk about and convey to fans, this also happened to be the first US Open to be broadcast on radio. However, what would be talked about was the fact that the big names would fade away and this major would come down to a marathon match between a pair of less-heralded, but quite talented players in their own right.

George Von Elm, a taciturn, chain-smoking native of Salt Lake City, after rolling 75 and 69 had the lead after two rounds. Billy Burke, a freckled, gregarious, cigar-chomper from Naugatuck, Connecticut, was just one back.

One of the more accomplished amateurs in an era (1920s) when that was the prevailing status, Von Elm enjoyed success early, winning the 1917 Utah Amateur title at sixteen. In 1921, he was suspended by the USGA for accepting expense money from supporters and for having a relationship with equipment company Spalding. However, when he returned to competitive golf in 1922, Von Elm was ready to prove himself on the national level.[1]

At the 1924, thirty-six-hole US Amateur championship at Baltusrol, he lost the title match to Bobby Jones. However, they would meet in the championship match for the same title again in 1926. While Jones was aiming for his fifth straight US Amateur crown (he had won in 1924 and 1925, and won again in 1927 and 1928), Von Elm stopped him, 2 and 1.[2]

Then on the international stage, at the 1926 Open at Royal Lytham & St. Annes Golf Club, he continued to perform very well against the greats of the day. In a tournament won by Bobby Jones, Von Elm finished in a very respectable tie for third with Walter Hagen. Von Elm's last big win in the amateur ranks was the 1930 French Amateur. He would turn pro later that year; though he'd have several runner-up finishes, he'd win only once on the PGA Tour.[3]

Burke played with a slightly unorthodox grip because of the loss of parts of two fingers on his left hand from an accident at an iron foundry where he worked. Still, had won six tournaments before this event. The son of Polish immigrants, Burke was born William John

Burkowski. He would be credited with eleven victories in his career. He worked as a club pro and noted golf instructor at the Cleveland (Ohio) and Clearwater (Florida) Country Clubs, and would be inducted into the PGA Hall of Fame in 1966.[4]

So with things really heating up at Inverness, the third and final day of regulation play featured thirty-six holes rather than eighteen, and the field of 144 golfers would be melted down to 63. By the end of the fourth round, the high temperature had taken its toll, and the tournament became a two-man competition.

On that triple-digit Fourth of July Saturday (remember, this was a time when many players wore long-sleeved, collared dress shirts with ties), the chain-smoker rolled a 73 in the third round to go ahead by two over the stogey man. But Burke, who had a cigar in hand throughout the tournament, claiming he used it to test the direction of the wind, was still very much in the hunt.

Though Von Elm had a two-stroke advantage at the end of three, Burke actually held the lead late in the fourth thanks to a pair of Von Elm bogeys at fifteen and sixteen. However, Von Elm, now a first-year pro, managed to birdie the seventy-second hole with a ten-footer, forcing a thirty-six-hole playoff on Sunday. Both were at 8-over 292.

On that sweltering Sunday morning, Burke opened up a four-shot lead on Von Elm, but by the time the pair broke for lunch after eighteen holes, his lead had been narrowed to two.

The afternoon's eighteen saw a seesaw battle. While Von Elm would sink four straight birdie putts, Burke stayed the course. After nailing a fifteen-footer at seventeen actually held a one-stroke lead as the gentlemen approached the last hole (or so everyone thought). However, once again needing a birdie at eighteen to continue play, Von Elm did just that to force another thirty-six.

One of the all-time great sportswriters, Grantland Rice, was on hand, and he wrote this in his column:

"Apparently they are going on forever. After the most sensational 36-hole playoff in the history of golf, they are still tied up in a two-ply Gordian Knot at 149 strokes each. There were enough fireworks in this contest to make the fall of Pompeii look like a single Roman candle."

In the second thirty-six-hole playoff, with thousands braving the heat to see who'd come out still standing, fatigue and the cumulative battle with the sun saw both players balloon to a 76 and 77 in the morning round.

Competing in triple-digit-temperature conditions, these two men were playing their way into golf history . . . and playing . . . and playing . . . and playing.

But in the afternoon Burke overcame his one-shot deficit with a closing 71, which included four birdies, to win the title.

You want numbers?

Seventy-two holes of golf and a tie at 292.

Thirty-six more holes and a tie at 149.

Thirty-six more holes. Billy Burke 148. George Von Elm 149.

A combined 1,179 strokes over 144 holes. And the difference?

One stroke.

Having just completed the equivalent of two full tournaments, after US Golf Association president Herbert H. Ramsay handed the trophy to Burke, the victorious but drained young man reportedly looked at Von Elm and said:

"I'm sorry it had to end this way."

The equally exhausted Von Elm could only muster a nod in agreement. Burke received the trophy and the winner's share of $1,000, while Von Elm earned $750.

A few weeks after the championship, a writer asked Burke, a burly fellow, how the players stood the physical torture of what amounted to two tournaments in one. "George Von Elm lost fifteen pounds," said Burke. "And you, Billy?" the writer asked. "I gained three," Burke replied.

Summing it up in his distinctive way, Rice wrote this:

"Not even the drama built up through the years by such eminent stars as Jones and Hagen could quite match the performance put on by Bill Burke, the winner, and George Von Elm, the loser by one stroke after one hundred and forty-four holes of pressure golf under blazing suns and through sudden winds and squalls of rain. Golf made good again to prove that the game must always stand above the player, to prove again that anything can happen, and that it follows no set laws. It is still the game of mystery, the game that will never be thoroughly understood."

40

SNEAD SNATCHES DEFEAT FROM VICTORY

JUNE 8–12, 1939
PHILADELPHIA COUNTRY CLUB
GLADWYNE, PENNSYLVANIA

S am Snead was the best athlete ever to play golf. He had the best
tempo I've seen. On top of it, he had a body made out of rubber.
And he had the strength of an American football player. What a
combination.

By the end of his career, Sam had won more tournaments than any
golfer who ever lived. He had won more prize money than any golfer
who ever lived. He also won seven majors, including three Masters
and three PGA Championships. And in his first visit across the pond,
he took an Open championship, in 1946.

By any measure that is an amazing career.

However, despite some outstanding performances, he was never
able to win a US Open, and thus he was unable to become part of
that exclusive club that have achieved the career Grand Slam. (I am
proud to be of those five.)

Slammin' Sam came close to winning the national championship
a half dozen times, including four runner-up results. This effort in

the 1939 event at the Philadelphia Country Club is perhaps his most gut-wrenching missed opportunity.

Golf history (and this book) is filled with examples of a major known more by the person who lost than won. The 1939 US Open is one of those.

Named after his maternal grandfather as well as Confederate general Stonewall Jackson, a distant relative, Samuel Jackson Snead was born the last of six children in 1922 in the tiny town of Ashwood, just outside of the small resort village of Hot Springs, Virginia, in the Appalachian mountains.[1]

Growing up excelling in sports including baseball and basketball, young Sam was also an avid outdoorsman who enjoyed hunting and fishing. And contrary to popular view, he was not double-jointed but simply had outstanding flexibility in his joints along with longer than normal muscles.

Golf for him began by his using a swamp-maple branch and clubbing any makeshift ball, usually some bundled-up rags. He caddied at a young age and then famously would sink empty tomato cans in his backyard to hone his chipping and putting.[2]

Fast-forward to the early days of the PGA Tour, publicist Fred Corcoran (who later became Snead's manager), had been building up Snead's success in an underdog mode of heroes of the day, like the racehorse Seabiscuit that caught the nation's imagination. The country had been mired in the depths of the Depression, and no one in the golf world had inspired them since Bobby Jones. Snead presented himself as a naïve, drawling-voiced hillbilly, but he had with the smoothest swing in the game, which was envied by the world's best players. He caught America's attention, especially when he won five tournaments in 1937. Going along with the backwoods image, the rather clever Snead made a bundle appearing in lucrative exhibitions as well as endorsement deals.

"He is a lot more complex than most people think, and I've always believed he's a little misunderstood," said Byron Nelson. "He was very good for the game—the first serious athlete who kept himself in top shape. They all do that on tour these days. But Sam was the first. There's never been a more gifted natural player."[3]

And that gift was on display from the first tee at the Philadelphia Country Club's Spring Mill course. Slammin' Sam would belt a 68 to earn the solo lead after the first round. Determined to stay on track and get that elusive national title, Snead maintained a one-stroke lead with a 71 halfway through. Horton Smith was one back and Craig Wood two.

Wood was due. Not only did he finish second in the inaugural Masters in 1934, but the following year at Augusta National he was the victim of Gene Sarazen's famous "shot heard round the world" and lost to him later in a playoff. He'd also lose to Denny Shute in a thirty-six-hole playoff at the Open in 1933, at the Old Course at St. Andrews.

Johnny Bulla, a good friend of Snead's, parlayed a 68 to take a one-stroke lead over his pal, who was now tied with Wood and Denny Shute in second place after three rounds. A powerfully built man at six foot three and 220 pounds, the native of West Virginia was a natural southpaw, but he learned the game right-handed due to a dearth of left-handed equipment. Sadly, Bulla's father, a Methodist minister, never forgave his son for pursuing professional golf and refused to speak with him for doing so.[4]

In the final round, Snead's play was speaking for itself. By the time he was standing on the tee at the seventy-second hole, all he needed was a par to earn that elusive US Open trophy. But since this match was taking place before the days of omnipresent giant leaderboards and pairing of the final-round leaders, he didn't know that. Sam thought he needed a birdie, and thus his strategy was more aggressive.

Things went awry right from the tee box as his drive on this par-5 eighteenth landed in the rough left of the fairway and a distant 275 yards from the green.

He topped his next shot, which landed in a steep bunker about 110 yards from the green. Though he would likely clear the five-foot trap face with a wedge, he didn't want to come up short of the green. So with a mighty lash of his eight-iron, he cleared the shower of sand to reveal the ball was now embedded near the top of the same bunker.

Snead slammed out, only to find his ball had landed in another bunker, now forty feet short of the flag. His fifth shot rolled across the green. The putter didn't help as he took three strokes with the flat blade. Eventually he settled for a triple-bogey eight.

Meanwhile Byron had made up five stokes and finished at 284. Craig Wood birdied the seventy-second hole. They would be joined by Denny Shute for a three-man playoff. Snead missed the playoff by two strokes.

Snead was crushed.

"That night, I was ready to go out with a gun and pay somebody to shoot me," he said in his book, *Slammin' Sam*. "It weighed on my mind so much that I dropped 10 pounds, lost more hair and began to choke up even on practice rounds."

Nelson and Wood each shot 68 in the first eighteen-hole playoff, then Nelson edged Wood by three strokes by shooting 70 in the second eighteen-hole playoff to capture his only US Open title.

I played that same eighteenth hole about twelve times in my career. You must remember there were no technical scoreboards like today. He thought he needed a birdie to win. And tried to hit it over the bunker. But he caught the face of it, and the ball fell back into the bunker. Had he known he just needed a par or even a bogey he would have won. He would have played well away from the bunker. He would not have even tried to take a shortcut. So, what a difference it makes when you have the information laid out for you on the golf course like we did. And that cost him the (career) grand slam.

But let me tell you something, if he hadn't had to go to war, Sam Snead would have won the Grand Slam.

41

A SOLDIER'S VICTORY

JUNE 12–16, 1946
CANTERBURY GOLF CLUB
BEACHWOOD, OHIO

I n the first US Open since 1941 (the event was suspended due to World War II), could there be any more appropriate victor than a war hero?

Lloyd Mangrum, who earned two Purple Hearts and four battle stars, including one after being wounded in the Battle of the Bulge, would have a different kind of fight on his hands, but after a tough and extended competition the decorated corporal would emerge victorious at the Canterbury Golf Club.

Pretty amazing, considering that while serving in Patton's Third Army he suffered severe wounds, including a permanently damaged left knee—memento of a German bullet— that creaked when he walked as well as a severely damaged shoulder. Doctors said he'd never play PGA golf again.[1]

And as the field arrived in Cleveland for the national championship in June of '46, the big favorites were Ben Hogan, Sam Snead,

Byron Nelson, and Jimmy Demaret. No one mentioned Mangrum as even a possibility.

That didn't bother Mangrum, who was a study in languid relaxation. A slim, debonair fellow with a world-weary expression and distinguished flecks of gray hair in his thick, wavy-black hair, he never hurried, never fretted, often sizing up putts with a cigarette dangling from his lips.[2]

But at the Canterbury Golf Club, the players risked neck fatigue from constantly swiveling their heads every which way trying to figure out those tricky greens. Perhaps Sam Snead said it best when he was quoted saying he'd "much rather face a rattlesnake than a downhill two-footer at Canterbury."

It had hosted the US Open before. In 1940, there was a controversial disqualification. Lawson Little, Gene Sarazen, and Ed "Porky" Oliver were tied after seventy-two holes at one-under-par 287. However, Oliver was then disqualified for beginning his final round ahead of his posted starting time. Oliver indicated there was a storm coming, and since the starter had given them their cards, they thought they could start early and beat the storm. Five other players started early and were disqualified, but the impact was devastating for Oliver.[3]

Little, who had won four amateur majors, won his only professional major here, beating thirty-eight-year-old Gene Sarazen in an eighteen-hole playoff. One of the favorites, Sam Snead, took the first-round lead with a blistering 67, but a closing 81 placed him well back.

In the 1946 version Snead once again started out well, as his 69 gave him a co-share of the first-round lead. However, he wouldn't be able to maintain that and would finish well back once again.

But emerging after their fine play in the second round were two other greats. Ben Hogan, on the strength of six birdies, rolled a 68 for a share of the lead at the halfway mark. Byron Nelson, who had revealed that the 1946 US Open would be his last, was sitting just two strokes behind the leaders after a pair of 71s.

Atop the leaderboard with Hogan was Vic Ghezzi. The New Jersey native was no stranger to success in the majors. He defeated Byron Nelson, the defending champion, in the title match by a 1-up score on the second extra hole to win the 1941 PGA Championship.

His memorable quote encapsulated the magnitude of his victory: "I won against one of the finest golf players we've ever had. I feel like a kid on Christmas morning."

One of the players he defeated to reach finals was Lloyd Mangrum.

Here in Cleveland, Lloyd started out 74-70, but after a 68 he found himself among the leaders. He and Ghezzi were just a shot behind leader Nelson, who had scored a 69 heading into the final round. And Byron's lead could have been larger if not for a rules violation.

On the thirteenth hole, trying to work his way through the crowd, after finally getting past the ropes, Nelson's caddy unfortunately stepped on the ball. The result was a one-stroke penalty for Byron, which would turn out to be quite pricey.[4] (Though some maintain the caddy was pushed off balance by the surging crowd).

It must be remembered that it was just one year prior that Nelson had produced one of the all-time great seasons, which included eighteen total wins and eleven consecutive victories, including a PGA Championship. He was still playing superbly.

Well, this championship would require a playoff to determine a winner because Nelson, Ghezzi, and Mangrum were all tied at 284 after seventy-two holes. Ben Hogan's three-putt bogey at the eighteenth hole ultimately cost him a spot in the playoff.

Somewhat less known, however, was the fact that there might never have been a playoff if Herman Barron, a player known to his golfing peers for his short game, had made a birdie putt on the seventy-second hole that would have won him the tournament. Even with a par he would've joined the other three in the playoffs. Alas, he three-putted and finished tied for fourth.

Despite being one of the taller players at six foot four, Ghezzi was not a long hitter, but like Barron he also was known for his play around and on the greens. Mangrum, also known as "Mr. Icicle" for his calm demeanor and relaxed swing, showed no signs of nervousness heading into the playoffs. Nelson, who led by two strokes with three holes to play, bogeyed the seventy-first and seventy-second holes to fall back into the tie. Nevertheless he was poised for extra innings.

The three-way playoff between Mangrum, Ghezzi, and Nelson would need more than the customary eighteen holes to decide the champion after each player shot an even par 72 in the morning.

In the afternoon's eighteen, Mr. Icicle showed signs of melting as he found himself trailing by three shots with just six left. This included a debacle at the ninth, where he nearly shot himself out of contention with an out of bounds tee shot, but a seventy-foot putt for bogey allowed him to minimize the damage. However, after birdies on thirteen, fifteen, and sixteen he climbed back in the race. Despite bogeys on seventeen and eighteen, the soldier was victorious, finishing with an even par 72, one stroke better than both Ghezzi and Nelson.

In a USGA interview years later, Nelson reflected on the incident that cost him.

"So, Lloyd won there in '46. But I really don't mean to take things away from Lloyd winning the tournament. But I really threw that championship away by poor concentration, and by playing those last six holes with a doubt in my mind as to what was going to happen."

Just as he said he would in Cleveland, two months after the championship, Nelson announced his retirement from the tour at age thirty-four, though he continued to play at the Masters through 1966. He also played twice again at the US Open (1949 and 1955), and once at the Open Championship in 1955.

Following this thirty-six-hole playoff, the USGA instituted a new playoff rule: If a scheduled eighteen-hole playoff ended in a tie, it would go to sudden death, rather than another full eighteen holes.

Speaking of playoffs, Mangrum lost a playoff for the 1950 US Open at Merion to Ben Hogan and his famous one-iron (see chapter 43). He was a runner-up in three majors and finished third in four more. The two-time Vardon Trophy winner finished in the top ten at the Masters Tournament ten consecutive years. His 64 in the opening round in 1940 was a Masters record that stood for forty-six years, until Nick Price's 63 in the third round in 1986.

He was a winner of thirty-six tour events, the leading money winner in 1951, and victorious in six of eight Ryder Cup matches, twice serving as captain. Yet sadly, Lloyd Mangrum is practically unknown to modern golf fans.

The decorated war veteran passed away from a heart attack at age fifty-nine in 1973. In 1998, a quarter century after his death, he was inducted into the World Golf Hall of Fame.

42

THE STAR OF STARS AT HOGAN'S ALLEY

JUNE 10–12, 1948
RIVIERA COUNTRY CLUB
PACIFIC PALISADES, CALIFORNIA

The 1948 US Open at the Riviera Country Club in Pacific Palisades, California, featured one of the all-time great courses where one of the all-time great players, Ben Hogan, shined like few others.

The term "Hogan's Alley" has been associated with such golf courses as the Colonial Country Club in Texas, where he won their Invitational five times, and at the Carnoustie Championship Course in Scotland, where he bravely took on the par-5 sixth hole during the 1953 Open Championship, driving the left side of the fairway between the sand bunkers in the fairway and the out-of-bounds markers. But it was the Riviera Country Club that was the first to be dubbed "Hogan's Alley."

Situated in the foothills of the Santa Monica Mountains between Malibu and Beverly Hills, about a few long-irons from the Pacific Ocean, the Riviera Country Club course was designed by George C. Thomas and opened in 1926. It's a gem that tests all aspects of a player's game—and try as they might, even Jack Nicklaus and Tiger Woods, two of the game's best players, were unable to win here.

It was here at the par-71, 7,020-yard course where Hogan won the Los Angeles Open in 1947. It was here on a non-tricked-up course made of great natural hole concepts that Hogan won the 1948 Los Angeles Open. It was here where, after winning the PGA Championship, he returned to become the first player since Gene Sarazen in 1922 to have won both the US Open and the PGA in the same year. And it was here in 1950, just thirteen months after his near-fatal car accident, when medical experts thought he'd never be able to play again, that amazingly he finished runner-up in a playoff to Sam Snead.

Located just off fabled Sunset Boulevard, the Riviera has enjoyed a long history of stars roaming its fairways ever since it opened, like Charlie Chaplin, W. C. Fields, Douglas Fairbanks, Elizabeth Taylor, Clark Gable, Gregory Peck, and Dean Martin, as well as Katharine Hepburn and Spencer Tracy (who both costarred in the 1952 golf film *Pat and Mike,* which was shot on this course). However, none have put on a show at this club quite like Bantam Ben.[1]

And this includes Humphrey Bogart who, when not playing, used to sit for hours under the sycamore tree out at the twelfth hole with a thermos containing his favorite beverage, watching the pros play through. Greta Garbo used to walk the course, sneaking out from her house on a ridge overlooking the thirteenth hole.[2]

No, there'd be no overlooking Hogan at this venue. Unsurprisingly, he arrived in mid-June a pretournament favorite, fresh from adding a Wanamaker Trophy to his collection.

And he started out like a favorite. Playing with the support of a devoted gallery, Hogan grabbed a share of the lead with an opening round of 67 (including a 4-under-par 31 on the outward nine).

Joining him atop the leaderboard was Lew Worsham. A club pro working in Maryland who would also have a long tenure at famed Oakmont Country Club in Pennsylvania, Worsham was the defending champion.

The vet, who served in the Navy during World War II, had battled Sam Snead at the 1947 US Open Championship to win by one stroke in an eighteen-hole playoff. Though Snead sank an eighteen-foot birdie putt on the seventy-second hole to shoot 70 and tie Worsham to force the playoff, it would be the second of four-runner up finishes for the Slammer (see chapter 40).

But Snead, fighting off the winds in the afternoon coming off the Pacific, matched his opening 69 with an identical score. His 138 total set a US Open record and provided him a one-shot lead over both Hogan and future four-time Open champion Bobby Locke of South Africa.

Another record was set when Ted Rhodes became the first Black player to compete in the modern era of the US Open. Growing up in Nashville, he learned the game of golf in his teenage years while working as a caddy in that city. Like Worsham, he also served in the Navy during World War II. Rhodes was the personal golf instructor to heavyweight champion Joe Louis, a single-digit handicapper himself.

Rhodes made the cut, and with a 70-76-77-79 performance, he finished in fifty-first place.

Riviera was the first venue to host a US Open on the West Coast. At the aforementioned 7,020 yards with a par of 71, at the time it was the longest-ever course for a US Open.

It was also still a time when Saturday meant thirty-six holes in determining a champion. And with a solid 68, Hogan regained the lead after the morning round. His fifty-four-hole total of 207 put him at 6 under, two shots ahead of two-time Masters champion Jimmy Demaret, three ahead of future PGA champ Jim Turnesa, and four in front of the great Snead.

The thirty-six-year-old was determined not to let the talented trio behind him get any ideas about overtaking him. Wasting no time, Hogan birdied the first and went out in 33 to start his afternoon round.

However, the colorful fellow Texan, Demaret, playing an hour ahead of Hogan, caught fire midway through final round, even coming close to tying Hogan at one point, but he could not keep the ball rolling. He concluded with a fine 69 but gained no ground as he finished second, still two strokes back of the champion Hogan.

And while Demaret's 278 and Turnesa's 280 totals eclipsed the US Open record by three and one, respectively, it was Hogan who set the new mark. His 67-72-68-69=276 broke the tournament record (previously set by Ralph Guldahl at Oakland Hills Country Club in Birmingham, Michigan, in 1937) by five shots.

History would not be as kind to him again when the US Open came to the West Coast again in 1955, at the Olympic Club in San Francisco (see chapter 44). But Hogan was the first golfer in US Open history to post three rounds in the 60s, and this would be the first of his four national championship titles.

To add some authenticity on the big screen, Riviera would also be a backdrop for a movie made about Ben's life. One of Hollywood's leading men, actor Glenn Ford, would portray the golfer in the 1951 motion picture *Follow the Sun*.

The Riviera will always be known as "Hogan's Alley" and to commemorate that, a statue of Ben Hogan was erected adjacent to the upper putting green by the clubhouse.

43

A MIRACLE AT MERION

JUNE 8–11, 1950
MERION GOLF CLUB
ARDMORE, PENNSYLVANIA

On February 2, 1949, Ben Hogan was the reigning US Open champion. However, Bantam Ben's chances of defending his crown were wiped out that day in a near-fatal car accident.

Ben and his wife, Valerie, were driving back home to Fort Worth, Texas, on a foggy day after he played in the Phoenix Open. A Greyhound bus was speeding in the opposite direction at them while its driver attempted to pass a slow-moving truck. Unable to avoid the head-on collision, Hogan instinctively threw his body across the front seat of the car to protect his wife. The force of the impact with the ten-ton bus drove the steering column of the Hogan car into the rear seat.

While his spouse escaped without serious injury, Hogan was not so lucky. He suffered:

· a shattered left collarbone
· a broken left ankle
· a double ring fracture of the pelvis

· broken ribs
· several deep cuts around his left eye
· severe shock

The news spread rapidly, including erroneous reports that he had died. Unfortunately, blood clots developed in his legs and began to move toward his heart, threatening to take his life. The emergency surgery left him with his largest vein, the vena cava, permanently closed. Hogan would have to endure poor circulation to his legs the rest of his life. His doctors told him that he would have acute difficulty walking, let alone playing eighteen holes.

Then again, the doctors didn't know their patient.

Despite being flat on his back for nearly two months, Hogan never gave up. He used the same determination that made him a great golfer to rehabilitate himself. As soon as he could walk, Hogan pushed himself to increase the distance every day. The golf game came back around slowly but steadily. In June 1950, just sixteen months after the accident, news came that the soon-to-be thirty-eight-year-old would be a part of the 165-player field at Merion.

However, his preparations included a lot more time away from the practice range.

"Hogan would get up in the morning and sit in a bath of Epsom salts for an hour. Have breakfast and then he wrapped both legs from his ankles to his crotch with an ace bandage. Then he had a much bigger one made that went from his belt to practically under his armpits," said John Capers III, chairman of the Merion Archives Committee. He learned this from conversations he'd had with Hogan's lawyer, Francis Sullivan, who was a longtime member of Merion.

Hogan was familiar with the course, having made his US Open debut there. But it was not successful. In 1934, at age twenty-one, the young man rolled a pair of 79s and missed the cut.

Located in Ardmore, not far from Philadelphia, Merion hadn't changed much since the days Bobby Jones dominated play there. As a teenager, he won two matches in the 1916 United States Amateur at Merion. Jones also won the 1924 Amateur and made history winning the US Amateur at Merion in 1930 as part of his Grand Slam season.

By US Open standards Merion was short—just 6,700 yards, but the par-70 layout challenged in other ways, with its wafer-thin fairways, unforgiving rough, small greens, and sprawling clumps of devilish dune grass around its strategic bunkering, which rewarded shotmakers.

On Hogan's first day, he used a collapsible chair between shots to rest his legs. He managed a 2-over 72, but the surprise leader was an unemployed former Army private from Alabama.

Having qualified for the last spot out of Birmingham winning in a playoff, twenty-six-year-old Lee Mackey, casually surveying his shots while puffing on a cigarette, was moving Merion's distinctive wicker-basket flagsticks with a record-tying round of 64, which included seven birdies.

Nearly three weeks of steady rain the month prior had added a good pitching softness to the greens, so the second round saw proven talent rise up the leaderboards. While Mackey would balloon to an 81, fading from the scene, Cary Middlecoff, Lloyd Mangrum, Julius Boros, and Ben Hogan would finish under par. On the strength of birdying four of his first ten holes, Hogan's 69 put him just two back of new leader E. J. "Dutch" Harrison.

An Arkansas native, the one-time farm boy learned the game as a southpaw and had been a pro for twenty years. And while Harrison would ultimately own eighteen career titles, this would not be one of them.

Meanwhile, Saturday's thirty-six-hole closing day would be a stern test for Hogan, given his current physical challenges.

But another former US Open winner, Lloyd Mangrum (see chapter 41), with his straight drives and superb play around the greens, would produce the only score in the 60s among the leaders in the third round. His 69 gave him a fifty-four-hole total of 211 and a one-stroke lead heading into the final round that afternoon.

Cary Middlecoff, the golfing dentist from Memphis and the defending US Open champ, produced his third straight 71 on a third straight boiling day in Pennsylvania for a share of third place. With another 72, Hogan was also just two back at 3 over par. After lunch, the heat and the exhaustion of three rounds of intense play was affecting Hogan as the fourth round unfolded that sweltering afternoon.

Despite battling intense pain that forced him now and then to simply stop in his footsteps, even clutch his legs on the hilly portions of the course, Hogan was holding his own on the scoreboard.

This was the first time Hogan competed in a thirty-six-hole day, grueling under any conditions, since his accident. David Barrett, author of the engaging *Miracle at Merion,* reminds us that on the twelfth hole Hogan almost fell down, and he could barely walk after that. Hogan himself would admit to almost quitting after the thirteenth hole, but his caddy pressed him to go on. Middlecoff later told reporters, "I thought for sure he was going to collapse."

But with Philadelphia native George Fazio and Mangrum the clubhouse leaders at 7-over 287, a determined Hogan fought on. Despite being bone-weary and walking on aching legs, Hogan still had a chance to win the tournament in regulation, but fatigue contributed a lot to missing a short putt at fifteen and then bogeying the par-3 seventeenth. Looking in trouble, the steely little Texan now needed par at Merion's notoriously difficult par-4 eighteenth hole to join Mangrum and Fazio in a playoff.

The eighteenth hole has a quarry running across it and a pin cut on the right side of the green, behind a bunker. After a fine tee shot left him over two hundred yards, he considered trying to cut a four-wood in there, but from a tight lie decided on a one-iron.

Summoning all his focus and dwindling energy, Hogan delivered what would be one of the most famous and clutch shots in golf history. It was brilliantly captured by photographer Hy Peskin, whose strikingly magnificent photo showed the outline of the bunkers and gallery in the distance while framing Hogan at the top of his follow-through.

The result of a perfectly balanced swing, Hogan's ball stopped on the left of the green to the roar of thousands of fans surrounding the final hole. Defying the pain, Hogan got down in two from about forty feet and thus joined the playoff scheduled for the following day.

In his book *I Call the Shots*, Johnny Miller called it "the supreme test of skill, guts and daring, the defining moment of Hogan's career."

To mark the historic shot, there is a plaque embedded in the middle of the eighteenth fairway at Merion Golf Club, about 213 yards from the middle of the green. The inscription on the plaque is simple. It reads:

JUNE 10, 1950

US OPEN

FOURTH ROUND

BEN HOGAN

1-IRON

However, according to the USGA, sometime after that fourth round a thief had stolen not only that instantly historic one-iron from Hogan's bag but also his shoes.

According to Capers, Merion's chief archivist, "Hogan did not have a backup. And I do not know if he put another club in the bag or not."

But how did that one-iron get in the bag to begin with when there was a maximum fourteen-club limit for the national championship?

"There was a fourteen-club rule for the USGA," pointed out Capers. "Because if you have a sand wedge, the one-iron was going to be a fifteenth club, but one which he normally carried. However, in the multiple practice rounds Hogan played with Sullivan, in his mind he determined there was no seven-iron shot at Merion. So Hogan played without a seven-iron for five rounds of the open."

Before we go further, let's take a quick look at the playoff participants.

Hogan's story has been well-chronicled: A high school dropout who turned pro in 1930, he struggled for success his first ten years, going broke several times in the attempt. But his tenacity, determination, and practice regimen helped cure a lingering hook. In 1940 he was the PGA Tour's leading money winner, and he earned the Vardon Trophy on his way to greatness.

Hoping to win in his birthplace of Philadelphia, George Fazio had two career victories and worked as a club pro among other places at the Hillcrest Country Club in Los Angeles where many of Hollywood's celebrities played.

After his playing days were over, Fazio went on to become a well-known golf course architect (Butler National Golf Club in Oakbrook, Illinois; and Turtle Bay Golf Club in Kahuku, Hawaii; among others) working along with his nephews Tom Fazio, Jim Fazio, and course designer Lou Cappelli. But right now he had designs on capturing a major.

In winning the 1946 US Open, Lloyd Mangrum already had a major but the rather expressionless player had, like Hogan, began as a caddy and had struggled for many years to make it as a tour pro.

But Mangrum knew about pressure, real pressure. After fighting in the Battle of the Bulge during World War II, Mangrum was the recipient of not one but two Purple Hearts.

Because of the blue laws in the state of Pennsylvania, the playoffs could not begin until two o'clock on Sunday afternoon. And they had to be finished no later than 7 p.m.

Staring down his own physical limitations as well as his opponents, Hogan played the steadiest of the three to open things. Heading to the back nine, he had a one-stroke lead at even par after thirteen holes. A bogey and double bogey at fourteen and sixteen dropped Fazio out of contention.

Playing steadily despite the pain, Hogan putted consistently and got his sixth straight par on the inward nine to stay in the lead at even par. The gritty Mangrum bounced back from a bogey at fourteen and birdied fifteen to remain one back at 1 over.

On the sixteenth hole, in his opponent's line, Mangrum marked his ball so Fazio could finish out. After Fazio putted out and replaced his ball on the green, but a bug landed on it. Marking his ball a second time, Mangrum picked it up gingerly between two fingers to show that he was not cleaning it and blew the bug off, then holed the putt for what he believed was a par to stay within one.

Mangrum teed it up for the next hole. Then Ike Grainger, the referee for the playoff and an executive committee member of the USGA, pushed his way through the crowd and told Mangrum, "We have a problem. You mismarked your ball a second time. According to USGA rules. And because of that you will be assessed a two-shot penalty."

According to the rules in 1950, the PGA Tour allowed a player to mark his ball at any time while on the green, but in USGA championships, marking a ball on the green in stroke play was only permissible when it was in another player's line.

Completing the miracle comeback, Hogan would seal his second US Open victory and fourth major with a fifty-foot birdie putt at seventeen, winning by four strokes.

As for the stolen one-iron?

According to the USGA, it showed up nearly thirty years later when it came into the hands of a collector who sent it to Hogan. He confirmed it and donated it to the USGA museum. No word about the missing shoes.

If that one-iron shot at the seventy-second hole, as Johnny Miller said, captured the essence of Hogan, one could certainly say his victory in golf's toughest event, just sixteen months after a near-fatal accident, is one of the most inspiring comebacks in sports history.

44

THANKS FOR THE CLUBS

Ben Hogan arrived at the Olympic Club in San Francisco determined to become the first five-time winner of the US Open (Scottish émigré Willie Anderson won in 1901, 1903, 1904, and 1905, as did Bobby Jones in 1923, 1926, 1929, and 1930).

A glance at Bantam Ben's record in this major over the past decade and a half reveals why most sportswriters saw him as one of the clear favorites in the 162-man field on the Lake Course at the Olympic Club:

1940—tied for fifth

1941—tied for third

1942–1945—(no US Open because of World War II)

1946—tied for fourth

1947—tied for sixth

1948—first

1949—injured

1950—first

1951—first

1952—third

1953—first

1954—tied for sixth

Yes, there'd be plenty of talent that included former and future major winners Tommy Bolt, Jack Burke Jr., Julius Boros, Gene Littler, Byron Nelson (who came out of semiretirement to play in his final US Open), and Sam Snead, among others, to offer some spirited competition. But little did the great nine-time major winner know an obscure thirty-two-year-old municipal course golf pro driving out from Davenport, Iowa, would have the ultimate impact on this tournament and the fabled Texan's record-setting quest.

Jack Fleck grew up dirt-poor outside Davenport, Iowa, where his family lost their farm during the Depression. He wore hand-me-down clothes that were held together by patches, and his shoes were stuffed with cardboard to cover the holes in the soles. A poster child for many of that era. He helped his family make ends meet early on by picking apples for pennies, then followed his older brothers by working as a caddy at Davenport Country Club. It generated a spark that would make the game his lifelong passion. To earn a princely sum of forty-five cents a round, the young teen would sometimes sleep overnight in the sand bunkers so he'd be first in line to get a bag.

Fleck never took a lesson, but he used some borrowed clubs, and his self-taught swing grew to become smooth and easy. He would spend hour after hour imagining he was roping his irons with the same nerveless, repeating precision as his idol, Ben Hogan.

After graduating from high school in 1939, he decided to head south to Texas to play golf and escape Iowa's harsh winters. But he was called to duty, serving in the Navy during World War II He was a crewman on a British ship that fired rockets at the Germans during the D-Day invasion of Normandy.

Shortly after the end of the war, Fleck returned to Davenport. Eventually he'd become the pro at a couple of municipal courses, and he began playing on the PGA Tour during the winter months.

Fleck would later say that when he first joined the PGA Tour, he would follow Hogan during his practice rounds, studying his mannerisms and techniques, trying to learn everything and anything he could about how his favorite player meticulously managed a course.

In contrast to his hero, Fleck stood nearly six foot two. He also had trouble controlling his short fuse, sometimes to the point where he would storm off in the middle of a round. He had a family to support, but he also dreamed of competing on the PGA Tour, and he was determined to make it happen. He drove all the way from Iowa to San Francisco with a goal of getting a top ten finish so he wouldn't have to qualify again the following year.

Fleck arrived the Saturday before, and though it took a while to get a lay of the land on this par-70, 6,700-yard course, he played many holes stretching into darkness to get a feel for the comparatively short but demanding layout. Comprised of narrow fairways and smallish greens that were well protected by tight entrances, there was a devilish mix of cypress, cedar, pine, and eucalyptus trees with an often fog-dampened turf that minimized fairway rolls. This created a much longer test than the scorecard indicated. On top of that, in hosting its first major, the club brought in esteemed golf architect Robert Trent Jones to bring it up to championship level. More and bigger traps, which were extended part of the way across the entrance to the green, increased yardage, higher rough, and a narrowing of the fairways made the Olympic course a difficult test, even by USGA standards.

Jones applied his pet "shot-value theory" in upgrading the Lake Course: the more dangerous drive makes for an easier second shot, and the easier drive makes for a more dangerous second shot. If you view the tough par-4 holes on the Lake Course now, you can see this happen on holes two, four through six, nine, eleven, and fourteen.[1]

And the results of the first round reflected that.

More than a few of the 162 players did not break 80 on the first day.

However, what those inflated scores did was make Tommy Bolt's 67 even more impressive. Well-known for a fiery disposition that earned him the nicknames "Thunder" and "Terrible Tommy"—he would break clubs during rounds, and his penchant for throwing clubs led to the adoption of a rule prohibiting such behavior—what wasn't as well known to the sporting public was that Bolt was one of the better players when the courses got tougher. And his competitors knew this. Requiring just twenty-five putts, Bolt was the only player under par and had a three-shot lead.

The mist and cool temperatures didn't help forty-two-year-old Hogan, whose ailing left knee was still plagued by a circulatory ailment from the car accident. Nevertheless at two-over 72 he was in the hunt at fourth place.

The fit, slender Fleck, who didn't smoke, drink, or eat red meat, often wore a somber façade behind some prominent dark eyebrows, became even more of a long shot after an opening 76. But keeping to his routine of practicing yoga (something he started a while back to control his short fuse and was years, no, decades ahead of his time) and relaxing by listening to the Mario Lanza records he had packed along with his record player in his Buick, Fleck found his groove for round two.

Even though Bolt zoomed to a second round of 77, he still maintained a share of the lead. With brilliant iron play, highly talented amateur Harvie Ward rolled a 70 and was 4 over, like Bolt, atop the leaderboard.

One of the favorites, Sam Snead, jumped into the fray with a solid 69, four back of the lead.

Despite putting not being one of his strengths, Fleck's 69 was largely due to a hot Bulls Eye flatstick, and it helped get him just one back of the lead halfway through. He was joined at 5-over with Boros, Hogan, and Augusta's Walker Inman.

The Iowan's other clubs would ultimately produce magical results, but perhaps just as interesting was how he came to own them.

Earlier in the year in Florida, at the St. Petersburg Open, Fleck was mesmerized by a set of irons in the clubhouse. Admiring the quality and design, he saw they were made by the Ben Hogan Golf Company, which was brand-new. He then asked a few other pros if they thought Ben Hogan would make him a set of clubs if he asked, and they basically said, "Don't bother." But after sending in his specs, and much to his surprise, Fleck received the irons in a follow-up visit to the Hogan offices the week of the Colonial National Invitation.

On top of that, the day they both arrived at the Olympic Club for the US Open, Hogan hand-delivered two factory-fresh wedges to Fleck and refused to take a penny for the entire set. While many established pros were scratching their heads as to why the obscure Iowan was shown such favor (the only other similar set used in the 1955 Open was by Hogan himself), years later Fleck himself was never really given an answer and eventually felt it was "that I had grown up poor and worked hard like he had."

The good fortune did not stop there for Fleck. In his autobiography, *The Jack Fleck Story,* the wiry golfer recounted something inexplicable that occurred on that Saturday morning, back when they played the third and fourth rounds in the same day.

"I was shaving, and suddenly a voice came out of the glass, clear as a bell. It said, 'Jack, you are going to win the Open.' At first, I thought I'd imagined it or maybe somebody was in the room with me. I looked around, then went back to shaving. By golly, if it didn't come a second time straight out of the mirror. Clear as day. 'Jack, you are going to win the Open!' I had goose bumps on me, as if electricity was going through my body."

(Or could it have been induced by listening to his favorite singer belting out his favorite tune on the record player: Mario Lanza singing, "I'll Walk with God"?)

In any event, Fleck played with a buoyed competitive spirit and hung tough. The leaderboard at the end of fifty-four holes was a who's who of some of the game's best players:

1	BEN HOGAN	72-73-72=217	+7
T2	JULIUS BOROS	76-69-73=218	+8
	SAM SNEAD	79-69-70=218	
T4	TOMMY BOLT	67-77-75=219	+9
	BOB ROSBURG	78-74-67=219	
T6	JACK FLECK	76-69-75=220	+10
	HARVIE WARD (A)	74-70-76=220	
	JACK BURKE JR.	71-77-72=220	
9	WALKER INMAN	70-75-76=221	+11
10	GENE LITTLER	76-73-73=222	+12

After a brief lunchbreak of soup, sandwich, and iced tea, Fleck headed out with the others for the final round.

One by one, the contenders faded away. By midafternoon it looked as if Hogan had that fifth championship. After he made par on the seventy-second hole, thousands of fans rose and roared their approval across the natural amphitheater. Most observers believed that he had already locked up the championship. After all, his 287 was five strokes better than Sam Snead, who had finished thirty minutes ahead of him and Tommy Bolt, who had finished thirty minutes behind him. They would be tied for second. Former champion Julius Boros finished eight back for a share of fifth.

Hogan acknowledged the crowd, and as he headed to the locker room, he offered the "winning" ball to a USGA official for their museum.

The NBC television network, which that year had the first contracted television coverage of a US Open, featured analysis from legendary player Gene Sarazen, who proclaimed Hogan the champion.

But what about Fleck?

Perhaps because he was unproven, Fleck was forgotten, even though he was just one stroke back at fourteen. Though he did fall two back after bogeying that hole, Fleck was determined to make a run at his hero. To do so, he would have to birdie two of the final four holes, something the vast majority of the field had failed to do all week.

Another secret to Fleck's success, besides yoga and the soothing sounds of Mario Lanza?

It would be the adrenaline rush he said he got from downing handfuls of sugar cubes every four or five holes provided by his longtime friend Dr. Paul Barton, an Iowa dentist Fleck had caddied for as a youth and who had come out to support him.

Freshly fired up with a new round of sugar cubes, Fleck drained an eight-footer for par on fifteen. On the massive 603-yard par-5, he was on in three and would two-putt from twenty-five feet for par. With the temperature suddenly dipping and dampness increasing on the grounds as the sun began to set, Fleck managed to hit a pair of fine wood shots on the difficult par-4, 461-yard seventeenth. He had a birdie try but the down- and sidehill putt lipped out of the hole, so he settled for par. Now it came down to needing a birdie on the seventy-second hole to force a playoff with his hero.

Teeing off on the 337-yard eighteenth using a three-wood, Fleck found himself about six inches in the first cut off the fairway. Not a terrible lie, and with the distance about 125 yards, Fleck flicked a three-quarter seven-iron on a low line and just cleared the bunker protecting the green out front. The ball finished about eight feet right of the cup.

Hogan had showered and put on a coat and tie. Thinking he had his much-coveted fifth title, he was telling writers and others gathered in the locker room that he would probably not compete on a regular basis anymore due to the mental cost and physical strain it took out on his hampered body. (He was also interested in building his golf club company.)

Then came a roar similar to what Hogan had enjoyed just a while earlier at the eighteenth green.

Wasting no time, Fleck calmly popped in the downhill right-to-left putt to force an eighteen-hole playoff with the superstar the following day. Hogan's 70 was the best score of the final round until Fleck walked off the seventy-second green shooting a 3-under 67, tying the lowest score of the tournament.

"A reporter whispered hoarsely: "The kid's sunk it!" Ben Hogan's head went down and he cursed softly. Then he lifted his head and looked around at them all. "I was wishing he'd either make a two or a five," he said. "I was wishing it was over, all over." He turned to an attendant, pointed to his clubs, and sighed. "Well, we might as well git those things back in the locker. Gotta play tomorrow, looks like."[2]

Despite being inundated with telegrams from Iowans admonishing him for prematurely calling Hogan the winner, Sarazen essentially shrugged the criticism off and said he wasn't wrong, just early, and that Hogan would get that fifth national title on Sunday.

Well, it would be Goliath who blinked first in the playoff. They matched pars until the par 4 fifth, when Hogan fell one back with a bogey. Even when he got it back with a tremendous fifty-foot birdie on eight, Fleck matched it with a two of his own. It was the first of three straight birdies for the underdog.

On the tenth, a par-4, 422-yard hole with a slight downslope and dogleg to the right, both made the fairway and each had birdie tries.

Hogan missed, but the seemingly carefree Fleck did a toe dance as his ball rimmed the cup and fell in. The twenty-footer put him up by three strokes at 3 under.

The combatants exchanged bogeys on eleven and twelve, but Hogan birdied the fourteenth to gain one stroke.

The seventeenth hole, a par-4 at 467 yards (a par-5 that had been converted to a par-4 for this championship) saw Hogan smash his longest drive of the day down the right center of the fairway. Then he followed that with a great three-wood to the edge of the very long fringe cut of the green. Meanwhile, Fleck found himself in the rough, short of the green. He then wedged it up still below the cup. However, Hogan, putting from the fringe at about twenty-five feet, sunk his par, and the crowd roared. After missing his short par effort, Fleckbogeyed.

Out of sugar cubes and trying to stay composed despite the thick, largely pro-Hogan crowds all around, Fleck arrived at the final hole with just a one-stroke lead against the four-time national champ. How would you feel at this stage?

In another bit of irony, down one, Hogan now aimed to tie Fleck on the eighteenth hole like Fleck tied Hogan on the eighteenth hole the day before. The short 334-yard, par-4 eighteenth required a very accurate tee shot for good position, as the fairway narrowed and the rough was long, wet, and heavy beyond the first fringe cut.

While he would later admit his foot slipped, Hogan pulled his tee shot left and it ended up thirty feet off the fairway in the exceptionally high rough about a foot high. Fleck followed with a three-wood straight down the fairway.

Essentially the tournament would be decided here. Hogan needed three strokes—one to uncover the ball he could only barely see, another to nudge it all of three feet, and finally a third to punch it laterally to the fairway. From there, he got up and down for a double-bogey 6. Fleck two-putted from twenty feet for par for a fairy-tale three-stroke victory.

The new champion acknowledged the tremendous ovation from the thousands of spectators storming the green and was graciously congratulated by Hogan.

Facing down the mighty Hogan, considered a sheer winner in pretty much any man-to-man duel, especially when the battleground was the US Open, it was a sweet victory—literally—for Fleck.

And in a tournament seemingly filled with a bucketful of irony, in his only two previous US Open appearances, the gangly, Lincolnesque Iowan missed the cut at Merion in 1950 and tied for fifty-third at Oakmont in 1953. Who was victorious on both those occasions? Ben Hogan.

After his defeat, Hogan, choked and almost in tears, told the crowd gathered at the presentation ceremonies about a decision he had come to based on the physical and mental price he paid and the emotional toll these efforts took on his wife, Valerie.

"I came here with the idea of trying to win. I worked harder, I think, than ever before in my life. It's too hard to train for a big tournament. I want to become a weekend golfer. When I play, it'll be for fun."

By beating the world's greatest golfers collectively, and the generally accepted top golfer individually, Fleck's victory evoked memories of the 1913 US Open when Francis Ouimet, a twenty-year-old American amateur, defeated the British stars Ted Ray and Harry Vardon in a playoff (see chapter 38).

It was the first US Open at the Olympic Club, but it would share something with several others when this venue hosted the national championship in the future. Interestingly, this would be the locale where the fan favorite somehow lost out to the less heralded challenger:

1966—Billy Casper rallied to beat Arnold Palmer

1987—Scott Simpson outlasted Tom Watson

1998—Lee Janzen edged Payne Stewart

In his autobiography, Fleck tells the story of how he was sought out by one of America's biggest golf enthusiasts before he left San Francisco.

At the request of President Dwight Eisenhower, who was in town for a United Nations meeting and wanted to meet the new US Open champion, the Secret Service found Fleck after searching the city for two days. He was sharing a room with Dr. Barton and had not registered in the hotel in his name.

They would have a brief conversation. A couple of weeks later, Fleck flew out to Washington, DC, and was part of a meeting at the White House for the President's Physical Fitness Council. (Presumably Fleck didn't push the nutritional value of the sugar-cube angle.)

Fleck won two more titles and finished his career with five second-place finishes, six thirds, and a total forty-one top ten finishes in 271 events, according to the PGA. The closest he ever came to winning another major on the PGA Tour (he would win the 1979 PGA Seniors Championship one year before the Senior PGA Tour was formed) came at the 1960 US Open at Cherry Hills in Colorado. After a gallant run, he'd finish with a share of third place behind Jack Nicklaus and winner Arnold Palmer.

In pulling off one of the most astounding upsets, the unheralded muni pro from Iowa reinvigorated the meaning of the term *open championship*. And to think, he did it with clubs from his idol.

Years later Hogan would quip, "Yes, Jack beat me with my own clubs."

"It was just unbelievable, the kindness he continued to show me. In a sense it is a shame that I used those very clubs to defeat him," Fleck would later say of this uncharacteristically kind gesture from Hogan.

45

THE CHARGE AT CHERRY HILLS

JUNE 16–18, 1960
CHERRY HILLS COUNTRY CLUB
CHERRY HILLS VILLAGE, COLORADO

It is very rare that you get three generations of great players coming down to the final few holes when competing for the title in the same major.

However, that would be the case here at Cherry Hills when my good friends Arnie and Jack, along with Ben Hogan, the player I grew up wanting to emulate, would emerge from a deep field to battle for the national championship.

Arnold Palmer arrived at the base of the Rocky Mountains here at Cherry Hills located in the suburbs of Denver, Colorado, with his game in top form. Not only had he won a second Masters title in April, but he had collected four other victories earlier in the season.

The dynamic thirty-year-old from western Pennsylvania, with the go-for-broke style that made the game seem more dramatic, helped bring the sport to the masses. His unmatched flair and charisma delighted his massive following, not just the spectators on whatever course he played (his huge galleries were labeled Arnie's

Army), but also the millions of viewers new to the sport watching on television.

The plainspoken son of a greenskeeper at a working-class steel mill town had become influential in changing the perception of golf from an elite, clubby pastime to a sport for one and all.

Another gentleman from humble beginnings, this one representing an earlier generation, was forty-seven-year-old Ben Hogan. A four-time US Open winner who had won three consecutive majors titles (see chapter 64) seven years earlier, was now a part-time player, full-time clubmaker, but with an endless passion for the national championship.

The third player in this drama was a twenty-year-old from Columbus, Ohio.

Though he was a good all-round athlete in his youth, Nicklaus showed a particular flair for golf. With strong encouragement from his father and help from teaching pro Jack Grout, the young sensation was making his mark in the sport by collecting numerous state and regional junior titles before winning the 1959 US Amateur.

At the 1958 US Open at Southern Hills in Tulsa, Oklahoma, where I made my national championship debut and came in second place, this stout eighteen-year-old was very impressive. Though he finished back in forty-first, I could see that Jack Nicklaus was on his way to great things.

However, while the 1960 US Open would ultimately reflect a convergence of three different eras vying for the title, early on Cherry Hills was owned by a tough former football player at Duke University.

Powerfully built Mike Souchak was already an eleven-time winner on tour. And the thirty-three-year-old had been leading here wire to wire for three rounds.

The par-71, 7,004-yard course was situated over 5,300 feet above sea level. With its small greens, well guarded by bunkers and water hazards (1958 US Open champion Tommy Bolt infamously threw his club in the lake at eighteen after a poor shot), Souchak's power and finesse matched anyone out there.

This guy was stronger than anyone on the tour. My goodness, was he strong. And he had a wonderful personality. Mike was the first player to buy me dinner when I was starting out. It was in Wilmington, Delaware. He took me to dinner in his brand-new Cadillac. Mike also traveled to Australia with me. We used to listen to the Everly Brothers song "Wake Up Little Susie" and the Platters' "Only You."

And even though his thirty-six-hole score of 68-67=135 set a new open record, Souchak would not be singing a happy tune come the fourth round. He struggled on the final hole of the third round; during his backswing a camera clicked loudly, and Souchak's drive soared out of bounds, and he took a double-bogey 6 for a 73. The big fellow would never regain his momentum. He'd close with a 75 and a share of third place.

Meanwhile both Nicklaus and Hogan rolled 69s to move to within three shots of Souchak. Heading into the final round it was a crowded leaderboard. Plenty of accomplished players would make a run, including Julius Boros, Jerry Barber, Dow Finsterwald, and Jack Fleck, all of whom were (or would be) major title holders.

I was even par to begin the final round, but I rolled a 76 and finished well back with a share of nineteenth place.

Palmer started the final day seven back and, with all the talent ahead of him, looked to be out of it.

It was an era when the final two rounds were played on Saturday. So, after the third round where he shot a 1-over 72, Palmer was sharing a lunch of cheeseburgers and ice tea on this sweltering day with two writers/friends, Bob Drum of the *Pittsburgh Press* and Dan Jenkins of *Sports Illustrated,* and he was thinking about what it would take to overcome everyone and win.

"If I drive the green and get a birdie or an eagle [first hole], I might shoot a 65. What'll that do?" Palmer asked.

"Nothing," said Drum. "You're too far back."

"It would give me 280," Palmer said. "Doesn't 280 always win the Open?"

"Yeah," laughed Drum. "When Hogan shoots it."

Displeased at the comment, Palmer walked out the door to the first tee with more determination than ever.

The first hole at Cherry Hills was a 346-yard par-4. It had not treated him well; as a matter of fact, he opened play with a double bogey after a wayward drive. But in keeping with his well-developed go-for-broke philosophy, looking for a way to build momentum and set a tone for surging past the fourteen players in front of him on the leaderboard, the bold and daring Palmer really let his shirt out with a mighty bang off the tee.

He drove the green then two-putted for birdie (there is a plaque beside the first tee at Cherry Hills, commemorating Palmer's drive to the heart of the green). At the second, he made a thirty-five-footer from the fringe for another. At the third, a brilliant approach shot led to yet another birdie. He would make it four straight by dropping an eighteen-footer. After a par at the par-5 fifth, Palmer produced back-to-back birdies at six and seven.

Six birdies in seven holes for 30 on the front nine.

A couple days before the championship began, Nicklaus's dad discovered that the odds on him winning were 35 to 1. Feeling good about his game, the young man asked his father to "quietly" put down $20, as he was getting married and could use $700.

Things were looking good for the wedding bonus as Nicklaus, who was paired with Hogan, scored an eagle and a birdie to finish the outward nine in 32 and a share of the lead. However, back-to-back bogeys at thirteen and fourteen dropped him out of the top spot.

At the same time, his wily playing partner was putting himself into contention for a fifth Open title. Though the aging wonder was still highly accurate to fairways and greens, at this stage of his career he was having trouble with his putter, but Hogan managed to sink a twenty-footer at fifteen. At 4 under par for the championship, he was tied with Palmer and Jack Fleck and a stroke ahead of Nicklaus. Having put on a ball-striking clinic all day Saturday by hitting thirty-four consecutive greens in regulation, the tough little Texan amazingly was right in the thick of things.

After a solid tee shot at the par-5, 548-yard hole, standing in the seventeenth fairway, Hogan had one more shot at glory. He faced an island green guarded by a twelve-foot stream, while Nicklaus played it safe to about twenty-two feet from the cup. Knowing his own recent putting shortcomings, Hogan wanted to get it closer. What he got was a disappointing result that would linger on his mind the rest of his life.

Gambling with the water hazard, using a pitching wedge and laying back the face, Hogan struck it likely just one groove higher than he wanted. Despite his making a very good shot under such enormous pressure, after the soft landing the ball trickled back into the water, missing the mark by just inches. As Boros and I watched from the fairway, Hogan then removed his shoe and sock so he could stand with his right foot in the stream and play his fourth shot. After splashing a fine effort out of the water, his par-save attempt went wide. The bogey dropped him one back.

Hogan's error combined with Fleck's bogey put Palmer in the outright lead.

With nothing to lose, Hogan stood at the tee of the 468-yard uphill par-4 final hole and let it all out—and hooked the drive into the lake. Instead of a birdie to tie, he ended up with a triple-bogey 7 that dropped him into a share of ninth, four strokes back.

Years later Hogan would say that the fateful shot at seventeen still haunted him. "There is not a day that passes that doesn't cut my guts."

Showing a lot of guts for a nonpro competing with the sport's very best, Nicklaus, with his third 71, finished in second place. It was the best showing by an amateur at a US Open in more than a quarter century.

Hogan was impressed by his young playing partner. Famously he told the press, "I lost another golf tournament, but I'll tell you something. I played 36 holes today with a kid—this Jack Nicklaus—who could have won this Open by 10 shots if he'd known what he was doing."[1]

Palmer knew what he was doing.

Playing conservatively (for him) on the back nine, after a birdie at eleven he consistently scored pars. With a score of 65, Palmer had shot the lowest final round for a winner in US Open history.

It was a very popular victory.

With this victory, Palmer had become the first player since Hogan in 1953 to win the Masters and the US Open in the same year. He'd finish second in the Open Championship and seven in the PGA later that year.

This was Palmer's only victory at the US Open. He would finish second four times, including three playoff losses in 1962, 1963, and 1966 (see chapter 49). But in a charge-filled career, the 1960 US Open charge was perhaps Arnie's most famous.

And of this seminal tournament, widely considered to be one of the best in history, one could say Palmer claimed the throne that Hogan had occupied for so long. But the new king had only to look over his shoulder to see a highly talented hungry phenom (and ten years younger, to boot) who would soon vie for that coveted crown.

Still, on this hot July day in the Rockies, a new era in professional golf had begun. And the sport was now led by perhaps the most popular king to date. A beloved monarch, one with a daring, swashbuckling way of taking command of a tournament, one whose signature go-for-broke style would make him a folk hero to millions.

It was the beginning of golf's golden era.

46

NICKLAUS NOTCHES MAJOR
VICTORY #1

JUNE 14–17, 1962
OAKMONT COUNTRY CLUB
OAKMONT, PENNSYLVANIA

E ven though we would become known around the world as the Big Three, despite being great friends (or, better yet, because we were like brothers), Arnie, Jack, and myself loved nothing more than trying to beat each other's brains out on the course. And the bigger the stakes (any major), the more intense the competition became.

And the 1962 US Open was a classic example of our uber-competitiveness in action.

In 1962, Palmer was at the peak of his popularity and playing abilities. Not only had he won four majors, he was fresh from winning his third green jacket (and five other tournaments that season). And now he was returning home to play a US Open on a course he knew better than anyone, having played it dozens of times.

The thirty-one-year-old son of a groundskeeper, who grew up in Latrobe, Pennsylvania, was being presented with a tailor-made homecoming opportunity that aimed to be a coronation of golf's new king. The Oakmont course was just over thirty miles from his hometown, so not only would he be staying in a familiar bed with home-cooked meals every night, but every day he'd be followed by thousands of fans who marched in from nearby Pittsburgh to cheer him on from hole to hole, round by round.

Even though it was a terrible loss for me (see chapter 6), losing out to Arnie as part of a playoff in that Masters in April served to drive me to best him here and win my first US Open championship.

Nicklaus, too, was plenty motivated to win his first US Open championship.

He had enjoyed the best amateur career since Bobby Jones. In his last three years as an amateur, the burly twenty-two-year-old Nicklaus twice won the USGA Amateur Championship (in 1959 and 1961), took both the National Intercollegiate and Western Amateur titles the previous, year, and led United States teams to victory in the most recent Walker Cup and World Amateur competitions. Showcasing his rare combination of smartly controlled strength and finesse, he nearly took the 1960 US Open, falling two strokes short of Palmer at Cherry Hills Country Club (see chapter 45).

However, since turning pro six months earlier, the personable PGA Tour rookie was winless, and it was eating at him.

Taking on the old, storied par-71, 6,894-yard course with its famously furrowed bunkers and undulating lightning-fast greens, Arnie and I opened with 71s and a share of fourth place. Jack was a stroke back at 1-over 72.

While the record opening round gallery of nearly 17,500 mostly followed the pairing of Jack and Arnie, it was defending champion Gene Littler who took the lead with a 69.

A former NCAA champion out of the University of Houston, Phil Rodgers, built like a shorter Nicklaus, had already won twice earlier in the year. He had a fine round going and was among the leaders when he came to the seventeenth.

Back in 1953, Ben Hogan drove the green on this short 292-yard, par-4 hole on his way to victory, but since then a small group of

spruce trees had been planted at the elbow of the dogleg to discour-
age the strongest hitters from doing that again from the tee. Never
one lacking in self-confidence, Rodgers, a chunky former marine,
tried the shortcut nevertheless. His tee shot was now actually lodged
in one of those trees. But rather than take an unplayable lie penalty of
two strokes, Rodgers decided to hit his ball out of the tree. Whacking
at the ball at chest-high level, he'd walk away from the green a few
swats later with a quadruple-bogey 8. To his credit, Rodgers battled
on and went on to finish the tournament in a tie for third place, only
two shots back.

With even more of his army present in the second round (nearly
twenty thousand spectators), Palmer did not disappoint his fans
and zoomed to the top to share first place with Bob Rosburg, both
with 68.

Looking like the King, with superb driving and tossing the ball off
his irons onto the greens with ease, Palmer scored the lowest round
of the day. He would later call it one of the best performances of his
career. His 3-under 139 halfway total put him three strokes ahead
of Jack and myself. We shared fourth place with future PGA major
winner Bobby Nichols.

On Palmer's second straight day paired with Nicklaus, fans standing five or six rows deep popped up their periscopes in order to see the
King in action. But there was an ugly side to all this. Many of the fans
from Steeltown had not been to many golf tournaments, and they had
more of a football-game mentality. To them, Nicklaus was more than
an opponent—he was the enemy who was threatening their king.

I remember fans barking out "Fat Jack," and a sign that said, "Hit
it here Ohio Fats." I remember when Nicklaus would hit a shot that
nestled just a few feet from the flag and there'd a quite smattering of
polite clapping, but when Palmer would follow and finish thirty-five
feet well back from the cup, the gallery would go crazy. They'd stomp
their feet and actually cheered when Jack made bogey.

It was a trying time for Jack, but he handled it amazingly well.

"It seemed like the whole population of not only Latrobe and Pittsburgh, the entire state of Pennsylvania turned out to root for him to win a second US Open," wrote Nicklaus years later in his book, *My Story*.

"I learned later that many in the crowd rooted loudly against me, but nobody talked to me about that at the time and it did not penetrate my intense concentration during play. So far as I was concerned, the noise was just that—noise."[1]

On Saturday, in an era when the closing thirty-six holes were played in the same day, Palmer managed to stay atop the leaderboard despite a 73, which he attributed to "putting with a wet noodle" despite hitting sixteen greens. His putting would be a significant factor in the outcome of this tournament.

In that morning round, Jack and I finished right on his tail. At 1-over 214, we were just two shots back heading into the final round. We lived for these situations!

However, despite multiple lead changes, with Rosburg, Rodgers, Nichols, and myself unable to make a strong enough move, Palmer still led Nicklaus as they made the turn.

With a birdie at eleven while his opponent bogeyed thirteen, Nicklaus was now tied for the lead. Each produced four straight pars. Now, if either could birdie the seventy-second hole, they'd win the national title.

Going first, Nicklaus's birdie try from twelve feet slid just past the left side of the cup. Now with a great chance to win at home, Palmer gave it a go. However, he missed from ten feet, thus forcing an eighteen-hole playoff the following day.

Palmer was exhausted from the heat and grind of competing against the game's top rising young star. Looking at Nicklaus, the King said with a weary smile, "I wish it were someone else. That big, strong dude. I thought I was through with him yesterday."

Though the clearly pro-Palmer crowd continued to taunt the twenty-two-year-old bulky upstart in the playoff, Nicklaus silenced them the best way he could, speaking through his clubs. After six holes he had built a four-stroke lead. Still, Arnie's Army remained devoted as they felt the charge was coming and that he'd emerge victorious.

Sure enough, with birdies at nine, eleven, and twelve, Palmer closed to within one. However, a three-putt bogey at thirteen (his third of the playoff and tenth of the tournament) proved to be costly for Palmer. Nicklaus was too strong and held him off, winning by three strokes, 71 to 74.

Afterward, Palmer mentioned to the media, "Now that the big guy is out of the cage, everybody better run for cover."

A US Open. Not bad for a professional's first tour victory.

That was a great battle (I finished in a tie for sixth). Then the world suddenly realized Nicklaus was the best young player in the world. I felt sorry for Palmer because it was basically in his hometown. And that always rubs salt into the wound.

As the Big Three, we have shared so many interesting times traveling around the world. China, Japan, Arnold, Jack, and me. And being competitive whenever we stepped onto a golf course no matter where it was around the globe. I remember battling it out to see who could win the most Australian Opens. I beat Jack by one, and I still have the Australian Open record today of 264. Shot a pair of 62s, and the record from 1965 still stands.

I remember when they came to visit me in South Africa. Arnold couldn't land his plane. With elephants, lions, and buffalo on the airstrip he couldn't land, so we had to get the game ranger to chase them off the landing strip.

We had great times together traveling the world and promoting golf because we loved the sport. Doing lots of exhibitions and raising millions for charity.

There will never be another Big Three like Arnold, Jack, and me. Yes, maybe there will be playing-wise. But not as brothers, living together in one another's homes. Riding horses on my ranches and going down into gold mines together, but still wanting to beat each other fiercely wherever we played around the world. It was quite an experience. In these days there's too much money. There's no way they can travel and live with each other like we did. It's a different world. A time that has gone. As they say, "Everything shall pass." It was a special time in golf history.

47

STAVING OFF VENTURI'S VULTURES

JUNE 18–20, 1964
CONGRESSIONAL COUNTRY CLUB
BETHESDA, MARYLAND

Where had it all gone? Three years removed from anything resembling glory and ready to call it quits and go sell cars for a living, golfer Ken Venturi was broken physically, mentally, and financially at age thirty-three in the summer of 1964. The buzzards were circling what appeared to be the end of a notable golf career.

After developing his game at San Francisco's popular public track, the Harding Park Golf Course, Venturi was city champion at just eighteen. And through his friendship with a prominent San Francisco auto dealer named Eddie Lowery (better known as the pipsqueak who carried the bag of Francis Ouimet in the 1913 US Open—see chapter 38), he came under the watchful eye of Byron Nelson, who helped the ambitious young man produce a repeating, graceful swing that would shape him into one of the best long-iron players in the game. He was also impacted by friend Ben Hogan in that he became quite a calculating student of the game, bringing a very analytical approach to each hole, each shot. (He also took to wearing a newsboy cap.)

Venturi won the California State Amateur at Pebble Beach in 1951 and 1956, and served in the Army in Korea and Europe between those two amateur titles. Nineteen fifty-six was also the year that the rest of the nation became aware of his talents.

Amazingly, golf's next Can't Miss Kid was looking to not only become the first amateur to win the Masters, but he was on course to do it in wire-to-wire fashion. However, the final round was played in very windy, tough conditions. Only two golfers broke par that day, and the amateur from San Francisco was not one of them. As a matter of fact, he closed with a soaring 80 to lose by a stroke to Jackie Burke Jr.

Disappointed but undaunted, Venturi soon turned pro. From 1957, his rookie year on tour, through 1960, Venturi won ten events, including back-to-back events in his first season as well as the LA Open and the Bing-Crosby Pro-Am. In his first five years on tour his money rankings were tenth, third, tenth, second, and fourteenth.

And in 1960 Venturi found himself with yet another chance to win the Masters.

However, Arnold Palmer, needing a birdie-birdie finish on the final two holes to secure the one-stroke victory over Venturi, came through and won a wire-to-wire victory.

The downfall began by accident in 1961—an auto accident, to be precise. Injuries to Venturi's wrist and back took their toll. The physical injuries (including pneumonia and a pinched nerve) affected his once-soaring confidence. The mental anguish and emotional strain was all part of a three-year slide. Unable to produce enough results to even pay caddy fees and hotel bills (he won less than $7,000 in twenty-seven starts in 1962 and collected less than $4,000 in 1963), by the spring of 1964, Venturi, a married man with two sons, was looking for work.

His game had plummeted to the point where he missed the US Open three straight years (despite a pair of top ten finishes in his first two appearances). Deciding to give it one more try, pulling down on his trademark white linen cap, Venturi dug deep and found just enough string-straight iron shots to barely qualify for the 1964 US Open at Congressional.

Little did he know that at Bethesda he would have to dig deeper than he ever could have imagined if he wanted to make his comeback complete. The buzzards had not flown away yet. The Congressional Country Club in Bethesda Maryland, not far from Washington, DC, at 7,053 yards (par 70) would be the longest course in US Open history.

The club was incorporated in 1921. Life memberships were snapped up by important people throughout the nation: the John D. Rockefellers, senior and junior; Vincent Astor, John Hays Hammond, Pierre S. and Alfred I. DuPont, Harvey S. Firestone, Bernard Baruch, and William Randolph Hearst, to name a few. In 1941 the club was leased by the government as a site for training espionage agents during World War II.[1]

As for the course, on the front nine, the most talked about holes would be the sixth and ninth.

The 456-yard sixth is the toughest par-4 on the course. On the right, there is out of bounds and a ditch. At the 270-yard mark there is a crest with a pair of fairway traps on the right side. The approach shot must fly over a pond and land softly on the green.

The 599-yard, par-5 ninth presents a major challenge to get on to the terraced green in two. There's a massive gully in front of the green area with woods on each side. And that valley, thick with rough, protects the front of the green. As for the green itself, it has two traps on the right side, one on the left, and one in the back terrace running from left to right.

The finishing hole at eighteen, a 465-yard, par-4 demands an accurate tee shot as a lake provides water hazards on three sides of the green which also has three bunkers.

With the help of having the club's top-rated caddy (William Ward) who literally took a measuring stick to the course beforehand, Venturi made a thirty-five-foot birdie at four and a par-saving pitch at eighteen after being up against the lake. He finished with a respectable 72. However, the first-round leader was the one who had provided Venturi some heartbreak at a previous major.

Arnold Palmer, with a 68, was the only player to shoot under par. And with a pair of back-to-back runner-up finishes in the previous two US Opens, the King was determined to wear this major crown again as he did at Cherry Hills in 1960.

Palmer followed that with a fine 69, but even so, he lost the lead when Tommy Jacobs came out of nowhere to roll a 64 for a 4-under 136. Jacobs, a former US Amateur champion, stroked three birdies in a row starting at thirteen, then finished off with a whopping sixty-foot putt at eighteen. His 64 equaled the all-time US Open record for a single round made by Lee Mackey Jr. at Merion in 1950.

Venturi completed round two with a 70 and was six back at 4 over and a share of fourth place. Defending champion Julius Boros and Deane Beman, a member of Congressional, were among those that missed the cut.

Largely due to slow play and insurance against weather delays that prevented rounds from being completed on the same day, the USGA would make a format change. Nineteen sixty-four would see the end of thirty-six-hole play on Saturday. Beginning the next year, the third round of eighteen on Saturday would be followed by a Sunday fourth round of eighteen.

Heavy rain late the second night softened the greens—as Mother Nature giveth so she takes away—and it literally turned up the heat (and humidity) for the last two rounds. With temperature readings rising in some areas to 108 degrees and near three-digit humidity, while the American Red Cross were answering calls to spectators with heat prostration, the players carried on.

Despite being the only player in the field with two subpar scores, Palmer, who had just won his fourth green jacket in April, wasn't feeling the heat with his putter (he three-putted four times). His 75 placed him six strokes back of Jacobs, whose 70 gave him the fifty-four-hole lead at 4-under 206.

Venturi enjoyed a great start to round three and was 3 under through five. Starting six strokes behind Jacobs, Venturi made it all up with a 30 going out. So impressive was his play that it did not go unnoticed by a rather prominent sports figure who was observing him as a member of the gallery.

In his book, *Getting Up & Down: My 60 Years in Golf,* Venturi tells this story.

Vince Lombardi, the legendary coach of the Green Bay Packers, told a friend that he was convinced I would be the champion.

"How can you tell?" the friend asked.

"Just take a look at him," Lombardi said. "His eyes are dead. They are the coldest I've ever seen. He beats them going away."

Over the years, a few of his players told me that Lombardi often brought my name up during his halftime speeches to motivate them. "You look into that guy across from you on the line," he would say, "and his eyes better know that your eyes own him. The greatest eyes I ever saw in my life were Ken Venturi's when he stared at that ball. I feel he made the ball move." Last time I saw Lombardi, about four years later, he was still talking about it. "I'll never forget that look on your face," he said.[2]

Well, twenty-one-year-old Raymond Floyd would never forget the face of his playing partner. Venturi's beautiful performance was quickly disintegrating as he struggled mightily to get through the morning round.

He scrambled for pars on fifteen and sixteen. While sizing up a short par at seventeen, Venturi, his face ashen and his eyes glazed, was shaking in his shoes with weakness. He looked to be, as Floyd would say, "on the verge of fainting." Looking disoriented, he gave away two shots in the last two holes. Still, he finished the round with a brilliant 66.

So, in addition to trying to negotiate narrow fairways, deep rough, fast greens, and the fragile emotions of a US Open, the stifling, suffocating, steaming cauldron conditions kept the buzzards around. Growing up in San Francisco, Venturi was more accustomed to fog, mist, wind, and rain, so he was quickly being undone by the deadly duo of heat and humidity.

During the lunch break between rounds, Venturi ate nothing and was lying on the ground in the locker room. Worried USGA officials looking on with deep concerns on their faces, as Venturi reread a handwritten inspirational letter from a friend of his, a golf-savvy parish priest in San Francisco, the Rev. Frank Murray. Dr. John Everett a Congressional club member and the Open's chairman of the medical committee, arrived, tended to him, then warned that "going back out there could be fatal."

"I'm already dying," Venturi responded, alluding to not only his health but also to his flailing career. "I have no place else to go."

Though he was two back of leader Jacobs but four ahead of a fading Palmer, Venturi's determination was fed by a burning desire to complete an incredible comeback, one in which he was so close to giving up the PGA for good.

So, literally coming off the floor, Venturi managed to drag himself to the first tee for the final eighteen. He would basically play in a trance, relying on instinct and experience while shuffling down the fairways, which he seemed to hit with astonishing regularity. He was helped by Dr. Everett, who joined him in the fourth round and, walking just inside the gallery ropes, applied cold towels and ice cubes between holes and made sure Venturi consumed salt tablets from time to time.

After Jacobs double-bogeyed the second hole, Venturi was tied for the lead. With a birdie at nine while his opponent bogeyed the same hole, Venturi now had a two-shot lead heading to the back nine.

Venturi was aided by the fact that Jacobs faltered with three straight bogeys beginning at thirteen. And that was where Palmer had a pair of back-to-back bogeys and then two more back-to-back at sixteen and seventeen. Unbelievably, going on feel and muscle memory, with six pars, a birdie, and a bogey, Venturi lurched to the seventy-second hole with a four-shot lead. On a day when he'd lose nearly eight pounds, the only thing stopping him now was himself.

After hitting his drive at eighteen, Venturi turned back, leaned over to an old friend, and asked how he stood. His longtime pal replied, "Just stay on your feet. We've got this."

After his ten-foot stroke fell into the hole, Venturi dropped his putter, removed his cap, let the tears flow, and uttered: "My God, I've won the Open."

Witnessing the performance firsthand was a future four-time majors winner. Ray Floyd called it one of the gutsiest performances ever.

"I didn't believe in destiny until Ken Venturi won the 1964 US Open," said Floyd, looking back many years later. "I was paired with him for the final 36 holes, and how he finished, I'll never know. It was the hottest day I've ever seen. Even people sitting down in the gallery were passing out. By the end of the morning round, Ken was in bad shape. In the afternoon, toward the end, he didn't know where he was. Part of the miracle was how he kept hitting the ball flush and pretty long, too. When he holed the final putt and I picked the ball out of the hole for him—he was too dazed and exhausted to do it—I had tears in my eyes. Some things are just meant to be."[3]

Having hydrated and feeling well enough to take on the media, Venturi entered, and surveyed the writers gathered at the press conference, and said: "The last time I saw any of you guys was when you were interviewing me at the 1960 Masters and someone yelled 'Palmer!' and you all ran out of the room and left me there sipping my Coke."

Then in a moment of reflection about his tailspin and ultimate redemption he stated: "If I had to do everything all over again and write a script or a book about it, I wouldn't change one thing that happened to me in my life. Nine months ago I was about to quit, and I didn't know what was going to happen. I've tasted the bitterness of defeat, and now I'm going to taste the sweetness of success."

Amazing, considering his condition, Venturi's last two rounds (66-70) tied the Championship record total of 136. On top of that, he was the only player in the field to finish under par.

Venturi went on to win twice more in '64. Later that year he won the PGA Player of the Year Award and was named *Sports Illustrated*'s "Sportsman of the Year," a tremendous achievement considering that it was an Olympic year.

"I'll tell you one thing," Venturi reminded the press, "Arnie may have his Army, but those cats out there with me today were solid supporters. I even had some of Arnie's outcasts. I used to have Venturi's Vultures!"

His vindication complete, Venturi's Vultures flew away with nothing.

48

MY PINNACLE: ACHIEVING THE
RARE CAREER GRAND SLAM

JUNE 17–21, 1965
BELLERIVE COUNTRY CLUB
ST. LOUIS, MISSOURI

Together, the Big Three would win thirty-four majors. In 1965 each of us had won three of the four majors. For Jack, the Open Championship was proving the elusive one. For Arnold it was the PGA. For me it was the US Open.

And, quite frankly, the record shows the United States national championship was dominated by Americans after some victories early on by Scottish and English players.

So, to have the opportunity to complete the career grand slam before Nicklaus and Palmer was a great challenge. We loved each other like brothers, but at the same time we were very competitive.

I never prepared for a tournament more diligently than for that US Open. I did something at Bellerive that I did not do at many tournaments. There was a giant scoreboard with a Wall of Champions that had a list of previous winners of the US Open, but the space for 1965 was blank.

So each morning I'd go down and stare at it. And Ken Venturi's name was ahead of mine as the previous year's winner (see chapter 47). But I just kept seeing my name there and visualizing "Gary Player" in gold letters up there in the 1965 winner's slot.

I arrived at the US Open early, largely because Jack insisted: "If you want to win the career grand slam before me, you better come and let's practice together."

I did so reluctantly. I had actually wanted to go to Greensboro and play (in a tournament) because I needed the money. But he convinced me to go prepare with him, and we had a wonderful week practicing at the Bellerive Country Club located west of downtown St. Louis.

Like one of the great US Open champions, Ben Hogan, I really, really studied the course. And it was a monster. At 7,191 yards it was the longest of any US Open golf course in history at that time. I would take copious notes and sketches of the course (which is routed round a winding creek and a feature that comes into play on nine holes) including the roughs off the fairways, bunkers, and greens, and then I would study them in my hotel room in the evenings.

The course was built on rolling Missouri farmland. It was designed by Robert Trent Jones and featured unusually large and subtly contoured greens.

This Open would also include other firsts. It would be the first broadcast in color. It would also be the debut of a new format. For the first time in history, the US Open would be played over four days. This new format not only provided increased television revenue and exposure, but it also solved the challenge of having the sixty-plus players who had made the cut complete thirty-six holes on Saturday.

There is an interesting note about how Bellerive was even selected to host the Open. The mayor of St. Louis, unaware of the selection process for awarding venues, approached Hord Hardin, then a key USGA executive and member of Bellerive, and asked if the event could be held in '65 to coincide with the bicentennial celebration in St. Louis.

After being told how the process works and that San Francisco's Olympic Club had already been awarded the tournament, the mayor actually called his counterpart in San Francisco and asked if Bellerive could host the event.

Being amenable, Mr. Hardin then approached the USGA and an agreement was worked out, with Bellerive hosting the '65 Open and the Olympic Club the '66 Open.

One other thing I did was to visit a Catholic church, and I am not a Catholic. I prayed for courage and patience.

I then patiently went through the course and was pleased with my opening round of even par 70, closing the back nine with three birdies to one bogey. That put me just two behind the leader, Kel Nagle, and one behind Mason Rudolph and two-time US Amateur champion Deane Beman, who also had won the British Amateur championship.

Despite Bellerive's length, long hitters seemed to gain little advantage in the opening round. In fact, Nagle and Beman were two of the shortest hitters in the field, yet they were also two of just three competitors to break par on Thursday. Nagle, from Sydney, had won the Canadian Open, the Australian Open, and the 1960 Open Championship at St. Andrews, but had not been victorious in the United States.

Nagle's balky putter led to a 73 on Friday, a score Beman also ended up with. Despite hitting a bad approach shot that cost me a bogey on the first hole. on the ninth hole I sank an eighteen-foot downhill putt for a birdie. Then, playing the steadiest of golf through the late afternoon, parred in for my second consecutive 70. So, again, by being patient, I took the lead at 140 halfway through.

Bellerive was one of the first US Opens to feature Bermuda grass, which stands up so the ball goes straight down, and is therefore tougher to get out of. There'd be some big names who had trouble with that rough and would not be among those playing on the weekend, namely Arnold Palmer and defending US Open champion Ken Venturi.

Interestingly, because this tournament marked the first time that the US Open was televised in color, some club officials ordered the seventeenth and eighteenth greens to be sprayed emerald green to make sure the course looked its best for the cameras.[1]

One thing the cameras could pick up by looking at the players with all the sweat and towels was the intense heat that is Missouri in the summer. But I was young and strong, and despite the broiling conditions, I also kept up with my regular workouts. I was lifting weights, including squatting 325 pounds. And I was determined to wear black and was not worried about the scorching weather.

Additionally, contrary to what some may have heard, I am not superstitious. I think you are crazy if you are superstitious and play pro golf. That doesn't work. I simply liked the feel of that specific black shirt. It was a certain type of material. So I washed it every night and wore it every day. Eventually, I gave the shirt to the club, and I believe it is on display at the locker room in Bellerive.

There had also been some talk about my use of fiberglass-shafted clubs. Well, when you think about it, the fiberglass was really inferior for a golf club. But at that stage, how do you know? You're a young man supporting a growing family. They paid me a lot of money to use it. In those days it was a massive contract. And I felt confident that I could play with anything. But frankly, I was quite relieved when the contract came to an end.

I made the shaft very whippy. I put a marble insert in my wood. And I had a "G" grip, which is funny looking.

Julius Boros, a two-time US Open champion, said to me, "That is the biggest miracle that will ever happen in golf if you could win on this golf course with those clubs." He added, "What you could do is use the same shafts and go fishing."

Technology in golf is ever evolving. At the time, it was my expectation that the fiberglass-shafted clubs would replace steel-shafted clubs, but obviously that didn't happen. Players will always have to adapt to new technology in this great game. But the main piece of equipment is the ball.

A golf ball today can travel so much farther than ever before, probably one hundred yards longer than when I won the US Open in 1965. New equipment will continue to shape golf, its strategy, and the physical course, for as long as we allow.

I continued to lead after the third round with a 1-over 71. Beard moved into a tie with Nagle two strokes back of me.

With three holes to play in the final round, I was three clear of Nagle stepping up to the tee at sixteen. Now in a moment where I forgot that being patient helped get me where I was, I rushed my shot and tried to belt a four-wood in between gusts. The impatience cost me—my ball was plugged in the greenside bunker. After I double-bogeyed the par-3 sixteenth, and then watched Nagle birdie the seventeenth, we were all knotted up. We both come up short on our long birdie tries at eighteen to win it in regulation thus came an eighteen-hole playoff on Monday.

Still, I went to sleep that night filled with confidence. I was in top shape and just twenty-nine, and my opponent was forty-four. I knew it was hot and I was playing beautiful golf. I was putting like Houdini. So, I was never more confident of winning than I was then. And like I've said many times, winning majors often comes down to two things—confidence and putting. The 1965 US Open would be no different.

So here we were, a South African and an Australian, vying for the US Open title. Nagle struggled to maintain the form he showed the previous four days. He three-putted the opening hole for bogey. And on the fifth, he unfortunately struck women spectators on two different shots and ended up with a double bogey. And while those fans would be all right, Nagle's game was not.

Meanwhile, I was finding the correct spots on the massive but undulating greens and rolling them in, scoring back-to-back thirty-five-foot birdies on holes two and three and another on eight. I built up a five-shot advantage, which I would not let go of, keeping on with that visualization of my name atop that scoreboard.

In taking the playoff 71 to 74, I became just the third player in history to win the Grand Slam, joining Gene Sarazen and Ben Hogan.

And though I wanted to beat Jack in our race to winning the career grand slam (he would achieve his the following year at the Open at Muirfield in Scotland), I also have to thank him for urging me to practice with him in St. Louis the week before the major. It was the Golden Bear's persistence that convinced me to take the extra time to study the details of Bellerive. I'm glad he did.

It was a great moment in my life. And it was made even more special by fulfilling a promise I made back in 1962. When I was walking down the eighteenth fairway with Joe Dye of the USGA at Oakmont, the famous course near Pittsburgh, I vowed to him, "When I win the US Open one day—which I am game to do, Mr. Dye—I am going to give all my prize money back to America for what they have done for me. For cancer, which my mother died of, and for junior golf, which is close to my heart."

Now this was not a normal major. This was to win the Grand Slam. So I was in the right frame of mind. Twenty-five thousand dollars, that was a lot of money back in those days, and after that a lot of players thought of doing it. And today it is quite a common procedure.

But I mention it only because there is tremendous satisfaction in giving something back in times of great success. And giving it away, I must tell you, felt wonderful beyond words. My mother passed when I was just eight years old, and it agonized me to see her suffer, so cancer was at the top of my charity choices. Because I suffered as a junior, youngsters were next on my list of charitable endeavors.

To be champion of the greatest country of the world. What an honor.

All tournaments are a test, but the majors are the ultimate because they are the final exam that you study for all year. And know this—excellence is timeless.

That is by far the best achievement of my career. You can't do anything better. I don't care who you are. One cannot do anything better than winning the Grand Slam.

The only thing you can do better is to win it again, but I wouldn't be doing it with fiberglass shafts!

And wouldn't you know it, Julius Boros came up to me afterward and said:

"I've just seen the all-time miracle—winning the US Open with a fishing rod."

49

ARNIE'S FADE AND CASPER'S COMEBACK

JUNE 16–20, 1966
OLYMPIC CLUB
SAN FRANCISCO, CALIFORNIA

This is the story of two supremely talented players competing in the game's toughest tournament who just happened to be at opposite ends of the charisma spectrum.

Arnold Palmer exuded a massive aura of charm that was magnified as the face of the sport as it took off via television, while Billy Casper came across as a rather colorless and droll fellow. Misunderstood. A bit of an enigma. And at the end of this tournament one can add *antihero*.

Perhaps Casper himself said it best in his book, *The Big Three and Me,* when he wrote: "We didn't look alike, we didn't talk alike, we didn't act alike, and we sure didn't play golf alike. His game plan was different than mine. He was aggressive; I was conservative. He aimed for pins; I aimed for position. His personality was different than mine. He thrived on crowd interaction; I tried to shut out the crowd.

"But we were after the same thing, and it wasn't to perfect our mechanics or shoot a good score. It was to win."

And neither was a stranger to being in the winner's circle of a major. Palmer had won seven majors, including the 1960 US Open in Cherry Hills in perhaps his most memorable comeback charge. Casper had won the 1959 US Open at Winged Foot, defeating among others Arnold Palmer. Would either be the first to win their second US Open here at Olympic Club?

Known as the Lake Course, it was not an overly long layout, running just over 6,700 yards. But it combined smallish greens and fairways lined with many kinds of looming trees with typical USGA-style rough, which certainly favored the accurate hitter over the bomber.

Three future stars of the game, three future majors winners, would make their Grand Slam event debuts here.

Homegrown San Franciscan Johnny Miller, a nineteen-year-old amateur starting his sophomore year at Brigham Young University, had grown up playing the course as a junior member of the Olympic Club.

The Olympic Course is a bit deceiving. With no water hazards and few bunkers that really affect strategy, and with the wind really not a factor, it is a bit of a deceiving layout.

"Like all truly great courses," Miller said, "its difficulties are subtle. It beats you testing your patience, persistence, courage, concentration, course management and creativity. You finish a round at Olympic feeling like you've just donated 3 pints of blood."[1]

For a young man who'd planned to caddy for the event, instead Miller qualified and impressively finished eighth, the low amateur.

Another collegian, Hale Irwin, an All–Big Eight defensive back when he wasn't hitting three-irons on the nose for his collegiate team at the University of Colorado, was really in awe of the place and happy to be there despite finishing well back.

Lee Trevino was less happy to be there.

"My first US Open in 1966 at the Olympic club was not one of my all-time thrills. I shot 303 for 72 holes tied for 54th won $600. I did not leave my heart in San Francisco. I had never played a great golf course like Olympic, a course with that kind of rough. I'd never hit a ball out of tall grass before. I had played municipal courses all my life and they didn't have rough. Or bunkers. I was not good hitting out of the tall rough because of my flat swing."[2]

The Merry Mex would be talking and playing a much better game after this experience. Just two years later Trevino would be US Open champion (see chapter 50).

I arrived as defending champion having won at Bellerive the year before, I made my chances here tougher by opening with a 78. And even though I closed with a 69, I ended up back in fifteenth place.

Unsurprisingly, the coleaders after the second round were Palmer and Casper, the only players under par. At 3-under 137, they had a three-shot lead, and the automatic draw placed them together in the third round and again in the fourth.

Before the tournament started, the USGA announced that in the interest of speeding up play it would assess a two-stroke penalty for slowness. One of the targets was Jack Nicklaus; "a walker" shadowed his group, which included Bruce Devlin and Tony Lema.

Despite having to wait on the players in front of them early on, a gap did begin to widen after they'd completed a third of the round so the designated USGA walker informed them that they needed to pick up the pace. Rarely, if ever, rattled on the course, always known for not getting too high or too low, Nicklaus fumed and uncharacteristically proceeded to produce four straight bogeys.

Philip H. Strubing, of Philadelphia, chairman of the USGA Championship Committee, conceived the idea of establishing a target time for a round played in threes. The players were advised that "the USGA believes the maximum times . . . should not exceed 2 hours for 9 holes and 4 hours for 18 holes."[3]

Nicklaus and his group had been in the rough often early in the round and finished in less than four and a half hours, which was still nearly an hour longer than others had taken.

The Golden Bear's anger and frustration spilled over into the press conference afterward when he said, "Golf is a very difficult game, and you have to maintain your tempo. If you get off your tempo trying to rush, it makes it that much harder. I think the game is a little slow and should be speeded up, but to have someone on your back for eighteen holes is too much."

But Jack kept his poise well enough to produce a pair of 71s and share of fifth place heading into the weekend. Ultimately, he'd finish in third place.

Still battling for first place after the third round were Palmer and Casper. But Palmer had created some separation; Casper was going the wrong way, and lucky his putter bailed him out so he could scramble for a 73. "After the way I played today, I'm just happy to be playing tomorrow," the San Diego native said afterward.

Palmer's fifty-four-hole total—3-under 71-66-70=207—put him three strokes ahead of second place Casper who was at even par.

Known for his great charges and ultra-aggressive play, even with a lead, the thirty-six-year-old Palmer knew no other way. His "go-for-broke" style cost him more than a few times throughout his career, but then again was precisely one of the reasons that Palmer was perhaps golf's most-beloved figure.

Palmer began the final round with a three-stroke lead over his playing partner, Casper. He started out just fine with a pair of opening birdies. After Casper bogeyed holes three and five, the King's lead was now seven. Making the turn in a sizzling 3-under 32, the ultrapopular player, who came from a steel-mill town in western Pennsylvania and played college golf at Wake Forest, turned his thoughts to beyond victory and to the record books heading down the homeward half.

With his eye on Ben Hogan's US Open scoring record (276 in 1948; see chapter 42), Palmer needed to shoot just 1-over 36 on the back nine for 275. As if things weren't difficult enough, there was no precedent for Casper to point to—in the long history of the US Open, nobody had ever overcome a seven-shot deficit with nine to play.

Ironically, Arnold Palmer had overcome seven strokes with a closing 65 to pass fifty-four-hole leader Mike Souchak to win the national title at Cherry Hills in 1960, but that was over eighteen holes, not nine.

So Casper, at this stage, was thinking about second place and was determined to stay ahead of Nicklaus and Lema (who were two behind him). However, Palmer bogeyed ten and thirteen, and birdied twelve and fifteen. Casper's mindset changed as he was now just three down with three holes to play.

Though he was not the most animated player out there, he did have fans, and as the competition grew tighter he attracted even more fans. He certainly had plenty of fans supporting him back home—he and his wife, Shirley, his childhood sweetheart, were raising eleven children. While the devout Mormon didn't drink or smoke, his exotic diet did draw a lot of attention from the media. In an effort to lose weight and deal with allergies, Casper maintained a regular menu that included elk, moose, bear, and buffalo.

Some began referring to him as Buffalo Bill. But what drew the attention of his peers was a great game out on the course.

"Billy was unflappable and methodical," said Hale Irwin. "If he wasn't set, he'd put the club back in the bag and start all over again. Being methodical, he'd check all the boxes, but once he was ready, he'd hit it pretty quickly."

And of course while he excelled in all facets of the game (though not exceptionally long off the tee), he was an acknowledged magician with the flatstick.

"Billy Casper was one of the greatest putters I had ever seen," said Lee Trevino.

Maybe in his rush for glory, Palmer forgot who he was playing with. Because as his game unraveled, Casper was steadily stalking his prey.

"In competition he never choked . . . If you found yourself playing head-to-head against him, you were in very deep trouble. He had almost no ego, and he didn't get nervous. He didn't care if you outdrove him or hit your second shot inside him," said fellow Mormon Johnny Miller. "He would grind along in a very businesslike way, rarely making a mistake, and eventually he would beat you."[4]

The man who was entirely self-taught and swung by instinct and intuition was making his own charge. At fifteen, he drilled a twenty-footer, while his opponent bogeyed for another two-shot swing. Down just three with three holes to play, the thirty-four-year-old Casper told himself, "I can win this tournament now."

For Palmer, his body language and demeanor had gone from flicking away half-smoked cigarettes with a smile while hitching his pants up cheerfully heading down the fairway nodding to fans confident in the knowledge that he could secure an eighth major in record-setting fashion to a lingering expression of anguish, knowing both goals were slipping away. Casper, who had been such a nonthreatening ghost so far back in the shadows on the front nine, was now spooking Palmer.

The massive sixteenth, the last par-5 of the layout, was a monstrous 604 yards. Casper pushed his drive into the right rough, while Palmer hit a duck hook into the trees on the left, which settled in deep rough. Unable to advance it any great length and only finding deeper rough, he now was forced to use a nine-iron and lay it back into the fairway. With a smash of his three-wood, Palmer struck a mighty blow. The ball sailed over 250 yards but found a greenside bunker with a fried-egg lie. He was now lying four.

Cool, calm, and collected, Casper hit his third shot to within twelve feet of the cup. Palmer blasted out of the sand to get to within five feet. But after Casper sank his putt for birdie and Palmer bogeyed, it was yet another two-shot swing.

Palmer's lead was now down to one with two holes left.

At the 443-yard seventeenth, Casper pushed his shot to the right while Palmer missed the fairway, short and left in deep rough. His next attempt came up forty yards short of the green in the right rough, but Casper also missed the green. But he would scramble for par while Palmer missed his ten-footer for par. After his fifth bogey on the back nine, Palmer's seemingly insurmountable seven-stroke advantage had evaporated, and they were now all tied coming to the seventy-second hole.

Casper's tee shot at eighteen settled on the right edge of the fairway, while Palmer's one-iron pulled the ball into the left rough. On the green with his approach shot, Palmer still had a delicate and tricky downhiller of over twenty feet. Casper's approach put him to within fifteen feet of the flag. They both made par and thus forced an eighteen-hole playoff the following day.

Palmer shot 4-over 39 on the inward nine, Casper shot 3-under 32, and the two tied at 2-under 278, seven strokes ahead of solo third-place finisher Jack Nicklaus. Visibly subdued and shaken, Palmer, sitting in front of his locker after Sunday's catastrophe, said, "It's hard to believe."

However, with the unwavering support of his army, in the next day's eighteen-hole playoff, Palmer got everyone believing he could recover and win this thing because under sunny skies with a pair of birdies, the King took a two-shot lead at the turn for home after posting a 2-under 33 to Casper's 35.

Nevertheless, it would be a familiar story of the back nine. Once again, Casper would pick up six shots on Palmer down the stretch, just as he had picked up seven the day before. With three bogeys and a double bogey to close out, Palmer eventually shot a 3-over 73 to Casper's 1-under 69. So the difference really came in the scores on those back nines the last two days, where it was 66 to 79 in Casper's favor.

On eighteen, Casper made birdie, his thirty-third one-putt of the tournament. As they walked off the eighteenth green after the play-off, Casper could only say, "I'm sorry, Arnold."

Palmer never won another major, and he told friends in subsequent years that this missed chance devastated him the most.

"I always thought if Arnold were playing against anyone else in the last two rounds, he would've won," said Miller. "But against Billy, Arnold knew he couldn't afford to make a mistake, which had to intensify the pressure he is already feeling. Billy had a way of doing that to people. He was a persistent, remorseless player who could stand up to anyone, anytime, anywhere."[5]

Yet the collapse did nothing to reduce Palmer's enormous popularity. If anything, what happened at Olympic strengthened it. For in this incredible defeat, he became real to fans, more human than ever. Combine that with his comparatively dry personality, Casper didn't get as much credit as he deserved for his tremendous play.

"Casper in my mind is the most underrated golfer of all time, hands down. He won 51 times in the PGA Tour from 1956 to 1975. Only five players had won more tournaments, and Billy's victories came against some of the best golfers of any era," said Miller.

50

SUPER MEX ANNOUNCES HIS ARRIVAL

JUNE 13–16, 1968
OAK HILL COUNTRY CLUB (EAST COURSE)
ROCHESTER, NEW YORK

Even though defending champion Jack Nicklaus (who set a new US Open scoring record with a 275 at Baltusrol the previous June) would make a late run to capture a runner-up position, this tournament was essentially between two very different players, Bert Yancey and Lee Trevino. Both were seeking their first major and in the case of the latter, his first victory on the PGA Tour.

A native of Florida, the twenty-nine-year-old Yancey had attended the United States Military Academy in West Point, New York, and was captain of the Cadet golf team. His golf swing certainly had a set cadence. He swung the same way. He took the club back slow. He set it. He made sure everything worked coming through then held his finish. When he walked down the fairway, upright and expression-less, it was as if he were part of a military parade march.

Stylish yet reserved, Yancey had won four tournaments, but the closest he came to a majors victory was leading after fifty-four holes at the Masters the previous year before finishing third.

Trevino, twenty-eight, had a different personality (and swing) than his main opponent. He was talkative, friendly, and with a keen wit, often smiling and interacting with the galleries. His self-taught flat swing wasn't classic nor long by any means, but it was quite accurate. He also experienced a very distinctive road to this point. The stocky Mexican American grew up near a country club, but it was far from that kind of lifestyle.

Never knowing his father, Trevino was raised by his mother and grandfather, a gravedigger. Living with two sisters in a floorless home without electricity or indoor plumbing, he began picking cotton at age five. It was a primitive existence that included using lake water to wash clothes and for baths.

They lived less than a football field from the seventh fairway at the Dallas Athletic Club. At about seven years old Trevino would pick up errant balls that came over the fence and sell them for ten to fifteen cents to help put food on the table. Soon he would hang around the caddy shed and began to learn about the game by carrying a bag. An eighth-grade dropout, he later worked at a driving range, whose owner, Hardy Greenwood, had noticed the youngster's golf skills. Over time their relationship grew, and Greenwood became a golf tutor and father figure.

Trevino joined the Marine Corps at seventeen. He began playing golf competitively for the first time as he represented the US Marines while based in Okinawa, Japan, in 1958. After his discharge in 1960, he returned to Dallas and tried to make a living at golf, mostly by hustling. It was where he came up with the telling quip—"You don't know what pressure is until you've played for $5 a hole with only $2 in your pocket." And later the stakes would be for a lot more during a well-chronicled gambling match with future superstar Raymond Floyd.

After working as a club professional in El Paso, Trevino eventually qualified for a PGA card. Though winless, he won $26,472 as a rookie, forty-fifth on the PGA Tour money list, and was named 1967

Rookie of the Year by *Golf Digest*. His fifth-place finish at the US Open also earned him an exemption into the following year's event.

Largely because of his hard-scrabbled path and coming comparatively late into the game, Trevino considered himself an outsider and an underdog.

"You have to understand I came into this world on a cotton farm. And I came in the Marine Corps and I got out at age twenty-two and went to work on a construction crew on a golf course. I really did not start playing golf until I was twenty-two years old," said Trevino. "And I didn't know anything about Arnold Palmer. I didn't know anything about Sam Snead. I didn't know anything about Gary Player, Jack Nicklaus. All these people, all these majors, I had no clue! I was trying to figure out who I was going to beat out of $10 tomorrow at Tenison Park. I tell people that and it is hard for them to believe."

He quickly made a believer of tour veteran Doug Sanders, an eight-time winner to that point.

"I played four practice rounds at Oak Hill, all with Doug Sanders and Doug says, 'Man, I'm gonna make a bet on you because I have never seen a man drive a ball this straight,'" Trevino recalled.

With two recent runner-up finishes, was the personable and talented Mexican American's luck about to change and get into the winner's circle?

Well for a man who considered himself an introvert off the course and who was happy putting on the carpet of a cheap hotel into the wee hours, Trevino did something he had never done before or since. After receiving a letter from a local family offering to host him, he decided to spend the week with company. Paul Karcher, a former minor league pitcher who had done well in the insurance business, invited the young player to stay with his family, which included five kids. One evening as everyone relaxed in the backyard, the youngest daughter found a four-leaf clover and offered it to her guest. The appreciative Trevino graciously put it in his pocket for good fortune.

And it would turn out he'd get some more luck. Rules in place until 1976 did not allow players to use their own caddies at the US Open. Instead, caddies had been drawn by lot from a pool recruited by the host club. And Kevin Quinn, a gangly student at Cornell who had just finished his freshman year, got Trevino's bag. He had caddied at Oak Hill for four summers and was the club's top-rated caddy.[1]

Finally, Trevino's confidence was at an even higher level. After the last practice round he declared, "That expression 'horses for courses' I found to be true for me here at Oak Hill."

Designed by Donald Ross and playing to a par 70 at over 6,900 yards, the East Championship Course was lush with oaks, elms, pines, and flowering trees. It had also hosted a US Open twelve years prior. In 1956, Dr. Cary Middlecoff was the winner with a score of 281 for seventy-two holes of play, one stroke ahead of Ben Hogan and Julius Boros.

It would be Yancey, with that graceful swing, who would feel at ease here as well. His opening 67 gave him a two-shot lead. But Trevino was splitting every fairway with his tee shots and combining that with solid chipping and putting. His game was under control and it showed. One of just three players to score under par, he also felt good with a 69, tied with Charles Coody at 1 under.

With the average width of the Oak Hill fairways just thirty-four yards and a premium on fairway accuracy, and with lush four-inch rough waiting in plain sight to challenge the errant, Trevino battled the rough a bit more this day, but his putter was shining. It was the flat blade that allowed him to finish with a 68. And while his 3-under 137 total gave him sole possession of second place, Yancey methodically marched down the course. He finished with a 68 of his own and made the record books. His 135 total tied the US Open record for the first thirty-six holes, made by Mike Souchak in 1960 at Cherry Hills in Denver.

Nicklaus was part of a large group in seventh place, seven back.

With that serious demeanor it was business as usual for Yancey.

By the end of the third day his 70 added up to another record. His 205-hole total broke an Open record; it was one stroke less than the 206 Tommy Jacobs had shot at Congressional in 1964. However, his playing partner had gained a stroke on him and really liked where he was at.

"I knew that I was the underdog and that nobody expected me to win," said Trevino.

He was excited about teeing it up for the final round. And to mark the occasion, which would become a tradition of his, Trevino's Sunday wardrobe would have what he'd call his payday colors. It included not only a red shirt and black pants (long before Tiger) but red socks and a red glove!

In his 1982 book, *They Call Me Super Mex,* Trevino tells the story that after winning a tournament in Sydney, Australia, he received a new car, which he gave to his mother-in-law. She had requested that it be a black-and-red one, and she named it Payday.

But the payday was a long way off for Trevino here in Rochester. Things didn't start well after he bogeyed the first hole of the final round. However, he kept plugging away, and after Yancey bogeyed his third of the first five holes, Trevino led by one. Palmer was on his way to a 75 after a third-round 79. Nicklaus at one point got to within three shots, but that would be the closest he'd get.

At the turn the steady Trevino, with eight straight pars, had a three-shot lead over Yancey. It would increase to five with back-to-back birdies starting at eleven. In a style uniquely his own, he would delight galleries with unending banter, all the while mesmerizing his fellow competitors with awesome displays of shotmaking.

As for the former, for example when he knocked an approach shot onto the green midway through the final round, he freely declared, "I'm trying to get a big enough lead where I can't choke it."

I have played with him in many rounds, and Lee was and is a chatterbox. There are some players like Ben Hogan who would not say a word to you during a round. Others, like Sam Snead, wouldn't look at your swing. So you do what helps to focus, to relax, to be comfortable as best as you can under pressure, and in Lee's case it's talking and talking and talking.

As for the shooting display, the numbers would bear this out in the end—Trevino was second in number of fairways hit, forty-two; ranked second in greens reached in regulation, fifty-five; and, perhaps most telling, especially at a US Open, no three-putts! But what was really happening under that assassin's smile was the rise of the killer instinct instilled in him via his hustling days in Texas. It was basically match play, and that was in a hustler's wheelhouse.

"Being the underdog. I knew I could shoot in the 80s and nobody would be surprised, but if I played well, it put pressure on Bert, who was expected to win," said Trevino.

The pressure showed, as four bogeys on the back nine sealed Yancey' s fate.

Meanwhile, Trevino saw another challenge he wanted to go after. If he parred eighteen, he would tie the record Nicklaus had just set the year before at 275. He did, and became the first player in US Open history to shoot all four rounds in the 60s.

The 1968 US Open wasn't just Lee Trevino's first win in a majors championship—the first of six majors (see chapter 70)—it was his first win of any kind on the PGA Tour.

Maybe the four-leaf clover did have some charm to it.

Perhaps much bigger than record-setting numbers was that by winning at Oak Hill, the affable Mexican American had opened up the game to a blue-collar world. Not bad for a kid born into poverty, who grew up sleeping five to a room.

"My family was so poor," Trevino joked, "when somebody threw our dog a bone, he had to call for a fair catch."

51

TREVINO SNAKES NICKLAUS

JUNE 17–21, 1971
MERION GOLF CLUB
ARDMORE, PENNSYLVANIA

While there'd be a young collegiate player who'd make a bold move to steal the title, this tournament really would come down to a pair of thirty-one-year-olds. But not just any thirty-one-year-olds.

Jack Nicklaus was an eight-time major winner, an established superstar on tour. Lee Trevino already knew how to win golf's toughest tournament, having been victorious at the 1968 US Open. Fearless and among the best ball-strikers in the game, the Merry Mex defeated the Golden Bear at that national championship at Oak Hill Country Club in Rochester, New York, by four strokes. And he arrived at Merion with a hot hand. He also got some encouraging words from the superstar: "When I arrived at Merion in June 1971, I was thinking about what Nicklaus told me in March: 'You just don't know how good a player you are. You can win anywhere.' I also remember what Walter Hagan once said: 'Any player can win a US Open, but it takes a hell of a player to win two.'

"I had thought about that a thousand times since I won at Oak Hill three years before. Merion is a great old course on the main line in the Philadelphia suburbs, and as soon as I played a practice round there I felt this might be the time for me to move up in class. I thought I had an excellent chance of winning because my game was starting to peak. At some point in the year your game will always peak, and mine at started to do it the past few weeks."[1]

In the seven tournaments he entered before Merion, Trevino came in second once, third twice, and had two victories.

Still, of all the players on tour, it was his main opponent that he had the most respect for.

"I remember in 1979–1980, Jack was not playing very well and the media was starting to get on his nerves I think a little bit. You know how they do that. Everything was—'What's wrong with Jack?'" recalled Trevino. "Then he comes out and wins two majors [US Open and PGA 1980]. I remember my first press conference after that. I said, 'Listen, I want to tell you all one thing. I'm a farm boy. And I have never hunted bear. But when bears are hibernating, goddammit don't wake them up! They will maul you to death and you all woke Jack up.'"

Emerging from his slumber, the Golden Bear managed the speedy greens on the par-70, 6,544-yard course for a 1-under 69, just two off the lead. Trevino was one back of him in a big group that included Johnny Miller and Tom Weiskopf.

Trevino shot 72 for the second round. And despite an adventure at eleven that resulted in a double bogey, Nicklaus also managed to finish the round 1 over.

For years Trevino had built up a regular routine after completing a round. After watching TV while he enjoyed his dinner in his hotel room, the Merry Mex would set up practice, but these days he had to improvise.

"You know, the worst thing that ever happened to us was when the Holiday Inn put shag carpet in," Trevino recalled with a laugh.

"You could chip off it, but you couldn't putt on it. I tell you what I did though, I got a putting mat. And a pool table bumper which was four foot long. Then I got a hockey bag and I would roll the carpet up, stuffed it in the bumper, and traveled with it. So, if I had a hotel that had a shag carpet, I had my own gear for putting."

It worked because in the third round Trevino rolled 2-under 69. However, Nicklaus bettered him by a single shot. But the story on this Saturday was a twenty-four-year-old entering his senior year at Wake Forest who bettered everyone.

Twenty-one-year-old Jim Simons, an amateur from Pennsylvania, zoomed into the lead at 3-under 207 after a 5-under 65, just one off the championship record. He converted seven birdies after making only two in his opening thirty-six holes.

It was shaping up to play out not unlike the 1954 Masters where two stars, Hogan and Snead, had serious competition with another amateur from Wake Forest—Billy Joe Patton (see chapter 4).

Young Simons hung tough, and at the turn of the final round still had the lead over Nicklaus and Trevino. However, after birdies at twelve and fourteen, the Merry Mex moved into the lead and was the only player under par. He was 1 under, while Nicklaus was even and Simons 1 over.

At eighteen Trevino smoked a three-wood approach through the green and had about an eight-footer for par to maintain the one-stroke lead.

He stood over the tricky putt as twenty thousand gallery members became deadly silent. Suddenly a kid who had climbed a tree for a better look crashed to the ground. Backing off, Trevino tied to re-group, but he missed the putt and had to settle for bogey.

Trevino refused to blame anybody but himself. "I was very worried about him and wanted to make sure he was okay," he said.

Still in contention at the seventy-second hole, needing birdie at the last to tie, Simons found the rough with his drive. He ended up suffering a double bogey that left him with a 76 and a tie for fifth at 283.

Finishing with a second straight 69 for even par 280, Trevino signed his scorecard then rushed to the locker room, while Jack sized up his fourteen-foot birdie at eighteen that would win him yet another US Open. With his eyes closed, Trevino heard the groans of the gallery and he grinned, knowing he'd be in a playoff.

Meeting with a handful of reporters afterward, Lee and Jack sat together in the steamy locker room.

"I don't recall what Jack said but then they turned to me and asked how I thought I would do in tomorrow's playoffs.

"I don't know I have got everything to win and nothing to lose. Number one I am playing the greatest player ever, and number two you've got your headlines written already anyway. But you better not print them yet."

The man unafraid of any competitor couldn't wait for the playoff the following morning. "I already felt like I had won because I had nothing to lose, and I always got extra motivated playing against Jack because he was the very best," Trevino said.

Monday morning's playoff had a slight delay that led to one of the more memorable preround incidents in majors history.

"I believe that was a first US Open that they broadcast all eighteen holes. To achieve that, they had to move TV cameras around on forklift trucks. And to do that there they had to lay plywood around throughout the golf course," explained John Capers III, the chair of the Merion Archives Committee. "Apparently the delay on the first tee of the playoff was due to the fact broadcasters were trying to position a TV camera at the end of the fairway of the first hole, which was a ninety-degree dogleg left. That is why Trevino and Nicklaus were sitting around. That is when Trevino pulled out the snake and threw it over to Jack."

Nicklaus had come out first and was sitting under a tree, his head down, silent, when out came Trevino full of energy. He waved to the crowd, beaming and rubbing his hands together in anticipation of the duel.

The Merry Mex then went over to his golf bag, unzipped a compartment, and pulled out a four-foot-long toy snake and held it up. The crowd gasped as Trevino laughed and tossed it at Nicklaus. Realizing it was a fake, Jack chuckled. So did the fans.

But there was a history behind the prank.

"My daughter had bought the snake at the zoo. I did some cameos on Tuesday for *SI* at Merion," explained Trevino. "If you look at some photos by *Sports Illustrated,* they wanted to show how tall and penal the rough was. I have a hatchet and a safari hat on with the fake snake resting on the hatchet. I forgot it was still in my bag. So, when I reached in there to get another glove, Nicklaus saw me hold it up and was laughing and asked that I throw it to him."

But then it got real. And Trevino opened the playoff with a bogey. However, exposing one of the few weak aspects of his game, Nicklaus had trouble getting out of the bunkers, and suffered bogey and double bogey on the next two holes. Suddenly Trevino had a two-stroke lead.

But what really gave him a boost came from above. After Nicklaus cut his deficit to one with a birdie at the par-4 fifth, crashing rain halted the competition for a spell.

"I felt I had a real big task in front of me because of how hard the greens were. They didn't water them," remembered Trevino. "[When] we went in for shelter. that is when I kind of perked up because I realized now I got a shot. Now his high shot will be no better than my low one."

Nicklaus cut into the lead several times, to within one stroke as late as the twelfth tee. But Trevino was a steady-rollin' man, hitting fairways and greens to produce no bogeys and a pair of birdies on the back nine. He never relinquished the top spot and would score a 68 to Jack's 71.

Having secured his second US Open triumph, Trevino has always been quick to give credit to Mother Nature.

"I have said this many times. I would never have beaten Jack in the playoffs at Merion if it didn't rain. After four holes we had a one-hour delay because it had become a downpour. Those were small oval greens, and Jack hit it so high it doesn't make any difference to Jack how hard those greens are. He's going to stop the ball," explained Trevino. "I can get on those greens, too, but I have to be more accurate than he does because I can only use the front of the green. I cannot go to the middle or back of the green. That downpour softened the greens. Mother Nature controls how difficult the golf course is going to play."

While Trevino's victory at Merion began a great three-week run where he also captured the Canadian Open and then the Open Championship at Royal Birkdale, the US Open victory was a very personal win for the personable man.

"Winning at Merion in the playoff over Jack was special," Trevino revealed. "You have to remember even though I had gone on tour full-time in '68, I really didn't feel like I belonged to the fraternity. Most of the players on tour were college graduates with great amateur records. I was a dropout, came from a cotton farm, and knew nothing about the greats of the game. I had no TV. But I qualified for the Open in '66, '67, and won it in '68. So, after defeating Jack under those circumstances, for the first time, I believed in myself and felt I really belonged."

Let me tell you something. The greatest golfer I ever saw from tee to green was Ben Hogan. There's also Sam Snead, but Lee Trevino is right up there. He's in the top three from tee to green. And I am so proud of what he has accomplished given such humble beginnings.

52

HERE'S JOHNNY!

JUNE 14–17, 1973
OAKMONT COUNTRY CLUB
OAKMONT, PENNSYLVANIA

I t is one of a handful of rounds that has stood the test of time as one of the greatest ever. We are talking about Johnny Miller's final round at the 1973 US Open at Oakmont.

I have played a lot with Johnny. And I will tell you, for two years Johnny was the best golfer in the world. No question.

He had an incredible backswing. He had the Ben Hogan backswing. He just fired those balls at the pins. It was like an arrow right at the target. It was something to see.

Born and raised in San Francisco, Miller took to the game early on. At age five he was taught to play the sport by his father, Larry. It started when his dad came home one day from a local army surplus store having bought a big green canvas tarp, which he nailed to the ceiling of the family basement. He also installed a large mirror and laid out instructional books by Sam Snead, Byron Nelson, and Ben Hogan.

With nothing but positive reinforcement from his father, young Johnny would pound balls with a cut-down club into that tarp for hours. He never stepped foot on a golf course for several years. He studied images from the book to compare grip, stance, and posture with those greats. This honed a fine sense of balance and tempo but also a terrific sensory recognition of making solid contact.

When he did eventually get to the course, he was hooked. His father had worked out an arrangement for his son to become a junior member at the Olympic Club. After school, the young teen would often take a cable car and bus to get in a few holes before homework.

In 1964 Miller won the US Junior Amateur. Two years later, the nineteen-year-old amateur just missed qualifying for the 1966 US Open at the Olympic Club. Resigned to caddying for that event, Miller got lucky. Finishing as first alternate in the field of 156, he wound up playing instead because there was a withdrawal.

With his extensive knowledge of the course, he made the most of the opportunity. Miller not only was low amateur but he tied for eighth.

After graduating from Brigham Young in 1969, Miller turned pro. He picked up his first PGA Tour victory event in 1971 and won again in 1972. In the majors, he finished runner-up in the 1970 Masters and recorded top-ten finishes in the 1971 and 1972 US Opens. He won twice more in 1973 before arriving at Oakmont.

The par-71, 6,921-yard course at Oakmont is located in the suburbs of Pittsburgh in western Pennsylvania. Though they are large, these are some of the fastest greens in the country, placing a premium on ball-striking, as one must keep the ball under the hole. And despite the rain early in the week, between the lush rough, 187 bunkers, and ground crew breaking out their heavy rollers and running them across the greens, making them even firmer and faster than normal, it set up to be a tough challenge even by US Open standards.

I was just overcoming my own challenge and trying to meet my own high standards. I was just rounding into shape after a couple operations, including emergency bladder surgery. At one point during the road back, it felt like I was trying to swing the club with a brick on it, but I started out well at Oakmont.

Hitting the right spots on the green, my putting was good, and I took the lead after an opening 4-under 67. No one else shot under 70.

Halfway through I still had a one-shot lead, but I faltered with a third-round 77. The leaderboard after fifty-four holes was very crowded, including forty-three-year-old Arnold Palmer as one of four coleaders with Julius Boros (age fifty-three), Jerry Heard, and John Schlee. Tom Weiskopf, who had won tournaments in three of the previous five weeks was one back and two-time US Open winner Lee Trevino two back.

Heard, from California, joined the PGA Tour in 1969 and had won three times, including the Colonial. Schlee, an astrology enthusiast, went to a star for help with his game, and it paid off. Before the event, he worked with Ben Hogan on his setup and backswing (Hogan won here in 1953).

Miller, who started the day just three back, forgot his yardage book back at the hotel, and it nearly cost him any shot at the tournament; Oakmont is one course on which you need perfect yardage for those tricky greens. While Miller's iron game was so well-honed that he could usually get within a couple feet of his yardage, with no reliable markers in that era, without his book, it became more of a guessing game. It showed because he made three bogeys and a double bogey over the first six holes. Fortunately, his wife Linda went to retrieve the book, so his 3-over on the back nine Saturday salvaged a 76. However, he would now start the final round six strokes back, and with the heavy hitters ahead of him, things looked bleak.

The clear crowd favorite was coleader Arnold Palmer. He commuted every day from home in Latrobe just thirty-nine miles away with his dad, Deacon, accompanying him. The King, who had not won a major since 1964, at age forty-three would get his last great opportunity here at Oakmont. Arnie's Army was hoping their man could summon one last charge. It would also be a way to get some measure of revenge if he could defeat his friendly rival Jack Nicklaus, who as a twenty-two-year-old rookie defeated Palmer in a playoff, winning his first major on this course at the 1962 US Open (see chapter 46).

In his book *I Call the Shots,* Miller revealed someone else called the shots just before teeing off for the final round.

"As I stood on the practice tee warming up on Sunday, a little voice in my head told me to fan my left foot open toward the target. I had never tried it before, but I decided to try it. It led to one of my best ballstriking rounds ever. I missed a bunch of putts and still shot 63. From then on, I trusted my intuition and my heart."

Despite the voice and the trusty yardage book in full support, the slender twenty-six-year-old dedicated Mormon was not sure he could overcome the stellar list of marquee players ahead of him.

"I was six shots out of the lead and all the greatest players were ahead of me: Nicklaus, Palmer, Player, Trevino and Weiskopf," said Miller. "I didn't think I had any chance to win when I teed off that final day."[1]

After teeing off an hour before the leaders, Miller birdied his first four holes to move into red figures. "For the first time it occurred to me that I could win," said Miller, after his fourth consecutive birdie. After three pars, he three-putted the par-3 eighth for bogey to go back to even. "I went from being nervous to semi-mad," said Miller. "That kind of got me focused again. I told myself, 'If you're going to win the US Open, you can't be nervous, so let's put the hammer down.'"[2]

Completing the front nine with his lone bogey of the day at eight and birdie at nine, Miller was three back of Palmer and Weiskopf heading to the back nine. But he continued to fire his irons at the flagsticks, and after three straight birdies starting at the eleventh, the San Franciscan was now in the lead by one stroke over Schlee. After adding another birdie at fifteen then barely missing birdie tries at seventeen and eighteen, Miller was the clubhouse leader at 5 under.

In shooting a stunning 63, Miller hit all eighteen greens in regulation and needed twenty-nine putts. Now, finishing over an hour ahead of the last pairing, it was a matter of waiting in the clubhouse to see if anyone could equal him. Believe me, I know that anguish of waiting! (See chapter 66.)

One by one they came and went. With two eagles and four birdies, Lanny Wadkins closed with a brilliant 65, but he was too far back to overhaul the leader. With a pair of birdies at sixteen and seventeen, Nicklaus closed well but finished fourth. Weiskopf fell short with a pair of back-nine bogeys. Boros and Heard both shot 73 and finished in a tie for seventh. Arnie's Army wilted in the heat as Palmer's hopes were dashed with back-to-back-to-back bogeys starting at the par-5 twelfth.

Even though he opened his round with a double bogey, John Schlee rallied with an eagle and five birdies. He had a chance to tie Miller and force a playoff at the seventy-second hole, but he missed his forty-foot birdie try and settled for second place.

The new US Open champion's super 63 was even more remarkable given that only three other players managed to even break 70 on the day.

"It was definitely no fluke," said Miller Barber, his playing partner during the round. "It was just an excellent round of golf. Everything he hit was right at the flag. He lipped out a few putts too. It very easily could have been a 60."[3]

A 60 in the final round of a US Open?! Well, to many observers that didn't sit well with the USGA who took pride in making their courses the most demanding in golf. Their setup the following year reflected that embarrassment.

It is still being debated half a century later, but in 2003, Johnny Miller told the *Los Angeles Times:* "My final round had more repercussions for the USGA than any other round in history. The next year, [the course] was off the charts. I guess they really took a lot of flak. I sure took a lot of flak from a lot of players, blaming me"[4] (see chapter 53).

Golf Magazine ranked it the greatest round in golf history.

Some numbers endure as the standard of excellence in a particular sport. Among those are:

- 8—consecutive NBA titles won by Bill Russell leading his Boston Celtics
- 56—Joe DiMaggio's hitting streak
- 100—Wilt Chamberlain's scoring total one night in Hershey, Pennsylvania
- 8—Michael Phelps's eight gold medals in the 2008 Olympics
- 511—pitcher Cy Young's career win record
- 31—the incredible number of lengths of victory by Secretariat at Belmont in his Triple Crown year of 1973

and to that add

- 63—Johnny Miller's final round score to win the national championship

"There have been 59s shot, I shot several 61s in my career," Miller said in a 2016 ESPN story. "But to shoot 63 at Oakmont on the last day to win by one is what makes the round what it is . . . It's nice to have that one round that people will remember."

53

ALL-HALE AS IRWIN EMERGES
FROM THE MASSACRE

JUNE 13–16, 1974
WINGED FOOT GOLF CLUB (WEST COURSE)
MAMARONECK, NEW YORK

The greens were slick, the grass was high, and the scores were higher. The so-called Massacre at Winged Foot happened this year with a winning score of 7 over par. Did the USGA set up Winged Foot with extremely thick rough and lightning-fast greens because of Johnny Miller's scorching 63 in the final round of the 1973 US Open? Many of the golfers in this tournament thought so: it was the USGA making sure nobody would do that again.

Located outside New York City, the Winged Foot Golf Club with its huge stone clubhouse, outdoor terrace, and beautiful elms is an incredible place to visit. It has hosted many championships, and the atmosphere is as good as anywhere.

The course itself? The par-70, 6,691-yard layout is just one mean hombre.

It was even more imperative here to keep the ball in play because the rough was so high. It was a hosel wrapper. The conditions were so tough, they were as difficult as any course I have ever seen. So, so tough. So it demanded extra patience. Look, you simply had to do everything well. So great is my respect for it that one of the best horses I've ever bred in South Africa was named Winged Foot.

Like the US Open the year before, I led the tournament after the first round, this time rolling an even par 70 on a day that no one shot a subpar round. Only twenty-three of the 150 golfers in the field scored better than 75, and forty-four of those golfers shot 80 or higher!

Jack Nicklaus four-putted off the very first green. I remember him telling me after the opening round, "These are the most severely undulating greens I have ever seen. They have obviously driven everyone up a tree." He finished with a 75.

One thing you don't want to be doing is knocking by that hole. For sure. First hole, you try to play short of the flag for an uphill putt, if anything because you don't want to be knocking it by. Because the greens were murder, absolutely murder. I have never seen greens tougher than those. Never.

And with a 73, I maintained a share of the lead heading into the weekend. And what a powerful leaderboard it was. Joining me at the top were Arnold Palmer, Raymond Floyd, and Hale Irwin at 3-over 143.

While the shaved, slick greens gave everyone fits, there was also the matter of the bunkers. Johnny Miller, the defending champion, was still in contention on Friday until he found the front-right bunker on the seventh hole and took four shots to get out, making a quadruple-bogey 7.

He was lucky to survive the cut (or was he?). Those flying out early included a handful of major winners. There were four former Masters champions: Doug Ford, Tommy Aaron, Bob Goalby, and Charles Coody. Add to that five former US Open champions who also missed the cut: Lee Trevino, Gene Littler, Ken Venturi, Billy Casper, and Tony Jacklin.

Unfortunately for me, like at Oakmont the previous year, I fell back with a third round of 77, but even with the very tough scoring conditions I stayed in contention.

If I'm not mistaken, on the fourth hole I hit a drive. I don't recall the club I used, but I hit the ball over the green half an inch out of bounds. Half an inch! We had to get a piece of string and tie it to the out-of-bounds stake, and it showed I was actually *less* than a half inch out of bounds. And that put the spoke in the wheel and prevented me from winning it. And it was probably my best chance at a Grand Slam, having won the British (see chapter 71) and Masters that year (fifth in the PGA).

Not only did the greens and bunkers provide their share of grief, there was also the infamous rough to deal with.

"I'll never forget Winged Foot that year, it was so penal, the rough was so high. As high as I had ever seen it," said David Graham, who won the Open in 1981 and tied for eighteenth in 1974. "If you missed the fairway, you were lucky to find your ball."

Still finding his ball in rather favorable positions was a young man from Kansas City via Stanford. Tom Watson took the third-round lead with a 69. Just twenty-four and seeking his first victory of any kind on tour, he had a one-stroke lead over Hale Irwin.

Irwin was a bespectacled, academic all-American and defensive back at the University of Colorado. Unlike others, he was not intimidated by Winged Foot. The former All–Big Eight Conference safety used an approach similar to how he might tackle a fullback.

"I remember arriving at Winged Foot and it was like that analogy of going up against a big opponent in football. You've got this 250-pound running back coming at you and you're wondering how am I going to tackle him," recalled Irwin. "At Winged Foot we essentially had a big bruising fullback running straight at us. You could see it in the locker room that 70 percent of the field had mentally checked out. The environment was just deathly [morbid].

"I remember telling myself, 'You hang in there. You only have to beat 30 percent of the field. Not that you are going to win, but you've got only 30 percent of the field kind of here, everybody else is moaning and groaning and complaining and they are already out.'"

By avoiding the big numbers and with a precious birdie at nine, Irwin took the lead at 5 over, one stroke ahead of Watson, as they headed to the back nine.

Irwin was no stranger to winning on tough courses, having been victorious at the Heritage Classic in 1971 and 1973, held on the formidable Harbor Town Golf Links in Hilton Head Island, South Carolina.

Palmer, forty-four, was the crowd favorite. He started out just three back, and to the joy of his thousands of followers he stayed right in the hunt this Sunday afternoon. But then he bogeyed three of the last six holes to finish with a 76 and a share of fifth place. He was joined there by Watson, who ballooned to a 79.

But Watson would overcome the major disappointment and the battle within himself with sheer determination, and he would earn the first of eight majors by winning the Open Championship at Carnoustie the following year.

Meanwhile, Irwin, who came to the game comparatively late and from left field, growing up in a place where there were no golf stars and baseball was the sport (near Commerce, Oklahoma, where Mickey Mantle came from), would apply the skills of straight driving, accuracy with long irons, solid bunker play, and patience to winning the first of three US Opens here.

But it would take all his skills, including being very consistent with a two-iron and sand wedge, to overcome the enormous challenges Oakmont presented.

"The fairways weren't overly generous. If you were wild off the tee, the trees would get you," explained Irwin. "So the problem was you had a long golf course with narrow fairways and heavy rough, and you were hitting long second shots into extremely firm greens with steep bunkers everywhere. Again, you just had to find the fairway. Then if you did, you had to find the green."

Irwin then talked about his approach to those slick greens: "Because the greens were so fast and had so many undulations, I found you had to cut the greens up in quarters. If the flag was in the back I wanted to be in the front part. If the flag was in the front part I didn't want to be way beyond it. If it was left or right, I just wanted to be in one of those quadrants as best I could."

One of his keys was simply trying to keep the ball under the hole so he wasn't putting downhill.

"Once you got on the green you just had to realize that you were going to make more bogeys than birdies. It is going to be an over-par golf course. If you made a double bogey, well, you just weren't ever going to come back from that," said Irwin, "Three putts were very common. In fact, Jack [Nicklaus] four-putted the very first green. Putted it right off the green and made double bogey. Now you don't think that news doesn't travel fast?!"

After Irwin passed Watson with a long birdie putt at the ninth hole, he'd "make more bogeys than birdies" by a two-to one margin on the back nine. He offset four bogeys with a pair of birdies, which was good enough to defeat Forest Fezzler, who finished two shots back at 9 over. Nine over for second place? That is almost double digits over par.

As a matter of fact, Irwin's 7-over 287 total was the highest winning mark in a major since the 1963 US Open at the Country Club in Brookline, Massachusetts, when Julius Boros won his second Open with a four-round total of 293. The 1974 scoring average of 76.99 was highest in relation to par in a major since the 1958 US Open. Even of the guys who made the cut, thirteen had rounds in the 80s, and forty-one guys couldn't break 300.

So it was no surprise that the combination of the narrow fairways, the fast greens, the deep rough, the pin placements, and the general setup prompted complaints before, during and after play.

The great sportswriter Jim Murray tells this story about the Golden Bear.

"I came upon Nicklaus on one of these forays as he was throwing a little 76 at the course one afternoon and he spotted me and stopped. 'How can you stand to watch this—I can hardly stand to play it!' he said, shaking his head. Nicklaus had 136 putts over the four days, the most of anyone in the tournament."[1] One player joked he once marked his ball only to see the quarter slide off the green.

More than a few players criticized the US Golf Association, claiming it was trying to embarrass them. Sandy Tatum, a USGA executive in large part responsible for the way the course played, brushed them off with his now famous quip.

"We're not trying to embarrass the best players in the game. We're trying to identify them."

I love that statement. And I endorse it 100 percent.

There's no question that setup they had was the toughest ever in the history of golf! No question. I mean the greens were hard. The rough was the highest you ever could wish to have it. And I want to tell you something: I have never in my life, in my seventy-three years as a professional, ever seen a tournament setup as tough as that. Ever. Ever.

That course, it was a a a massacre. But that is the examination paper that's put in front of you. And that's what you've got to accept. Somebody's gonna win.

And Hale Irwin? When I think of fierce competitors, I think of Ben Hogan, Jack Nicklaus, Tiger Woods, Raymond Floyd, and Hale Irwin. Fierce, fierce competitors.

Winged Foot played extremely difficult throughout the tournament, leading sportswriter Dick Schaap to coin the phrase "the Massacre at Winged Foot," the title of his ensuing book.

Many players and quite a few in the media held the view that when the best players in the world shoot 7 over par and that's the best score they can shoot, then maybe the USGA set the course up a little too tough.

"If anyone went out to their backyard and weeds were anywhere from eight to twelve inches tall, but very thick, that's what the rough was like with fairways just twenty-five to twenty-eight yards wide," explained Irwin. "For a green, go rumple up a tight, shagless rug in your room, try to take a golf ball and spin it on your linoleum floor. That is what it was like. And when you throw that all together you can sense what the players were trying to accomplish. But if I could remind people there were only two players in the entire field that finished in single digits over par. Again, if you could've been in the locker room, you would have felt the death pall in the room. It was that palpable. It reeked of death."

Well to many observers, Johnny Miller's record 63 closing round at the previous year's US Open at Oakmont didn't sit well with the USGA. They took pride in making their courses the most demanding in golf, and their setup here at Winged Foot was a devilish reflection of that embarrassment.

The USGA's Tatum explained his organization's perspective.

"I remember one night I was walking down the hall in the hotel and I came upon two players. One of them said, 'Boy, Sandy, you look tired.' And the other player said, 'You'd look tired too, if you had been out there all night on your knees waxing the greens.'"

Regarding the term "Massacre at Winged Foot," which endures, Irwin said: "Well, I think it was probably an appropriate term. Yes, we were in a battle with Winged Foot. The USGA won't say they prepped that course because of the year before, but I think all the players will disagree."

For the twenty-nine-year-old Irwin, this win launched him to elite status and a brilliant career that would include three US Open titles (and later a record-setting turn in what is now known as the Champions Tour).

"I had won before but always the big challenge was to get to that majors championship level. And now I had done it and I knew what it felt like. What a supreme feeling. And now you want to do it again!

Patting yourself on the back saying, 'Boy you did it' better last about five seconds because you've got to move on and play the next tournament. And then the next major championship.

"So for me, it was the turning point in my career. It was a great week, but it was also very difficult because it was one of the most trying weeks I've ever had. It was an achievement of a lifetime ambition, but because it was so much fun even though it came with a lot of difficulty, it gives you the confidence and excitement to move on and do it again. And again. And again," said Irwin. "Still, I can't imagine Jack and Tiger winning that many majors. It's just unbelievable."

It was an era of persimmon and balata gear, but far more than any other modern Open, Winged Foot 1974 even fifty years later is still remembered not for shotmaking, but for how so exceedingly difficult it played.

54

A ONE-SHOT WONDER

JUNE 17–20, 1982
PEBBLE BEACH GOLF LINKS
PEBBLE BEACH, CALIFORNIA

Five-time Open champion, five-time leading money winner, three-time Vardon Trophy winner, two-time Masters winner, six-time PGA Tour Player of the Year, and a Hall of Famer, Tom Watson has produced a tremendous number of achievements in this game. However, the number by which most fans around the world will remember him by is one.

Jack Nicklaus would call it a thousand-to-one shot.

Yet, even though what many experts thought was a miracle chip in from the rough on the seventeenth hole in the fourth round of the 1982 US Open to give him the stunning upset over the Golden Bear, Watson felt it was more the result of confidence built from hundreds of hours of effort playing the course going back to his college days.

And it all began with donuts.

"Monterey had a little donut shop," Watson recalled. "They were little glazed donuts. I would get a dozen and a quart of milk and that was my breakfast. I ate those before I got to Pebble Beach."[1]

After a tough week of hitting the books, the psychology major would be grateful to share his pastries with an individual who provided him entry to paradise at a time when it was way beyond a starving student's budget.

"When I went to Stanford, I had the opportunity to play Pebble Beach a number of times thanks to Ray Pargett, who was a starter that let me play for free," explained Watson. "I used to call him up and say, 'Ray, can I come down and play the course this Saturday morning and could I be the first off?' And he'd say, 'Sure, come on down.'

"Ray was a member of the Forty Thieves. It was a group of golfers who just loved the game. He kind of just took me under his wing. Always been grateful for that."

Like many players, Watson would imagine himself in a pressure situation to see how he'd produce in the clutch.

"No matter how poorly I was playing [at Pebble], I'd always get to the fifteenth tee and say, 'All right, the game's on now. I have to par the last four holes to win the US Open against Jack Nicklaus. That's the truth,'" said Watson. "I never did either. I never succeeded in parring the last four holes to win the US Open, no matter how many rounds I played there as an amateur."

Well, as a pro there in 1982, he opened with pars. That is, two rounds of 72, which put him in a share of eighth place with a group that included Nicklaus.

Australia's Bruce Devlin was the leader, five strokes ahead of Watson. An eight-time winner of the PGA Tour, he was on the downside of his career. This would be the last of his sixteen top ten finishes in a major (he'd garner a share of tenth).

On Saturday, Watson zoomed to the top with a third-round 68. He was now tied for the lead with a fifty-four-hole tally of 212. He and Bill Rogers were 4 under. Nicklaus would start the final round three back.

Though he was up against a pair of titans, Rogers knew how to win the big events. The slender native of Waco, Texas, was the defending Open champion, having defeated Bernhard Langer by four strokes at Royal St. George's.

The 1981 PGA Rookie of the Year was paired with Watson, three groups behind Nicklaus. With a birdie at four, Rogers took a one-stroke lead. However, starting at the par-4 third, Nicklaus stormed into contention with five straight birdies. And trouble loomed for Rogers at the turn, specifically holes nine and ten. The wiry Texan three-putted the former and failed to get up and down from a green-side bunker on the latter.

Though David Graham and Dan Pohl would move up and both would get it to 3 under at one point, the back nine essentially came down to another Nicklaus vs. Watson showdown.

After that marvelous par save from the edge of a cliff at the tenth, Watson birdied from twenty-two feet at the eleventh to go 5 under. That gave him a two-stroke lead over Nicklaus, who earlier had bogeyed eleven. But Watson gave back a stroke right away with a bogey at the next hole. Then at the par-5 fourteenth, a par 5 of 565 yards; despite his third shot resting short of the green, stopping on the collar at the back, Watson rammed home a thirty-five-footer for birdie. But in the seesaw battle, Nicklaus birdied fifteen. After Watson pushed his driver into a fairway bunker with a steep front wall, and having no shot forward, he ended up dropping a shot at sixteen, so they were all even again at 4 under.

As Watson arrived at the seventeenth, Nicklaus had completed his round. Parring the last two holes, he finished with a round of 69 to post 284. He was feeling good about winning his fifth national title here.

Meanwhile on the 210-yard seventy-first hole, Watson pulled his two-iron left. He knew it was in the tall stuff but upon arriving found it was not a bad lie.

"I felt that I could get the ball up softly enough. It was a lie that I had practiced because I knew I wasn't going to hit the greens very well the way I was hitting it, and as a result I played a lot of practice shots from downhill, deep grass lies from around the greens, and I was hitting that shot pretty well," explained Watson.

Could all those donuts and practice rounds through the years at Pebble, with him imagining going against Nicklaus, help pull off the improbable here?

"I went up to hit the shot and Bruce [Edwards, his caddy] said, 'Get it close,' and I said, 'Get it close? Hell, I'm going to hole it.'"

With approximately six feet from the edge of the green, he had about ten feet of green to work with. Using a similar technique he'd use for a shot from a bunker, Watson opened the blade of his sand wedge and delicately slipped it under the ball. And with a surgeon's touch, his effort got the ball to immediately pop up high and short to land gently on the green.

Quickly picking up speed on the downslope, it proceeded to crash into the flagstick and dropped in.

As the gallery roared its approval, Watson, beaming from ear to ear, jogged around the edge of the green in celebration. Then he turned around, pointed a finger at Edwards, and said, "Told you so!"

He now had a one-shot lead over Nicklaus heading to the final hole. Nicklaus, who had been watching Watson's progress on a TV monitor in back of the eighteenth green, had turned away for an instant. Then after hearing the roar, he had to ask what happened.

After Watson sealed the victory with a birdie on the closing hole to win by two, Nicklaus shook his hand on the green and said with a smile, "You little SOB, you did it to me again. You're something else."

He was referring to the fact that at the 1977 Masters, Watson held off Nicklaus to win the green jacket, then did the same at the US Open championship in Turnberry in 1977.

Watson would often refer to that chip at seventeen as "the best shot, the most important shot I ever made in my life."

The fact that it came at a US Open meant even more to Watson.

"Honestly, the US Open was the one tournament I wanted to win the most," said Watson, a five-time Open Championship champion.

"It's our National Open. I live in this country and I am an American citizen, born here, so it naturally meant just a little bit more to me. It's the benchmark of my career as far as what I wanted to do in the game."[2]

Sometimes an entire major can be captured in just one shot. That chip shot will be talked about in the same sentence with Gene Sarazen's double eagle in the 1935 Masters and Jack Nicklaus's one-iron that rattled the flagstick on the seventeenth at Pebble Beach in the 1972 Open.

Speaking of Pebble Beach, I wonder if Watson sent Mr. Pargett a box of glazed donuts as an expression of gratitude.

55

STRANGE BACK-TO-BACK

JUNE 15–18, 1989
OAK HILL COUNTRY CLUB (EAST COURSE)
ROCHESTER, NEW YORK

Seven. That's all. In the 129 years since the first US Open was held, just seven players have managed to win the event back-to-back.

Unquestionably, part of the explanation is simple competition. This is the biggest tournament of the year for the world's best golfers, and it's simply quite difficult to prove you're the best of the best in consecutive years.

And with the rotation of courses every year, one year's course can really suit your eye, but the following year's course may not.

One thing those seven players share is grit and toughness. An ability to grind. Curtis Strange certainly fits that mold.

"I met Curtis when he was a freshman at Wake Forest. And I recognized that right away. I was in the gallery when he won the NCAA Championship in San Diego as a freshman. He eagled the last hole to win the national title by one shot," recalled Peter Jacobsen. "He just had that never-give-up, never-say-die attitude that you need to win back-to-back US Opens."

The year before at the Country Club at Brookline, Massachusetts, it looked as though Curtis Strange might falter in his quest to win his first major. After bogeying the seventy-first hole, he dropped down into a tie with Nick Faldo. Then on the final hole, he hit into a bunker. However, he got up and down for par to preserve the tie and won by four strokes in an eighteen-hole playoff the following day with steady play.

Strange came from a golf family. His father, Tom, was an accomplished club professional who owned the White Sands Country Club in Virginia Beach. Curtis and his twin brother, Allan (who would also play on the PGA Tour) began playing at age seven.

Tragically, when he was fifteen, Curtis lost his father to cancer. He would lose himself in the game and become a three-time All-American. Professionally, in 1985 he had an ugly start at the Masters, opening with an 80. However, he fought back with rounds of 65 and 68, and he actually had the lead by four strokes heading to the back nine at Augusta on Sunday. However, he'd end up losing to Bernhard Langer. In the ensuing years he would play well and earned a lot of money. In 1988 he became the first tour player to win more than one million dollars in official money in a season, and in the process he earned PGA Player of the Year honors.

Arriving at Oak Hill to defend his title, the thirty-four-year-old Strange put on his well-known game face and went about his business like Hogan, with an air of being stubborn, steely, mum, and intimidating. Or as his caddy, Greg Rita, preferred to say, "He came focused."

Strange began the defense of his title with a 71. But in the second round he opened with back-to-back birdies and fired a 6-under 64 to tie the course record, set in 1942 by Hogan. Halfway through, his 5-under 138 was good enough for a one-stroke lead over Tom Kite, who shot 67-69.

The second-round action also provided an extremely rare occurrence for a US Open. In less than two hours, four players (Jerry Pate,

Nick Price, Doug Weaver, and Mark Wiebe) recorded a hole-in-one at the 167-yard sixth hole. Each had used the same strategy. All four took a seven-iron, each shot landed to the right and beyond the flag, then spun back into the cup.

Meanwhile, Mother Nature would put her spin on things. Due to heavy overnight rains that thoroughly soaked the already saturated course, there was a four-hour delay in starting the third round (some began calling it Soak Hill). Squeegee crews mopped up the wet track, and even the local fire department was enlisted to pump water off the flooded East Course.

As a result of the prolonged setback, instead of pairs, the players went off on split tees in groupings of three, a first at the US Open.

At the end of the day, with his third round in the 60s, Kite took over the lead. His 5-under 205 was one better than 1987 US Open winner Scott Simpson and three better than Strange.

Eighteen. That was the number of times Kite had finished in the Top Ten in the majors, including a pair of runner-up finishes at the Masters. Could the thirty-nine-year-old Texan finally break through here?

Things looked promising early in the final round when he birdied hole three to go 6 under. Diminutive Welshman Ian Woosnam, who'd win a green jacket at Augusta National two years later, moved up the leaderboard here by opening with back-to-back birdies. And after Kite triple-bogeyed the fifth, Woosnam was just two shots off the pace.

Meanwhile, the man wearing the Hogan-esque demeanor let the others make mistakes. After nine straight pars, Strange made the turn tied for the lead with Kite at 2 under. After his opponent bogeyed the tenth, Strange had the lead that he'd keep a stranglehold on.

Kite would double-bogey thirteen and fifteen, dropping him from contention. His resulting 8-over 78 placed him back in ninth place. Continuing his steady play as others fell around him, Strange, after fifteen consecutive pars, birdied sixteen. This gave him a two-stroke lead over Chip Beck and Mark McCumber.

Strange knew the national championship game formula very well by now. And despite a closing bogey, his unwavering patience and perseverance was rewarded with a rare back-to-back title.

Having been in the hunt once again until a late meltdown, Kite was disappointed yet philosophical about the situation.

"What can I say? My golf stunk," he said. "I will survive it, I promise you. It is a bitter pill to swallow. You don't like having a chance of winning any tournament, much less a major championship, and perform the way I did today."

He would add later, "Will I come back to win a major? Damn right I will." On that he was right, as Kite would take the US Open at Pebble Beach in 1992.

Now all smiles and downright jovial in the posttournament press conference, Strange described his accomplishment in becoming the first player since Hogan in 1951 to win back-to-back Open championships.

"It's not so much what Ben Hogan did, but what others have not done. The great Arnold Palmer, Jack Nicklaus, and Tom Watson have not won back-to-back Opens. It feels fantastic," said a beaming winner.

Jacobsen, a keen student of the history of the game and a seasoned broadcaster, had this observation about why his friend was able to achieve such rare status in winning consecutive US Opens.

"I think you've got to have a mean streak in you," said Jacobsen. "Kind of like a Hogan or Tiger, Curtis could stare the paint off a wall. He would just refuse to lose. He was just going to figure out a way to get it done."

Strange is just one of seven in the long, long history of the game to figure it out.

56

⌐

PEBBLE, CENTENNIAL, AND TIGER— MASTERPIECE THEATER

JUNE 15–18, 2000
PEBBLE BEACH GOLF LINKS
PEBBLE BEACH, CALIFORNIA

The one hundredth US Open in 2000 was a milestone that featured the game's best player at the game's most magnificent venue.

In this defining performance on the game's toughest stage, the centennial US Open featured Tiger Woods at Pebble Beach. That's it. There's no need to talk about the competition (there was none) be- cause this was a history-making accomplishment by a man who was in a league of his own. It was a 156-man field, but this week it was all about one player.

How good was his game before arriving here? Woods won, yes, was victorious in eleven of his last twenty PGA events and had thir- teen wins in his last twenty-four tournaments worldwide, simply a tremendous winning percentage.

One of those victories came at Pebble Beach back in February. Seven strokes behind with seven holes to play, Woods rallied and sparked by an eagle on the fifteenth hole. He won the Pebble Beach

AT&T Pro-Am, making him the first player since Ben Hogan in 1948 to win six straight tour events.

One of the reasons for his great success was never being satisfied. After tuning up his game with some practice rounds out in Las Vegas, Woods felt his putting was off. So the night before the first round of the US Open, he took some extra time on the practice green at Pebble Beach with coach Butch Harmon.

It seemed to work. The number one ranked player in the world opened with a 65, which included six birdies and no bogeys.

"Yesterday, actually since I've been here, my stroke hasn't been as comfortable as I'd like to have it. I was making putts, yeah, but there are certain ways of making putts. Either they go in properly, or you just kind of scoot them in. I didn't like the way I was rolling the ball," said Woods.

"I was making quite a few putts in practice rounds, but the ball wasn't turning over where I'd like to see it roll. And I worked on it for about a couple of hours yesterday and found that my posture was a little off, my release wasn't quite right, I wasn't releasing at the right time, and I just needed to get, basically, some reps in. Once I get enough reps, I feel a little more comfortable; and today I putted beautifully."

It was a beautiful performance on one of the world's most beautiful golf courses.

Shaped along the stunning bluffs above Stillwater Cove and Carmel Bay, where the rugged Monterey coastline meets the Pacific, the course offers long and short holes, varied elevation changes, and smallish yet tricky greens. But there's no margin of error, no bailouts. Of course, besides rain and fog, things get a whole lot more challenging when the fickle winds pick up and look to wreak havoc on those playing in such pristine surroundings.

On top of that, the twenty-four-year-old had first played this course at age thirteen. That was long enough to learn the par-71, 6,846-yard course plays differently at different times of the year.

"It's playing quite a bit differently than it did during the AT&T. All of the fairways are drier, they are faster, the greens are harder and firmer," Woods said earlier after a practice round. "The so-called three-and-a-half rough is a little different than the three-and-a-half inches of rough that everyone had said prior to the tournament. It's going to be a very difficult week."

Difficult for whom? Certainly not Tiger.

Not unlike the great racehorse Secretariat in the 1973 Belmont Stakes, Woods simply began pulling away from the field.

Building on that 65, the lowest score ever shot at Pebble Beach during a US Open, and despite fog delays affecting the completion of the first and second rounds, Woods, seemingly almost impervious to the conditions, followed with a 69 and increased his lead to six shots.

The only real drama was something only his caddy, Steve Williams, knew at the time. After sinking a thirty-foot birdie try at twelve before dark halted play, they returned to finish the second round Saturday morning. When they came to the eighteenth tee, Woods hooked his tee shot into the Pacific.

Williams pleaded with him to play it safe and tee off with an iron. A puzzled Woods would have none of it and insisted on staying with the driver. So, nervously, Williams handed him the ball. Why was the caddy on edge?

Between forgetting to return balls back to the bag the night before after a putting session on his hotel room carpet and giving a few scuffed balls to kids during play, Woods was playing with his last ball, and he didn't know it!

If that last ball found a watery grave, penalty strokes would have come into play, as Woods would have faced asking one of his partners for a ball (penalty for playing a different model of ball, two shots), or had his caddy run to the Lodge and whip out his credit card (likely an undue delay penalty, two shots).

After the ball landed safely in the fairway, Williams's racing pulse lowered slightly.

Marching on relentlessly, Woods was increasing his lead in the third round when he suddenly had a hiccup. On a day that was brutal for scoring, with the wind blowing hard and the rough even more difficult to manage, Tiger showed he was not immune to the USGA's devilish twists on the tall stuff at Pebble Beach.

After a poor tee shot on the par-4, 337-yard third hole, Woods then required multiple shots to get out to the rough and ended up with a triple-bogey 7. Now, in normal circumstances, few players can win a tournament making a triple bogey, even fewer a major championship, especially a US Open. But Woods still led by six, and he eventually finished with a 71, which made him the new owner of a ten-stroke lead, the largest fifty-four-hole gap of any US Open.

On a day when seventeen players failed to break 80, Ernie Els, with the day's low round of 68, was in second place at 2 over. Woods's total so far was 65-69-71=205 and 8 under.

I have always maintained throughout my career that putting and confidence go hand in hand if you want to win a major, and Tiger certainly proved that in closing out this tournament. He started out the final round with an outward 35 by missing only one fairway and one green, while his opponents fumbled about on the challenging poa annua greens. Woods began the homeward half with a birdie at ten and then three straight birdies at twelve, thirteen, and fourteen to move to 12 under. With birdies on four of the first five holes on the back nine, his lead soared from nine to thirteen. The extra putting session with Harmon was paying off.

Woods would not three-putt all week, while one-putting thirty-four of the seventy-two greens. He played the first twenty-two holes without a bogey, as well as the final twenty-six.

"Those big-par putts, you have to make them in the US Open," said Woods. "If you miss a green here, or any US Open championship, excluding Pinehurst, it's hard to control out of the rough. You're going to have the eight- or ten-footers or longer for par. If you make those, those feel better than a birdie. And you build on the momentum you've built on, or it can turn the tide around. And this week, there comes a point in time during the round that you have to make one of those putts. And I was able to step up and bury one of those putts."

He buried his competition.

Finishing with a 67, Woods's 272 was fifteen strokes ahead of runners-ups Ernie Els and Miguel Ángel Jiménez.

"Before we went out, I knew I had no chance." Ernie Els said about Tiger Woods's ten-stroke advantage at the beginning of the final round.

Said Ernie Els afterward, "Whatever I say is going to be an understatement. At the moment, he's just a great player. He's only twenty-four years old. It seems like we're not playing in the same ballpark right now. When he's on, you don't have much of a chance. This week, myself, with my own game, I played one good round of golf. But still, I guess if I played out of my mind, I probably still would have lost by five, six, seven. He's a phenomenal player. That's an understatement, probably."

Nick Faldo, a six-time majors winner, who came in a distant seventh place, had this to say about what he witnessed that week:

"Tiger was the ruthless example of once he got the lead he kept piling on birdies and nobody could catch him. He was so good at that. He led in not just a wire-to-wire win, no that wasn't enough. He has a six-shot lead halfway through then a ten-shot lead after fifty-four, and he just kept pushing himself. That is the ability of the great players when there's nobody out there and nobody is pushing you and it is just you and your caddy, and he's going like, 'I have to make this' and he does."

This was also the first tournament in Woods's "Tiger Slam," his streak of four straight wins in majors from the 2000 US Open through the 2001 Masters. One month after winning his third major and first US Open, Woods became the youngest player (topping Jack Nicklaus by two years) to complete the career grand slam with a masterpiece in the Open Championship. At the Old Course at St.

Andrews, Scotland, Woods continued his dominating play, finishing at 19 under—another record—and eight shots clear of the two who tied for second—Thomas Bjorn and Els, the last two players he played with at the US Open. The eight-shot win tied the largest winning margin at any Open since 1900.

A month later Woods successfully defended his PGA Championship title at Valhalla Golf Club in Kentucky by beating Bob May in a playoff. He went on to win the Open, the PGA Championship, and then the 2001 Masters to have sole ownership of all four. The year 2000 is often regarded as the pinnacle of Woods's career.

The man that broke up Tiger's streak, at the 2001 US Open, Retief Goosen, was impressed by his competitor's ability to completely focus his attention under pressure in an almost serene-like state.

"Tiger is like Jack Nicklaus, mentally extremely strong. It seems like the bigger the stakes, the calmer they both appeared. And the more focused and the better they performed. Which is all mental," said two-time majors winner Goosen. "Some players cracked under the pressure, and can't control their emotions, whereas Tiger and Jack actually just seem to be getting calmer as the pressure mounts. Their ability to stay in the present moment were strong traits of theirs."

A peek into Tiger's mind after his victory here reveals a never-ending search to improve his game, all fueled by a bottomless competitive fire.

"I can tell you one thing, this is something I've said, and I will continue to say, is I'm going to try to—I'm going to try to get better. You're always trying to work on things in this game of golf, trying to get a little bit better. Always trying new equipment or trying new techniques. There's always something you're trying to get better. We all understand that. If we all play golf, we all have a bug—we're all trying to get better somehow."

I applaud his hunger to want to better his game, but I always say if Tiger Woods had never had another lesson after this, he still would've won twenty-two or twenty-three majors championships.

And would've gone down as the greatest athlete, man or woman, the planet had ever seen.

Now can you imagine Tiger Woods playing some of the greatest golf the world has ever seen in the history of the game and going along for lessons from guys who are club pros and not really people who played big major tournaments for a long time?

Still, knowing how tough to win any major is, the way Tiger dominated one of the toughest tests in golf that week at Pebble Beach is very, very impressive.

57

"I'M SUCH AN IDIOT"

JUNE 15–18, 2006
WINGED FOOT GOLF CLUB (WEST COURSE)
MAMARONECK, NEW YORK

What we have here at the 2006 US Open is another example of a major known more for who lost than who won.

San Diego native Phil Mickelson already started playing in the national championship when he was just a sophomore at Arizona State. As an amateur at Medinah in 1990, the young phenom finished at even par in a tie for twenty-ninth. In the ensuing sixteen years he had three runner-up results, the last being 2004.

At that event, in Shinnecock Hills, competing on the infamous greens that were baked after three days and extremely fast—many claiming it bordered on unplayable on some holes in the final round—Mickelson nevertheless birdied the fifteenth and sixteenth holes and led Retief Goosen by one with two to play. However, he then three-putted from five feet for a double bogey on the seventeenth. It was the South African's second US Open victory.

But this other great New York venue, Winged Foot, was filled with potential glorious opportunities for Lefty.

A Mickelson victory here meant history. As the winner of three straight majors (he had won the 2005 PGA Championships and the 2006 Masters), there'd been a lot written and talked about regarding the potential of a "MickelSlam" because that'd be something only his rival Woods had accomplished in the previous fifty years with his "Tiger-Slam" (2000). Jack Nicklaus (1971–1972) and Ben Hogan (1953) were two other players to win three consecutive majors in the modern era. (Bobby Jones's grand slam in 1930 came before the Masters had been founded and included the US and British Amateurs. See chapter 63.)

It is widely believed that the US Open is the most difficult and, according to many, the most coveted of golf's majors championships. The course setup (primarily its deep rough, narrow fairways, undulating greens, and daunting pin placements) demands the most from golfers. It is not only the most challenging, it is the most mentally exhausting.

And in Mamaroneck, New York, Winged Foot is a poster child for those aforementioned challenges, stirring up even more stress and pressure than most majors. Designed by A. W. Tillinghast, it opened in June 1923 and hosted its first US Open in 1929, which Bobby Jones won in a playoff.

Winged Foot is one of the great courses in the world, and I know it well because I have played there a lot. I was leading the US Open there in 1974, after the first thirty-six holes. Hale Irwin won with a 7-over-par total of 287, which gives some idea of the difficulty of the layout. It was the toughest setup ever in a tournament. The greens were murder, absolute murder. I have never seen greens more tough than those. Never.

Flying in under the radar for the 2006 version at Winged Foot was Australian Geoff Ogilvy.

Having never seen let alone played the course, during a tournament break in nearby Westchester just the week before, the native of Adelaide made a brief visit and became a quick study after his preparations and came up with this view:

"It is all about the greens. Starting with the first. It might be one of the most craziest, most difficult greens there are in all of golf. A relatively straightforward hole, but if you tried to build that green again they'd lock you up and never let you work on a course again," said Ogilvy. "All through the course it's all about making sure your approach shot lands below the hole for your par putt. Very difficult. If you get in the wrong spot around the greens, it's trouble time. The rest of the course is beautiful and lovely, but the challenge lies in the last two shots on every hole more than the first two shots."

Colin Montgomerie was certainly loving it (at least early on in the tournament). The Scotsman took the first-round lead with a fine 69. He was the only player to break par, a 1 under, and had the lead for the first time in nine years. One of the reasons he attributed it to was being under the radar, so less expectations to deal with.

"You know, I think the expectation of me in the '90s to win this thing was very high, and I gave it a go a couple times and was not quite close. I think the expectation was lower this particular year or the last few years that I haven't contended, and it does make a difference where you are more relaxed. It won't change me, my life, or whatever if I do very well here this week, but it might have done in the '90s. So that was more expectation and pressure on me then than there is now. It's nice, I can go out and sort of free-wheel, if you like, and not worry about things the way I used to do in the '90s."

Four times Monty had finished in second in a major. The most recent came in the previous year's Open Championship at the Old Course at St. Andrews. Owner of a record eight European Tour Order of Merit titles, could this be the major that the World Golf Hall of Famer would break through for a victory?

Well, in that relaxed mode, Monty showed the first round was no fluke when he followed that 69 up with a solid 71, and he was just one off the lead midway through.

Mickelson, who had opened with a 70, a solid start, followed that with a 73, but he tried to remain optimistic about heading into the weekend tied for seventh.

Tiger Woods, in his first major since the passing of his father, would have no chance. He did not fare very well and he suffered the first missed cut of his career in grand slam play with rounds of 76-76, missing by three shots. He was joined by such fellow stalwarts as two-time US Open champion Retief Goosen, Nick Price, and Sergio Garcia, as well as defending champion Michael Campbell in not making the weekend.

However, the weekend started out quite nicely for Phil. While Monty ballooned to a 75 on Saturday's third quadrant, Mickelson was tied for low round with 69.

After Lefty, a favorite of the New York crowd, deftly found the hole from fifteen feet for a birdie at sixteen and subsequently moved right to the top, the spectators bellowed their appreciation as he shared the fifty-four-hole lead with Kenneth Ferrie, a thirty-seven-year-old Englishman (competing in his first US Open, Ferrie would fade after a final-round 76).

But Phil the Thrill was right on schedule for his date with destiny, and so many New Yorkers were hoping to witness it.

"I'm very excited and happy to have fought hard on the back nine to get back into contention and tied for the lead. It should be a fun day tomorrow. I'm really looking forward to it," said the coleader. He added, "It's such a tough course, I don't know what number it will take. I'm not really entering it with a number in mind, but I'm just going to try to make a lot of pars, maybe a birdie here or there."

Ogilvy, with a steady 71-70-72 placing him at 3 over, just one back of the leaders, said the key was to plod along and avoid the big number. "That's sort of the way it's set up. You've got to really take double bogeys out of the equation, make smart decisions."

He expressed his pleasure about his efforts so far would provide his first experience playing among the final groups for the national championships. "Anyone who asked before I started, what do I want out of this week, I said I wanted to be in contention on the weekend and play in one of the last few groups just to see what it was like. I've played in the last few groups a lot but not at the US Open. Whatever happens, I just want to play well."

And Mickelson added a note of how his focus is on the here and now: "I've got one round to go, eighteen holes, and there's a lot of guys right there, a lot of good players that are making pars and fighting, just like I'm trying to do. I'm not thinking about those past tournaments. I'm trying to just play one more good round."

One more good round would prove elusive for just about all the final contenders. Still, this was to be one of the most thrilling finishes in US Open history.

Five players would have at least a share of the lead during the final round, with fifteen lead changes. However, it would be more about contenders stumbling than one-upping each other. Because, as is so often the case, the guy who wins a US Open is more often the player who makes the least mistakes.

Mickelson tied for the lead at the 2004 US Open, fell with a double bogey on the seventy-first hole. But make no mistake: Even though they went home unrewarded from Shinnecock Hills, the throng at Winged Foot were hoping to see their Phil raise the trophy.

It would be a good but dissatisfying round for Jim Furyk. While he garnered a pair of birdies to get to a couple under, he gave them back with bogeys on seven and nine. But after a long par save on ten followed by a pair of birdies on eleven and twelve, he suddenly had a piece of the lead. However, he just couldn't get any putts to fall on the way in, and though he finished with a fine 70, it would not be enough.

Furyk, a two-time All-American who led the University of Arizona to an NCAA title, reflected on the closing hole, his last missed opportunity: "[At] eighteen, I got a bad kick, landed the ball at least five, six yards in the fairway and almost ended up going in the long rough, hit a great second shot and missed my little putt, which looks like actually might cost me a shot at a playoff tomorrow. I'm disappointed. I played my heart out and it didn't work."

Paired with Furyk in that final round, Padraig Harrington stayed one back of the lead by sinking his par putt at the tricky thirteen. Arriving at sixteen, needing just three pars to finish for a likely victory, Harrington instead would go on to bogey the last three holes and finish at 71.

However, he managed to take some positives out of coming up short, saying that the self-belief gained from the experience at Winged Foot was what would propel him to great success.

"Well, believe it or not where my confidence came from was actually the 2006 US Open at Winged Foot," he said reflecting on it years later. "I hit the last three fairways, but finished with three bogeys to lose. Three pars would've won it outright for me. Two pars would've put me in the playoffs. Psychologist Bob Rotella was there to console me. I just looked at him and said after the round, 'Now I know I can win a major on my own.'

"Up to that moment, I always felt I needed somebody else's help to win a major. After seventy-two holes at Winged Foot, I felt I didn't play my best yet, just a couple pars away from making the playoffs. That had never happened to me before. Everything fell into place and I could see, 'Hang on a second, I am good enough to win these without anybody else's help.'"

It worked. The following year Harrington won the Open Championship at Carnoustie and the year after that he was victorious in two more majors—the Open Championship at Royal Birkdale and the PGA Championship at Oakland Hills, the same venue where I won the 1972 PGA Championships.

Then there was poor Monty. He was one of the players so closely associated with majors championship failure. But despite his first three-putt of the week at fourteen, he battled back. At seventeen Monty was in the trees, but he got it out and skipped it onto the green seventy-five feet from the pin. His putt swung way out left and fell into the cup, and now he was actually tied for the lead while playing the par-4 eighteenth.

Could this be it? Could this be the temperamental, talented Scot's moment of glory?

After all, he put himself into optimum position by getting the tee shot onto the right-center of the fairway, despite the requirement not suiting to his standard left-to-right ball flight. Now having accomplished that awkward challenge, with the pin placed on the back right of the green 171 yards away, it looked like with his natural power fade that a birdie for the win or at the very least a par for playoff was a certainty.

However, this sport offers very few certainties.

While his playing partner, Vijay Singh, awaited a ruling, instead of asking to play on, Monty stood there pondering and pondering. At the last instant, believing that adrenaline would be a factor, he switched from a six- to a seven-iron.

Johnny Miller, a former US Open champion himself, commentating for NBC-TV at the time, told the national audience: "I'm surprised he just switched clubs when you've had ten minutes to figure it out."

He caught it a bit heavy, and it veered right.

Apparently, he had not figured it out. Observing his shot, and not liking what he was seeing, a TV microphone picked up Monty's reaction—"What kind of shot is that?"

It was a shot that would start the downfall. Coming up short and right of the pin in high grass, he then pitched thirty-five feet past and then three-putted, missing an eight-foot comebacker. Monty had double-bogeyed from 171 yards. Game over.

Though he'd skirt the edges, the twenty-nine-year-old Ogilvy, entering the week ranked fiftieth in the world, would avoid a similar calamity. With his effortless swing, creative short game, and words of wisdom at a pivotal moment from his caddy, Alistair "Squirrel" Matheson, Ogilvy would experience a different result.

The key was his belief about producing in the clutch in the biggest events.

"I had won the World Match Play Championship earlier that year, and as anyone who has gone deep into the Match Play will tell you, that week gives you more experience hitting shots under pressure than any other event combined," said Ogilvy. "And with results like being T-16 at the Masters, T-5 in the 2005 Open Championship at St. Andrews, and T-6 in the 2005 PGA Championship at Baltusrol, I was getting belief in myself at the majors. I felt if I did play well, I could get myself into contention. And if I did get into contention, I feel good enough about my game that I could hang around a bit. That was the feeling. I felt good about my game."

Ogilvy was hanging around, all right, and his final round began with him hanging a bit longer than usual in the players' fitness trailer.

It was there that he became enthralled with a World Cup football match on TV, with powerhouse Brazil taking on his home team, Australia. Ogilvy still got in sufficient warm-up time.

A happy distraction also came in the form of Ogilvy's playing partner in the second-to-last group, the colorful Englishman Ian Poulter. When Poulter turned up with a pink bag and a pink outfit, he stole all the attention, which helped and was certainly better for Ogilvy than having to play with Mickelson in front of a partisan New York crowd. And of course, Poulter took all the razzing in good stride and later recalled one zinger from the spectators when a man in the crowd shouted, "It's Father's Day, not Mother's Day!"

It certainly would be a memorable day for Ogilvy.

He got off to a really good start with birdies on five and six. He led by two strokes after seven holes, but he lost his advantage with four bogeys in seven holes. He clearly remembers heading to fifteen being a crucial moment of his tournament.

"Walking off the fourteenth hole, I had just bogeyed it and I believe I was now two back, and was having a bit of a letdown then Squirrel, my caddy, I tell him, 'Oh well, maybe next week,' and he said, 'What do you mean? No one's going to par the last four holes, so just go par the last four holes,'" recalled Ogilvy. "He was just basically telling me, 'Let's finish this off with a little bit of dignity,' not that we're going to win, but he didn't want a crash with all bogeys. The whole week had disappeared for me, and I just had this nice little goal now of closing with four pars."

After pars at fifteen and sixteen, Ogilvy was halfway there. However, after a poor tee shot at seventeen landed in the right rough, he had no angle to the green.

"That hole had my number the entire week," said Ogilvy. "I don't think I hit the fairway once. But this was way in the trees, and I can only move it to a better spot still in the rough. I'm 120 yards to the green in the heavy rough. And I think it is definitely over now.

"I could not get the shot to the green because of the angle I had. The third shot up to the left of the green about pin high. My caddy Squirrel says, 'Why don't you just chip it in?' I had a chuckle to myself, but lo and behold it went in. It surprised me more than anybody else."

If Ogilvy could get that fourth straight par at eighteen, it would likely guarantee a spot in the playoffs.

He found the fairway with his tee shot, but it came to rest over an old divot. So, using a nine iron from about 155 yards, Ogilvy thought he had stiffed it—he even recalled thinking, "That's the shot that wins the US Open." However, the sand on the lie had its effect, and the ball landed a couple yards short on the false front and rolled back all the way down about thirty yards.

Nevertheless, once again, in the clutch, Ogilvy hit a fine chip and remained in the hunt.

All that was left was to awaiting the results of the lone challenger remaining—Phil Mickelson.

Stubbornly sticking with his errant driver, Mickelson missed the fairway again at seventeen, well over the gallery and into the trees. Finding his ball way left and amazingly inside a trash bag, Mickelson received a free drop. He was able to have a long go at birdie, but he settled for par.

Mickelson, who was in the top fifteen on tour in total driving yet ranked ninety-ninth in driving accuracy, stepped to the tee box at eighteen needing just a par to win and a bogey for a playoff. The 450-yard dogleg-left was playing to a stroke average of 4.471 for the week, making it, along with number one, the most difficult hole on the course.

It didn't help that Mickelson had driven the ball terribly all week. Finding zero on the back nine this Sunday and only twenty-four for the entire tournament placed him in a tie for fifty-first among the sixty-three players who made the cut. He would end up losing invaluable strokes by having six pars and two bogeys on the two par-5s for the tournament.

If I was Phil's caddy, I would have put a three-iron in his hand and run down the fairway with the bag on my shoulders, and I would not have come back to him.

His tee shot went so far left that it clattered through the trees by a hospitality tent. Still trying for par, he went for the green with his second shot but hit a tree, and the ball advanced just twenty-five yards.

His third faded into the greenside bunker, buried with a "fried-egg" lie; the fourth shot from the sand to win had no spin and rolled off the other side of the green into the rough. Phil's chip for bogey and a Monday playoff with Ogilvy rolled six feet past the hole. He had now tied Sam Snead for the most second-place finishes by a player who has never won the US Open with four. (He'd later also finish runner-up at the US Opens in 2009 and 2013.)

Phil's 6-over 286 put him in a tie for second with Montgomerie and Furyk.

What happened to the New Phil? When it came down to it, he lost as the Old Phil when he did his "Phil the Thrill" thing with a stubborn, reckless attempt to get himself out of another jam.

Phil Mickelson, trying to win a third straight major with arguably the best opportunity to claim what has become an elusive US Open title imploded on the seventy-second hole, ending the round with a double bogey (like Monty) when par would have secured the victory. He had a two-shot lead with four holes to play, but seemingly all in a New York minute, the finish was stunning and merciless.

Coming out of the scorers' area, Mickelson was still dazed and quite disappointed about what just occurred.

"I just can't believe that I did that. I am such an idiot. I can't believe I couldn't par the last hole. It really stings. This is going to take a little while to get over."

He went on to say: "This one hurts more than any tournament because I had it won. I think the biggest reason why this is so disappointing is that this is a tournament that I dreamt of winning as a kid, that I spent hours practicing—I mean, countless hours practicing. I came out here weeks and months in advance to get ready and had it right there in my hand, man. It was right there and I let it go."

One of the most wild, shocking, and heartbreaking US Open finishes of all time, especially knowing that heading into 2024 Mickelson still has not conquered the national championship, compiling a record six runner-up finishes in this major.

These events last seventy-two holes, not seventy-one. That's the harsh reality. Still, Mickelson almost pulled it off in distinctly Phil Phashion.

But in fairness, we've all been there. He makes that mistake there, but we all make mistakes, so you can't isolate it down to certain players. Colin Montgomerie and Jim Furyk also had a chance in that same tournament.

Nicklaus finished second in nineteen majors! Arnie, ten; Greg Norman and Tom Watson, eight each. I've been runner-up six times.

Trevino, Hogan, Snead—you can go down the line about the

greats that have come in second in a lot of majors. But what we all share is a determination to keep on being in contention again and again, and Phil has done that with distinction.

Remember the saying: "When you finish second, only your wife and your dog remember it. And that's if you've got a good wife and a good dog."

58

EYE OF THE TIGER STARES DOWN ROCCO AS ROCKY

JUNE 12–16, 2008
TORREY PINES (SOUTH COURSE)
SAN DIEGO, CALIFORNIA

Tiger Woods, the number-one-ranked player in the world, arrived in San Diego in a wobbly state.

After a brilliant 2007 season in which he won an incredible seven official PGA Tour events of the sixteen he entered (including his thirteenth major—the PGA) and three runners-up as well, he ruptured his ACL while running near his home in Orlando. He tried to manage the injury, but his continued golfing competition exacerbated it. He also had some cartilage damage, so even with three more wins in early 2008, he was forced to shut it down after the Masters and the surgery prevented him from competing. The rehab did not go so well and actually caused further damage. Although his doctors strongly advised him against it, Woods, who was determined to keep his life-long dream of capturing majors titles progressing, limped onto Torrey Pines with a double stress fracture in his left tibia and a torn left ACL.

The fact that this major was being held at a familiar course certainly must have factored in his decision.

Woods had won at Torrey Pines four years in a row. He had won six of the last seven Invitationals. Nearly 10 percent of Tiger's Tour wins had come at Torrey Pines. His success goes way back. He won at Torrey when he was too young to drive a car (the 1991 Junior World Golf Championship at age fifteen).[1]

Out of the 155 other players he would compete against, it would be a not-so-young, irrepressible, paunchy forty-five-year-old Pennsylvanian with a creaky back that would end up being the one going the distance with the thirteen-time majors champ.

Rocco Mediate grew up a few par-5s from Latrobe and in his late teens got to play with Arnold Palmer at the Latrobe Country Club. Soon thereafter he would team up with future two-time US Open champion Lee Janzen to help Florida Southern College win a Division II national team championship.

Though he'd go on to become the first PGA player to win on tour using a long putter (the 1991 Doral-Ryder Open), Mediate had long been plagued by back problems. He missed years of his prime due to a ruptured disk that required major surgery. But the affable battler fought on, getting his fifth tour victory in 2002. Unfortunately, the back problems resurfaced and he would go MIA again for a long period.

But driven by the goal of winning a major, Mediate picked himself up off the canvas and stepped into the big-time arena—in this case, the longest course in majors history at 7,643 yards. He played well enough with a 69 to finish the first round just one shot off the lead.

Meanwhile Woods, with a 1-over 72, admitted (with a wink) to a terrible start with a double bogey on the very first hole, the 448-yard par-4.

"Getting into the flow of the round, it helps when you hit six shots on the first hole to get into the flow. [Laughter.] That's a lot of shots to get into a flow. So, yeah. It's just a terrible way to start. It's one thing to hit the ball left off the first tee, that's fine, pitch out. But the wedge shot, I had all the room short of the hole, and I fly it past the hole. That's just a terrible mistake."

Closing with a 30 in the second round, Woods overcame his early mistakes and competitive rust by climbing right into the fray at the top. His 68 put him just one shot back of leader Stuart Appleby, who was 3 under at 139.

Meanwhile, the self-effacing Mediate was enjoying interacting with the fans while at the same time also relishing the course layout as he, too, was just one shot off the lead after a 71.

"I enjoy talking and I just go over and—especially, like, if I'm sitting there waiting a few times, I go over and say hi or what's up or make fun of somebody or they make fun of me. Whatever. It's fun," said the veteran.

What he saw in the third round was another formidable contender entering the fight. After finishing with a 70, Englishman Lee Westwood became the only player to shoot par or better in all three rounds. His fifty-four-hole total of 211 put him in second, one ahead of Mediate, who shot 72 but one back of the new leader.

Despite grimacing from the searing pain in his leg after all-you-got tee shots, and occasionally using his club as a cane, Tiger Woods nevertheless put up some amazing shots that resulted in two eagles and a chip-in birdie from the rough on the seventeenth. They resulted in a round of 70. And at 3-under 210 he had the lead heading into the final round.

And that is not insignificant, because Woods was 13-0 in majors when he had the lead after fifty-four holes.

Still, Westwood, one of the few people in the world who had prior experience coming back and beating Tiger Woods on a Sunday (it was the 2000 Deutsche Bank event in Germany) was hoping to draw on that success.

At a press conference the night before the final round, Westwood said with confidence, "I shot a 64 that day, so hopefully I can do the same tomorrow."

Westwood, who owned a pair of second-place finishes in the Masters as well as one in the Open Championship, was bidding to become the first European to win America's national championship since Tony Jacklin in 1970.

Mediate was well aware of Tiger's dominant finishes, but he gave himself a fighting chance heading into the fourth round.

"It's going to take a ridiculous round by one of us to beat him. If we go out and shoot 4 or 5 under par one of us, you never know. But you can't ever count anything. It's just you can't really predict anything that's going to happen," said Mediate. "It's not over yet. And I'm sure he'll tell you the same thing. Because this is a US Open course and you just don't know what the heck is going to happen sometimes."

What happened to Woods was not a good start. After clanging into trees on a pair of shots, he once again double-bogeyed the first hole. And he followed that with a bogey. Mediate's birdie at number two gave him a one-shot lead. However, after back-to-back bogeys, Rocco lost his lead to Westwood, who parred seven of the first eight holes.

After ten holes there was a three-way tie with everyone at 1 under. But Mediate played steady from there to finish with a par 71 and was the leader in the clubhouse.

Arriving at the seventy-second hole, a 573-yard par-5, Woods and Westwood were both just one back of Mediate. Both hit their drives into bunkers and had to lay up. Both reached the green with their third shots, leaving them with birdie putts to force an eighteen-hole playoff with Mediate. Once again, a crucial moment in the majors came down to the putter.

Westwood, fifteen feet away, went first. In arguably the biggest stroke of his very successful career, but still seeking his first major, he comes up short the ball bending left in front of the cup.

Now, with Mediate anxiously looking on outside the scorer's room, Woods, with his amazing undefeated streak on the line, had to sink his twelve-foot putt to extend play. The ball lipped the hole slightly before dropping in, and NBC-TV sportscaster Dan Hicks exclaimed, "Expect anything different?!" We now had an eighteen-hole playoff the following day to determine a winner.

The journeyman underdog challenger had nothing but admiration for the champ.

"The thing that's most amazing is the man I'm going to play tomorrow has won thirteen of these. It's amazing how much it takes. I gave all of what I had today and I can't complain. I knew he'd make that putt," said Mediate. He added, "Oh, my God, I get to play for the National Open against the best player on earth, that maybe has ever played. How much more could you ask for?"

The fans witnessing it on-site and the TV viewers couldn't ask for anything more, as the two combatants traded leads throughout the playoff.

It went back and forth with three lead changes on the front nine alone. But after back-to-back bogeys on nine and ten, the challenger was on the ropes, finding himself suddenly down by three. But he climbed back to within one as he parred the next two holes while Woods bogeyed both of them.

Mediate continued his rally. And after three straight birdies starting at the massive 614-yard, par-5 thirteenth, now had the lead at even par.

After both parred sixteen and seventeen, they came to the eighteenth hole with a similar situation as the day before. Woods needed birdie to extend play or his streak would be over.

Mediate's tee shot landed in a fairway bunker. Woods, with eagle-birdie the last two times at this hole, hit safely onto the fairway then was easily on in two. Mediate managed to set up a birdie try.

With thousands looking on and expressing support for both players, Woods putted first. An eagle could give him the lead. He missed. Now with a putt to achieve his dream of winning a US Open, the 158th-ranked Mediate also missed, but made his par to force sudden death.

Beginning at the seventh, a dogleg-right par-4, Woods hit a drive in the fairway and knocked his approach on the green to about twenty feet from the cup. Mediate hit his drive into a fairway bunker, then followed that with an approach shot that veered left and into the spectator grandstand. He would receive a free drop.

"Is the Cinderella story about to end?" NBC's Hicks wondered.

Tiger stroked a nine-iron from 157 yards onto the green. Mediate couldn't get spin on his ball, so his pitch rolled past the flag, forcing a twenty-footer.

Woods's outright winning putt fell a couple inches short. Mediate's effort to stay alive rolled his eighteen-footer past the right side of the cup. His dream of becoming the oldest US Open champion at forty-five years, six months rolled away with it.

"It was just unreal," Woods said with a lot of respect for his challenger. "It was back and forth, back and forth. And ninety holes wasn't enough."

Disappointed but proud of his effort, Mediate said, "I never quit. I never quit. I've been beaten down a few times and came back, and I got what I wanted. I got a chance to beat the best player in the world. And I came up just a touch short."

Tiger went on to have surgery soon after and missed the remainder of the 2008 season. It was his sixty-fifth career victory, passing Ben Hogan for third all time, but he would not win another major until more than ten years later (at the Masters in 2019).

"I think this is probably the best ever," Woods said, admiring his hard-fought-for trophy. "All things considered, I don't know how I ended up in this position, to be honest with you. It was a long week. There was a lot of doubt, a lot of questions going into the week. And here we are ninety-one holes later."

In the sport's most demanding tournament, lose focus, lose ground. There was no doubt, it was the eye of the Tiger . . . again in the end.

59

A CLASH (THEN CRASH)
OF TITANS AT TORREY

JUNE 17–20, 2021
TORREY PINES GOLF COURSE (SOUTH COURSE)
SAN DIEGO, CALIFORNIA

The 2021 US Open got off to a late start, but when the fog cleared, they had to complete the first round on Friday, and the leaders who emerged at the halfway point of this major would not be the titans the spectators expected to see . . . not yet.

Heading into the weekend at the top of the leaderboard were Russell Henley and Richard Bland, tied at 5-under 137 through thirty-six.

Henley, thirty-two, a seven-time winner on tour, hailed from Georgia, where he won the 2010 Haskins Award as the most outstanding collegiate golfer at the University of Georgia in Athens. An avid guitar player who has actually played onstage with some known bands, he was hitting all the right notes. He took the outright lead at 6 under after hitting his approach shot to the par-3 eighth hole (his seventeenth hole of the round) to seven feet and making the putt for birdie. But he could not maintain his advantage, and he bogeyed the par-5 ninth to finish at 1-under 70.

Bland, a journeyman from England, got into the Torrey field by becoming the oldest first-time winner in European golf history (in his 478th start!). But here in San Diego he made three birdies in a five-hole stretch. So at the age of forty-eight, Bland became the oldest player to hold a share of a thirty-six-hole lead in US Open history.

Neither would maintain the momentum to contend. Though the Georgian played well enough to share the lead through fifty-four holes, his final-round 76 placed him in a tie for thirteenth. Bland did not make a birdie in the third round and shot 6-over 77, which essentially ended his chances there.

Canadian Mackenzie Hughes, on the strength of a sixty-three-foot putt for eagle, finished with a 68 for a share of the third-round lead. He'd roll a 77 the following day to finish tied at fifteenth. The cream was rising as the stars got their measure of Torrey Pines.

The previous time this course hosted the US Open (2008), the game's biggest star had risen in the clutch. With a torn ACL and a broken leg, and through sheer will, Tiger Woods outlasted journeyman Rocco Mediate over a grueling ninety-one holes to win his fourteenth major and third career grand slam (see chapter 58).

The course at Torrey (whose pines are distinctive to the area) was originally designed by William Bell Sr. in 1957, and is home to the Farmers Insurance Open PGA Golf Tournament along with the North Course. In 2001 and again in 2019, Torrey Pines' South Course was renovated and redesigned by Rees Jones. With the most recent renovations, Torrey Pines South is longer and plays more difficult, with the South's teeing areas extending the length of this course to up to 7,800 yards.[1]

In 2019, those renovations included fairways and bunkers being shifted on holes four, nine, ten, twelve, and seventeen, and all bunkers refurbished.[2]

The main grasses of Torrey Pines are kikuyu overseeded with rye in the fairways with the greens primarily Bentgrass with Poa annua.

And it is with those greens that Jones made some of his more compelling moves. What he did was devise assorted internal contours—greens within greens—mandating precise approach play. Like any US Open where driving is at a premium, it became even more crucial with fairways pinched in by both penalizing rough and deep bunkers.[3]

This is a public course that hosts ninety-two thousand rounds of play annually. Not many US Open venues test the concentration of the competitors with distinctive ocean views that include the distracting sights of hang-gliders and paragliders soaring and hovering at the edge of the cliffs on the south end of the layout.

Bethpage in New York was the only other public facility that hosted a US Open, and the 2002 event was also won by Tiger Woods.

Woods was unable to play here, as he was still undergoing physical therapy after suffering significant injuries in a car crash the previous February. Still, there were plenty of marquee players moving into contention after some sparkling third-round play.

Louis Oosthuizen, who had a share of the lead after the first round, grabbed a piece of the third-round lead after making a fifty-one-foot eagle putt on the eighteenth hole.

However, the 2010 Open champion, who since had come in second five times in majors, knew there was a hungry group of talent nipping at his heels.

Speaking at a press conference after the third round, Oosthuizen said, "I need to play well. I need to go out—there's a lot of great players up there that's got a chance of winning this, and I just need to go out and play as good as I can tomorrow."

Also fighting back were a host of accomplished winners.

Former US Open champion Rory McIlroy, on the strength of four birdies on the back nine, including a chip-in from the rough to the right of the green on the twelfth, tied for the lowest round of the day at 4-under 67. He was just two back of the lead. As was defending champion Bryson DeChambeau, whose bogey-free round of 68 tied him with McIlroy.

Scottie Scheffler was within three of the leaders. Just four back were former major winners Dustin Johnson and Collin Morikawa along with hometown talent Xander Schauffelle.

And while it was not his hometown, San Diego and particularly Torrey Pines had been great to Spaniard Jon Rahm. Not only had he won his first PGA title there (the 2017 Farmers Insurance Open, after holing a long eagle putt on the final green) but he proposed to his wife, Kelley, on the beach just below the adjacent North Course. And now with his ten-week-old son, Kepa, on the grounds, along with his father, Edorta, Rahm was hoping to make this the ultimate Father's Day for him.

Growing up in Barrika, Spain, he spent most of his youth participating in soccer, canoeing, jai alai, and kung fu. But after countryman Seve Ballesteros captained Europe to a Ryder Cup victory in 1997 in Spain, the teenager focused on golf.

A burly man with massive thighs, Rahm's distinctive short swing was developed as a way to overcome a defect.

Right after birth, it was noted that Rahm's right foot had a clubfoot deformity, and doctors began treatment with serial casting. As a result, he had a shorter right lower leg and didn't have the stability and mobility of his right ankle. These limitations caused Rahm to create a shorter-than-normal swing.[4]

There were no limitation to the world's number-three-ranked player about his mindset. "I feel like, when you're a couple shots back, you have nothing to lose early on. So I feel like you can be a little bit more aggressive and try to get some birdies," said Rahm. "There will be somebody who gets a fast start, and hopefully that's me tomorrow, and I get a fast start, and I get it going fast."

Well, that turned out be exactly the case.

Rahm opened with back-to-back birdies, cutting the lead to just two even before the leaders had teed off.

"I could just tell, just going down the fairway after that first tee shot, that second shot, and that birdie, I knew there was something special in the air. I could just feel it. I just knew it. That's why I played as aggressive as I did because it was like, 'Man, this is my day; everything's going to go right.' I just knew that I could do it and believed it."

La Jolla–born Xander Schauffele, the sixth ranked player in the world, having played this course many times throughout high school and college, opened with a birdie to go 2 under and right in the mix.

Defending champion DeChambeau birdied at five. On the Par-3 eighth, he arced a high right-to-left tee shot that nearly dropped in for a hole-in-one. His tap-in birdie gave him the sole lead at 5 under.

Brooks Koepka, winner, winner, and runner-up in his previous three US Opens, was on fire. With three birdies on the front nine, he was just two shots off the lead at 3 under.

After scoring his third birdie on the ninth, 2020 PGA champion Collin Morikawa was suddenly 4 under and just one back heading into the back nine.

It was a real horse race, with some of the game's top thoroughbreds coming down the stretch.

The final round was so tight that six players had a share of the lead at one point, and there were ten players separated by a single shot. And while it certainly turned into a clash of the titans, what developed on the back nine was that the marquee leaderboard continued to shift by the minute. However, for the most part, it became a crowded downward spiral of bogeys and double bogeys.

Morikawa, considered one the best ball-strikers in the game and whose strength was his iron play, thinned a wedge on the par-5 thirteenth, which pretty much ended his title run.

Koepka's three bogeys on the backside hurt his chances.

The biggest fall came from the big guy. After a pair of birdies had given him a share of the lead with Oosthuizen at 5 under as he headed to the back nine, Bryson DeChambeau's close was atrocious.

He had back-to-back bogeys on eleven and twelve. On the par-5 thirteen, the defending champion sailed his bunker shot over the green and ended up with a double-bogey. Four dropped shots in four holes. After a quadruple bogey on seventeen, DeChambeau's 8-over 44 on the back nine tied him for twenty-sixth place.

"I didn't get off the rails at all. It's golf. People will say I did this or did that, and it's just golf."

Another US Open winner, Rory McIlroy, wasn't having much luck on the back nine, either.

After getting into a share of the lead, his downfall came with a double bogey on the twelfth, after his second shot plugged in the greenside bunker. That knocked him from a shot out of the lead to four shots back in a hurry.

With the pack of decorated challengers falling back, that left a two-man race between a Spaniard (Rahm) and a South African (Oost-huizen) for the US national championship.

It would be a thrilling close.

After seven consecutive pars, Rahm came to the par-4, 434-yard seventeenth at 4 under, still one stroke back of the leader.

With an offline tee shot that landed him in a fairway bunker at seventeen, Rahm rammed a hard gap wedge and spun it onto the green to provide him with a chance at a birdie.

Having grown up in Spain on greens that had lots of slope, Rahm was more accustomed to dealing with twisting lines than straight-ahead putts. So, this was in his wheelhouse. He dropped the twenty-four-foot left to right bender for a birdie and a share of the lead.

"The last time I won here, I finished birdie-eagle, and I knew I could finish strong again. I knew history could get close to repeating itself. I was aware hitting that putt. I stayed patient all day," explained Rahm. "I hadn't made many long putts all week. I made one on Thursday on fourteen, but that's the kind of putts I like. I've made a couple of long left-to-righters in the past in some clutch moments."

The seventy-second hole was a par-5, 545-yard test. If Rahm could birdie there, it would give him the clubhouse lead. It was a hole he had played well all week, each time with a birdie result.

Things were looking a little dicey after he found the right greenside bunker. But Rahm gathered himself and decided to play it safe, and play out to the right of the hole. If he did otherwise, he could easily watch his ball (and potential title) race downhill into the water lurking beyond.

And sure enough his conservative play set up for his favorite type of putt (besides the universal tap-in): a left-to-righter.

"I trusted my read, and as soon as I made contact, I looked up and saw where the ball was going," Rahm said. "It was exactly the speed and line I visualized. I told myself, 'That's in.' If you could see my thoughts with ten feet to go, in my mind, I'm like, 'That's in the hole.' And it went in."

The roar of the crowd certainly got the attention of Oosthuizen, who was back at fifteen going for his fourth straight par. After another par at sixteen, he came to the penultimate hole one back. Ranked eighteenth in the world, he certainly had shown that he had the all-around game to win.

Oosthuizen found trouble off the tee at seventeen, landing in a penalty area in the canyon left of the fairway. However, he made a brilliant recovery to set up a must-make par putt. Unfortunately, his stroke skidded just past the cup. The bogey put him now two back, forcing him to make an eagle to get into a playoff. (But remember he'd eagled that very hole the previous day to give him a share of the lead.)

The thirty-eight-year-old still had a chance, but his tee shot at eighteen found the rough; thus he was forced to lay up. He needed to hole out his approach shot to force a playoff, but his wedge shot from sixty-nine yards failed to go in. Oosthuizen's birdie secured the familiar second-place finish, and Rahm won his first major.

Louis Oosthuizen is as nice a person as I have met. Yet he's never won a tournament in America. That would have been a privilege for him to win the US Open.

Rahm, now the world's number-one-ranked player, just felt something good was coming his way ever since an unexpected setback likely cost him a tournament victory just a few weeks prior.

Then, Rahm had tied the fifty-four-hole record at the Memorial and had a six-shot lead, only to be notified as he walked off the eighteenth green that he had tested positive for the coronavirus and had to withdraw. He remained in isolation until June 12. Then, eight days later, he was at the trophy presentation at Torrey Pines celebrating his first major championship and Spain's first US Open title.

"I'm a big believer in karma," said Rahm. "And after what happened a couple weeks ago, I stayed really positive knowing good things were coming. I didn't know what it was going to be, but I knew we were coming to a special place, I knew I got [my] breakthrough [PGA Tour] win here and it's a very special place for my family, and the fact that my parents were able to come, I got out of COVID protocol early, I just felt like the stars were aligning, and I knew my best golf was to come."

THE OPEN CHAMPIONSHIP

THE OPEN CHAMPIONSHIP, ALSO KNOWN AS THE BRITISH Open, is not only the oldest of the four majors (teeing off in 1860), but it is really a different type of game from the other tournaments that make up the Grand Slam.

From the early winners over a century ago like Tom Morris Sr., Tom Morris Jr., Willie Park Sr., James Braid, and John Henry Taylor to modern-day champions like Tiger Woods, Ernie Els, Padraig Harrington, and Collin Morikawa, how they all were able to succeed was an ability to judge the nuances of links-style golf.

Unlike other types of courses, links golf is simply a more adventurous way of experiencing the game.

Generally built on sandy coastland that naturally offers a firmer playing surface than parkland courses and located primarily in England, Ireland, and Scotland, the prominent elements of wind, rain, and cold (and also heat and sun on occasion) create a constantly evolving

environment. The playing conditions are always changing and without end.

Not only does it harken back to the roots of the game with the
ongoing importance of mastering the bump-and-run shot, what sepa-
rates the winners from the also-rans is having the imagination to look
beyond premeasured distances, get a feel and solid judgment about
the roll of the ball, and meet the demands of a layout that involves
the entire range of shotmaking.

I've had the good fortune to win three Claret Jugs on three different courses over three decades, and I love the distinct challenges these
links layouts offer. From deciphering the constantly fluctuating winds
off the sea, to judging the rolls on the hard and narrow fairways, to
the penal pot bunkers and undulating greens, the Open offers a complete test of one's game.

When I look at the Claret Jug, emblematic of the Champion Golfer
of the Year title that goes with it, to see my name etched on it with
some of the greats of the game like Vardon, Jones, and Hagen fills me
with pride.[1] It also reminds me how the Open is such a treasure trove
of great history and tradition that continues to be one of the world's
great sporting events.

60

ALL IN THE FAMILY

SEPTEMBER 23, 1868
PRESTWICK GOLF CLUB
SOUTH AYRSHIRE, SCOTLAND

Though this would be a small field (twelve would finish), compared to today's enormous lineups that average more than 150 competitors, it would eventually come down to a rather historic father-son duel for the title of this, the ninth Open Championship.

Old Tom Morris (referred to as Tom at the time—it wasn't until later when historians began using Old Tom) was pivotal in producing the inaugural Open Championship in 1860. Morris worked as a greenkeeper, golf instructor, ballmaker, clubmaker, and course designer before going on to dominate as he claimed the top prize four times over the following seven years.

Unsurprisingly, going into the contest in 1868, Old Tom was a heavy favorite to capture the Challenge Belt. But it must be remembered that in 1868, he was the defending champion—and the oldest. He had won the previous year at forty-six years and 102 days old, a record he would hold until 1968, when Julius Boros won the PGA Championships at forty-eight years, four months, eighteen days.

Though his father was Champion Golfer of the Year for the fourth time, Young Tom (referred to as Tommy at the time) was a teenage prodigy determined to make a name for himself.

The story goes that the son showed his emerging talents by defeating his father during a match at St. Andrews when the youngster was just thirteen. Young Tom would make his Open debut in 1865, then produce a ninth-place and a fourth-place finish in the successive years, so he was ready.

And Prestwick, with its crisscross design, was a familiar layout for both.

"The first 12 Opens were all played at Prestwick and both men won all of their Championships at Prestwick—four titles each," noted Hannah Fleming, museum and heritage assistant curator at the British Golf Museum. "Tom was Keeper of the Green at Prestwick, which meant he was in charge of the course, he laid out the course and knew it very well, while Tommy learned to play at Prestwick. So there was already an awareness of Tommy when he was a teenager and these appearances as a 15- and 16-year-old, there must have been talk at the time that he was on a good roll."[1]

It would be a record-setting roll indeed. Young Tom bolted to the lead with a record-setting 51 in the opening round for a two-shot advantage.

Now there'd be no "moving day" Saturdays on this twelve-hole layout because this midweek championship began and ended on Wednesday after the combatants had played three complete rounds.

And Old Tom would remind everyone who was the reigning king, as he'd break his son's just-set record with one of his own. Along with Willie Park Sr. (already owner of three Open titles), the defending champ scored a 50, which provided him with a one-stroke lead over his son.

That final round in this family duel took another record-setting turn when Young Tom topped his father's unprecedented lead-grabbing second-round score with a tremendous 49. Young Tom was the winner, and Old Tom the runner-up with three strokes back—the only time in majors history a son-father team would finish first and second.

Young Tom remains the youngest Open winner in history, and his father is still the oldest. At just seventeen (almost four years younger than anyone else ever to win the title), the son had dethroned the father. And this would be no fluke; Young Tom would also win four Open titles just like his old man.

And there could very well have been a few more, but tragedy struck the Morris family. Young Tom died on Christmas Day, 1875, at age twenty-four from a pulmonary hemorrhage. Though that was the official cause, some say it was a broken heart.

As he was wrapping up a match play event teaming up with his father in mid-September, Young Tom received an urgent telegram that he return home immediately. His pregnant wife, Margaret Drinnen, had gone into a difficult labor. But when he reached her bedside, it was too late. Both his wife and newborn baby were dead.

Despite the tragedies, Young Tom made a lasting impact on the sport. With his flair for the dramatic and aggressive style of play, some say he was a precursor to the charismatic Seve Ballesteros. Not only did this pioneer raise the standard of play with his enormous skill set, but word-of-mouth from the spectators who witnessed his well-publicized challenge matches throughout Scotland, along with extensive coverage from major newspapers across Britain, served to provide a massive increase in the popularity of golf for spectators and participants.

61

VARDON GETS HIS GRIP ON THE CLARET JUG

JUNE 10–11 AND JUNE 13, 1896
MUIRFIELD
EAST LOTHIAN, SCOTLAND

Harry Vardon's enduring global impact on golf would really tee off with his performance here at Muirfield in 1896. While it would not be easy (he trailed the entire way and fought to get in the playoffs which were uniquely delayed) he would earn his first of six Open crowns here by defeating J. H. Taylor who was attempting to win his third straight Open Championship.

Vardon and Taylor along with James Braid became known as the "Great Triumvirate." They ruled the golf world during their prime (the mid-1890s to the mid-1910s) and collectively won sixteen Claret Jugs. Their ongoing success and rivalry had quite an impact on increasing the public's interest in the sport.

Nicknamed "the Stylist" by his peers, more for the smoothness of his tempo than his fashion-setting attire (more on that later), Vardon was known for his exceptional accuracy and control with all the clubs. He achieved it with a more upright swing (with a decidedly bent left arm) that resulted in not only a higher ball flight and more carry, but the end result was a softer landing.

With his higher and more balanced finish, Vardon's upright swing overall was fairly distinctive for the times and resembles more of today's PGA Tour styles.

Back then a more commonly used swing was called the "Saint Andrews Swing," a shorter, lower motion that was employed to keep the ball deeper down in the windy conditions. As a result, one would more often than not finish off balance.[1]

Muirfield, unlike its equally famous US Open hosts, Carnoustie and St. Andrews, is not a public course and is home to the one of the world's oldest and most exclusive golf clubs, the Honourable Company of Edinburgh Golfers (formed in 1774).

While there are no blind shots and few trees at Muirfield, there is a certain openness of the layout. But ever-lurking is the harsh rough, which devilishly waits for the next errant shot. And being a links course, overlooking the Firth of Forth, Muirfield undoubtedly plays significantly tougher when the wind blows off the sea.

And don't think you've caught a break if the gales subside, because the track at Muirfield is also well-known for its more than 160 bunkers. Quite a few of those have steep turf walls that are sure to stick in your memory should you find yourself in one of those just once. You'll also have to keep your concentration all the way to the clubhouse because the long par-4 eighteenth is one of the toughest finishing holes of any in the Open rotation.

Vardon's concentration was a little off in the opening session when he rolled an 83. This put him six behind Taylor and eleven behind leader Sandy Herd. Herd, who had spent years apprenticing first as a baker, then as a plasterer, before turning to golf, would popularize waggling the club during setup. (It must've helped in some way because the St. Andrews native was the most prolific acer of his era, credited with seventeen holes-in-one.)

After the third round, Herd still led Vardon by four and Taylor by three.

Besides a comparatively distinct swing, Vardon also popularized a grip, and though he did not create it, it does bear his name. Even though historians generally agree it was probably invented by amateur golfer Johnny Laidlay, a Scotsman who won the British Amateur Championship in 1889 and 1891, the Vardon Grip is commonly used today.[2]

Essentially, the Vardon Grip, which is also referred to as the overlap grip, involves both hands anchored through the right pinky finger. The right pinky then lies on top of the depression between the index and middle fingers of the left hand.

Getting a grip on his game after three rounds at Muirfield, Vardon was putting things together for a final run. With Herd taking himself out after an 85, Taylor shot 80 in the final round to grab the clubhouse lead. Vardon shared the lowest round score, finishing with a 77, good enough to tie Taylor and force a playoff.

On a side note, just days before his seventy-fifth birthday, Old Tom Morris, playing in the Open for the thirty-fourth and final time, withdrew after failing to break 100 in his first three rounds.[3]

While the elder statesman of the game gave it an admirable final effort, Vardon and Taylor were about to square off to see who'd win the Claret Jug. However, there is an interesting note regarding the playoff.

In something unimaginable taking place in today's game, despite the tournament's final round ending on a Thursday, the playoff wasn't played until Saturday. That was because Taylor and Vardon were engaged in a thirty-six-hole tournament at North Berwick on Friday. Taylor finished as joint winner of the North Berwick tournament, with Ben Sayers and Willie Fernie.

Would Taylor go two-for-two in the title department that week?

It did not look promising. After just eight holes of a thirty-six-hole playoff, Taylor was already six shots back. He did rally and closed to within two of Vardon at the end of the first eighteen. With a two-stroke swing, Taylor got the upper hand on the very first hole of the afternoon round, but Vardon grabbed the advantage back over the next few holes. The event was finally decided at the seventeenth, where Vardon holed a twelve-yard putt to take a three-shot lead, then gained another stroke on eighteen to win by four (157-161).

Vardon garnered six titles between 1896 and 1914. Now, more than a century later, he remains the most decorated golfer in the history of the Open Championship.

More than one of the all-time great players, Vardon was a promoter of the game. During his career, Harry Vardon made three well-received visits to North America—1900, 1913, and 1920.

The first trip, in 1900, included an exhibition tour by Vardon and Taylor throughout the United States and Canada. It was a pioneering effort in that Vardon became one of the first players with a sponsor deal. Sporting goods giant A. G. Spalding underwrote the trip. Throughout the tour, Vardon promoted his Vardon Flyer, a Spalding gutta-percha golf ball.

Genial, modest, charismatic, highly respected among his peers, and quite gracious, the natty knickerbocker-clad Vardon had become the sport's first global celebrity. His journey throughout North America played a gigantic role in sparking golf's growth there. Oh, and to top it off, Vardon entered and won the 1900 US Open, edging his rival Taylor by two shots at the Chicago Golf Club.

Thirteen years later, Harry Vardon and Ted Ray were on an exhibition tour of the United States. The two Brits were such big stars that the USGA delayed the 1913 US Open until September just so they could make it to the tournament. But in one of the great upsets in sports history, then-little-known amateur Francis Ouimet, who grew up across the street from the golf club, instead won in a playoff over Vardon and Ray at the Country Club in Brookline, Massachusetts.

However, there's a lesser-known story tied to this.

Vardon and Ouimet would face each other again the following year at the 1914 Open Championship, when Ouimet made the trip to Prestwick in Scotland with the help of funding from friends.

Vardon and the defending champ, J. H. Taylor, were tied at five Open wins each entering this tournament. During that meeting, Vardon defeated runner-up Taylor by three strokes and crushed Ouimet by twenty-six in garnering his record-setting sixth Open Championship.

Returning to play the 1920 US Open at Inverness in Ohio, the amazing Vardon nearly won another major at age fifty. Alas, it was another close runner-up finish, as he finished one shot back of winner Ted Ray.

Again, to put it in perspective, Vardon, J. H. Taylor, and James Braid won seventeen majors in twenty years and became known as the Great Triumvirate of their era. Some call Sam Snead, Ben Hogan, and Byron Nelson, who collected twenty-one majors, as the American Triumvirate. All were predecessors to Arnold Palmer, Jack Nicklaus, and myself who were known as the Big Three of the modern era. Together we accounted for thirty-four victories in the majors.

In tribute to the great player after his passing in 1937, the PGA of America created the Vardon Trophy, which continues to be awarded annually to the professional with the lowest stroke average on the PGA Tour.

62

THE FIRST YANKEE

JUNE 22–23, 1922
ROYAL ST. GEORGE'S GOLF CLUB
SANDWICH, ENGLAND

In the fifty-six Opens leading to the 1922 tournament, no American-born player had won the coveted crown. The early years had been dominated by Scotsmen like Old Tom and Young Tom Morris, Willie Park Sr. and Willie Jr., along with the Great Triumvirate of James Braid, Harry Vardon, and J. H. Taylor.

That all was about to change. The floodgates would be opened by a dashing and dapper young man out of Rochester, New York, by the name of Walter Hagen. The son of a blacksmith, Hagen learned the game beginning at age nine, working as a caddy for ten cents a round at the Country Club of Rochester.

Wearing his hair slicked down in the fashion of the movie stars of the day, the young man was also a very talented shortstop and pitcher. It was reported that he canceled a 1914 tryout for the Phila-delphia Phillies in order to play in a golf tournament, and after win-ning that year's US Open in wire-to-wire fashion, he hung up his spikes and put away his infielder's glove forever.

And golf was the better for it as the charismatic, very natty dresser created a larger-than-life aura around himself while living extravagantly. Combined with his success, it made him sort of the Babe Ruth of golf as a showman and partier, always traveling about in style. He would famously say years later: "I never wanted to be a millionaire. I just wanted to live like one." And after becoming the first golfer to win $1 million, he said with a wink, "I was also the first to spend $2 million."

Hagen made his debut at the Open Championship in 1920, where he would become a pioneering figure in the development of professional golf.

His career came in an era of sports long dominated by amateurs, including golf; professionals were often treated poorly in comparison. This was especially true in England, where golf professionals were not allowed to use the clubhouse facilities and were not permitted to enter the establishment by the front door.

So, at the 1920 Open Championship, held at Royal Cinque Ports Golf Club in Deal, Kent, Hagen had to hire a Pierce-Arrow car to serve as his private dressing room after he was refused entrance to the clubhouse dressing room. He also hired a chauffeur, and parked the expensive car in the club's driveway. It had the effect he was looking for, as this behavior raised a few eyebrows in class-conscious Britain.[1]

It would only be the beginning, but Hagen, who would become known as the "father of professional golf," would get much-deserved credit for raising the dignity for the professional golfer and gaining equal access to locker rooms. By the time his brilliant career was over, the Haig was instrumental in bringing more publicity, elevated status, bigger prize money, and lucrative endorsements to the sport that are so evident today.

The Royal St. George's course is situated among towering sandhills overlooking Pegwell Bay in southern England. It really has the player at its mercy if any wind kicks up off the channel.

Despite calm, sunny conditions Hagen scored an unimpressive 76 to lead things off. Not good when considering the leaders were no flukes. Three strokes ahead were Ted Ray and J. H. Taylor.

Royal St. George hosted the first-ever Open Championship to be played outside of Scotland in 1894, and the winner was the aforementioned Taylor. Now, twenty-eight years later, Taylor was amazingly right in the thick of the fight. His 73 provided him a share of the opening-round lead with Ted Ray.

Ray was an interesting figure in his own right. With a pipe clenched between his teeth, the burly Englishman was resplendent in his regular attire of felt trilby hat, plus fours, waistcoat, and flapping jacket.

Friendly, optimistic, and daring, Ray combined a bit of John Daly, Phil Mickelson, and Seve Ballesteros. Like Daly, the UK's original grip-it-and-rip-it guy was known for length off the tee. Like Mickelson, he was very aggressive, and that attacking style along with his engaging personality made him a crowd favorite. Finally, like the charismatic Ballesteros, Ray had a terrific ability to get himself out of trouble. Captain of Britain's original Ryder Cup team of 1927, Ray had also won a pair of majors before arriving here.

Those mighty credentials didn't seem to worry Hagen. He reportedly had been up the night before until the wee hours with a few other Americans in a high-stakes putting competition on the hotel lobby carpet. They had been trying to line up their shots through the haze of their cigar smoke and maintaining their balance after a bit of drinking.

The format then was they played for two days, thirty-six holes each. The afternoon round of the first day saw the wind pick up, and while many in the field elevated to the high 70s and even mid-80s, Hagen rolled a fine 73, beating the Brits at their own game. After two rounds, the American was now in the lead and two strokes ahead of Taylor and Jim Barnes.

However, the following day it looked as though Hagen was through. He finished the third round with a 79, and even that required some magical saves to avoid rising into the 80s. But the damp and blustery conditions applied to everyone, so there'd be no runaway victors in this weather.

Jock Hutchison was born in St. Andrews in 1884 and played his first rounds of golf on the Old Course. But when he returned to win The Open at the Home of Golf in 1921, he was an American citizen. In a morning round filled with miserable weather and just-as-miserable scores, Hutchison showed why he was defending champion when he took the lead heading into the final round by posting a remarkable 73. Hagen was two back in third, while Taylor had a share of second place.

With wind and rain ever-present throughout the closing round, it was more about grinding, and it took a toll on more than a few players.

The great Taylor, who had won his first Open way back in 1894, was now fifty-one years old. He was feeling it in his tired legs, and he scored 77 to close, falling back to finish fifth. Hutchison would fail to repeat when he ended with a 76.

So it really came down to a battle of familiar foes: Hagen vs. Barnes.

Barnes had won the first two PGA Championships, in 1916 and 1919 (there was no tournament in 1917 or 1918 because of World War I), as well as the 1921 US Open. Known as "Long Jim" for his unusual six-foot-four height (quite tall for the times), the future Hall of Famer's winning margin at that US Open was nine strokes, a record which was not broken until the year 2000.

At the 1921 PGA, Hagen defeated Barnes in the championship match by a final score of 3 and 2. It was Hagen's third major victory, but the first of his eventual five wins in the that major.

But here at Royal St. George's, Barnes, who had finished early with a 73, looked to be the winner. Scotsman George Duncan, winner of the 1920 Open Championship, had ballooned to an 81 in the third round, but with birdies at sixteen and seventeen he closed with a brilliant 69, the only round under 70 in the tournament to earn him a tie for second place.

However, determined to make this long journey across the Atlantic pay off, Hagen, with clutch pars on sixteen and seventeen, produced a gritty 72 and won the Claret Jug with a four-round score of 300, one ahead of Barnes.

I like Mr. Walter Hagen. I was a big fan of his. I mean he was a very charismatic person. And we need more people like that today.

One night during this major he was out having his drinks. He was standing at the fireplace when one member of the party said: "Mr. Hagen, you know all your opponents are sleeping and here you are drinking at the bar."

Hagen: "They might be in bed, but they're not sleeping."

How good would he have been if he played with the equipment of today? And had access to today's travel luxuries?

I used boats and propeller airplanes. Young people have no idea that those conditions even existed. Today they travel nonstop on a flight that took me four stops and forty hours. With kids in tow. No movies, no headphones. No beds. Sleeping on the floor. Imagine the daunting travel logistics of Mr. Hagen and his era. Still, what a player.

This victory made him the first man to win all three professional majors, having won the PGA Championship the previous year and the US Open in 1914 and 1919. The Haig's victory at Royal St. George's (his first of four Claret Jugs) along with those of Bobby Jones and Gene Sarazen, represented the growth of the game on the international level as well as a sign of things to come. Americans would win eight of the next ten Opens.

63

ON THE ROAD TO THE "IMPREGNABLE QUADRILATERAL OF GOLF"

JUNE 18–20, 1930
ROYAL LIVERPOOL GOLF CLUB
HOYLAKE, ENGLAND

As great an accomplishment as it was to win back-to-win Open Championships in 1926 (pulling away from then two-time champ Walter Hagen) and 1927 (taking the title in wire-to-wire fashion at the Old Course at St. Andrews, Scotland), American Bobby Jones would take this Open victory and combine it with wins in the three other biggest tournaments of the day to make 1930 one of the most historic years any golfer has had.

With wins at the US Open, US Amateur, Open Championship, and British Amateur, what the twenty-eight-year-old-native of Atlanta accomplished was hard to put in words. (The Masters had not yet been formed, and Jones was not eligible to compete in the PGA Championship, as this event was open only to professionals.) Wordsmiths of the time felt since it was an accomplishment largely because no one had thought it possible, terms like *major* and *grand slam* just didn't capture the magnitude of it.

The *Atlanta Journal*'s O. B. Keeler would later write: "This victory, the fourth major title in the same season and in the space of four months, had now and for all time entrenched Bobby Jones safely within the Impregnable Quadrilateral of Golf, that granite fortress that he alone could take by escalade, and that others may attack in vain, forever."

However, what is undertold is that forever performance almost didn't happen, because just a few weeks before he arrived at Hoylake, Robert Tyre "Bobby" Jones Jr. almost lost the British Amateur held at St. Andrews.

Jones had to persevere through three tough, tough matches that could've gone either way before finally defeating Roger Wethered in the final, 7 and 6.

Speaking of St. Andrews, it was here as a nineteen-year-old at the 1921 Open Championship, that Bobby displayed his volcanic side. After having shot a 46 on the front nine in the third round, the steam was rising from the young man. After following that with a double-bogey six on ten, he erupted and picked up on eleven when his third shot on the par-3 hole was still in a bunker, and he simply stormed off the course.

Time, helped make that a distant memory for Jones, as he gathered more experience on links play and achieved success.

The Open Championship would not be any easier.

The Royal Liverpool Golf Club at Hoylake was founded in 1869, and is the second oldest seaside links course in England (only Royal North Devon is the more senior). It is certainly one of the tougher layouts of the British rotation. Only six holes are in the dunes—otherwise there is little protection from the ever-changing wind, and harsh run-off areas abound, as do punishing bunkers.

The newly crowned British Amateur champion would also face a formidable field, which included Leo Diegel (back-to-back PGA championships 1928 and 1929), Fred Robson (runner-up to Jones in the 1927 Open at St. Andrews) and Horton Smith (the only golfer to defeat Jones during the latter's Grand Slam year of 1930, at the stroke play Savannah Open in February, as well as future two-time winner of the Masters).[1]

Nevertheless, with an opening round of 70, Jones grabbed a share of the lead with Macdonald Smith and Henry Cotton.

Cotton, a future three-time winner of the event, emulated his hero Walter Hagen in terms of being a flashy dresser and a high roller, often playing cards for significant sums all night and beyond until his tee time beckoned.

But he ballooned to a 79 and fell seven off the pace. Jones, whose fluid swing of easy grace was developed at East Lake Golf Club in Atlanta, where he first learned the game as a young child, produced a 72. This was good enough to give him the sole lead by one-shot lead heading into the third round.

Round three was a bit uneven for the Georgian, but he fought more than usual to keep control of his shots and avoid the big numbers that could happen easily on this layout. He finally settled for a 74. It cost him the lead, and he would trail Archie Compston, whose 68 made him the only player under par heading into the final round.

Compston, from Wolverhampton, England, was an instructor to royalty. He played more in Europe than on the PGA Tour, and had won the British PGA Matchplay Championship in 1925 and 1927. In 1928 he played another great match player, Walter Hagen, winner of the previous four PGA Championships, in a seventy-two-hole challenge match, and defeated the American 18 and 17. However, just two weeks later Hagen rebounded to win his third Open title. Compston finished third, three behind, with Gene Sarazen the runner-up.[2]

Compston could not come close to matching his 68 and blew up to 82 in the final round, dropping to a share of sixth place.

Jones was not exactly knocking the cover off the ball (oh wait, that is a baseball term). After a disastrous triple bogey on the 527-yard par-5, he uncharacteristically took five strokes from just short of the green. The Claret Jug was up for grabs.

Over the last five holes at Hoylake—wind-whipped holes which are well trapped and measure 511, 443, 532, 419, and 408 yards, respectively, as rough a finish as there is in golf—Bobby fought his way home, 4-5-4-4-4 against an approximated par of 5-4-5-4-4, for a 75. Jones's 3-over 291 tally was two better than Leo Diegel and Macdonald Smith.[3]

The second part of the Quadrilateral was now secured.

Interestingly when the trophy presenter made the announcement to the crowd introducing the winner, he called it the "British Open Championship," and the "Winner of the British Open Championship" instead of "the Open Championship" and the "Champion Golfer of the Year," which the British have long, long insisted it be called.

After Jones and Mary returned Stateside in early July on the SS *Europa* with the Open Championship and British Amateur titles, he was accorded a ticker tape parade up Broadway to New York's City Hall, as thousands of fans filled the air with cheers and confetti.

He'd then go on to win the US Open (his fourth) at Interlachen in Minneapolis, and then the US Amateur at Merion to complete his unprecedented crowning glory. At just twenty-eight years old Jones promptly retired from competitive golf for the most part, except for later playing in his own tournament at Augusta National.

From 1923 to 1930, Jones won thirteen of the twenty-one national championships he entered. In eleven of his twelve Opens, British and American, he either won or finished second. Seven were victories. Two of his losses were in playoffs. During that same period, 1923 to 1930, he played in only seven non–majors championship tournaments. He won four of them.[4]

And even though there are solid arguments that the current version, the "Pro Grand Slam," is a much tougher challenge, and some of the game's other greats have put together unforgettable efforts (Hogan's three majors in a row in 1953; Nicklaus's three out of four in 1971–72; and the Tiger Slam in 2000–2001), the fact remains no has been able to win the Open, the US Open, the Masters, and the PGA Championships all in one season.

So, for a young man who practiced law by day and bested some of the game's best all-time professionals on the weekends before choosing to walk away from competitive golf at the age of twenty-eight, yes, the Impregnable Quadrilateral of Golf is a legendary achievement by a legendary player.

It was that rare something that transcended golf, because Bobby Jones was the champion of a nation at a time when sport helped the American public escape the despair of poverty and lingering anguish in the midst of the Great Depression.

I so enjoyed meeting Bobby Jones, who arguably was the greatest player that ever lived. Playing golf with a walking stick and using a ball that went eighty yards shorter. No modern-day machinery to keep the course fresh. Lots of spike marks on the greens. Fairways hardly cut short. No jets to travel in. You think about what he did and it was quite remarkable.

64

THE WEE ICE MON AND
GOLF'S TRIPLE CROWN

JULY 8–10, 1953
CARNOUSTIE GOLF LINKS
ANGUS, SCOTLAND

In the summer of 1953, if you went by his record, one would not know that six-time majors winner Ben Hogan was still recuperating from a near-fatal car crash four years earlier.

Though he played in limited tournaments, it must be remembered at the time of the accident Hogan had suffered a broken collarbone, a broken rib, internal bleeding, a double-fractured pelvis, head abrasions, a broken ankle, and contusions to the left leg. Doctors wondered if Ben would ever walk again—if he even survived.

However, as a testament to his courage and determination, the forty-year-old Texan would endure a lengthy and painful rehab. When he was able to play again, he would receive daily deep-tissue massages, then wrap both legs heavily and carry on through his trademark quiet grit and fortitude. Bantam Ben won that year's Masters with a record low score. His 274 total broke the previous record by five.

Hogan then proceeded to win his fourth US Open, crushing the field led by Sam Snead at one of the national championship's most demanding venues, Oakmont, by six strokes. Even more impressive was that this one was done in wire-to-wire fashion. The fourth crown tied the tournament record shared by Willie Anderson and Bobby Jones (Jack Nicklaus later joined them).

Adding majors seven and eight to one's career—not a bad start to 1953.

Now there was no real talk of a professional grand slam until Arnold Palmer's play in 1960, but the rare possibility of winning three majors in the same year was right there in front of Hogan. (More about conflicting major tournament schedules later on.)

However, Hogan was not inclined to make the long journey to England and play the Open. And though several well-respected individuals in the sport made calls to convince him to go, he didn't decide to compete until one of the all-time celebrated players reminded him that his greatness would never be assured until he possessed a Claret Jug. That player? It was four-time Open champion Walter Hagen.

Now, once committed, Hogan was well-known for his preparation and attention to detail, but here's one aspect of the plan that did not involve his swing or clubs (but of course both of those could have been adversely affected if the following didn't happen):

Knowing how harsh and unforgiving Carnasty—er, Carnoustie—could be bone-chilling cold even in midsummer, Hogan ordered two pair of long-handled cashmere underwear costing $95 each from New York retailer Abercrombie and Fitch (that's more than $1,000 each in today's dollars).

Of course, the underwear story made news so A. J. Anderson Co., of Hogan's hometown of Fort Worth, gave him two pair of red long johns made of cotton and wool. Not to be outdone, BVD sent him three pair.[1]

From wool underwear to cashmere sweaters, the now well-layered, always dapper Hogan arrived in Scotland two weeks before the championship got underway to learn how to play links golf and compete with the smaller British golf ball. He'd play long into the extended daylight at a course called Panmure, just down the road from Carnoustie.

Hogan's stamina would be tested early because it was an era where there were no exemptions for the Open. Every player had to earn their place, and so Hogan had to go through the tough challenge of a thirty-six-hole qualifier just to make the field.

CBS radio broadcaster John Derr, just one of a very few American journalists there, walked the practice rounds with him and thus became a confidant of Hogan's. With no scoreboards, he'd occasionally duck into the press tents to provide the golfer with scoring updates during the final rounds.

Carnoustie, often called the most difficult of all Open Championship courses, would be especially tough with the windy and damp conditions Hogan and his competitors would face. I've played the course many times and won the Open there in 1968. It is brutally long at more than 7,200 yards and is made even tougher by the winds that whip off the sea. What really grabs your attention is that no more than two consecutive holes head in the same direction, so the player has to cope with the wind from all angles, which makes it tough to get into any sort of rhythm. On top of that, you have two streams, Jockie's Burn and the infamous Barry Burn, that meander their way through the course and naturally can cause their own brand of mayhem.

The putter caused Hogan mayhem in the opening round as he settled for a 1-over 73 that put him in a share of seventh place. American amateur Frank Stranahan grabbed the lead with a 2-under 70, while three-time Open champion Bobby Locke of South Africa and future five-time Open winner Peter Thomson of Australia were lurking just two back at an even-par 72 (see chapters 65 and 68).

Stranahan was an interesting character. An early proponent of strength training, he came from a wealthy family (owners of the Champion Spark Plug Company in the fast-growing days of the automobile industry) and was a member at the Inverness Club in Toledo, Ohio. Byron Nelson, one of the best players in the world and conveniently the club pro at Inverness between 1940and 1944, was one of his teachers.

A two-time British Amateur champion with four top ten finishes in the majors, Stranahan traveled with weights and argued passionately for the benefits it brought his game at a time when most of his peers were still concerned that it would reduce their flexibility. I am proud to call him my fitness mentor, friend, and inspiration.

Essentially, he was a pioneer. Eventually his fitness regimen would be adopted by the PGA Tour, which would supply staffed workout facilities to players at Tour events by the 1980s. And we've all seen the extended fitness regimens of today's best players.

In the second round, Stranahan fell back with a 74, and he'd join Thomson for a share of fourth place. But an interesting phenomenon was developing for that other member who also found himself in fourth after his 71.

Hogan had one of Hollywood's most iconic entertainers following him around. Superstar Frank Sinatra, who was performing at a concert in Dundee, was in the gallery for day two and told the media that "all America is rooting for Hogan."[2]

Something bigger was happening, though. Though Hogan came across as somewhat cold and aloof to many Americans, the Scots quickly embraced him for his tremendous game and his approach to the sport. As the gallery grew and grew, he became known as "the Wee Ice Mon."

But he'd had a head cold sneaking up on him for several days. On the night before Friday's final day of play—thirty-six-holes—it erupted with a fury, shooting his temperature to 103, and he didn't get much sleep. In the morning, his feet were numb and his head was dizzy, but a shot of the new wonder drug penicillin, administered by a Dundee physician, seemed to help a bit.

Struggling physically, Hogan still had an excellent morning round. He shot 70, and a birdie at eighteen put him in a tie for the lead with future Open champion Roberto De Vicenzo of Argentina (see chapter 7). Between rounds he sat in the locker room alone, took an aspirin with a glass of lukewarm ginger ale, and ate half a ham sandwich with a few orange wedges. Feeling better after a brief rest, he calculated that another 1 under might secure the championship.[3]

One of his key calculations throughout the tournament was figuring out how to play the tough par-5, 567-yard sixth hole, which he was playing a half shot over par. It featured a split fairway; the right-hand side was the far safer option, but the left-hand side had a better route to the green. Despite limited circulation in his legs, which were magnified by the cold, damp conditions, Hogan chipped in for birdie at the fifth and took sole possession of the lead.

Then at the aforementioned sixth, with the wind dead into the player's faces. Hogan had the confidence in his game and that his shotmaking skills were perhaps never better displayed than at this hole, where he routinely avoided out of bounds on the narrow left side. It would be the same in the final round. Like he did in each of the previous rounds, he birdied it. The story goes that his afternoon tee shot finished in his divot from the morning round. (The sixth would later receive a plaque naming the hole "Hogan's Alley.")

Battling the flu as well as the competition, Hogan would open up a two-shot lead with a birdie at the thirteenth, and this fueled him to the finish. One of the better players with the lead, bone-tired Hogan would fend off any contenders.

Try as they might, Stranahan, Thomson, and another Argentine, Antonio Cerda—who had set a course record of 69 in the third round—would finish a distant four strokes back of the new Champion Golfer of the Year.

With nearly twenty thousand spectators gathered around the eighteenth hole while several million listened in for updates on BBC radio, Hogan finished the tournament with a birdie. His final-round 68 produced a 282 total, which crushed Carnoustie's existing tournament record by eight strokes: 73-71-70-68. Hogan had lowered his score with each succeeding round.

In a radio interview with Derr of CBS, the Wee Ice Mon Hogan was appreciative of the fans' support. "The people have just been wonderful to me over here. I never saw such crowds. I think the whole of Scotland was actually pulling for me to win."

Not until Tiger Woods in 2000 would a player match his three majors titles in the same year. It was the ninth and final major of Hogan's career.

As far as any Grand Slam, that would've been impossible in 1953 for Hogan to achieve for several reasons. The PGA Championship that year was held at the Birmingham Country Club outside of Detroit. Given Hogan's physical limitations, especially his weakened legs, the match play format was more of a marathon, calling for two eighteen-hole rounds on the first day, followed by thirty-six-hole matches the following four days. Hogan knew it and didn't even sign up to play. Also, the overlapping qualifying and tournament schedules made it impossible for Hogan to be in two places at once.

One place he did arrive at was for an unusual ceremony in New York City. After the win, Hogan and his wife, Valerie, were passengers on the SS *United States* westbound to New York City, where he received a ticker tape parade. Yes, Broadway became a fairway for the day and exclusively Hogan's Alley.

With the Claret Jug, Hogan now joined Gene Sarazen as only the second player to win the career grand slam. (I am proud to have joined that club along with Jack and Tiger later.)

One could argue that Hogan's 1953 was the best year a golfer ever had—five tournaments, five victories, and three of them majors. Ben Hogan, the Wee Ice Mon, had scored a Triple Crown.

65

IT WAS A LOCKE BETWEEN THESE RIVALS

JULY 3–5, 1957
THE OLD COURSE
ST. ANDREWS, SCOTLAND

With the setting being one of the sport's most historic venues, this was perhaps golf's most underappreciated rivalry, and it would provide the lucky spectators in attendance to see Australia's Peter Thomson and South Africa's Bobby Locke vie for supremacy.

What was in store for the fans walking the Old Course was two titanic talents, both three-time Open champions, each looking to defeat the other (and the rest of the field, of course) to become a four-time Champion Golfer of the Year.

Famous for being a fancy dresser in his plus fours but also a tremendously slow player, Locke would earn World Hall of Fame numbers with seventy-five victories worldwide, including fifteen in a brief stint on the PGA Tour in America. And this despite missing several years of his prime by serving in the South African Air Force during World War II.

Just how good was Bobby Locke? He actually came up with the now-universal phrase, "You drive for show and putt for dough."

Growing up in South Africa, I used to watch him like a hawk. He had a very distinctive putting style. Generally, he'd have a closed stance with the left foot clearly ahead of the right, place the ball on the toe of the putter to ensure he would not cut across the ball, then aim to the right and he'd hit up at the ball, which would impart the best roll. Very wristy with essentially no follow-through. It worked magic for him.

Peter Thomson, who'd eventually own five Open titles (see chapter 68), had a top five finish in both the Masters and the US Open. As the only golfer in the twentieth century to lift the Claret Jug on three consecutive occasions, he was the clear favorite to win the coveted Champion Golfer of the Year title again.

A cultured man who appreciated the arts, the longtime resident of Melbourne generally kept to himself and was regarded a premiere strategist who approached the game in simple terms. A player with a fluid swing who would make the rounds with an imperturbable air of self-control, he was a man of enormous, quiet confidence and subdued ego.

In essence, Thomson knew he was good and that was all he needed to know. And his dominant record made it easy to see why. Now with the course knowledge of having won the Open when it was held at St. Andrews just two years prior, the Australian was ready to give it a go again.

Normally in the British course rotation, the Old Course would not have been the venue again in such quick fashion. However, a rather interesting circumstance led to it hosting again just two years later.

The 1957 event was actually set for Muirfield, but the Suez Crisis in Egypt in late 1956 led to serious fuel shortages in Britain and rationing of gasoline. Earlier that year, the Royal and Ancient governing body decided that St Andrews, on a railway line, would be an easier place for players and spectators to get to than Muirfield, and so the tournament was moved. Muirfield was allocated the 1959 event (when I won; see chapter 66).[1]

Spurred on by missing the cut the previous year at Hoylake (where his rival Thomson had won for the third year in a row), Locke was even more motivated to grab the Claret Jug. Producing scores of 69 and 72 to place him just two shots off the lead halfway through the tournament, the thirty-nine-year-old South African followed that up with a third round of 68, taking the lead by three strokes over Thomson, who was tied with Eric Brown in second with a fifty-four-hole total of 212.

Since the rivals both finished the final eighteen with a 70, Locke won his fourth and final Open Championship by three strokes.

It was not without some controversy at the seventy-second hole.

Lying two, Locke was only four feet from the cup when he moved his ball marker one putter-head length to avoid the line of fellow competitor Bruce Crampton's putt. After Crampton holed out, Locke forgot to replace his ball to its original position and sank his putt. He could have been disqualified. Only much later were officials made aware of Locke's mistake. In the end, the Championship Committee decreed that no advantage had been gained and that the result, and Locke's three-stroke victory, stood.[2]

Locke's competitive career was shortened by a serious car accident in 1959. And as a result of recurring headaches and sight issues thereafter, he never fully recovered his top game. Still, take it from two of the game's very best: Bobby Locke was an all-time great player in a Hall of Fame career that included five top five finishes in the US Open.

About the South African, Ben Hogan once said, "Everyone examines greens, but only he knows what he's looking for."[3]

In 1946 a South African financier, Norbert Erleigh, paid Sam Snead to come to South Africa for a series of exhibition matches. Of sixteen, Locke won twelve, Snead two. They halved two.

"Everything he played was a hook," Snead said years later. "I could beat him from tee to green 15 times out of 18 and still lose. He was the greatest putter I have ever seen. He'd hit a 20-footer, and before the ball got halfway, he'd be tipping his hat to the crowd. He wore out his hats tipping them."[4]

Bobby is probably the best putter the world has ever seen. And he didn't putt on the smooth greens that we have today. The greens we have these days are smooth as a snooker table.

One six-foot putt, for my life? I'll take Bobby Locke. I've seen them all, and there was never a putter like him.

66

FROM GLOOM TO GLORY:
WINNING MY FIRST MAJOR

JULY 1–3, 1959
MUIRFIELD
GULLANE, SCOTLAND

My dreams of success in this sport really began when I was sixteen after I broke my neck jumping into a compost pit while showing off for friends. During my convalescence, I would look into a mirror and repeat the phrase, "You are the greatest golfer in the world."

I had some early success winning in Egypt and Australia, but part of being great is winning majors. I was driven to win majors, to say I had beaten the best in the world at the game's highest level.

As a young South African, winning the Open seemed the ultimate prize in golf to me. During my teenage years countryman Bobby Locke was dominating the Open. This was the game's oldest championship, so being a subject of Britain's "empire," I'd play it over and over in my head from distant Johannesburg that "this putt is for the Open Championship!"

Winning the Claret Jug at the Open was a challenge I was determined to meet. It would mean sacrifices, however. I arrived at

Muirfeld at just twenty-three and basically with no money. My wife, Vivienne, had just had out first child. And I did not have the funds to fly all the way back to South Africa to be there with her, which I wanted to do.

You must remember, just four years earlier, I had only £200 in my pocket that my father had given me that I had to stretch my entire trip abroad. He worked in a gold mine twelve thousand feet underground and never earned more than £100 a month in his life. I later found out that he got an overdraft to help me. So, when I arrived in Scotland to play the Open at St. Andrews I couldn't find a cheap room, so I put my waterproofs on and slept in the sand dunes. And during play I wore a sweater on a hot day because I didn't want others to see I was wearing a tie for a belt.

Things didn't start out well at Muirfield. My plan was to get in some practice rounds early. The winds here are quite tricky, and you wanted to work out the distances involved with each hole and the clubs that would be required in any possible situation. I met the man in charge at the clubhouse. Brian Evans-Lombe, a former cavalry colonel, was the club secretary. And I remember the conversation like it was yesterday.

I said, "Good morning, sir."

He said, "What do you want here?"

I replied, "I have flown thousands of miles to come to practice for the Open."

He said, "You are not practicing here. This is Muirfield. You have no right just to walk in here and say you are going to practice."

"My wife has just had a child," I said. "I'm very poor. And I'm going to win the Open."

He looked at me. "Not only are you not going to practice here, but you're an arrogant young bastard as well."

So I went on my hands and knees on the floor.

"I beg you to let me practice," I said. "I really am poor. I need to win."

He relented and later became a dear friend. In fact, he helped me enormously because the fifteenth hole was a driver and wedge in the practice rounds, but after seeing me do that he suggested, "When the wind comes up you can use a three-iron there."

Founded in 1744, a decade before the Royal and Ancient Golf Club of St. Andrews and home to the Honourable Company of Edinburgh Golfers, the original course was laid out in Leith, moved to Musselburgh in 1836, and then rebuilt at the present site in 1891. Golf was first played on eighteen holes laid out by Old Tom Morris at Muirfield in 1891. When it hosted the first of its sixteen Open Championships in 1892, Muirfield was the first Open to be played over seventy-two holes.

Through the decades, some of the sport's biggest names have won the Open Championship at Muirfield. Harry Vardon would win the first of six Opens here. James Braid would win his first of five here. Later on, Jack Nicklaus, Lee Trevino, Tom Watson, Nick Faldo, Ernie Els, and Phil Mickelson would also earn a Claret Jug on this course.

I must say, from my very first practice rounds in 1959 and after competing in subsequent Opens here in later years, I agree with many others who say this course is perhaps the fairest test of all the Open venues.

One of the reasons is that with two circuits of nine rotating in opposite directions, the back nine loops inside the front nine, ensuring that golfers never face the same wind direction on two consecutive holes. But a competitor must constantly take into consideration the wind, from whichever direction, before deciding on a club.

You never what's going to happen in the Open, and there's no such thing as yardage. You might hit a pitching wedge 160 yards and the next day hit 160 yards with a two-iron. So, it is a matter of feel. Using your judgment. Using your eyes. It's so different. You have so much adversity in the tournament. You get in the bunker, you have to play out backward. You play in the morning and you play in perfect weather, but in the afternoon you play in a strong wind. You've got to battle the elements. You've really got to use what I call your natural instinct when playing.

It is the ultimate test. That's what I love about that major.

Yes, I had to win at Muirfield—I needed the money, even more so since I flew in my wife and young daughter, but there were some prominent opponents in the field who had their own ideas. Namely the likes of the aforementioned Bobby Locke, whose name was already on the Claret Jug four times, including just two years previous, and the defending Peter Thomson, also a four-time Champion Golfer of the Year.

And let's not forget Henry Cotton, a three-time past champion. Englishman Fred Bullock, whose daughter Sandra was caddying for him, was a definite threat. He had three top ten finishes already at the Open Championships. As a matter of fact, Fred had the lead outright or a share of it after each of the first three rounds here.

On top of that you had that crafty veteran from Belgium, Flory Van Donck, who was playing in his twenty-first and final Open Championship. Entering this event, Flory had four straight top five finishes at the Open Championship. He was self-taught, and his swing was so smooth and rhythmic he was often called "the Sam Snead of Europe."

After two rounds, I had shot 75-71 and was eight strokes behind the leaders. On the eve of the final round, I told Pat Matthews of Slazenger (a prominent sporting goods manufacturer) in no uncertain terms that I was going to win the Open.

Pat responded, in a sort of dismissive tone, "My young man, at your age? That's a little ambitious, isn't it? And besides, you're eight shots back."

Back in those days we played thirty-six holes on the final day. It was quite a windy day. To illustrate how the course can change day-to-day, hour-to-hour, minute-to-minute, during a practice round I'd played the fifteenth hole in practice with a drive and a sand wedge. In the morning of round three, I hit a drive and a three-iron, and in the afternoon a drive and a two-iron. Both times I got a birdie.

Heading into the final round I was just four strokes back, but there were still nine players ahead of me. By now the wind was howling and the weather got worse; nevertheless, I set a goal of 66 for the closing round.

I hit the first green with two driver shots into the wind and made four. On the par-5 fifth I was just four feet away in two and picked up two strokes right there. Another key was the ninth. Devilish not just because of the heavy wind—there's a gray stone dyke running all along the left side, so if you find yourself out there you're out of the championship running. And the right side of the narrow fairway was no bargain, either; with thick rough, it was ringed around the green with a half dozen traps, and the green itself was almost five hundred yards away. Again, I remember using a driver for my second shot and got lucky landing on a narrow strip of turf between bunkers. Happy to settle for par, I had scored 34 for the outward nine.

I continued my good play on the closing half.

I birdied ten and twelve, as well as the short thirteenth thanks to a fine tee shot that landed eight feet from the cup. After a birdie at sixteen, I was thinking that if I could close with a pair of pars, I'd reach my goal of 66. Things didn't look great at seventeen after my four-wood second shot went over the green and eventually required me to sink a rather nerve-wracking twenty-footer. I managed to do so.

I now arrived at the seventy-second hole just needing par for 66. It wasn't meant to be. After driving my tee shot into the bunker, I'd eventually three-putt for a double bogey. Even though it was a 68, I thought I had given away my best chance at a major to date.

Even with Vivienne trying to console me, I held my head in my hands with thoughts gloomier than the weather.

Because the leaders were playing two hours behind me, I spent much of that time with very taut nerves desolately pacing back and forth along the four-hundred-yard entrance road near the clubhouse. I eventually left for the hotel feeling I had blown the tournament. I tried to soothe my nerves by taking a cold bath. Then I changed into a white suit and tie and returned to the clubhouse, where George Gibson, the PGCA secretary, took me to a balcony to watch the last players come up the eighteenth green.

It turns out the other leaders were struggling as well. One by one the other competitors finished out of the running. It came down to Flory Van Donck and Fred Bullock, who would need a three at the 427-yard home hole to tie me. Each took five.

I became the youngest man to win the Open over seventy-two holes. And I must say I felt so privileged when I was told I had tied the record . . . set by Ben Hogan. I became the only man in history to match Mr. Hogan's 1953 achievement of winning with four rounds each of which was lower than the one before. Hogan at Carnoustie had 73-71-70-68=282; at Muirfield I had 75-71-70-68=284.

But most of all, I had Vivienne and my daughter Jennifer to share in the victory. Now we'd be able to afford the large family we wanted. I just wished my father could've been there.

The long hours of toiling under the South African sun, all the travel spanning the globe, and the unswerving support of family and friends now seemed validated.

What appeared to be a terrific ending, however, was in fact only the beginning. I now had the first leg of the Grand Slam and was on my way to success at the highest level in the sport. I'm thankful that my hunger to win never left me.

67

THE KING'S IMPACT

JULY 12–15, 1961
ROYAL BIRKDALE GOLF CLUB
SOUTHPORT, ENGLAND

This a story less about victory and more about the charisma and fortitude of one legendary player who personally revived American player interest in the game's oldest major. (Of course, holding up a Claret Jug goes a long way, too.)

Americans certainly had a history of performing well at the Open Championships. In 1922, Walter Hagen became the first American-born champion of the Open, and he went on to claim the championship three more times in the decade (see chapter 62). Bobby Jones won it back-to-back starting in 1926. Then in 1930, that talented amateur from Georgia won his own unique "Grand Slam" as he claimed both the US and British Opens and US and British Amateur Championships in the same calendar year (see chapter 63). That success was carried on with wins by Gene Sarazen in 1932 and Denny Shute in 1933. However, the Great Depression and increasing political and economic instability in Europe limited the number of top Americans participating in the tournament over the remainder of the

1930s and throughout the 1940s and 1950s. Except for Sam Snead making a trip and winning in 1946 (and a sixth-place result in 1962) and Ben Hogan taking the title in his lone visit in 1953, most American players had stopped making the trip due to travel concerns (long and arduous in the days of no private jets), the comparatively low prize money, the qualifying, the food. the dreary wet weather, and comparatively spartan accommodations. There were various other reasons, too, such as unfamiliarity with links play and handling the smaller ball, where differences in trajectory, distance, and control were extensive.

Enter Arnold Palmer.

Palmer's father, who worked as a greenskeeper at the Latrobe Country Club in western Pennsylvania, had told him, "You'll never be a great player unless you play well internationally." And in 1960, after he won the Masters and the US Open, there was talk of his winning the professional "Grand Slam." Palmer was doubly motivated to challenge for the Open.

And at the Open, played at St. Andrews that year, not only did Palmer go through qualifying and deal with the other conditions that held back other Americans from making the trip, but he had a great showing.

After the first nine holes of the final round, Palmer still trailed by four. But he then charged, including a birdie on the final hole. Australian Kel Nagle needed to par the final two holes to win, and that was what he did. Word spread quickly, and with Palmer's attacking style and charisma capturing the British public and press, he'd return in 1961 to try and improve on his runner-up finish.

The Royal Birkdale venue, a par-72, 6,844-yard track, was located on the Lancashire coast a few miles north of Liverpool. The winds and rain hitting the course off the Irish Sea can be counted on to challenge even the best golfers in the world, especially since many of the tees are high up on the sand hills exposed to the full fury of those strong gusts that steadily lash the area.

But Palmer's lashing long-iron play, which was a strength of his game, bored through those winds. However, gale-force winds caused scores to soar during the second round on Thursday. Still, Palmer managed to secure a share of second place with defending champion Nagle, as both were just one off the lead at 1-under 137. Welshman Dai Rees and South African Harold Henning were tied for first.

It should be remembered that Palmer would have had a share of the lead halfway through if not for a penalty he called on himself.

After a fine drive at the par-5, 510-yard sixteenth, Palmer's approach bounced off the green into a bunker. Just as he was near the contact point, the wind blew the ball slightly backward. He hit squarely on it, but blasted it over the green. He reported it to an official and the ultimate result was 73 instead of 72.

Unfortunately, after the second round I had to withdraw for the first and only time in all my years of competing in the majors. I had some beef jerky that was brought from South Africa. It got moldy and I puked my heart out.

The weather got increasingly nasty as heavy rains washed out both rounds on Friday. It was so bad that rare cancellation was a possibility; however, the weather let up just enough to play the third and fourth rounds in showers on Saturday.

Palmer, leaning on his strength of often using a one-iron, that difficult club he controls so well, still gave him a distance advantage off the tees. Then he'd follow that up with a wind-boring low ball flight approach that still managed to have enough backspin to hold the greens.

An example of both his power and aggressive play that so excited British fans was exemplified by a shot he took at the fifteenth, which would be commemorated with a plaque that is still there to this day. (After renovations it is now the sixteenth hole.) An errant drive found a stubby bush. And though his caddy felt the best option was to wedge it out, Palmer wanted to go for the green, so he pulled out a six-iron. The surrounding gallery let out a slight gasp then quickly quieted down, anxious to see if he could pull it off. Hitching up his pants, Palmer sized up the situation one last time. Then with a mighty lash the plant just disintegrated, and 165 yards later the ball was on the green.

That combination of power, risk-taking, and finesse procured a 69. Heading into the final round, Palmer now had the lead at 4-under 212, one ahead of Rees. That would be the winning margin.

One year after making his Open Championship debut, Arnold Palmer had scored his first victory in golf's oldest tournament.

That performance had more wide-ranging impact than any drama on the course. Besides being the first American champion since Hogan in 1953, the King's efforts did more to increase the status of the Open in America than anything before. A champion who truly believed in the importance of the sport's history, Palmer forever changed how the tournament was viewed in the eyes of his fellow American pros.

And after Palmer made it cool with his magic touch, and then won it again the very next year, Americans would go on to win the Open thirty times over the next sixty years.

"I think it's very clear the change in the attitude of the players is because of Arnold Palmer when he won the Open Championship and had to qualify the next year," Tom Watson said in a conference call years later. "He put that much emphasis and importance . . . and the rest of the players followed."

Arnie was like Jack, myself, Tom Watson, Lee Trevino—guys that want to win tournaments. We weren't concerned about inconveniences.

You will never be recognized as a superstar if you don't win the Open Championship. It is as simple as that. It is historically the most important tournament in the world. And if you think about it, it is the greatest test. For example, on day one you hit a driver and a seven-iron to the first hole. The next day you had a driver and a three-iron to the first hole. Yardage does not mean a thing. You have learned to hit it short of the green. Yet you learn to roll it up to the green from a long way away. And you have to learn to carry the ball onto the green sometimes. And every day is a different test. One day the weather is perfect and the next it is lousy, and when combined with everything else, it's a test of golf you don't get anywhere else in the world.

68

|

THOMSON'S TERRAIN

JULY 7–9, 1965
ROYAL BIRKDALE GOLF CLUB
SOUTHPORT, ENGLAND

Peter Thomson won his first Open Championship in 1954 on the very course he would win his fifth and final Claret Jug—Royal Birkdale. Located on the northwest coast of England, Royal Birkdale has hosted the Open ten times and has become one of this major's most renowned and challenging venues.

Growing up on the hard-and-fast conditions of the fine courses that dotted the sand belt of Melbourne, with their many sand ridges towering over the fairways, this Australian seemed a natural on a landscape filled with undulating dunes and thick brush. And with his keen ability to keep the ball below the winds on this track in Southport, they might have well called it "Thomson's Terrain" because (and it is worth repeating) twice during his career, Royal Birkdale hosted the Open and he won it both times. (And it certainly didn't hurt Thomson's career by having a job in his youth at Spalding Sporting Goods working in their research laboratory, which included testing golf balls.)

But in 1965 the test at Royal Birkdale would be competing against such proven players as Arnold Palmer, Kel Nagle, Jack Nicklaus, Sam Snead, Bob Charles, and myself, all past Open champions. The first-round leader with a 68, Tony Lema, was also the defending champion, which is a story in itself.

After several years of struggle on the PGA Tour, late in the 1962 season, the native Californian's first official win came in late September at Las Vegas in the Sahara Invitational Golf Tournament, three strokes ahead of runner-up Don January (himself the future winner of the 1967 PGA Championships). Four weeks later, on the eve of his playoff victory at the Orange County Open Invitational in Costa Mesa, California, the bubbly Lema joked to the media that he would serve champagne if he won that week's PGA Tour tournament.

Sure enough, after sinking an eleven-foot birdie try on the third extra hole for the victory over Bob Rosburg (another future PGA Champion), he brought champagne for the media. From then on, Lema was known as "Champagne Tony." And he kept on winning. From September 1962 through May 1966, Lema won twelve times on the PGA Tour, had six other wins, and finished in the top ten in eight of the fifteen majors he played, including a runner-up performance to winner Jack Nicklaus in the 1963 Masters.

Lema would get some measure of revenge against the Golden Bear by turning the tables, this time at the 1964 Open Championship in St. Andrews. Amazingly, for someone who had never previously visited Britain or played links golf (he did get an assist from caddy Tip Anderson, who once caddied for Arnold Palmer), the rising star dominated the proceedings at the Old Course, winning his first major. Nicklaus, a three-time Open champion, came in second, a distant five strokes back.

Back at the '65 event, Thompson opened with a 73. Despite a fine 68 the following day, he still trailed Lema, who shared the lead with Bruce Devlin halfway through. However, using his vast experience in playing in foul weather throughout the UK, Thomson scored a modest 72 in the third round. With the other competitors ballooning, it was enough to send him into the lead after the morning's third round.

Paired together in the final round, the four-time champion and the defending champion fought it out. After Thomson had built a three-stroke cushion deep into the front nine, Lema made some birdies of his own to close to within one. He even had an opportunity to square things; however, he just missed a birdie putt on the sixteenth.

That would be as close as Lema got, because there'd be a three-shot swing between the pair over the last two holes, thanks largely to a pair of Thomson birdies.

As the victor, Thomson joined James Braid and J. H. Taylor (and now Tom Watson) as a five-time Open champion (including three in row from 1954 to 1956). Only Harry Vardon had ever done better, with six titles.

Tragically, just over a year later, right when he was poised to become one of the truly elite players in the game, Lema was killed when the small plane in which he was traveling crashed onto a golf course outside of Chicago.

Thomson, the Hall of Famer from Australia, who played primarily in Britain and Asia, competed comparatively little in the United States in his prime (which included a fourth-place finish in the 1956 US Open and a fifth-place performance at the 1957 Masters). He did, however, have a successful turn later on, stateside with the PGA's fledgling senior circuit known nowadays as the Champions Tour (in 1985 he won nine times).

He laid out his views about the differences between the courses and the style of play in England and the United States during a *Sports Illustrated* interview.

"For reasons of my build and my style I find it more to my liking on seaside links," he said with typical analytical detachment. "The major difference between British courses and American is that the ball bounces as far as it rolls in England. In America it doesn't. I greatly prefer close turf because I strike my shots hard downwards and I get a lower line of flight than most. Playing British-style courses requires extremely delicate judgments, rather more exacting assessments of each shot. It is not a question of fixing your eyes on the flag and swinging. It is a more sensitive game."[1]

69

A SHOT AT GLORY SLIDES BY

JULY 8-12, 1970
THE OLD COURSE
ST. ANDREWS, SCOTLAND

As the home of golf, down through the generations, whenever St. Andrews hosts the game's oldest major, the sport's biggest names all arrive with the same special dream of hoisting the Claret Jug at this fabled course. The 99th Open Championship in 1970 would be no different, but in the end it would feature two stars and a peacock.

Having won the US Open two years before, Lee Trevino didn't know what to expect when he crossed the Atlantic to play links golf in the British Isles. Turns out it was love at first sight.

"I played all my golf at Tenison Park East [Dallas], you had to hit the ball straight. You could not land the ball on the green because they wouldn't hold. They were very small oval greens. And they were as hard as a brick. So you had to bump and run. And that is how I played," said the Texan. "When I went over to the British courses, I thought I was playing Tenison East only without trees. It was easy for me. Really easy right from the start. They played like a hand in a glove for my game."

Indeed, the Merry Mex would be very successful with seven top ten finishes, which would include winning the first of two consecutive Opens in 1971 (see chapter 70).

Seven-time major winner Jack Nicklaus had turned thirty and had not won a Grand Slam event in three years. Realizing how precious few opportunities there really are at winning a major, and enduring his longest drought to date, the Golden Bear used two things to help propel him to greater heights starting with this tournament.

First, Nicklaus had always looked up to Bobby Jones, and he was well aware of the legendary player's view that he considered a victory on the Old Course a necessary validation of a golfer's greatness.

The second was the memory of his late father, who had passed in February 1970 from pancreatic cancer at fifty-six. Charlie Nicklaus was the guiding force in his son's development as a man and golfer, and he simply was Jack's closest friend.

In his autobiography Jack expressed the depth of their relationship, calling his father "my guide, my companion, my mentor, my supporter, my defender, but always most of all my closest and surest friend."

The peacock of this story is Doug Sanders. He grew up dirt-poor in a small Georgian town during the Great Depression, a youngster whose family couldn't afford to buy him shoes. Sanders walked around barefoot helping his parents make ends meet by picking cotton. Unable to afford food, let alone golf lessons, Sanders learned how to play after begging to be allowed to caddy at a worn and shoddy nine-hole course, sneaking in self-taught swings when he could.

It certainly would be an unorthodox motion, with its short backswing and follow-through. Some called it a "phone booth" swing. Didn't matter; it worked for him.

Good enough to earn an athletic scholarship to the University of Florida in Gainesville, where Sanders led his team to an SEC title. After winning the Canadian Open as an amateur, Sanders then launched a very successful pro career, winning eighteen tournaments by the time of the 1970 Open Championship.

With all that success, Sanders made up for those barefoot and hand-me-down clothes. He created a distinct style that would earn him the nickname "the Peacock of the Fairways" for his flamboyant apparel.

Considered by many to be way ahead of his time on the fashion front, Sanders would be profiled in golf and nongolf magazines that would feature photos of his closets filled wall-to-wall with hundreds of shoes, pants, shirts, and sweaters in bright ensembles, representing a cross between an Easter-egg hunt and a rainbow.

Once named by *Esquire* as one of America's "Ten Best Dressed Jocks," the self-proclaimed playboy was often seen with one beautiful date after another, and at age thirty-six he showed no signs of slowing down. But despite the money and fame, he still could not break through the winner's circle at a major.

Twice he came in third at the PGA Championship and finished runner-up in that event in 1959. He came close in the US Open, ending up second in 1961. In a bit of irony, he lost the 1966 Open at Muirfield to Jack Nicklaus by one stroke. Déjà vu all over again?

Trevino, Nicklaus, and Sanders all opened with 68s, just three back of the lead. By duplicating his 68 the following day, Trevino, battling the wind and rain, took the lead halfway through the tournament at 8-under 136. Nicklaus was just one back and Sanders three.

Britain's twenty-six-year-old Tony Jacklin, the defending Open champion and current US Open titleholder, was certainly in the mix as he was tied with Nicklaus for second place, much to the delight of the crowd.

Back in the first round Jacklin was on fire. After a record-tying outward 29, including birdieing the first three holes then holing out a wedge from one hundred yards for an eagle at the par-4 ninth, the popular Brit was eight under par and looked all set for a solid 62 or 63. Unfortunately the weather drowned out his heated play, as a rainstorm caused suspension of play. When competition resumed the following day, Jacklin would bogey three of his remaining five holes to finish with a 67.

All the aforementioned stayed in the race with fine third rounds. Trevino kept his lead following a 72. Nicklaus and Jacklin were still tied for second place. But now Sanders, with a second straight 71 (despite a double bogey at seventeen, where he pitched into the infamous road bunker), joined the two others for a share of second heading into the final round.

Leading both the second and third rounds, Trevino's rare unforced error at the fifth hole of the final round would cost him dearly. After roping a shot to the wrong flag on the massive par-5, 567-yard hole, he immediately recognized what he had done and slapped himself in the forehead, saying, "I done hit to the wrong stick." Now he had to putt eighty feet to the correct flag. The resultant three-putt was part of a day where he finished with a 77 and fell to a share of third place. Jacklin, too, went high with a 76 to end in fifth.

Meanwhile, Nicklaus had employed a swing strategy to combat the feisty crosswinds that wreaked havoc with his standard fade on nearly half the course by toeing in the clubface slightly at address, rather than mess with his setup or swing. Still, the 50 mph winds that conveniently showed up for the final round affected Nicklaus most on the greens, where he had several three-putts, including on the eighteenth. He finished with a second straight 73, still a good score considering the conditions.

So the always sartorially splendid Sanders had destiny in his own hands.

On the previous day he had double-bogied hole number seventeen, widely considered the scariest par-4 in golf. Today, Sanders would produce what was perhaps the shot of his career here in the final round. He faced a poor lie near the back edge—downhill, it required getting the ball up quickly and stopping it on the shallow shelf of the green.

Sanders delivered the blow by sliding through the sand at the optimum angle. His shot took one big hop and came to rest less than a foot from the hole. the crowd roared its approval of that brilliant

effort. Now, the lanky Georgian could win his first major by finishing with a par.

Just four shots from a Claret Jug, he struck a fine tee shot at the
par-4, 350-yard closing hole. Next up, a ninety-eight-yard pitch to
the flag in the middle left of the green. Playing safe, he finished on
the back of the green. It left him a fairly long lag effort in order to get
down in two to claim his first major championship.

Showing no outward signs of the pressure he must have been feeling, Sanders delivered a solid putt to within thirty inches of the cup.
The next one, the potential Open winner, would be one of the most
famous putts in history.

Approaching his short putt, Sanders recalled what he was thinking.

"I walked up to my ball, looked down at the line, and saw what
I thought was a pebble. I bent over to get it but it wasn't a pebble, it
was just where the sun had burned the grass."

What happened next was that he never really regrouped and was
not in his proper stance when he struck the ball. Trying to rush it to
get it done, he knew he missed it right away. As the ball went rolling
past the hole, Sanders kind of lurched toward it.

His playing partner, Trevino, had a clear view of the debacle.

"He was shaking so bad that when he was holding the putter, he
actually had his hands inside his right thigh, so he couldn't take the
putter back. So, by not taking the putter back, he had to release the
putter and he released it open."

Though he gallantly came back to give Nicklaus a run for the jug in
the following day's eighteen-hole playoff (he had four bogeys to Jack's
thirteen straight pars to open things, but closed with three birdies in
the final five holes), Sanders would lose, again, by one stroke to Nicklaus in an Open.

Nicklaus was back on track (and what a track—he'd finish with a
record eighteen major victories). After sinking the winning birdie at
eighteen, so excited to have won at the Home of Golf and being able

to win for his father, Nicklaus uncharacteristically threw his putter way up in the air, leaving others to duck for cover.

Unfortunately for Sanders, there'd be no ducking for cover from the haunting memory of the short, missed putt sliding past the cup at the seventy-second hole.

I have often said that many majors come down to one stroke, and just as often it comes down to the shot on the green. Doug's failure to get it the ball the hole—just thirty inches from the cup—is arguably the most famous miss in golf. Those are the breaks in this game, and everyone who plays at the highest levels has suffered plenty of them, including myself.

The colorful Sanders, who'd never win a major on tour, would carry on in his good-natured way. Hiding the blues behind the vibrant colors he continued to wear into his later years, Sanders would inevitably be asked the same question wherever he went—"Doug, 1970 Open—St. Andrews, do you ever give your closest brush with majors immortality much thought?" and the imperturbable Sanders would inevitably reply, "Very rarely, I mean you know, sometimes five or six minutes can go by in a day without me thinking about it . . ."

70

TREVINO EARNS BACK-TO-BACK JUGS

JULY 12–15, 1972
MUIRFIELD
GULLANE, SCOTLAND

ee Trevino was one of the straightest hitters I ever saw in my life. He also had the perfect game for the Open because he hit the ball very low. I knew, even though I had won my first major here at Muirfield and was feeling good about my game, that the Merry Mex would be a formidable opponent.

Trevino defeated Liang-Huan Lu, Tony Jacklin, Jack Nicklaus, Billy Casper, and myself to win the previous year's Open at Royal Birkdale, which was the one hundredth time the tournament was played. Arriving as the centennial champion, Trevino was brimming with confidence. Not only did he have three top three finishes, including a victory in the weeks before flying over to Scotland, but the links layout fit like a hand to a glove for the Texan.

Jack Nicklaus also had good success early on. As a matter of fact, he had already won the Open twice, in 1966 at Muirfield and 1970 at St. Andrews (see chapter 69).

For a competitor who from the start of his career focused his formidable talents on success at the majors, Nicklaus had extra motivation to take the 1972 Open. Having won both the Masters and the US Open (leading in every round), playing on some of his favorite venues—Augusta National, Pebble Beach, Muirfield, and Oakland Hills (the site of the PGA held later that summer), this was quite possibly the best chance he'd likely have at winning the coveted and elusive Grand Slam.

Led by the facts that he had won the first two majors of the year and had already mastered Muirfield, Nicklaus was the odds-on favorite to win the 1972 Open. Now because he also held the PGA Championship title from February 1971, with a victory at Muirfield, Nicklaus would become the first to hold all four major titles at once.

So, the cagey Trevino went to the first tee convincing himself there was more pressure on Nicklaus to achieve such a rarified accomplishment than for him to defend his crown.

Nicklaus and Trevino didn't really cross paths; they had opposite tee times and were never paired together for any of the rounds. Still, despite the Golden Bear's ever-looming presence, Trevino was not intimidated. He had the reputation of never backing down from anyone, and in the biggest win of his career, he had defeated Nicklaus in the 1971 US Open, something that elevated his confidence against the eleven-time majors winner (see chapter 51).

In his book *They Call Me Super Mex,* Trevino talked about both competing against Nicklaus at the US Open earlier in the year as well as his unorthodox prep for his upcoming title defense.

"In the month before I defended my British championship, I trained very hard. I took my family with me to Central Texas, rented a house and trained on Orville Moody's place in Killeen. I was up at five every morning, running through the hills, and then I played golf. The greens superintendent had a twelve-year-old daughter, a mute who read lips, and she drove the cart with my bag on it. I didn't ride. I ran between shots and I played 36 holes a day. I was determined to be sharp for Muirfield."[1]

Lee and I shot even par 71 in the first round, three back of the lead, while Jack was one better at 1 under. While Jack and I were tied for third place at 142 even par after round two, Britain's Tony Jacklin, already the owner of a pair of majors, rolled a 69 and had a share of the lead at 1 under.

Atop the leaderboard with the popular Jacklin was Trevino. The affable Texan would often whistle, sing, and talk to himself and anybody else around as a way of relaxation while walking down the fairways. He got on a hot stretch and closed out his round with five straight birdies, including an astonishing hole-out of a sand shot at sixteen. He later admitted that should have been a double bogey, as well as the sinking of a thirty-foot chip on the last green.

The coleader halfway through talked about the keys to his fine play so far.

"I realized I couldn't use the driver very much. And I had a one-iron, believe it or not," said Trevino. "The course was completely dry. They had a two-year drought. There was virtually no rough whatsoever. The fairways were so dry that you could see the powder from where the ball landed. I was driving the ball with a three-iron or a one-iron. And I was driving it three hundred yards easy. A lot of the other guys were getting in trouble with the driver because they were finding bunkers they had never seen before. The ball wouldn't stop."

Unfortunately for Doug Sanders, the ball wouldn't stop at eighteen. After a long birdie at fifteen that got the crowd fired up, then another at seventeen, the literally as well as figuratively colorful Sanders, seeking his first majors win, took a two-shot lead to the tee at eighteen.

However, errant tee and approach shots and trouble getting out of a bunker led to a triple-bogey 8. The three-shot swing cost him the lead; he would gamely hang on and ultimately finish the tournament in fourth place.

Another colorful American out on the Scottish links was Ken Harrelson. The twenty-seven-year-old had retired just the year before from Major League Baseball, where he was an all-star first baseman-outfielder. He made it through qualifying only to miss the cut by one stroke.

I had a poor third round and fell back with a 76, and Nicklaus stayed in the hunt with an even par score. But the day's finest performances were delivered by Jacklin and Trevino.

Paired together, these two went at it. Jacklin started out well early with an eagle at the fifth. But Trevino showed some of his brilliant short game, particularly on the back nine. After back-to-back birdies at fourteen and fifteen, Trevino hooked the ball into a greenside bunker at sixteen. Lying on a downslope with no shot to a very shallow pin and no green to work with, he intended to get it past the hole, let it roll back, then settle for bogey. He popped it out, and the ball simply dropped in the cup. As the crowd yelled their appreciation, Trevino tossed his sand wedge and threw his hat to the ground in pleasant disbelief. Instead of bogey, his birdie moved him to 4 under, and he was now tied for the lead with his playing partner.

At eighteen, both were 5 under. However Trevino's six-iron approach shot rolled hard through the green and came to rest on a bank of chunky grass in back. From that position he tried to simply get up and down for par, but the ball rolled toward the target, and Trevino ran excitedly as it dropped in for a birdie. With a phenomenal 66, he took a one-stroke lead into the final round over Jacklin.

Nicklaus had started the final round six shots back, but it was time for the others to beware of the bear.

He had played defensive golf the first three rounds, but he was well aware that he had to go on the offensive if he was to have a chance to track down the leaders.

He started out well, with birdies at two and three. After another birdie at the par-5 fifth, he quickly cut his deficit in half at 3 under. With a birdie at nine, Nicklaus went out in 32, and the appreciative crowd energized him.

In a rather unusual circumstance, an energetic jackrabbit cost Trevino the lead early on. Just as he was in midstroke, the hare ran right behind Trevino, wrecking his concertation and sending his putt past the cup. Trevino slammed down his putter, put his hands on his hips, and stared at the ground dejectedly. He ended up with a bogey.

After birdieing the tenth, the Golden Bear had made up his big deficit and now actually had the lead.

It would be game on, as the afternoon had lots of jockeying at the top. Even though I closed with my best round by far in the tournament with a 67, I had too much ground to make up and wound up in sixth place.

But that reminds me: Experts are quick to count people out. At the 1956 Masters, Jack Burke Jr. rallied from a tournament record eight shots back to pass Ken Venturi, who had led the entire tournament. At the 1978 Masters, I overcame a seven-shot deficit going into the final round, shooting a record-tying 64 to win my third Masters and ninth majors championship (see chapter 10).

Meanwhile, back at the 1972 Open Championship, Trevino quickly regrouped. With an eagle on nine, he was back in the lead at 6 under. Jacklin stayed right behind him with his own eagle. All this was happening just as Nicklaus was getting ready for his birdie try up at eleven. The roar he heard forced him to back off and go through his routine again. By sinking it he was tied with Trevino for the lead with Jacklin one back at 5 under.

Now as Nicklaus was getting ready to belt his tee shot at fifteen, there was another roar. He had to back away again. This time Jacklin birdied twelve and grabbed a share of the lead.

Proof that it is a game of inches and illustrating just how thin the margins are between being the victor or the runner-up, Jack's birdie try at fifteen lipped out. It would be a key blow. And he would bogey the short par-3 sixteenth, his first of the round. After a par at seventeen, still just one off the lead, Nicklaus could only manage par on the seventy-second hole. His Grand Slam dreams now rested on the closing performances of the two leaders still out on the course. And what riveting action that would produce.

I walked around the last three holes of that tournament. I'm saying I saw all that drama unfold with my own eyes. You could not repeat what Lee Trevino did with a thousand tries.

The worst thing I ever saw in golf was Jean Van de Velde's crash at the 1999 Open in Carnoustie, a three-shot lead with one hole to go (see chapter 74). Another one was Arnold Palmer's blown six-shot lead over Billy Casper at the Olympic Club in San Francisco at the 1966 US Open (see chapter 49).

But the worst of anything that has ever happened was Tony Jacklin and Lee Trevino here at Muirfield. In the other two cases, Palmer and Van de Velde did it to themselves. Here Trevino did it to Jacklin.

When they were on the sixteenth hole in the final round, Trevino was two shots back of Jacklin. Jacklin hit first, and it settled just twelve feet from the hole. Trevino put it in the bunker. Now the flag in those days was a wooden pole. Very thick. Hard to get the ball into the cup. If Trevino's shot from the bunker did not hit the flag, he would go into the rough two-feet high and the best he could do was make double-bogey. The rough at Muirfield has always been and always will be high. Trevino got in the bunker and bladed the ball. The odds of it going in were 1 in 1000. It hit the flag and dropped down in the cup.

At seventeen Trevino hooked his tee shot into the bunker. Jacklin's shot was right down the middle. Trevino, groaning and mumbling, knocked it out. Then he knocked his third shot over the green. Jacklin knocked his second shot onto the green. Trevino got up sulking and not really trying. He semi-duffed the chip. The ball caught a five-foot bank in the back, rolled down, and dropped into the hole. Meanwhile, Jacklin three-putted and lost the Open. He was never the same again. It destroyed his entire career as a golfer. That was the worst I ever saw in my lifetime.

It is a moment the Brit will remember forever, nearly on in 2 but down in 6, while Trevino was off in 4 but down in 5.

Trevino had done it. He earned back-to-back Claret Jugs and was the first to successfully defend his title since Arnold Palmer in 1962.

It was the third of four times that Nicklaus was a runner-up to Trevino in a majors championship. Nicklaus had this to say about that experience at Muirfield:

"As always in golf I had control of my own destiny. It hurt, but life would go on, there was nothing I could do but get on with living. In golf you will always lose a lot more than you win, and if you want to retain your sanity and protect the sanity of those around you, you just have to conjure up enough fatalism to live peacefully with that fact."[2]

For Jacklin, on the other hand, it was a devastating blow.

Years later, in an interview with a British newspaper, Jacklin admitted he was never the same after what happened in that tournament: "Again, I reacted thinking, 'He's not going to beat me like that.' But I took a rush at my birdie putt and hit it an awkward distance past. Circumstances being what they were, I missed the return and the rest is history.

"I never really featured in major championships after that. And for me golf is all about winning majors. It changed my outlook somehow. I always believed to succeed all you needed was to dedicate yourself and put your time in. I was competitive, mentally tough, but obviously not tough enough to endure that."[3]

At the very least, Jacklin can proudly look back at winning two majors: the 1969 Open at Royal Lytham and the 1970 US Open at Hazeltine.

Though he would not win another Open, Trevino looked back with a chuckle as he pondered what might have been had he found links golf earlier in life.

"Well, I always thought that if I had played the Open from the time I was twenty, I'd have won five or six," he said with a hearty laugh.

I remember afterward the writers asked Trevino, "How did you do that two out of three holes?" And he said, "Ladies and gentlemen, don't forget—God is a Mexican."

You know I love being with Lee because we laugh all the time.

71

SAME PLAYER AS FIFTEEN YEARS PRIOR

JULY 10–13, 1974
ROYAL LYTHAM & ST. ANNES GOLF CLUB
LYTHAM ST. ANNES, ENGLAND

Running along just inland from the Irish Sea near the blue-collar resort of Blackpool on the Lancashire coast lies one of the quirkiest courses in the Open rotation. It's whipped by cold, doused by rain and constantly changing crosswinds, starts with a rare par-3, and closes out with six consecutive tricky par-4s. Contestants at Royal Lytham are presented with knee-deep roughs that are unbelievably hazardous, undulating fairways, and several blind tee shots as well as more than two hundred bunkers that guard everywhere you're trying to get to.

It is not a favorite of most players, but I love the wind, and I went into this tournament with a positive mindset. After doing my homework, I developed a reliable game plan.

I haven't really elaborated on this before, but I was as deeply prepared for this tournament as any I ever played. In practice rounds I experimented to get a better pulse on how to gauge those distinctive winds, and I realized my best course of action would be to rely on the one-iron as much as possible. There were plenty of naysayers, but I gave them no mind. I knew from practicing in these gale force winds that club was the best for me because it helped keep the ball low as well as maximize the ball's run.

The results of sticking to my game plan were evident. I opened with rounds of 68 and 69. So halfway through, I was the only contestant under par. And at 5-under 137, I had a five-stroke lead. Fellow South African Bobby Cole and England's Peter Oosterhuis were at even par 142.

I hit these one-irons to these narrow bumpy fairways. And I reminded myself, "Yes, you're hitting a much longer second shot to the green, but if you drive into the rough, and now you come out, you've got to put your third on the green. You can't make a mistake. By staying in the fairway, you've got a chance to make par."

My playing partner for the first two rounds, Hale Irwin, who came over as winner of the tough US Open (see chapter 53) found the layout here quite challenging.

"I think all the Open courses for me were difficult in that my eye preferred narrow fairways, big trees, targets that were defined. So you go to play in an Open Championship like Lytham and your target is more like skyline to skyline," said Irwin. "You have mounds, lots of pot bunkers, but I could never really get my target lines straight in my mind. That was an ability I just didn't have. [Also,] I'm not a great cold-weather player. Wind I don't mind. It was cold and rained quite a bit, so when you're wearing glasses and it is raining sideways, *that* makes it more difficult," said the American with a laugh. (He'd finish twenty-fourth.)

Unlike traditional links layouts, Royal Lytham also differs in that the routing changes direction no fewer than twelve times. Crosswinds can make judgment of distances extremely risky, and most of the drama takes place on the back nine where most of the winds come right at you, making it play longer and even harder to judge club selection.

Most people don't know that this was the first time in the Open it was compulsory to play with the larger 1.68-inch ball, which had been used in America for many years and was less easy to control in the wind than the smaller ball. And the wind obviously has a lot more effect on it. It's like when they played the Ryder Cup and they said to Ben Hogan, "You have a choice of the big or small ball." And he said, "Anyone who takes the big ball in the wind is an idiot." And he was right.

Big ball, small ball, I was really focused. The key factor was that throughout the rounds I kept the ball in play. And I always *loved* playing in the wind! So psychologically I told myself, "This is great for me," because a lot of people don't like playing in the wind.

I remember hitting a shot at the twelfth hole; I believe it was a par-3. One of the best I ever played. And guys were hitting out of bounds there because the wind was so strong. I just loved competing in the wind.

After I finished with a third-round 75, with such a star-studded field, I told the press, "You can be ten behind and still win. The pressure is on you far more when you are leading than when you are charging. Three shots is nothing. It's gonna be a helluva day tomorrow."

Johnny Miller and defending Open champion Tom Weiskopf moved to within striking distance. So did Jack Nicklaus with a stretch that included a birdie, a birdie, and an eagle, coming from nine strokes back to within four. With a 73, Oosterhuis continued his steady play that kept him in second place, three off my pace. Nevertheless, I continued to be the only competitor under par heading into the final round and was quite confident in my game.

And it helped to have a familiar face on my bag.

My longtime caddy was Alfred "Rabbit" Dyer. I brought him over from America, where he became the first black caddy to appear in the Open. With colorful pants, a straw plantation hat, and a quick wit, Rabbit became a popular figure. He made friends with everyone, and was sought out by fans for an autograph.

I will never forget how his humor was on display after the third round. When he went to be interviewed, he kept saying, "*We* did this, *we* did that . . ." in front of 150 members of the press. But the day I shot 75 in the third round, he told the press, "*He* did this, *he* did that . . ." *We* shared a lot of laughs.

I opened the final frame with back-to-back birdies, and suffered a couple bogeys. But I drilled a two-iron onto the green at the sixth hole to within seven feet and scored an eagle to make the turn in 32. The highlight of the back nine was a chip-in birdie at thirteen. No one was going to catch me on this day. Not even Nicklaus nor the Englishman Peter Oosterhuis, as the closest challengers could never get within three strokes in the closing round.

Walking to the seventeenth hole, I had a six-shot lead. I turned to Rabbit and said, "Can we win from here?" because I was so focused on just getting birdies. And—I will never forget—he said, "Win from here? Ray Charles could win from here."

At the par-4, 453-yard seventeenth, I hit a fine tee shot that put me in excellent position, but my six-iron second shot went wild and landed in knee-deep rough, which caused a frantic search to beat the five-minute rule and avoid a two-stroke penalty. I was down on my knees pawing through the rough, but at the last minute a marshal found the ball. Bogey.

At the par-4, 386-yard eighteenth, I teed off with what really got me into my commanding position, the one-iron. However, my five-iron second shot pounded right through the green and came to rest right up against the old brick wall of the clubhouse.

The officials told me that since it was not a hazard or ground under repair, the ball had to be played where it was. Fortunately, it was slightly plugged in the dirt. I hit it left-handed with my putter, and it popped out over the flowerbed wall and rolled to a stop on the green just ten feet from the cup. Two putts gave me a bogey for the hole. Not the most glamorous finish, but good enough for a four-stroke victory on a very tough course. I was the only competitor under par (2-under 282).

I still had as much of the competitive fire, wealth of enthusiasm, dedication, and desire as I had fifteen years prior in winning my first Claret Jug at Muirfield in 1959.

And I have long said an underrated measure of success is winning over a long period of time. With my triumph in 1974, I now shared with Harry Vardon and J. H. Taylor the distinction of claiming the title in three separate decades.

Then when we left the tournament taking a train back to London (we didn't have jets waiting for us), Rabbit realized he'd forgotten the trophy!

I said, "Rabbit, we're going to be the first players to ever have lost the trophy." Fortunately, he eventually found it.

I am very proud of this achievement, for I have always felt money does not define your life or success—accomplishments do.

72

"THIS IS WHAT IT'S ALL ABOUT . . ."

JULY 6–9, 1977
AILSA COURSE AT TURNBERRY RESORT
AYRSHIRE, SCOTLAND

It's remembered as the "Duel in the Sun," which says all you need to know about the 1977 Open Championship at Turnberry. It beautifully captures golf's version of two great heavyweight prize fighters. One a thirty-seven-year-old legend, winner of fourteen majors, and the other a twenty-seven-year-old rising superstar. Both were equally determined to show the world that they had the nerve and guts to emerge victorious. Both were merciless in a dog-eat-dog environment that they felt right at home in. It was to be a showdown of epic proportions.

The former, Jack Nicklaus, reflected on the circumstances he found himself in that unusually warm, dry week along the west coast of Scotland against the latter, Tom Watson.

"Nineteen seventy-seven Turnberry, Watson and I knew we were probably the two best players in the game at the time. Now we are playing together, head-to-head. We both played pretty good golf," said Nicklaus. "The fun *is* the competition. I felt I could add to my résumé, but there was a young fellow named Tom Watson who felt otherwise."

The gap-toothed young gun from Kansas, with his belying, freckle-faced Tom Sawyer–ish look and innocent grin, had already shown his mettle against the game's luminary three months earlier. At Augusta National, Watson held off Nicklaus to win his first green jacket at the Masters.

Now coming into his own, especially with a game and temperament so well-suited for links play, Watson, who had already won a Claret Jug just two years earlier at Carnoustie, had no fear of the Golden Bear as the battle began. After the first round, they had matching 68s, and at 2 under they already were high atop the leaderboard, sharing third place with Lee Trevino, himself a two-time Open champion (see chapter 70).

This was the first Open championship ever played on the Ailsa course at Turnberry. Less than fifty miles from Glasgow, it is located on the magnificent Ayrshire coast, by the Firth of Clyde, off the North Channel of the Irish Sea and graced by a distinctive lighthouse. The course, whose fairways were used as runways during World War II, had been affected by the unusually dry summer.

The earth, scorched from a combination of lack of rain and comparatively high temperatures, yellowed the grass, and made the rough more wispy and the fairways rock-hard. As for the course layout, what you have is that it heads out toward the water for eight holes, runs along the shoreline for three, then winds its way back inland. Some have compared it to Pebble Beach that way.

As you wind down your round and get closer to the clubhouse, the huge luxury hotel looms above you. In addition to the iconic lighthouse, Ailsa Craig, a few miles out at sea and over a thousand feet high, is a massive rock and bird sanctuary. Regarding Turnberry's natural defenses, a lot of holes that made difficult from crosswinds as well as the cold and rain.

"I think trying to pick the right club is the hardest thing because you'd never really know if it's [the wind's] going with you or against you," said Nick Price, a future Claret Jug winner at Turnberry.

A comparatively tight and narrow course, one that requires the skills of being able to hook and slice it into the wind, this is definitely a ball striker's layout.

American Roger Maltbie was striking it well enough to take the thirty-six-hole lead with a 66. But it was another American, Mark Hayes, a two-time All-American at Oklahoma State University, who produced a record-setting round. Rebounding from a poor 6-over 76 opener, Hayes, the winner of the Tournament Players Championship, rolled a 63. That result established a new single round record at the Open Championship by two strokes.

With both shooting even par, Nicklaus and Watson were just one back of Maltbie. With identical scores of 68-70, they would be paired for the third round. Maltbie would later close with 80 for nine-over 289 in a tie for twenty-sixth place.

The weather continued to heat up, and the third round saw the mano a mano Watson-Nicklaus duel get even hotter. In what was building up into one of the greatest head-to-head shotmaking and low-scoring battles in golf history, both finished at 5-under 65 for a 7-under 203 total.

With identical rounds of 68-70-65, they were now three shots clear of Ben Crenshaw and six ahead of the remainder of the field after fifty-four holes.

The fight picked up right where it left off when they teed off for the final round. Nicklaus jumped out to a three-stroke lead after four holes, but Watson did some scoring of his own. Counterpunching, the young lion birdied three of the next four to tie. Then Nicklaus steadied himself to lead by one at the turn. After a birdie at the par-4 twelfth hole, the Golden Bear had a two-stroke lead. But he was unable to put his opponent away, and Watson retaliated with birdie at thirteen.

Watson and Nicklaus had left the rest of the field in their dust awhile back. At this stage, they were the only two under par. Their nearest competitor, Hubert Green, who had won the US Open just a few weeks earlier, was ten strokes back!

So with just a few loyal friends and perhaps some family members making up the galleries of the sixty-two other players, the majority of spectators raced to follow the history-making exploits of these two titans.

However, at one stage, the normally respectful crowd, in their ever-increasing attempts to get closer to the action, spilled onto the fairway. Feeling concerned for his safety from the frenzied mass, Nicklaus refused to play on until the crowd was back under control.

Once that happened, there was no letup in the epic battle. After four hours of heavy punching and counterpunching, the riveting play wound its way to a legendary conclusion. Still one back with just four holes to play, from well off the green, Watson used his putter in that classic Texas wedge style, and from seventy feet away he gave it a helluva send-off. As the ball gained steam like a locomotive engine, it looked like it was headed for London until it slammed into the flagstick and rammed into the cup. He had delivered a body blow, as the birdie tied the match yet again with just three holes left to play.

The energy from the crowd was electric, and it spurred on the two combatants, who were simply miles ahead of everyone else and locked in a personal battle. Now standing on the sixteenth tee, Watson, really sensing the moment, turned to Nicklaus with that knowing grin and said:

"This is what it's all about, isn't it?"

Jack smiled back and said:

"You bet it is."

They both scored par and came to the seventy-first hole knotted at 10 under.

After their tee shots at the par-5, 500-yard seventeenth, Watson hit a magnificent second shot. His iron dropped right over the flag and settled on the green about twenty feet for eagle, at least a sure birdie. Nicklaus could not match that; his shot missed the green short and right, which would hand him an awkward chip. But the two-time Open champ showed his fine touch and rolled it up to with five feet. However, he missed the short birdie putt. Watson made his and, for the first time in the entire tournament, had the lead.

After identical 68-70-65 (203) totals, matching each other stroke for stroke in a world of their own each of the last two rounds, all that separated them after seventy-one holes was one shot.

On the par-4, 431-yard eighteenth, after the young challenger's long-iron tee shot settled on the left side of the fairway, Nicklaus dialed up his power game and pulled out his driver. Unfortunately, he came up and off it, pushing the ball to the right. It settled in some rough, but just as disconcerting was that it sat beside some nasty gorse brush, which could make a full swing problematic. In an uncharacteristic manner, Nicklaus whacked the club down angrily to the ground and stormed down to see the damage it had wrought.

Like a boxer in the ring stepping back to assess the state of his opponent, or a marathoner looking into the eyes of his fellow runner as he moves past him in the waning stages of the race, Watson walked over to examine Jack's lie. Suspecting Nicklaus would have some kind of play, Watson played his second shot first. The confident young man in the lime-green shirt and yellow-and-green checkered pants and white shoes proceeded to deliver a fantastic shot under enormous pressure.

As the roar of the crowd confirmed, the ball settled less than a couple feet from the flag.

With his opponent on the green with almost a gimme birdie, Nicklaus had some fortune come his way. He had a clean backswing and a straight shot to the flag. Taking out a huge chunk of grass, he managed to land it on the right corner of the green.

The crowd rushed en masse across the eighteenth fairway to gather around the final hole. Nicklaus waved both hands to acknowledge the massive gallery, as did Watson. In maintaining absolute drama to the end, Nicklaus drained his thirty-two-foot putt, forcing Watson to make his.

He did.

To the rain of steady applause from the more than twenty thousand appreciative spectators, Watson and Nicklaus left the eighteenth green arm in arm, each now a two-time Champion Golfer of the Year.

Even though I finished way back with a share of twenty-second place, can you imagine shooting 65-66 at Turnberry and losing? That's self-explanatory. We don't have to say another word.

Watson's seventy-two-hole total of 268 established a new Open Championship record by eight shots. For Nicklaus, it was the sixth of a tournament-record seven times that he finished runner-up in the Open. And think about this—his 269 total was seven strokes better than anyone had ever shot before, but it was still not enough.

The historic performance was perhaps summed up best not by the victorious Watson nor by the defeated Nicklaus, but by Hubert Green, the only other player to finish under par and a distant eleven strokes behind the winner. When asked for his thoughts on his opponents' battle, he quipped: "I won this golf tournament. I don't know what game those other two guys were playing."

73

SEVE TAKES HISTORY FROM WATSON

JULY 19–22, 1984
THE OLD COURSE
ST. ANDREWS, SCOTLAND

Tom Watson was the man. He was the player that the press, fans, and competitors pointed at to make even more history on these hallowed grounds at the 113th Open Championship.

And why not?

After all, the eight-time majors winner had won the last two Claret Jugs (back-to-back wins at Royal Troon in 1982 and Royal Birkdale in 1983), and most observers knew he had the ideal game and approach for the crazy bounces of links play to win it again.

"Watson had a bad shot and it did not seem to bother him one way or the other. He'd just go find it and hit it again. That's how all the great players did it," said Larry Nelson, a three-time majors winner.

"Tommy is just a great competitor and very solid ball striker," added Fuzzy Zoeller. "And I think that's one reason why he's won the British Open so many times. He very seldom missed the golf ball. Just very consistent hitting the ball solidly."

While the Kansas City native with the famous gap-toothed grin was a solid pick among prognosticators to earn his sixth Open title and tie Harry Vardon's record, there was a determined Spaniard who had other notions.

Having won the Masters the previous year, Seve Ballesteros also had experience winning the Open, being victorious five years earlier at Royal Lytham. And after a second round of 68 to go with his opening 69, Ballesteros had a share of second place with Nick Faldo and Lee Trevino at 137, 7 under. Watson was two back at 5 under.

Tall, lanky young Australian Ian Baker-Finch threatened to sneak in and take the crown from everybody. He not only led at the thirty-six-hole mark, but he held a two-stroke lead after fifty-four holes. He would share the lead with Watson, who rolled a 66.

Heading into the final round, Ballesteros and Germany's Bernhard Langer were just two behind them. When Finch made the turn with a 41 on the way to a final 79, it really was a battle between the American, German, and Spaniard. Though Langer tried to battle gamely and stayed in the mix, it eventually came down to Ballesteros vs. Watson for the Open title.

Ballesteros had a couple birdies on the front nine and a one-shot lead at one point, but he also made a pair of three-putts that kept the others in the game. Slamming into the nasty gorse on the short, par-4 twelfth, Watson needed a drop and thus suffered a penalty stroke there, but he quickly got it back and a tie for the lead with a birdie at thirteen.

As they were playing just one group apart and battling within a stroke of each other most of the day, it looked like they were headed for a tie and playoff. Then came the seventeenth—the infamous Road Hole.

With its narrow green fronted by a well-visited pot bunker, a road on the right, and heavy rough on the left, where landing there will make it near impossible to get on in two, and framed by the Royal and Ancient Clubhouse and the town of St. Andrews, the uniqueness of this long par-4 has resulted in shots that don't happen anywhere else in the world. The wrecker of many a player's dreams.

And if the past few days were any indication, Ballesteros's chances could've been dealt a death blow here; in each of the previous rounds he had dropped a stroke at the par-4, 461-yard seventeenth. But knowing it was all on the line here, the daring Spaniard stroked a risky approach from the left-hand rough, enabling him to two-putt and head to the seventy-second hole with a par.

The pressure was now on the American to get through the danger zone painlessly. It started out okay with a drive that set up a decent angle for his second shot. But as Ballesteros was soaking up the roars of approval heading toward the green at eighteen, Watson was getting ready to take aim at the green with a two-iron.

Ballesteros then judged his right-to-left putt from around twelve feet perfectly. The ball hesitated on the lip, like sort of a final bow before the curtain fell, then it toppled in. In one of the classic celebrations in golf, the animated Spaniard, with a huge smile, pumped his fist several times then hugged his caddy.

Meanwhile back at seventeen, Watson's two-iron was too strong. From an uphill lie, his approach bounded over the green, across the road, and perilously close to the stone wall. Lucky to make bogey, Watson would now have to eagle eighteen to force a playoff.

That didn't happen. Though he'd come close (see chapter 75), Watson would never win another major.

With millions of viewers around the world watching on television, Ballesteros's famous fist pump after his last putt is one of the enduring images of golf. Years later in his autobiography, Ballesteros would write: "This was the happiest moment of my whole sporting life. My moment of glory, my most fantastic shot."

74

SACRE BLEU IT: THE COLLAPSE
THAT WILL LIVE IN INFAMY

JULY 15–18, 1999
CARNOUSTIE GOLF LINKS
ANGUS, SCOTLAND

It would be the last Open of the decade and indeed the twentieth century, but it will live on forever. Why? Because it included the most infamous collapse in major championship history.

Van de Velde.

A name synonymous with fiasco.

Jean Van de Velde, a thirty-three-year-old from Saint Martin, France, came to this event as an unheralded golfer ranked 152nd in the world. The slender, amiable Frenchman, who spoke English with a charming Gallic accent, suddenly had the golf world's attention after rolling a second-round 68 and sat atop the leaderboard halfway through the major.

Some of the fairways were just fifteen yards wide—as Lee Trevino once said, "Our group had to walk single file down the fairway to stay out of the rough." The combination of these high, rough, narrow fairways with postage stamp–sized landing areas, rock-hard greens, and vexing, gusty crosswinds made scoring conditions extremely difficult.

On the first day, scores on the par-71, 7,361-yard course included five-time champion Tom Watson, who had won here in 1975, finishing with an 82. Defending champion Mark O'Meara had an 83.

In round two, Sergio Garcia, who opened with an 89, followed with an 83. The average score was 78.31. Add it up and there were 55 players in the field of 156 who had scores in the 80s.

The Frenchman had a 75, Combined with his subsequent 68, Van de Velde was in first place at 1-over 143. But heading into Saturday for third round play, looming among others were such familiar marquee names as Tiger Woods and Greg Norman.

The Carnoustie course continued to play mean, and no one was under par after three rounds. But Van de Velde, made two massive birdie putts—a seventy-footer on fourteen and a forty-five-footer at eighteen. With a solid 70, he had now expanded his lead heading into the final eighteen. At even par, he was five strokes ahead of Australia's Craig Parry and America's Justin Leonard. Woods was seven back and Norman eight.

While sports are as intrinsic to French culture as wine and croissants, and they do excel in cycling, handball, and football, this nation of 67 million has not historically produced many world-class golfers. However, Van de Velde had the comfort of knowing there was a precedent of success for his country in the Open's history.

Ninety-two years earlier at Royal Liverpool Golf Club in Hoylake, Arnaud Massy, a native of Biarritz, France, became the first non-Briton to win an Open Championship. That victory in 1907 would be his only major title, but it was an impressive two-shot-winning performance over the runner-up, three-time Open champion J. H. Taylor.

If he was nervous, Van de Velde certainly hid it behind a casual approach when he spoke to the media before the final round.

"It's the biggest tournament ever in the world and I'm leading, what can happen?" said the affable Frenchman. "I can lose it or I can win it. Either way, I'm having a good time. That's the main thing. I know there are a lot better players than me who have had a more commanding lead and still lost. Maybe I am going to blow it tomorrow. What do you expect? I'm not the No. 1 player in the world . . . not yet."[1]

Not yet. Van de Velde certainly had a sense of humor to go with his lone victory in over 280 tournaments to that point (the 1993 Roma Masters).

How strong would the French resistance be when facing some sharpshooting playmakers?

Though Woods and Norman would not challenge for the lead, Parry—the stout Aussie from Sunshine, Victoria, paired with Van De Velde on this final round—was 3 under through ten holes while the Frenchman was 3 over. And after his playing partner Van de Velde bogeyed the next hole, Parry had the outright lead. The five-stroke lead was now gone.

Meanwhile, way up ahead, Paul Lawrie from nearby Aberdeen had been slowly chipping away at the ten-stroke deficit he'd started the day with. After getting his fifth birdie of the day at fourteen, he was now four back of Van De Velde, at 7 over.

He shot a sixth birdie at seventeen. When he came to the seventy-second hole, the thirty-year-old former club pro, ranked 159th in the world, found a greenside bunker. However, a brilliant up and down gave him a round of 67, equaling the best of the tournament, set by Parry the day before.

In the clubhouse at 6 over, Lawrie would spend much of the time at the practice range with his coach Adam Hunter, because he knew the closing stretch of holes would not be easy for the remaining contenders.

Van de Velde suffered back-to-back bogeys starting at the eleventh.

But after finding high grass at twelve, Parry would end up with a triple bogey and go from 2 over to 5 over. After he bogeyed the next hole, this opened up things for Justin Leonard, who briefly took the lead after a birdie at fourteen put him at 4 over. But the lead changed yet again as Van de Velde birdied that same hole. Leonard, the 1997 Open champion, bogeyed fifteen.

At eighteen, Leonard's second shot landed in the Barry Burn, and he finished the round with a bogey tied at 6 over with Lawrie. Parry had a double bogey at seventen, while his partner parred it. Argentina's Ángel Cabrera had a chance to join the clubhouse lead, but narrowly missed a birdie putt on eighteen.

Now coming to the seventy-second hole, the Frenchman had destiny in his hands. Standing at the tee of the par-4, 487-yard home hole, Van de Velde had a seemingly insurmountable three-stroke lead, meaning he could double-bogey and still win the Claret Jug.

In perhaps a reflection of his gallant Gallic nature, and to the dismay of American television broadcasters who strongly voiced their concerns, the Frenchman did not play it safe off the tee and chose instead to go with his driver. That was where the trouble started.

He pushed his tee shot far to the right, over the water bordering the right side of the eighteenth fairway, and onto the seventeenth hole. Van de Velde stood over his ball and surveyed the scene, then waved away the spectators standing around down toward the green. The prudent play would have been to use a wedge to get back onto the fairway. Instead, he decided to go for it and selected a two-iron for his second shot.

His bullet veered left, blasted off the face of the grandstand by the green, hit a metal railing about the width of a golf ball, bounced backward sixty yards, then off the rock wall, holding the burn before finally settling down in knee-deep rough. A bit of misfortune because if the ball stayed in the grandstand, he would have been able to drop without a penalty.

Now trying to free himself from the thick stuff, Van de Velde only managed to find the burn that fronted the green. Sitting at the edge of the burn, Van de Velde stared at his ball in the water. He then proceeded to take off his shoes and socks and stepped down into it.

As the tragicomedy built, there was a mix of howls and moans and supportive applause from unbelieving and sympathetic fans trying to grasp something no one had seen before. He stood with hands on hips down in the burn, his pants rolled up, and stared from behind the ball, considering an attempt to play it from the water.

"As I walked forward, I could see the ball was sitting on the sand," explained Van de Velde later in an *R&A* podcast. "Half of the ball was outside of the water, so I'm going to go and play! I mean, it's a bunker shot, literally. There's nothing to it!"[2]

He decided against it and instead took a drop (fourth stroke), at which point he hit his fifth shot into one of the deep greenside bunkers.

But drawing inspiration from Parry, who holed out from nearly the same spot in the bunker, Van de Velde knew he could actually still win if he did the same thing.

He didn't. His ball ended up about six feet from the hole. Van de Velde would sink his seventh shot, which spared the Frenchman temporarily from the guillotine and forced a three-man playoff between himself, Lawrie, and Leonard.

In the four-hole aggregate playoff starting at fifteen, Van de Velde would double bogey, bogey, birdie, and bogey. Lawrie would complete the biggest comeback in championship history with back-to-back birdies at seventeen and eighteen.

There have been some notable downfalls throughout the long history of the majors. Some may point to Sam Snead, who made a triple-bogey 8 on the final hole of the 1939 US Open and missed a playoff that was eventually won by Byron Nelson.

Arnold Palmer's 1966 US Open debacle (a seven-shot lead lost on the final nine holes) or Adam Scott's Open Championship dropout in 2012 (he bogeyed the last four to lose by one) but they were also very successful players overall. Given the derisive phrases that have emerged from his debacle—including the term "pulling a van de Velde" to describe similar events—the gallant Frenchman will be forever remembered for one of the greatest meltdowns in majors history.

"It just came out to be a nightmare," said Van de Velde.

75

FIFTY-NINE-YEAR-OLD WATSON: LIVING PROOF YOU CAN WIN FOR LOSING

JULY 16–19, 2009
AILSA COURSE AT TURNBERRY RESORT
AYRSHIRE, SCOTLAND

t's like how they do those flashbacks in the movies. In this case it is Tom Watson addressing his ball, wearing rather colorful, yellow-checkered pants and a loud lime shirt. He gets ready to hit his approach shot to the eighteenth hole in the final round of the Open at Turnberry in 1977. We see the ball in the air as the camera cuts back, and then we're transported forward in time thirty-two years. Now we see him in conservative dark trousers and a traditional blue sweater, reacting to his approach shot at that same hole.

In the earlier moment, Watson was on his way to defeating Jack Nicklaus in one of the all-time great major contests. In the latter, amazingly, at the age of fifty-nine, Watson was in position to pull off one of the greatest performances in the history of the game.

So, would this have a Hollywood ending?

It certainly had the makings of a blockbuster. The lead character, nearly sixty years old, was going up against hungry, highly talented competitors half his age. Besides, he had not won a major on tour in twenty-six years.

Coming into the tournament Watson was a 1,500–1 shot to hoist the jug for the sixth time. On top of that, he was still recovering from hip replacement surgery.

What's this old gunslinger thinking?

"The older guys have an advantage. We've played under these conditions and we kind of get a feel for it. And that feel is worth its weight in gold when you're playing," said Watson after opening with a superb 65 for a share of second place.

And there's both a physical and mental boost when you've had success on a given course, especially when it was a major win against arguably the game's greatest player.

"I have to admit that I do remember and do—I maybe play off some of the memories of '77 here, and that helps me," explained Watson. "Whenever you play a golf course and you have success there, you hit quality shots and—I can remember every darn shot I hit in '77, the last round. And it's of record that Jack [Nicklaus] couldn't remember any of them of his," the eight-time majors winner added with a laugh.

"But that helps you. I can stand up there on the fifteenth hole and say I cut this four-iron in there against a crosswind and held it right in the middle of the green. I know that helps me. When you play a golf course where you played cruddy, you don't remember the duck hook in the left rough on the thirteenth hole, no. You want to forget that one. And it does help you."

And those recollections continued to help during the second round, when high winds and scattered showers pushed the scoring average more than two strokes higher with just seven subpar rounds.

Even though he struggled through the front nine, Watson carried on with superb play late in the round. By holing long putts at the sixteenth and eighteenth, in producing three birdies, he was now tied for the lead halfway through at 5-under 135.

Watson was one of the better foul-weather players of all time. Another edge he held on links courses was his ability to handle the inevitable tough breaks of the path of the ball.

"He loved crazy bounces you get in the British Open. Most golfers can't help but expect justice when they had a good shot and they become annoyed when the ball caroms off a knoll. But bad luck did not faze Watson one bit," said former Open champion Johnny Miller.

"I asked him once how he is able to play so well in the British Open what with the lousy weather, bad bounces, and all that, and he answered, 'I love bad bounces' and walked away," recalled the long-time broadcaster in his book *I Call the Shots*.

Fellow American Stewart Cink, who was seeking his first major win, battled the restricting elements to pull to within three of the lead. He was impressed but not shocked about seeing who was in first place.

"Definitely experience plays a big part in low scoring. Watson, what can you say about his experience. It's second to very few. Tom Watson is one of the best ball-strikers of all time. He knows the way around here, and I'm not surprised to see him up here."

Despite fine performances from British players Ross Fisher and Lee Westwood in particular, Watson maintained his lead after third-round play by one stroke. After three days "out on the range," the aging gunslinger was finding that his aim was still pretty accurate, and he was encouraged about Sunday's showdown.

"The first day here, yeah, let the old geezer have his day in the sun, you know, 65. The second day you said, 'Well, that's okay, that's okay.' And then now today, you kind of perk up your ears and say, 'This old geezer might have a chance to win the tournament,'" said Watson.

Could it happen that thirty-two years later Watson does it again?

It began as a sentimental journey down memory lane shared by throngs of supportive fans, but as the week progressed there was a real chance that Watson would have a fantastic new memory to enjoy. Same venue. Same result. Victory.

Having won his first Open at Carnoustie, on the country's east coast, in 1975 (when main challenger Cink was just two years old), Watson continued to be a great favorite of the Scottish fans. However, there were several British players who had their own ideas about the Claret Jug.

Fisher, who began the day just one back, started off hot, opening with back-to-back birdies. Taking a two-shot lead to the fourth hole, he made bogey. But a quadruple-bogey 8 at five ended his chances. Fellow countrymen Luke Donald and Chris Wood would play quite well, but in the end England's best chance fell to Lee Westwood.

On the strength of a birdie at six and an eagle at seven, Westwood made the turn in the lead by two.

Americans Cink and Watson made their moves on the back nine. Cink, the tall, lanky, and amiable native of Huntsville, Alabama, was without a majors title at this point, but he did have eight top ten finishes in the Grand Slam events. With three birdies coming back, he was 1 under with a chance for birdie at the last.

The thirty-six-year-old talked about what he was going through in facing the tricky eighteen-footer, which he'd sink for the birdie that would tie him with Watson at 2 under for a share of the lead.

"[I'd] been working really hard the last two or three months on my putting and my whole mental approach to golf. And that was just another test, you know, that I had to try to pass, and I passed that one. And it just came at a great time. I had a good solid routine there. I knew what I was looking at, and I hit that putt with really—really without a care in the world of whether it went in or whether it missed.

"But a blank mind like that is the best way to approach a pressure-packed situation, and I was proud of myself the way I handled that."

Watson and Westwood were paired together. Despite being among the leaders most of the round, Westwood bogeyed three of the last four holes, including a three-putt on eighteen. This dropped him to 1 under and one stroke behind clubhouse leader Cink.

Although he bogeyed two of the first three holes, Watson carried on with his trademark "no worries" grin. With the huge support from the massive galleries he kept at it, producing a couple birdies along with way. And after another birdie at seventeen, the old man was in control of his own destiny. A par at the seventy-second hole, and victory would be his.

On the threshold of becoming not only the oldest winner of the Open but of any major, Watson struck his approach shot. It was on line, but it rolled past the flag to the collar on the back of the green.

Still, no problem, right? Just an up and down in two was all Watson required to make par for the victory and become only the second man after Harry Vardon to win six Claret Jugs.

Facing a slightly downhill shot with the ball resting partially in higher grass at the edge of the green, Watson chose to pop it out with his putter. It was not his best effort, as the ball settled about eight feet past the hole.

Now with a huge, hushed crowd looming and big, big history weighing heavy on his shoulders, Watson would later admit he made a poor putt. Coming up short and right.

The ensuing playoffs were anticlimactic. Perhaps feeling every one of his fifty-nine years, it seemed the legs and spirit of the old gunslinger were spent. With a pair of bogeys and a double bogey in four playoff holes, Watson couldn't keep up with the man twenty-three years his junior. Cink clearly earned his first major victory with a terrific close-out, birdieing the last two playoff holes to going 2 under to his opponent's 4 over overtime score.

Cink, the world's thirty-third-ranked player, had broken through to win in his forty-ninth majors try. He'd had just one Top-10 finish at the Open (tied for sixth at Carnoustie in 2007), and he was well aware of the sentimental story that had been unfolding all week. He had this to say to the media afterward:

"I can understand the mystique that came really close to developing here, and the story," said Cink, "But in the end, you know, it's a tournament to see who lasts the longest . . . It's a survival test, and I don't know what else to say. I don't feel ashamed. I don't feel disappointed. I'm pleased as punch that I've won, and also very proud of the way Tom Watson played."

Despite the twist in this Hollywood movie, the script at this point might call for direction to misdirect the audience.

(Enter laughing)

With that famous grin, the old gunslinger walked in to a press conference filled with saddened faces.

"This ain't a funeral, you know," Watson stated.

"It would have been a hell of a story, wouldn't it? It would have been a hell of a story. It wasn't to be. And yes, it's a great disappointment. It tears at your gut, as it always has torn at my gut. It's not easy to take."

Watson talked about his playoff performance and what he'd remember most about the tournament overall.

"The playoff was just one bad shot after another, and Stewart did what he had to do to win. And I didn't give him much competition in the playoff," said Watson.

"But you're going to ask me, what do I take from this week? Well, I take from this week just a lot of warmth, a lot of spirituality in the sense that, you know, there was something out there. I still believe that. It helped me along. It's Turnberry. Great memories here. This would have been a great memory."

When asked by a reporter if he could help with a good headline that might capture one of sport's all-time greatest nearly moments, Watson paused. Then he said with a grin:

The Old Fogey Almost Did It.

Watson's memory of that tremendous performance would be enhanced well beyond the outpouring he received from the overflowing viewing stands at Turnberry. He would go on to receive thousands and thousands of letters from all over the world. The majority of the letter writers basically said they gave up things they love because of their age. They thought they were too old, but his efforts had inspired them to rethink the possibilities and return to pursuing their passions. In losing, Watson inspired countless others.

76

PHIL FINALLY SCORES A JUG

JULY 18–21, 2013
MUIRFIELD
GULLANE, SCOTLAND

After trying unsuccessfully nineteen times to win the sport's oldest major, why would this one end any different for the now forty-three-year-old Phil Mickelson?

Well, Lefty had a couple things going in his favor this time.

For one, he had the huge confidence boost that he could compete at a high level on links-style courses after he won the Scottish Open the week before. Secondly, it was more about *how* he won that would boost his mindset the most heading into this major. It took a while (many years, in fact), but even though he had the talent, it was more about a shift in thinking and approach to playing links-style courses that set him right here. As Bob Seger would say, Phil was "running against the wind" for too long. Towering, cloud-bursting drives and spinning irons was not the formula here. So, in his ongoing education, Phil finally tuned into the Open's special idiosyncrasies, and one of his biggest changes was simply to leave the driver at home.

Instead, he went with a standard-issue thirteen-degree Callaway X Hot 3Deep three-wood (at 43.25 inches) as his longest club in the bag. (At the other end of his bag, Mickelson carried five wedges, including a Callaway Mack Daddy 2 sixty-four-degree model.)[1]

Of course, winning is always an elixir for whatever is ailing one's game.

Phil's week at Muirfield began with a solid 2-under 69. While playing under skies more suited to their native land than Scotland, a pair of Spaniards went low. Rafa Cabrera-Bello rolled 67 while countryman Miguel Ángel Jiménez carded a 68. But the low man of the first day was American Zach Johnson, whose eagle at 5 started a birdie fest that gave him the lead with a 5-under 66. Defending champion Ernie Els also won when the Open was held at Muirfield in 2002. This time, he would open with his first of three rounds at 74 and would not therefore be a factor.

Mickelson credited an early tee time to help with his good score.

"I got very lucky to play early today because as the day wore on and we got to the back nine, about a third of every green started to die and became brown. And the pins were very edgy, on the slopes and whatnot, that the guys that played early had a huge, huge break. Because even without any wind, it is beyond difficult."

While Muirfield can be difficult, playing 7,192 yards to a par 71, it is a fairly straightforward layout. In addition to the penal, steep pot bunkers, the real challenge can be club selection based on properly calculating the constantly swirling winds coming off the sea.

Aided by a putting tip from former Open champion Ian Baker-Finch, Lee Westwood was raising his countrymen's hopes that his first major would be the Open. Following a second-round 68, he made a long eagle putt at the fifth and became the fifty-four-hole leader by two strokes with a 3-under 210, after a 70 on Saturday.

Despite Australia's Adam Scott, America's Tiger Woods, and Sweden's Henrik Stenson moving up in the standings, the Englishman still felt good about his chances of finally scoring a victory in a Grand Slam event. (He had been runner-up twice to that point.)

"I'll think about winning the Open Championship tonight at some stage, I'm sure. I don't see anything wrong with that, picture yourself holding the Claret Jug at the final tee and seeing your name at the top of the leaderboard," said Westwood. "When it comes to tee off, I should be in the same frame of mind as I was today. I didn't feel any pressure today and felt nice and calm out there and in control of what I was doing."

And even though he shot 72 and was five back, Mickelson felt he was still confident he would win it.

"I have to play a really good round. If I can shoot something in the 60s, I think that will be enough."

A prophet, too?

The aforementioned challengers stayed in the mix for a while, but Woods would produce three bogeys on the back nine. Scott's chances faded after four straight bogeys starting on thirteen, despite his having the lead briefly after a birdie at eleven. Westwood's sluggish round of 75, which included just one birdie but five bogeys, took him out of the running.

But another Englishman was running in from no man's land. Ian Poulter got crazy hot, starting with an eagle on hole eight, then followed that with three straight birdies. His 67 was bettered by only one person.

In what his long-time caddy, Jim "Bones" MacKay, would call "the best round of his career," Mickelson in fact did shoot "something in the 60s."[2]

After completing the front nine at 2 under, Mickelson then stroked back-to-back birdies at thirteen and fourteen, which earned him a share of the lead. But to make it complete, he would earn a three-stroke victory by producing back-to-back birdies at seventeen and eighteen.

His 66 was the lowest of the day. It was perhaps his tee shot at fifteen that showed how much Lefty was in control of his game. With no driver in his bag, he smashed a five-iron that rumbled for 330 yards! Now that was being on a roll literally.

And to prove that was no fluke, the real clincher came at seventeen.

On the par-5, 575-yard hole, Phil whipped a three-wood sans spin through the wind that left him an uphill lie to the flag. His approach then rolled onto the green to huge cheers from fans who knew the value of that effort. As his caddy would later say, "He hit two shots of a lifetime consecutively," and he was rewarded with an easy birdie and the knowledge the Claret Jug was finally his.

There would be no 2006 US Open collapse here. Mickelson soaked in the well-earned standing ovation from the appreciative crowd as he strolled down the seventy-second hole fairway. Then he finished the tournament with another birdie.

Henrik Stenson would come in second with a 70, three shots back of Phil. The outcome would be different when they would meet a few years later at Royal Troon. But on this day, after more than twenty-one years of coming up short, this was Phil's finest hour.

"I'm so proud to be your champion," he said at the trophy ceremony. "I never knew if I'd be equipped, if I'd have the shots, if I'd have the opportunity to win this tournament. To play some of the best golf of my career, and break through and capture this Claret Jug is probably the most fulfilling moment of my career."

77

JORDAN RULES

JULY 20–23, 2017
ROYAL BIRKDALE GOLF CLUB
SOUTHPORT, ENGLAND

Golf can sometimes be a high-wire act because there's no one there to catch you when you fall. Sure, caddies can help in several ways as part confidant, counselor, and cheerleader (and in this case, Michael Greller certainly did that for Jordan Spieth), but in the end they can't swing the club.

So, given the deep level of competition out there, it is very rare, even for wire-to-wire majors winners, to not have close calls at some point over a grueling four-day seventy-two-hole test that could ruin a winning campaign. That would be the case here at Royal Birkdale, where a record-breaking crowd of 235,000 spectators were treated to all the ranges of weather this major can offer, swirling winds and mixes of sunshine and rain, and they were rewarded by some of the best closing play by any competitor in the majors—but only after a near-catastrophic shot at a key moment on the back nine on Sunday.

After winning the Travelers Championship less than a month earlier, Jordan Spieth took holiday to Cabo San Lucas and chilled with, among others, perhaps the two most accomplished athletes named Michael. Swimmer Michael Phelps has the most Olympic gold medals ever won (twenty-three) and Michael Jordan won six NBA championships with the Chicago Bulls.

Some of that winning aura rubbed off on him in the resort city at the southern tip of the Baja California Peninsula, in the Mexican state of Baja California Sur. It certainly didn't hurt the Texan when he arrived at the Royal Birkdale Golf Club situated in North West England, at Southport, Merseyside. As a matter of fact, when the tournament was on the line for the twenty-three-year-old, Spieth's caddy would cleverly draw on that champion pedigree holiday to propel his player to victory.

Spieth shared a large rental home with Rickie Fowler, Justin Thomas, Jason Dufner, and Zach Johnson, where a lot of gin rummy and snooker was played. Refreshed and relaxed in these comfortable accommodations, he was ready to take advantage of the early sunny conditions of Royal Birkdale.[1]

And the two-time majors winner (2015 Masters, 2015 US Open) certainly did capitalize on the favorable scoring circumstances. Spieth's 5-under 65 put him in the lead (along with Brooks Koepka and Matt Kuchar). He was pleased with his effort, but knew he had to take advantage now, since the weather predictions for the next few days was gloomy.

Conditions on day two were not nearly as ideal and with gusty winds and strong showers saying hello, many who shot in the 60s to start things, rolled in the 70s.

However, Spieth, who like his fellow competitors had to contend with heavy rain (enough to cause a brief suspension), was undaunted. While only eight players scored under par for their second rounds, the first day's leader finished with a 69, and his 134 two-day total gave him a two-shot lead at 6 under.

Opening the round with a birdie, Spieth then had two bogies on the front nine but back-to-back birdies on eleven and twelve plus a magnificent eagle on fifteen led to his two- stroke edge over Kuchar.

The leader at the halfway point talked about taking advantage of the breaks in inclement weather as having a large impact on his good scoring result.

"We had a stoppage of play and it got a little calm for about an hour or thirty, forty-five minutes. And that right there from the chip-in on ten until we got through twelve was really, really important. I was fortunate there. We had less wind for maybe—I would say a total of two hours today we had less wind than the guys had this morning, which makes a significant difference. And fortunately we were able to take advantage of those holes and that was key."

After beginning the defense of his crown with a 69, 2016 champion Henrik Stenson went up to 73. Tough to blame the Swede if his concentration wasn't all there. You see, thieves burglarized his rental home while he was playing his first round. Good thing he had already turned in the Claret Jug.

"They got obviously a lot of valuables, watches, and other things. But they were clearly targeting me, because they were there when I was out playing, and they figured out that the house was empty when I was away, and they stole all my gear. Normally I don't think burglars would take clothes. That doesn't feel like the normal kind of thing that you would take. But all my gear is gone," said Stenson.

"I still had some dirty laundry in another bag, so I managed to wash some of that up." he added with a bit of humor. Stenson was later provided more apparel by his clothing sponsor, Boss. He'd finish the tournament tied for eleventh.

With the winds slightly more benign coming off the Irish Sea for round three, Spieth, the world's number-three-ranked player, handled the undulating terrain with aplomb, scoring his second 65 in three days. This gave him a three-shot lead heading into the final round.

Even though South African Branden Grace scored 62, breaking the long-standing men's majors championship record of 63 and moved up to fifth place (he'd ultimately finish tied for sixth), the player going forward who would duke it out for the coveted title Champion Golfer of the Year would be fellow American Matt Kuchar. The tall, lanky native of Florida, who attended Georgia Tech in Atlanta, where he was a two-time first-team All-American on the Yellow Jackets' golf team, finished one back with a 66. That result put him in second place, three behind Spieth but three ahead of the next group heading into the fourth round.

Kuchar talked about his approach in being in the final group paired with the leader, Spieth, for the final eighteen.

"Again, I'll be playing with him, but not focused on him. My goal is to go out and play Royal Birkdale. I'll know exactly where we stand, but I don't know how much that ever helps you. You just have to go out and hit the best shot for the situation. I've been on some good form. The formula has produced a lot of good golf, and I hope it continues to produce some good golf tomorrow."

Neither one started out the last day in top form.

Spieth, who had made just four bogeys in the first three rounds, had three in his first four holes on Sunday! Could this be a British version of the 2016 Masters, where he blew a five-shot lead with nine holes to play?

And though he got one back with a birdie at the par-4 fifth, Spieth bogeyed again at nine. Meanwhile, with a pair of birdies on the front nine, Kuchar had tied Spieth heading to ten. It was a two-man contest, as both were 8 under heading to the thirteenth tee, a 499-yard par-4. What followed in essence turned out to be the greatest bogey of Spieth's career to that point, and it would catapult him to a super finish worthy of a Claret Jug. But that is getting ahead of things.

In blocking his tee shot, he wound up way right of the fairway, and the ball disappeared into high, thick grass, forcing him to take a penalty drop. A rather unusual one. After a lengthy ruling that took more than twenty minutes to be made, Spieth had to play his shot from Royal Birkdale's driving range.

He hit his approach from 235 yards by some equipment trucks, and despite a massive sand dune blocking his view of the green, he managed to eventually sink a bogey putt. Spieth left the green behind for the first time. But the poise and experience he showed going forward yielded brilliant results.

Spieth nearly scored a hole in one on fourteen, eagled the par-5, 542-yard fifteenth with a fifty-foot putt, then proceeded to fire consecutive birdies at sixteen and seventeen. This gave him a two-stroke lead coming to the seventy-second hole. With his closing par and Kuchar's bogey, Spieth had won the Open by three strokes and, with it, the third leg of the career grand slam.

The new champ talked about how a key moment in his victory came long before the closing holes.

"Michael [Greller] did a great thing today. He said, 'Do you remember that group you were with in Cabo last week [Michael Phelps, Michael Jordan],' in a picture that I posted. He goes, 'You belong in that group.' This is when I was 3 over through four. I'm sorry, this was on seven tee box. We walked off seven tee box, and he made me come back. He said, 'I've got something to say to you: He said do you remember that group you were with? You're that caliber of an athlete. But I need you to believe that right now because you're in a great position in this tournament. This is a new tournament. We're starting over here.'"

Only five men have won all four of golf's modern majors: Gene Sarazen, Ben Hogan, Jack Nicklaus, myself, and Tiger Woods.

As of this writing, Jordan is still one short. However, his victory at Birkdale was the greatest miracle of all majors championships that I ever saw in my life and that I will ever see in my lifetime. He was all over the place!

When I say "all over the place," I mean like no other golfer in the history of the Open. He had a round that should've been 78, 79. But instead he turned in a low score to win the Open. I admire that. I take my hat off to that. That's talent.

I've only seen twenty players in my lifetime that have got "IT." What the hell is "IT"? Nobody can define it. Everybody likes to think they know what "IT" is. Everybody knows a helluva a lot about nothing. Nobody can define "IT." "IT" is something you're born with. Jordan Spieth has got "IT."

If Jordan had to work on the right fundamentals of the golf swing, unquestionably he'd be number one on the tour because he's got a short game that is way above anybody else's. He's a competitor. He's got charisma. I'm just praying that he will find the right way to swing the club. And the fact that he hasn't continued to win majors proves that he hasn't found the right answer to his swing.

Will he find it? Yes. I think he will.

A PLACE IN THE SUN

I

f I think of one word to define my life despite all the adversity I had to endure, the word would be *gratitude*.

I am grateful that I have been able to globe-trot for well over sixty-five years. I have seen the world's wonders, met presidents and dignitaries, rubbed shoulders with leaders of industry, and had experiences beyond my wildest dreams. To have traveled more miles than any person ever has been an epic journey. I have learned to understand and respect other cultures, which has been an education unlike any other.

The people of the world continue to give me love and support to this day. I wish I could say thank you in a manner commensurate with what I have received, but I do not believe it is possible.

Many often pose the question: *What is your legacy?* I was bestowed a gift that allowed me to reach the pinnacle of achievement on the golf course. And I am most proud of the fact that I am the only player in history to have won the career grand slam on both the PGA and Senior Tours. I could list several others, but those achievements are not what I want to be remembered for.

My legacy is helping change the lives of people around the world who are less fortunate. For more than thirty years, my work with the Gary & Vivienne Player Foundation is what I am most proud of. In those years, the Foundation has raised millions of dollars to help underprivileged children.

As a result of my good fortune on the golf course through the gifts bestowed upon me, I had a duty to give back to those who need it most. And it is the work I have done to fulfill that responsibility of which I am most proud. It would be remiss of me to not state that the culture of giving in the United States of America has helped me make a difference. However, even in the United States, the greatest country in the world, one out of every six children are living in poverty and do not have their basic needs met. There is much work left to be done.

Benjamin Disraeli once said, "The Youth of a Nation are the trustees of posterity." Those words have echoed in my head for many years. The younger generation is responsible for the future. So, I want to go to my grave knowing that because of the difficulties I encountered as a young man and my subsequent good fortune, I have helped give others an opportunity at a better life and the tools to achieve their dreams.

That is my legacy.

ACKNOWLEDGMENTS

Throughout my career and to this day, there are countless people to thank for my success. Golf is typically viewed as very much an individual sport. But to the contrary, during the actual tournaments it is the player and caddy who must have a chemistry akin to team sports. And beyond that, to reach the level of a majors champion, no doubt the amount of people who helped pave my path along the way deserve recognition.

My ultimate gratitude first goes to my late wife, Vivienne, who passed away from pancreatic cancer in 2021. I first glimpsed my future bride over a fence, and I told my brother that I would marry her one day. He thought I was crazy, but my heart chose its soulmate right then and there. She was a talented golfer herself and once had two hole in ones in a single round. We wanted to have a big family, and Vivienne gave up her life to support my dreams. Six children, twenty-two grandchildren, and two great-grandchildren and counting. Without her, there is no Gary Player.

I would also like to thank four others who are now in heaven: my mother, Muriel Player, who passed away from cancer when I was just eight years old; my father, Harry Player, who sacrificed so much for our family and taught me the value of hard work; my brother, Dr. Ian Player; and my sister, Wilma, who always supported the dreams of their younger brother.

I really must also thank so many who taught me how to be a professional athlete and looked after my career on and off the golf course: Mark McCormack, Alastair Johnston, and Marc Tudhope.

Two of my closest friends and competitors, who I traveled the world with promoting our wonderful game: Jack Nicklaus and Arnold Palmer. I'm confident that together we made our mark on golf that will live on for generations.

Thank you to all of my sponsors over the years, especially Rolex and Berenberg.

And to the professional golfers, tournament executives, organizers and volunteers, business leaders, media, and fans who make it possible for us to earn a living playing a simple yet sophisticated game.

And to my dear friend, Dave King. I am forever grateful for our friendship.

To the talented leadership at HarperCollins/Dey Street led by: Liate Stehlik, Carrie Thornton, and Ben Steinberg along with Owen Corrigan, Melanie Bedor, Allison Carney, and Andy LeCount. And inestimable are the skills of editor Nick Amphlett. You continue to produce outstanding material and I appreciate your trust in this book.

And lastly, to Randy O. Williams, my coauthor. He displayed remarkable dedication and unwavering commitment to make this book possible. A true champion author, and I am thankful for his devotion to uncover the secrets of golf's major championships.

—Gary Player

This book has been a team effort and on the roster are a varied group of talented individuals who brought distinct skills and unstinting support to make it happen.

In gratitude to friends, family, and associates:

Marty Zager, Al Ruddy, John Alexenko, Mark Turner, Craig Cacek, Travis Cranley, Gerry Cranley, Al Petersen, Jim Glen, Dan and Linda Finklea, Ian Lawrence, Dan Aranguren, Paul and Joan Fantazia, Jim and Mari Davis, Jerry Rice and Sasha Taylor, Geoff Nathanson, Steve Jergentz, John and Deann Grogan, Bob and Debbie Sharka, Jim Bernard, Lee Barton, Ciao Jianjie, George and Tabia Gabriel, John and

Karen Loesing, Greg Bettencourt, Kevin and Stephanie Adkins, Lisa Davis, Steve and Shelli Goodrich, Rob Miller, Dan Shepherd, Miles Hopkins, Sydney Shiffman, Fred Wallin, Steve Rusmisel, Jamie Stockton, Rick, Mark, Susan, and Roger, and especially Monica Herdoiza.

Anthony Mattero and Mariam Jansyan for their sharp, intuitive business skills.

James Throssell for making the creation of this project possible (along with Bo Wood).

Debbie Longenecker, Marc Tudhope, Chantal Frans, and Jennifer Keene as indispensable team members.

Nick Coffman and his legal team.

To the talented leadership at HarperCollins/Dey Street led by: Liate Stehlik, Carrie Thornton, and Ben Steinberg, along with Owen Corrigan, Melanie Bedor, Allison Carney, Andy LeCount, and Mark Steven Long.

Inestimable are the skills of editor Nick Amphlett, whose zeal for shaping sports stories helped make this tome well-rounded. And to Matt Daddona for providing the tee time.

Golf historian Matt Ward for being a terrific sounding board. Curator Travis Puterbaugh. Gary Cypres of the Sports Museum of Los Angeles. And Scott Tolley.

To the fine folks at the governing bodies—USGA: Maggie Lagle, Tara LaWare, Beth Major, Jonathan Coe, Katie Boyce, Jose Lopez, and Victoria Nenno. PGA of America: John Dever. R&A: Stuart Moffatt. Augusta National: Regina O'Brien and Patrick Kravitz. PGA Tour's Doug Milner and Chelsea Kottke.

And for help in covering the sport's great venues, much appreciation to: Alex Podlogar, Tim Freund, Steve Brady, Chad Ellis, Tim Meussle, Jessica Smith, David Penske, Mike McCullough, John Capers III, Chris Wirthwein, Tony Pancake, and Christian Lovecchio, among others.

Shirley Ito and Michael Salmon of the LA84 Sports Library.

My road crew . . .

The scores of journalists and broadcasters who shared their keen perspectives.

To the many players whose clear expression for their love of the game and competing at the highest levels resonated in our conversations.

Finally, I would like to convey my deepest appreciation to Gary Player for embracing the challenge and spilling his passion all over the pages.

Thank you.

—Randy O. Williams

NOTES

1: THE SHOT HEARD 'ROUND THE WORLD

1. "An Ace Is Special, but an Albatross Is in Another Class," *Austin American-Statesman*, September 26, 2018, https://www.statesman.com /story/news/2016/10/14/an-ace-is-special-but-an-albatross-is-in-another -class/9927701007/.

2: FORT WORTH'S FINEST: BEN VS. BYRON

1. Byron Nelson, *How I Played the Game* (Dallas, TX: Taylor Publishing, 1993), 119.

7: "WHAT A STUPID I AM"

1. Rich Tosches, "Breaking Silence: Two Decades Later, Goalby Finally Talks About De Vicenzo, 'Clerical Errors' and the '68 Masters," *Los Angeles Times*, April 2, 1989, https://www.latimes.com/archives/la-xpm-1989-04-02 -sp-1531-story.html.
2. Bill Dwyre, "Appreciation: Bob Goalby's Life Added Up to So Much More Than an Odd Piece of Masters History," *Los Angeles Times,* January 23, 2022, https://www.latimes.com/sports/story/2022-01-23/appreciation -looking-at-life-of-bob-goalby.

8: NICKLAUS-WEISKOPF-MILLER = MAGNIFICENCE

1. Gil Capps, *The Magnificent Masters: Jack Nicklaus, Johnny Miller, Tom Weiskopf and the 1975 Cliffhanger at Augusta* (Boston: Da Capo Press, 2014), 32.
2. John Boyette, "1975 Masters Produced Unforgettable Sunday Drama," 2022 Masters, *Augusta Chronicle*, April 7, 2015, https://www.augusta .com/masters/story/news/1975-masters-produced-unforgettable-sunday -drama.
3. Jack Nicklaus with Ken Bowden, *My Story* (New York: Simon and Schuster, 1997), 335.

12: LOCAL BOY MAKES GOOD

1. David Moffit, "Maltbie Serious About Golf, but Draws Laughs," *Sunday Times-Sentinel* (Gallipolis, OH), April 12, 1987, C-2.

2. Sam Weinman, "The Inside Story of Greg Norman's Masters Collapse," *Golf Digest,* April 19, 2022, https://www.golfdigest.com/story/the-sharks-collapse-20-years-later.

15: THE DAY THE SHARK DROWNED

1. Rick Reilly, "Master Strokes," The Vault, *Sports Illustrated,* April 22, 1996, https://vault.si.com/vault/1996/04/22/master-strokes-nick-faldo-won-a-third-green-jacket-but-only-after-greg-norman-suffered-the-worst-collapse-in-major-tournament-history.

20: A MAJOR BREAKTHROUGH FOR GOLF-MAD JAPAN

1. Dan Rapaport, "Masters 2021: Will Zalatoris Continues to Find Success by Bucking Conventional Wisdom," *Golf Digest,* April 8, 2021.

21: GOLF'S NEWEST MAJOR DEBUTS WITH A DRAMATIC FINISH

1. Associated Press, "Cyril Walker a Pocket-Sized Ben Hogan of His Golfing Day," *Spokesman-Review* (Spokane, WA), August 23, 1948, 8.
2. "Presenting Two Golfing Extremes—Fastest and Slowest Pro," *Pittsburgh Press,* February 3, 1927, 26.
3. United Press, "Cyril Walker Dies; Beat Bobby Jones," *Toledo Blade,* August 7, 1948, 10.
4. "Six Professionals Tie for Five Places," *Evening Journal* (Delaware), September 14, 1916, 9.
5. "Jim Barnes Gets Wanamaker Trophy," *New York Times,* October 15, 1916.

22: HAGEN VS. SARAZEN: THE GREATEST 38-HOLE MATCH PLAY CHAMPIONSHIP OF ALL-TIME

1. PGA Metropolitan Section, https://www.met.pga.com/8a5a1d2de38819693cd7591cdcd61dd4.html.
2. "1922 PGA Championship Winner and Scores," Golf Compendium, https://www.golfcompendium.com/2018/12/1922-pga-championship.html.

23: THE HAIG'S UNMATCHED FOURTH STRAIGHT PGA TRIUMPH

1. Rachel Stone, "102-Year-Old Cedar Crest Golf Course Stays True to Neighborhood amid Gentrification," *Oak Cliff Advocate,* June 1, 2021, https://oakcliff.advocatemag.com/2021/06/cedar-crest-golf-course-history/.

25: BARBER RAZOR SHARP ON THE GREENS

1. Al Chase, "Olympia Fields Acres Expected to Be Homesites," *Chicago Daily Tribune,* June 23, 1946, B, part 3.
2. Bill Nichols, "January Lives with That Sinking Feeling," *Pittsburgh Post-Gazette,* June 11, 2003, D-2.
3. Alfred Wright, "Rain, Strain and a Win," *Sports Illustrated,* August 7, 1961, 10.
4. Associated Press, "Barber Defeats January by 1 Stroke to Win PGA Championship in Playoff," *Pittsburgh Post-Gazette,* August 1, 1961, 16.

5. Tom Emery, "Looking Back: When Woodson's Jerry Barber ruled the PGA," *Telegraph*, August 13, 2015, https://www.thetelegraph.com/sports/article /LOOKING-BACK-When-Woodson-s-Jerry-Barber-ruled-12565504.php.

28: THE OLD ACCOUNTANT DENIES THE KING'S QUEST FOR A CAREER GRAND SLAM

1. Dan Jenkins, "The Junkman Cools It," The Vault, *Sports Illustrated,* July 29, 1968, https://vault.si.com/vault/1968/07/29/the-junkman-cools-it.
2. Ibid.

30: TWAY HAS A BLAST AT LAST

1. Steven Pye, "How Bob Tway Won the 1986 US PGA," *Guardian,* August 5, 2014, https://www.theguardian.com/sport/that-1980s-sports-blog/2014 /aug/05/bob-tway-1986-us-pga-championship-greg-norman-golf.

34: THE EAGLE THAT LANDED A MAJOR

1. "History," TPC Harding Park, https://tpc.com/hardingpark/history/.

37: KOEPKA'S COMEBACK

1. Neil McLeman, "Brooks Koepka Shares Gruesome Details of Nightmare Knee Injury After Flying Masters Start," *Mirror,* April 7, 2023, https://www .mirror.co.uk/sport/golf/brooks-koepka-knee-injury-masters-29653523.

38: GOLF'S GREATEST UPSET

1. Christopher Klein, "The Greatest Upset in Golf History," History Channel, June 13, 2013, https://www.history.com/news/golfs-greatest-surprise.
2. Bill Pennington, "At the US Open, Saving the House That Golf Built," *New York Times,* June 14, 2022, https://www.nytimes.com/2022/06/14/sports /golf/us-open-francis-ouimet-house.html.

39: MARATHON MEN

1. "George Von Elm: Bio of the Amateur Golf Champ," Golf Compendium, https://www.golfcompendium.com/2021/11/george-von-elm-golfer.html.
2. Ibid.
3. Ibid.
4. UPI, "Billy Burke, Open Champ, Dark Harbor Pro, Is Dead," *Bangor Daily News,* April 21, 1972, 15.

40: SNEAD SNATCHES DEFEAT FROM VICTORY

1. James Dodson, *American Triumvirate: Sam Snead, Byron Nelson, Ben Hogan, and the Modern Age of Golf* (New York: Alfred A, Knopf, 2012), 39.
2. Ibid., 119.
3. Ibid., 17.
4. Sean Fairholm, "The Unapologetic, Trailblazing Life of Johnny Bulla," Global Golf Post, February 17, 2022, https://www.globalgolfpost.com /featured/the-unapologetic-trailblazing-life-of-johnny-bulla/.

41: A SOLDIER'S VICTORY

1. Al Stump, "The Story of Lloyd Mangrum," *Elks Magazine,* May 1954, 7.
2. Ibid., 48.
3. "1940," Canterbury Golf Club, https://www.canterburygc.org/about/history/1940.
4. "1946," Canterbury Golf Club, https://www.canterburygc.org/about/history/1946.

42: THE STAR OF STARS AT HOGAN'S ALLEY

1. Randy Williams, "Riviera Is Where the Stars Come Out to Play," *Montreal Gazette,* February 16, 2012.
2. Ibid.

44: THANKS FOR THE CLUBS

1. "The 1955 U.S. Open at the Lake," *Olympic Club Newsletter,* March 1987, 3.
2. Herbert Warren Wind, "Jack the Giant Killer," *Sports Illustrated,* June 27, 1955, 22.

45: THE CHARGE AT CHERRY HILLS

1. Dan Jenkins, *Jenkins at the Majors: Sixty Years of the World's Best Golf Writing, from Hogan to Tiger* (New York: Doubleday, 2009), 36.

46: NICKLAUS NOTCHES MAJOR VICTORY #1

1. Jack Nicklaus with Ken Bowden, *My Story* (New York: Simon and Schuster, 1997), 73.

47: STAVING OFF VENTURI'S VULTURES

1. "The Congressional Story," *Golf World,* June 12, 1964, 9.
2. Ken Venturi and Michael Arkush, *Getting Up & Down: My 60 Years in Golf* (Chicago: Triumph Books, 2004), 150.
3. Raymond Floyd, "My Shot: Raymond Floyd," *Golf Digest,* June 4, 2018, https://www.golfdigest.com/story/us-open-2018-my-shot-raymond-floyd.

48: MY PINNACLE: ACHIEVING THE RARE CAREER GRAND SLAM

1. Michael Trostel, "Great Moments: 1965 U.S. Open," USGA, March 29, 2015, https://www.usga.org/history/great-moments--1965-u-s--open.html.

49: ARNIE'S FADE AND CASPER'S COMEBACK

1. Johnny Miller with Guy Yocum, *I Call the Shots* (New York: Gotham Books, 2004).
2. Lee Trevino and Sam Blair, *They Call Me Super Mex* (New York: Random House, 1982).
3. Joe Dey, "The Open Pace Quickens," *USGA Journal,* July 1966.

4. Johnny Miller with Guy Yocum, *I Call the Shots* (New York: Gotham Books, 2004).
5. Ibid.

50: SUPER MEX ANNOUNCES HIS ARRIVAL

1. Adam Schupak, "Trevino, Caddie Recall Win at Oak Hill in '68," August 5, 2013, *Golfweek,* https://golfweek.usatoday.com/2013/08/05/oak-hill-lee -trevino-1968-u-s-open-win/.

51: TREVINO SNAKES NICKLAUS

1. Lee Trevino and Sam Blair, *They Call Me Super Mex* (New York: Random House, 1982), 119.

52: HERE'S JOHNNY!

1. Michael Trostel, "A Round for the Ages: Johnny Miller in 1973 U.S. Open," USGA, April 21, 2016, https://www.usga.org/history/great-moments--1973 -u-s--open.html.
2. Ibid.
3. Ibid.
4. Thomas Bonk, "The Greatest Round," *Los Angeles Times,* June 12, 2003, https://www.latimes.com/archives/la-xpm-2003-jun-12-sp-miller12-story .html.

53: ALL-HALE AS IRWIN EMERGES FROM THE MASSACRE

1. Jim Murray, "Return to the Scene of the Crime," *Los Angeles Times,* August 14, 1997, https://www.latimes.com/archives/la-xpm-1997-aug-14-ss-22511 -story.html.

54: A ONE-SHOT WONDER

1. Bob Harig, "Watson Prepared for Pebble Finale," ESPN, May 26, 2010, https://www.espn.com/golf/usopen10/columns/story?columnist=harig_bob &id=5218751.
2. Dave Shedloski, "Watson Executed When It Mattered Most at 1982 U.S. Open," USGA, February 14, 2015, https://www.usga.org/articles/2010/03 /watson-executed-when-it-mattered-most-at-1982-us-open-2147485795.html.

58: EYE OF THE TIGER STARES DOWN ROCCO AS ROCKY

1. John Garrity, "The Sky's the Limit," The Vault, *Sports Illustrated,* February 4, 2008, https://vault.si.com/vault/2008/02/04/the-skys-the-limit.

59: A CLASH (THEN CRASH) OF TITANS AT TORREY

1. "Torrey Pines Golf Course South," Torrey Pines.com, https://www.torreypines .com/torrey-pines-south-course/.
2. "Torrey Pines (South)," Top 100 Golf Courses, https://www.top100golfcourses .com/golf-course/torrey-pines-south.

3. M. James Ward, "Four Holes to Watch at Torrey Pines: U.S. Open 'Doctor' Weighs In," *Golf Today,* June 16, 2021, https://golftoday.co.uk/us-open -2021-four-holes-to-watch-at-torrey-pines/.
4. "Unique Reason Behind Jon Rahm's Unusual Golf Swing," Brucato Foot & Ankle Surgery, https://drbrucato.com/unique-reason-behind-jon-rahms -unusual-golf-swing/.

THE OPEN CHAMPIONSHIP

1. Golf Channle Digital, "History of the Claret Jug, Golf's Oldest Prize," NBC Sports Golf, July 15, 2022, https://www.golfchannel.com/news/british-open -history-claret-jug-golfs-oldest-prize#.

60: ALL IN THE FAMILY

1. "1868: The Story of the Open," The Open, October 31, 2018, https://www .theopen.com/latest/2018/10/the-story-of-the-open-1868.

61: VARDON GETS HIS GRIP ON THE CLARET JUG

1. "Harry Vardon: Golf's First International Celebrity," Professional Golfers Career College, https://golfcollege.edu/harry-vardon-golfs-first-international -celebrity/; "Golf—The Open Golf Championship," *Times* (London), June 15, 1896, 9.
2. "1896: Muirfield," The Open, https://www.theopen.com/previous-opens /36th-open-Muirfield-1896.
1. "Golf—Professional Tournament," *Times* (London), June 13, 1896, 15.

62: THE FIRST YANKEE

1. Will Grimsley, "Pros Toast Walter Hagen," *Sumter (SC) Daily Item,* August 7, 1980, 2B.

63: ON THE ROAD TO THE "IMPREGNABLE QUADRILATERAL OF GOLF"

1. Robert A. Erwin, "Horton Smith Beats Bobby Jones by One Stroke in Tourney," *Palm Beach News,* February 23, 1930, 5.
2. "Archie Compston: Bio of English Golfer, Teacher of Royalty," Golf Compendium, https://www.golfcompendium.com/2022/08/archie-compston -golfer.html.
3. "1930: Royal Liverpool," The Open, https://www.theopen.com/previous -opens/65th-open-royal-liverpool-1930/.
4. Shav Glick, "St. Bobby: Sixty Years Later, Jones' Spirit Lives On at His Favorite Course—St. Andrews," *Los Angeles Times,* July 15, 1990, https:// www.latimes.com/archives/la-xpm-1990-07-15-sp-405-story.html.

64: THE WEE ICE MON AND GOLF'S TRIPLE CROWN

1. Thomas Bonk, "The One and Only," *Los Angeles Times,* July 15,1999, https://www.latimes.com/archives/la-xpm-1999-jul-15-sp-56359-story .html.
2. "1953: Carnoustie," The Open, https://www.theopen.com/previous -opens/82nd-open-carnoustie-1953/.

3. James Dodson, *American Triumvirate: Sam Snead, Byron Nelson, Ben Hogan and the Modern Age of Golf* (New York: Alfred A. Knopf, 2012), 314.

65: IT WAS A LOCKE BETWEEN THESE RIVALS

1. "Open Switched to St. Andrews," *Glasgow Herald,* January 19, 1957, 9.
2. "1957: St. Andrews," The Open, https://www.theopen.com/previous-opens /86th-open-st-andrews-1957.
3. Tom Humphries, "Dark Journey a Four-Time Winner of the British Open, Bobby Locke Was Celebrated as a Hero in His Homeland, but He Left Those He Loved a Legacy of Sadness and Tragedy," The Vault, *Sports Illustrated,* April 2, 2001, https://vault.si.com/vault/2001/04/02/dark-journey-a-four -time-winner-of-the-british-open-bobby-locke-was-celebrated-as-a-hero -in-his-homeland-but-he-left-those-he-loved-a-legacy-of-sadness-and -tragedy.
4. Ibid.

68: THOMSON'S TERRAIN

1. William Johnson, "A Loner's Crusade," *Sports Illustrated,* July 15, 1968.

70: TREVINO EARNS BACK-TO-BACK JUGS

1. Lee Trevino and Sam Blair, *They Call Me Super Mex* (New York: Random House, 1982), 138.
2. Jack Nicklaus with Ken Bowden, *My Story* (New York: Simon and Schuster, 1997), 291.
3. Chris Cutmore, "You Can't Forget Choking at a Major, I Was Never the Same Again . . . I Felt Disabled: Jacklin Recalls His Muirfield Meltdown with Words That Will Chill Westwood and Co," *Mail Online,* July 15, 2013, https://www.dailymail.co.uk/sport/golf/article-2364401/THE-OPEN-2012 -Tony-Jacklin-recalls-Muirfield-meltdown-words-chill-Lee-Westwood-Co .html.

74: SACRE BLEU IT: THE COLLAPSE THAT WILL LIVE IN INFAMY

1. Thomas Bonk, "Van de Velde Breezing with a Five-Shot Lead," *Los Angeles Times,* July 18, 1999, https://www.latimes.com/archives/la-xpm-1999-jul-18 -sp-57254-story.html.
2. "The Story of 1999: Van de Velde, Leonard and Lawrie Recall Final-Round Drama," The Open, October 12, 2022, https://www.theopen.com/latest/the -story-of-1999-carnoustie-van-de-velde-lawrie-leonard.

76: PHIL FINALLY SCORES A JUG

1. Luke Kerr-Dineen, "The Clubs Mickelson Used to Win the Open," *Golf Digest,* July 21, 2013, https://www.golfdigest.com/story/the-clubs-mickelson -used-to-wi.
2. Bob Harig, "Lefty Captures Claret Jug, 5th Major," ESPN, July 21, 2013, https://www.espn.com/golf/theopen/story/_/id/9496665/phil-mickelson-wins -open-championship-1st-brilliant-66.

77: JORDAN RULES

1. Steve DiMeglio, "Jordan Spieth Puts Together Incredible Finish to Win British Open," *USA Today*, July 23, 2017, https://www.usatoday.com/story /sports/golf/2017/07/23/british-open-jordan-spieth-has-incredible-finish-win -title/502929001/.

SELECTED BIBLIOGRAPHY

Adams, Matthew. *In the Spirit of the Game: Golf's Greatest Stories*. Essex, CT. Globe Pequot Press, 2008.

Barkow, Al. *Gettin' to the Dance Floor: An Oral History of American Golf*. Springfield, NJ: Burford Books, 1986.

———. *The History of the PGA Tour*. New York: Doubleday, 1989.

Benedict, Jeff, and Armen Keteyian. *Tiger Woods*. New York: Simon and Schuster, 2018.

Bisher, Furman. *The Masters & Augusta Revisited: An Intimate View*. Birmingham, AL: Oxmoor House, 1976.

Capps, Gil. *The Magnificent Masters: Jack Nicklaus, Johnny Miller, Tom Weiskopf and the 1975 Cliffhanger at Augusta*. Boston: Da Capo Press, 2014.

Clavin, Tom. *One for the Ages: Jack Nicklaus and the 1986 Masters*. Chicago Review Press, 2011.

Clayton, Ward. *Men on the Bag: The Caddies of Augusta National*. Ann Arbor, MI: Sports Media Group, 2004.

Companiotte, John. *Byron Nelson: The Most Remarkable Year in Golf*. Chicago: Triumph, 2006.

Daly, John, with Glen Waggoner. *My Life in and out of the Rough*. New York: HarperCollins, 2006.

D'Antonio, Michael. *Tour '72: Nicklaus, Palmer, Player, Trevino: The Story of One Great Season*. New York: Hyperion, 2002.

Dodson, James. *American Triumvirate: Sam Snead, Byron Nelson, Ben Hogan and the Modern Age of Golf*. New York: Alfred A. Knopf, 2012

———. *Ben Hogan: An American Life*. New York: Doubleday, 2004.

Feinstein, John. *A Good Walk Spoiled: Days and Nights on the PGA Tour*. New York: Little, Brown, 1995.

———. *Moments of Glory: The Year Underdogs Ruled Golf*. New York: Little, Brown, 2010.

Flaherty, Tom. *The Masters: The Story of Golf's Greatest Tournament*. New York: Holt, Rinehart and Winston, 1971.

Fleck, Jack. *The Jack Fleck Story*. JC Publishing, 2002.

Frost, David. *The Match: The Day the Game of Golf Changed Forever*. New York: Hachette Books, 2007.

Glover, Tim and Peter Higgs. *Fairway to Heaven: Victors and Victims of Golf's Choking Game*. Edinburgh, Scotland: Mainstream Publishing, 1999.

Graubart, Julian. *Golf's Greatest Championship: The 1960 U. S. Open*. Taylor Trade Publications, 2009.

Gregston, Gene. *Hogan: The Man Who Played for Glory*. Englewood Cliffs, NJ: Prentice-Hall, 1978.

Hill, Dave, and Nick Seitz. *Teed Off*. Englewood Cliffs, NJ: Prentice-Hall, 1977.

Hobbs, Michael, with Peter Alliss. *Golf to Remember*. Garden City, NY: Doubleday, 1978.

Hogan, Ben. *Five Lessons*. New York: A.S. Barnes, 1957.

Hopkins, John, ed. *Golf—The Four Majors: An Anthology of the Best Contemporary Writing on Golf*. London: Heinemann Kingswood, 1988.

Janke, Ken. *Firsts, Facts, Feats, & Failures in the World of Golf*. Hoboken, NJ: John Wiley and Sons, 2007.

Jenkins, Dan. *Jenkins at the Majors: Sixty Years of the World's Best Golf Writing, from Hogan to Tiger*. New York: Doubleday, 2009.

Jones, Robert T. Jr. *Golf Is My Game*. New York: Doubleday, 1960.

Keeler, O. B. *The Bobby Jones Story*. Chicago: Triumph Books, 2003.

Lazarus, Alan, and Steve Schlossman. *Chasing Greatness: Johnny Miller, Arnold Palmer and the Miracle at Oakmont*. New York: New American Library, 2010.

McCord, Robert. *Golf Book of Days: Fascinating Facts and Stories for Every Day of the Year*. Citadel Press Books, 1995.

Miller, Johnny, with Guy Yocum. *I Call the Shots*. New York: Gotham Books, 2004.

Nelson, Byron. *How I Played the Game*. Dallas: Taylor Publishing, 1993.

Nicklaus, Jack, with Ken Bowden. *Golf My Way*. New York: Simon and Schuster Paperbacks, 2005.

Nicklaus, Jack, with Ken Bowden. *My Most Memorable Shots in the Majors*. Trumbull, CT: Golf Digest, 1988.

Nicklaus, Jack, with Ken Bowden. *My Story*. New York: Simon and Schuster, 1997.

Nicklaus, Jack, with Herbert Warren Wind. *The Greatest Game of All: My Life in Golf*. New York: Simon and Schuster, 1969.

O'Connor, Ian. *Arnie & Jack: Palmer, Nicklaus and Golf's Greatest Rivalry*. Boston: Houghton Mifflin, 2008.

Olman, John. *The Legendary Golfing Life of Gene Sarazen*. Cincinnati: Olman Enterprises, 1987.

Owen, David. *The Making of the Masters: Clifford Roberts, Augusta National, and Golf's Most Prestigious Tournament*. New York: Simon and Schuster, 1999.

Palmer, Arnold, with James Dodson. *A Golfer's Life*. New York: Ballantine Books, 1999.

Peper, George. *Golf in America: The First 100 Years*. New York: Harry N. Abrams, 1988.

Price, Charles. *A Golf Story: Bobby Jones, Augusta National and the Masters Tournament*. New York: Antheneum, 1986.

Roberts, Clifford. *The Story of Augusta National Golf Club*. Garden City, NY: Doubleday, 1976.

Rosaforte, Tim. *Tiger Woods: The Makings of a Champion*. New York: St. Martin's Press, 1997.

Rubinstein, Lorne, and Jeff Neuman. *A Disorderly Compendium of Golf Wisdom, Folly, Rules, Truths, Trivia and More*. Toronto: McClelland and Stewart, 2006

Sampson, Curt. *The Masters: Golf, Money and Power in Augusta, Georgia*. New York: Villard, 1999.

Sarazen, Gene, and Herbert Warren Wind. *Thirty Years of Championship Golf.* Englewood Cliffs, NJ: Prentice-Hall, Inc, 1950.

Snead, Sam, with George Mendoza. *Slammin' Sam.* New York: Donald Fine, 1986.

Snead, Sam, with Al Stump. *The Education of a Golfer.* New York: Simon and Schuster, 1962.

Sommers, Robert. *Golf Anecdotes: From the Links of Scotland to Tiger Woods.* New York: Oxford University Press, 2004.

Sounes, Howard. *The Wicked Game: Arnold Palmer, Jack Nicklaus, Tiger Woods and the Story of Modern Golf.* New York: William Morrow, 2004.

Steel, Donald. *The Open: Golf's Oldest Major.* New York: Rizzoli, 2009.

Trevino, Lee, and Sam Blair. *They Call Me Super Mex.* New York: Random House, 1982.

Venturi, Ken, and Michael Arkush. *Getting Up & Down: My 60 Years in Golf.* Chicago: Triumph Books, 2004.

Venturi, Ken, with Oscar Fraley. *Comeback: The Ken Venturi Story.* New York: Duell, Sloan and Pearce, 1966.

Wartman, William. *Playing Through: Behind the Scenes on the PGA Tour.* New York: William Morrow, 1990.

ADDITIONAL SOURCES AND REFERENCES

Websites including: apnews.com, asapsports.com, cbssports.com, espn.com, foxsports.com, gettyimages.com, golfchannel.com, golfcompendium.com, golf .com, golfdigest.com, masters.com, nbcsports.com, pgachampionship.com, pga .com, randa.org, si.com, smithsonianmag.com, usga.org, youtube.com.

The following is a list of assorted periodicals, news services, and newspapers that provided assistance in the formulation of various stories:

The *Arizona Republic,* Associated Press, *Atlanta Journal Constitution, Augusta Chronicle, Chicago Tribune, Cleveland Plain Dealer, Columbus Dispatch, Dallas Morning sNews, Ebony, Esquire, Fort Worth Star-Telegram, Golf Digest, Golf Journal, Golf Magazine, Golfing Magazine, Golf Monthly (UK), Golf Week, Golf World, Golf Plus (India), Golf World, Guardian, Life, London Daily Express, London Daily Mail, London Daily Telegraph, Los Angeles Herald Examiner, Los Angeles Times, Miami Herald, Newsweek, New Yorker, New York Daily News, New York Herald Tribune, New York Times, Oakland Tribune, PGA Magazine, Philadelphia Inquirer, Pittsburgh Press,* Reuters, *San Diego Union-Tribune, San Francisco Chronicle, Saturday Evening Post, Sport Magazine, Sporting News, Sports Illustrated, Time, Times (London),* United Press International, *Washington Post.*

PHOTO CREDITS

Grateful acknowledgment is made to the following for the use of the photographs that appear in the art insert: public domain (page 1, top); Pelham Country Club (page 1, bottom; pages 2–3); Merion Golf Club Archives (page 4); Sam Snead Jr. (page 5); Oakmont Country Club Archives (page 6, top left; page 8; page 10, top right and middle right; page 11, top left, top right, and bottom right); The Olympic Club (page 6, top right, bottom left, and bottom right; page 7, top left, bottom left, and bottom right); The Olympic Club/Tom Vano (photographs) (page 14); Aronimink Golf Club Archives (page 7, top right; page 9, bottom); Getty Images (page 9, top and middle; page 10, bottom right; page 15; page 16, bottom left and bottom right); Gary Player Collection (page 10, middle left); Randy O. Williams Collection (page 11, middle left); Crooked Stick Golf Club (pages 12–13); TPC Harding Park (page 16, top); and Kiawah Island Golf Resort/ Mic Smith Photography LLC (page 16, middle).